Reading Material Culture

Social Archaeology

General Editor
Ian Hodder, University of Cambridge

Advisory Editors
Margaret Conkey, University of California
at Berkeley
Mark Leone, University of Maryland
Alain Schnapp, U.E.R. d'Art et d'Archaeologie, Paris
Stephen Shennan, University of Southampton
Bruce Trigger, McGill University, Montreal

Published
MATERIAL CULTURE AND MASS CONSUMPTION
Daniel Miller

EXPLANATION IN ARCHAEOLOGY
Guy Gibbon

READING MATERIAL CULTURE
Structuralism, Hermeneutics and Post-Structuralism
Edited by Christopher Tilley

In preparation
THE ARCHAEOLOGY OF INEQUALITY
Edited by Randall H. McGuire and Robert Paynter
WOMEN IN PREHISTORY
Edited by Joan Gero and Margaret Conkey
IRON AGE SOCIETIES
From Tribe to State in Northern Europe
Lotte Hedeager
THE DOMESTICATION OF EUROPE
Ian Hodder

Reading Material Culture

Structuralism, Hermeneutics and Post-Structuralism

Edited by Christopher Tilley

Basil Blackwell

First published 1990

Basil Blackwell Ltd
108 Cowley Road, Oxford, OX4 1JF, UK

Basil Blackwell, Inc.
3 Cambridge Center
Cambridge, Massachusetts 02142, USA

British Library Cataloguing in Publication Data

A CIP catalogue record for this book is available
from the British Library.

Library of Congress Cataloging in Publication Data

Reading material culture: structuralism, hermeneutics, and post
-structuralism / edited by Christopher Tilley.
p.   cm.
Includes bibliography references.
ISBN 0–631–16081–7; 0–631–172858 (pb)
1. Material culture. 2. Structural anthropology.
3. Hermeneutics. I. Tilley, Christopher Y.
GN406.R43   1990
306—dc20   89–3589
                                                              CIP

Typeset in 11½ on 12pt Garamond
by Footnote Graphics, Warminster, Wiltshire
Printed and bound in Great Britain at
The Camelot Press plc, Southampton

Contents

Contributors

Henrietta Moore, Department of Social Anthropology, University of Cambridge, Free School Lane, Cambridge CB2 3RF, UK.

Bjørnar Olsen, Institute of Social Science, University of Tromsø, PO Box 1040, N-9001 Tromsø, Norway.

Eric Kline Silverman, Department of Anthropology, University of Minnesota, 215 Ford Hall, 224 Church Street SE, Minneapolis, Minnesota 55455, USA.

Christopher Tilley, Department of Archaeology, St David's University College, Lampeter, Dyfed, SA48 7ED, UK (formerly Department of Anthropology, University College London).

Timothy Yates, Department of Archaeology, University of Cambridge, Downing Street, Cambridge CB2 3DZ, UK.

Preface

This book has been written by a group of anthropologists and archaeologists who have their primary interests in material-culture studies but it transcends the concerns of these two disciplines as they are normally understood. Material-culture studies constitute a nascently developing field of enquiry which systematically refuses to remain enmeshed within established disciplinary boundaries. The field of material culture studies is one concerned with the relationship between artefacts and social relations irrespective of time and place. It aims to explore systematically the linkage between the constitution of social reality and material-culture production and use. Material-culture studies inevitably require a series of refusals. Minimally, four of these can be distinguished. The first has already been mentioned: disciplinary allegiance. Any distinction between matters 'sociological', 'anthropological', 'philosophical', 'archaeological', 'psychological' or 'literary' is arbitrary and unhelpful. The second is any attempt to separate out philosophical and theoretical questions from the practical business of research. Theory *is* practice and all practice *is* theoretical. Both theory and practice *are* philosophical in nature. The third is to subscribe to a subject-object dualism, that the investigator can be neatly separated out from that being investigated. The fourth is the reification of categories of analysis into separate spheres such as politics, economics, ideology or more specifically, art, literature, utilitarian artefact, etc., which then desperately have to be linked back together in some way.

This book is an exploration of a number of important contemporary positions in the human sciences which appear to have great relevance to material-culture studies: structuralism, hermeneutics and post-structuralism. These labels, in a very real sense, remain just that — empty of much specific content — and there seems very little reason to 'fill them up' and compare and contrast the results here. In the very moment of their employment it is necessary to abandon them. There are many types of analyses and authors which might be slotted into these categories. Equally there are many studies, positions and authors which transcend them. Post-structuralism is undoubtedly the most contentious label of all. As the name implies, it is simply something 'post', developing out of structuralism, and with a highly ambiguous relationship to 'it'. A certain degree of deconstruction is therefore necessary at the outset.

The approach taken in the book is to analyse and discuss the work of individual 'structuralist', 'hermeneutic' and 'post-structuralist' authors rather than attempt to generalize a distinctive series of positions to be fitted into each of these slots. All the chapters are selective and critical in approach, an engagement rather than a compilation. A 'straight' account or summary of the massive body of literature each author has generated is not intended. Furthermore no attempt is made to reconstruct an entire intellectual genealogy for each author tracing influences to other authors or positions or the general historical and intellectual circumstances in which their work took place. This ground has been all too well trodden to be repeated here. Furthermore there is little reason to consider such an approach to be an automatic or particularly useful strategy to be followed. The concern in each chapter is with the particular sets of concepts, categories and arguments each author employs. The first chapter, on Lévi-Strauss, differs somewhat from the others, which deliberately concentrate solely on the work of the author being discussed; in it I consider in some detail a hermeneutic critique of his work by Ricoeur, and Derrida's post-structuralist critique. This secondarily serves to introduce themes explored at much greater length in the rest of the volume.

The treatment of the book is thematic throughout. Each chapter considers a core of central issues and the manner in which these are confronted by the writer being discussed. These are:

1 Questions of time, history, cultural change and continuity.
2 Discourse, style and textuality: processes of reading and writing the social.
3 The constitution of the subject and subjectivity in relation to social totalities and cultural practices.
4 Politics and the sociopolitical role of the intellectual.
5 The manner in which a consideration of the first four points relates to an understanding both of material culture and the manner in which material-culture studies are at present constituted within disciplinary forms, in particular archaeology and anthropology.

Naturally, some of the authors considered are more concerned with certain of these themes than others, and this is reflected in the individual discussions.

The choice of which writers to include in this book, apart perhaps from Lévi-Strauss, whose structuralist project has remained at the centre of debate in the human sciences for the last four decades, was a difficult one and it is useless trying further to justify it. Lacan might have been substituted for Foucault, Gadamer for Ricoeur and so on. In addition the book might have been extended to cover Critical Theory in a consideration, for example, of the work of Adorno or Habermas. Limits had to be posted, and a personal selection made.

The book aims to provide a wide variety of different perspectives on the five issues mentioned above. A drawing of these together into some new kind of totalizing theoretical unity for material-culture studies to follow in a guide-book fashion is impossible, and the attempt undesirable. The positions advocated in the conclusions to the individual chapters, by the writers of this book, are not necessarily accepted by the other authors. The book is intended to stimulate debate, not to forge a spurious consensus.

It is the hope of the contributors that the book will both aid an understanding of the work of the various authors discussed and prompt the reader to read *them*. Each chapter has an extensive series of references to primary and secondary literature which may be followed up. Abbreviations of book titles are used throughout and these are annotated in the bibliographies. We have attempted to make the various discussions as 'accessible' as possible without providing a parody of complex arguments. But this work is an interpretation of interpretations in which the inherent difficulties of any process of reading and writing are emphasized. Reading and writing are not natural activities that are as obvious and unproblematic as eating or drinking. All the authors considered are generally thought to be in various ways 'obscure', 'difficult', 'complex' and highly 'theoretical'. However they all read, criticize, interpret and write with inordinate care and attention to detail. This obsession with language provides the major thread linking them all together. It is not just a rhetoric of style but a realization that language does not just transparently convey the 'order of things' but actually helps to constitute and problematize them.

The idea for this book had its origins in a series of advanced research seminars which took place in Cambridge during 1986. However the book bears only a very tangential relationship to those events, both in terms of contributors and in many of the substantive arguments put forward. I would like to thank Ian Hodder and Virginia Murphy at Blackwell for consistent support, patience and faith in the book.

Christopher Tilley

Part I
Structuralism

1

Claude Lévi-Strauss: Structuralism and Beyond

Christopher Tilley

I

Lévi-Strauss's Vision of a Structural Anthropology

The work of Lévi-Strauss has had a profound impact on the development of the human sciences during the last forty years. Any critical
appraisal of the manner in which conceptualization and theory
construction in disciplines as diverse as psychology and archaeology,
geography and literary criticism, has taken place ignores it to their
great loss. The 'interminable' nature of the myths that Lévi-Strauss has
so extensively studied finds its correlate in the interminable discussions of his own work. A bibliography on Lévi-Strauss and his critics
published over a decade ago (Lapointe and Lapointe 1977) contained
almost 1,400 entries, and the appraisals, including the present one,
have not dried up since. There is hardly a worker in the human
sciences today, who has not been directly or indirectly influenced by
Lévi-Strauss in either a positive or a negative direction, including all
the other authors discussed in this volume.

The father of contemporary structuralism and semiotics in areas
other than language, Lévi-Strauss has worked in three main areas: the
study of kinship, totemism and classificatory systems, and myth in
small-scale non-industrial societies. Of these, the last two today
appear to be of the greatest significance and interest, and in what
follows his studies of kinship will only be mentioned in passing. That
being said, absences rather than presences define the chapter: a taste
rather than a flavour. The text does not attempt transparently to
convey an essential Lévi-Strauss but is rather an engagement with
important aspects of his thought.

3

The major concern here is with sets of ideas and theoretical positions adopted by Lévi-Strauss and not with influences on his thought. An entire pantheon of writers including Durkheim, Mauss, Rousseau, Marx, Freud, Jakobson and Saussure can be mentioned (for discussions see Badcock 1975; Glucksmann 1974; Rossi 1974) but of these, only the last two appear to be absolutely crucial to an understanding of the development of Lévi-Strauss's structuralism and post-structuralist and other perspectives that attempt in various ways to go beyond it. In some respects Lévi-Strauss's work can be considered to be a unique combination of pre-existing intellectual materials available to him from the late 1930s onwards and it is the effects of this distinctive piecing together and extension of the materials in relation to particular sets of problems that provides the main focus of this chapter.

In this section aspects of Lévi-Strauss's work are discussed in detail. Three different lines of critical objection from perspectives within Critical Theory, hermeneutics and post-structuralism are then outlined in Section II, providing a link between this chapter and the others in the book. In Section III some of the contributions a consideration of Lévi-Strauss's structural approach can make to material-culture studies are outlined.

Structure

In the preface to *SA1*, Lévi-Strauss, citing a review of Pouillon, states that he would like to be remembered for emphasizing the structural character of all social phenomena and following such a position through to its logical conclusion in a systematic manner (*SA1*: vii). There can be little doubt about this but what is rather surprising is the lack of a rigorous theoretical definition and discussion of structure and structural analysis in much of his work. In various places the term 'structure' is used in relation to discussions of individual myths and also at a much more abstract and general philosophical level. The concept as used by Lévi-Strauss, suggests both a substantive theory purporting to explain the organization of the social world and a set of strategies for the analysis of that world. In other words, it plays a double role within both theory and methodology.

The concept of structure has a long genealogy in the human sciences. Lévi-Strauss's use of the term inaugurates a fundamental break with an empiricist tradition in which structure is conceived as an empirically observable and specifiable set of social relations making up, on the basis of biological analogies, a kind of 'skeletal' support for the social organism. In the 'structural–functional' theory of Radcliffe-

Brown and others, individuals and/or groups form the basic units of social structure. Human beings form points in the structure and structural analysis is concerned with the manner in which persons are arranged in relation to each other. Social structure can only be specified through rigorous observation of recurrent regularities in the networking of social interaction in an anthropological field situation. The term 'structure' becomes more or less equivalent to 'organization' or 'arrangement'. It remains a descriptive concept without explanatory significance, based either on direct observation or on empirically derived abstractions. Naturally, any concept of social structure has to be based on an analysis of the patterning of social relations but this does not imply that it has to remain at that level.

For Lévi-Strauss, structure has much more to do with models based on empirical realities than a description based on those empirical realities themselves (*SA1*: chapter 2). In other words in order to understand social relations, or any other aspects of human culture, it is necessary to probe beneath the observable to a more fundamental ontological level which can be shown to generate what the anthropologist or sociologist actually sees. The concept of structure becomes, therefore, generative and explanatory rather than descriptive. Structure becomes a social logic underlying and giving meaning, sense and significance to that which may be empirically observed. It exists through its effects on social life but is not itself empirically observable.

Lévi-Strauss derives essential features of his approach from contemporary structural linguistics, providing paradigm examples for a structuralist approach. The originality and importance of much of his work is to demonstrate how models drawn from linguistics can be used to understand and explain areas of human culture other than language. A positivist archaeology and anthropology in essence wishes to model its approach to the social world on the apparent success of the natural sciences, and physics in particular: the natural sciences provide a model to be emulated by a successful social science. Lévi-Strauss subscribes to a similar thesis except that he takes as an example to be followed the most rigorous and 'scientific' of the social sciences: linguistics. Underlying both positions is a naturalist thesis suggesting the possibility of the unity of the sciences in terms of one central programme. Linguistics is, of course, primarily concerned with processes of human communication, and so also is anthropology according to Lévi-Strauss. The social is above all a domain loaded with signification, symbolism and meaning: it is a vast verbal and non-verbal communication system. All culture, although not simply reducible to language, shares the same fundamental characteristics, or at the very least, a series of striking homologies: different aspects of human culture, such as kin relations, exchange systems, art, myth, ritual, culinary practices, etc., are structured like a language. Language is not only the primary characteristic distinguishing people from animals, it also provides an analogical foundation for understanding the rest of human culture (*SA1*: 62).

Lévi-Strauss explicitly bases his approach on Saussurian linguistics as modified by Troubetzkoy, Jakobson and others – what he terms the 'phonological revolution' (*SA1*: 33). Saussure's work involved a division between *parole*, the utterances of individual speakers, and *langue*, an underlying system of language making possible any particular speech act. Any act of speech is only comprehensible in terms of the system as a whole and at the same time this system itself only exists in a multiplicity of individual speech acts. The system itself exists through its effects, through its realization in the speech of individuals. It is not reducible to these individual speech acts but its systematicity makes the speech acts comprehensible. To understand language, then, requires an analysis not of the utterances of individual speakers but the underlying system that makes speech possible. Similarly, in order to understand chess, we do not analyse a series of concrete moves or games but the rules and conventions making any game of chess possible. The rules of chess exist independently of any chess game, only acquiring concrete form in the manner in which pieces are moved in any particular game. To understand the moves we need first to reconstruct the system on which they are based and so too with language. The underlying system is the structure of a language.

For Saussurian linguistics the nature of language is not to be understood by an atomistic analysis of it as a mechanical sum of units utilized in actual speech (as in nineteenth-century linguistics), nor in tracing historical changes in the units, but in slicing through it synchronically or horizontally which alone permits a comprehension of the entire system or structure.

This structure consists of a series of units or signs with two sides or faces: the signifier (a sound image) and a signified (a concept or object). The sign 'pig' consists of a signifier, the sounds 'p-i-g', and a signified, a conception of a pig, or a four-legged pink grunting animal. The important thing about this conception is that it reveals first the *arbitrary* relationship between a signifier and a signified. The link is a matter of historical and cultural convention. There is no natural link between a sound and a concept. Second, the linguistic sign links two elements which are nevertheless produced simultaneously. The sign 'pig' is only comprehensible by virtue of its *difference* from other signs: the fact that it is not 'rat', 'dog', 'rope', 'cat', etc. A linguistic sign only becomes comprehensible because it constitutes part of a significative system characterized by differential oppositions. It is the structure of the system which allows signifiers and signifieds to possess signification or meaning. This structure can therefore be defined as *a system of difference*. It is the *relationships* between the signs in the system that are of essential importance, not the signs themselves. Any person talking is not consciously aware of this structure, nor does she or he set out to employ it. Nevertheless the structure makes any speech act comprehensible: it resides in the *unconscious* mind. An unconscious system of differences and oppositions has to be postulated to account for this fact.

Saussure suggested that since language was a system of signs, linguistics would one day form part of a much broader science of signs – semiology – and Lévi-Strauss regards his own work as directly furthering the development of such a science:

> We conceive anthropology as the *bona fide* occupant of that domain of semiology which linguistics has not already claimed for its own. (*SA2*: 10)

> structure exhibits the characteristics of a system. It is made up of several elements, none of which can undergo a change without effecting changes in all the other elements ... for any given model there should be the possibility of ordering a series of transformations resulting in a group of models of the same type ... the above properties make it possible to predict how the model will react if one or more of its elements are submitted to certain modifications ... the model should be constituted to make immediately intelligible all the observed facts. (*SA1*: 279–80)

> The method we adopt ... consists in the following operations:
>
> (1) define the phenomenon under study as a relation between two or more terms, real or supposed;
> (2) construct a table of possible permutations between these terms;
> (3) take this table as the general object of analysis which, at this level only, can yield necessary connections, the empirical phenomenon considered at the beginning being only one possible combination among others, the complete system of which must be reconstructed beforehand. (*T*: 16)

In the short passages cited above Lévi-Strauss advances in a condensed (and somewhat oblique) manner most of the major tenets of Saussurian linguistics discussed above. The emphasis is on discovering basic relationships between the elements of that which is under consideration. While his use of the term 'model' is somewhat surprising given the connotations of this term within positivism it is quite clear that the terms 'analysis' or 'method' would provide close substitutes. For Saussure's terms 'signifier' and 'signified' Lévi-Strauss typically employs instead 'code' and 'message', suggesting a somewhat less arbitrary relation. Human culture consists of a series of codes conveying messages. It is the nature of these codes and messages and the principles or rules underlying their operation, that Lévi-Strauss wishes to determine.

From Jakobson's work Lévi-Strauss was influenced by a specific approach to the linguistic sign as a pattern of speech sounds. Jakobson argued that binary oppositions formed the basic principle of the organization of distinctive features of language at a phonemic level. This approach lays the basis for Lévi-Strauss's analysis of structures as consisting of sets of binary oppositions.

Kinship

The central feature of kin relations for Lévi-Strauss is that they may be conceived as arbitrary representational systems. Kinship systems are rule-governed sets of familial and group relations. Such relations can be considered to be homologous with linguistic structures. Kinship and language constitute different types of communication systems in the societies in which they arise. Both may be produced by identical unconscious structures (*SA1*: 62). To analyse kinship systems adequately it is necessary to consider them as structured sets of relations between terms or units. What, then, is the building block or elementary structural unit of kin relations? Lévi-Strauss rejects the definition of the kinship unit which might seem self-evident on empirical and biological grounds, proposed in the structural–functionalist theory of Radcliffe-Brown, that it resides in an 'elementary family' consisting of a woman, her husband and their children from which 'second-order' types of relations might be deduced, such as connections between such elementary families provided by common members, e.g. mother's brother, wife's sister, etc. For Lévi-Strauss the elementary unit of kinship consists of four terms, each connected with a relational function: brother (uncle), sister (mother), nephew (son), brother-in-law (father). While the correlation between the different avunculate forms (roles played by uncles) and descent types is not universal, he maintains that, regardless of any particular descent mode (patrilineal, matrilineal, etc.), if all the four terms of this relational system are taken into account, a definite connection does exist between the four types of relation within such an elementary unit: husband and wife, brother and sister, father and son, and mother's brother and sister's son. If we know one pair of these relations we can infer all the others.

Consideration of these relations allows him to solve a problem occurring in traditional anthropology: that of how to understand the relationship between a mother's brother and a sister's son. Two primary forms of such a relation occur. In some societies the uncle is feared and respected by his sister's son and has definite rights over his nephew. In other societies a joking relationship of familiarity occurs. These relations are inversely correlated with the attitude of the sister's son towards his father. Why? Radcliffe-Brown attempted an explanation of this phenomenon by noting a series of empirical regularities between the mother's brother and the sister's son in relation to other social variables, especially to types of descent. However, such correlations did not always hold good. Radcliffe-Brown's error was to begin and end his analysis with the relation between the mother's brother and sister's son rather than consider this as part of a wider structure: 'the relation between maternal uncle and nephew is to the relation between brother and sister as the relation between father and son is to that between husband and wife. Thus if we know one pair of relations, it is always possible to infer the other' (*SA1*: 42). Lévi-Strauss is able to put forward a new framework to consider the role of the avunculate in differing societies by considering the relations between the terms rather than concentrating on the terms themselves. This is a hallmark of his structuralist approach. Kinship systems form networks of systematically structured and structuring sign systems relating individuals and groups to each other. Rather than attempting to engage with the enormous complexity of the analyses of kinship undertaken in *ESK* Lévi-Strauss's approach to structure can be better approached by considering his analyses of totemism and myth.

Myth

Lévi-Strauss's most comprehensive and detailed structural analysis is of myth published in the four volumes of *Mythologiques* (*RC*; *HA*; *OTM*; *NM*), in three other books *WM*, *JP*, *AM*, and in articles reprinted in *SA1*, *SA2* and *VA*. No useful compression can be provided here of this massive and immensely stimulating body of work. The discussion will instead concentrate on delineating a number of fundamental principles underlying the individual analyses.

Myths tell stories dealing with such themes as the origins of the world and the place of humanity in it, the relationship between people and animals, sibling and parent—child relations, etc. Attempts to understand myth by other authors have primarily set myth within a functional and/or symbolic perspective. Myth can thus be viewed as a verbal expression of ritual practices which may work to maintain social solidarity and its emotive and expressive narrative content are usually stressed. Alternatively it may be written off as mere fantasy: defective primitive thought processes contrasting with a rigorous scientific logic.

Lévi-Strauss takes a different line. Myth and science are parallel ways of acquiring knowledge and the former is a supreme example of *bricolage* (*SM*: 18; see p. 26 below). Myths constitute a relatively autonomous realm of cultural practices and any individual myth can only be adequately explained in terms of its relations with other myths rather than with other aspects of culture external to it. Attempting to derive the meaning of myth from technoeconomic conditions or from particular sets of social practices existing in a determinate social setting constitute an unacceptable form of reductionism which fails to appreciate the essential characteristics of mythic structure.

The first and most fundamental principle of Lévi-Strauss's analysis, then, is to explain myth primarily *by* myth. This is very closely related to two other principles: *there is no original myth* and *the manner in which a myth is narrated by an individual is irrelevant* (*NM*: 626 and 644). These principles effectively remove any necessity to conduct a historical analysis of mythology – the attempt to trace myths back to some 'pure' form or point of origin – or to give analytical importance to variations in which the same myth may be told differently by individual speakers. For Lévi-Strauss myth is only comprehensible because it constitutes an overall system and forms part of a *collective* oral tradition: the nuances of narration by individual speakers do not matter since a particular myth to remain recognizable must retain a certain level of structuring of events and relationships. It is these fundamental events and relations which are the focus of concern in a structural analysis and not the manner in which they may be embroidered by an individual speaker.

Individual myths form elements of a total set or system and their meaning is to be derived from their relationship to this mythic system. The system as a whole forms a 'language' of myth. When myths are narrated by a speaker this act of *parole* gains meaning and significance and can only be understood by consideration of the overall language of myth of which the individual myth is a part and to which it relates and is to be ultimately derived. Although it is necessarily the case that each myth must have a point of origin, i.e. a story is told by a narrator for the first time, such origins are now irrevocably lost contingent events which even if they could be reconstructed would add little or nothing to our understanding. Contemporary myths existing in the ethnographic present are subject to a double determination. (i) By other myths: the relationship may both be temporal (previous versions) and spatial (myths derived from patterns of cultural contact). (ii) By constraints arising outside the mythological system itself (referred to as 'infrastructural determination') which may demand modification and/or reorganization of particular elements; e.g. two myths in different cultures may be identical apart from the substitution of one animal species for another for the reason that the geographical extent of the myth is greater than that of a particular species playing a specific role within it. The same may apply to technologies or other mythic elements.

Of these two forms of determinism the first is of far greater significance:

> either the infrastructure is identical with the kind of things which it is supposed to bring into play and, in that case, it is as inert and passive as the things themselves, and can engender nothing; or it belongs to the realm of lived-in experience and is therefore in a perpetual state of imbalance and tension: in this case, the myths cannot derive from it but through a causality that would very rapidly become tautological. They should be seen rather as constituting local and temporary answers to the problems raised by feasible adjustments and insoluble contradictions that they are endeavouring to legitimize or conceal. The content which the myth endows itself is not anterior, but posterior, to this initial impulse: far from deriving from some content or other, the myth moves towards a particular content through the attraction of its specific gravity. (NM: 629)

Myths primarily determined by other myths and acting so as to resolve contradictions (see p. 15), may make local adjustments but the form and nature of these is already built in and determined by the mythic system itself and its inbuilt capacities for transformation. Individual myths possessing meaning by virtue of their relations of difference to an overall mythic set cannot have their narrative line explained by mere reduction to the social context in which they occur. Furthermore although particular myths may occur in particular cultures, each myth is always already a transformation of previous or foreign myths. This will always be the case especially in view of the fact that virtually no social groups exist in isolation. In this sense Lévi-Strauss claims that myths transcend social and cultural context. Every myth is either a transformation of a previous myth and/or a translation (thus involving modification) from a neighbouring foreign culture. Myths do not come into being *in* a language or *in* a culture but rather at their points of articulation. So while every myth is a 'completed' product it is also forged from the remnants of prior productions, it is both primary and derivative. Myths do not belong to particular social or linguistic contexts but transcend them. Accordingly they translate well since they are already translations and that of essential significance is the *story*, which may be rendered equally well in any language, and even a poor linguistic rendition of the events related will still retain its mythic significance (*SA1*: 210).

The telling of a myth is an act of *parole* to be related to its *langue*. Sophocles' *Oedipus Rex* derives from the *langue* of the total Oedipus myth. The Oedipus myth at a wider level forms part of a more general mythic system in a relation of difference to this total set. Myths can only have an empirical existence in their *versions*, in acts of *parole*. Consequently mythic discourse in the telling is open-ended. Every myth may have a sequel and many variants and myths may be borne and die. This openness of myth at the level of *parole* contrasts with the closedness of the *langue* when viewed synchronically. A specific analogy here is the manner in which a cylinder (representing the *langue* of myth) may be said to constitute a closed surface, and would remain so even if extended indefinitely through time at one end, this temporal extension representing repeated acts of *parole* (*NM*: 633).

How, then, do we approach an individual myth? First, we must be aware of it as only a version and we need to take into account other variants. Second, we must be aware of it as a unit in an overall mythic system and analyse the manner in which it relates to other myths within the confines of a synchronic system. Although each myth is necessarily an incomplete fragment, when it is considered as forming part of an overall mythic system, it can be seen to encode basic oppositions and messages about the meaning and significance of humanity's place in the world. Third, analysis requires separation of the stability of *langue* within the myth from the fluxes of *parole* within versions: a search for constant and recurrent order: an underlying and embedded structure. This structure will inhere in relations between terms or units in the story which require isolation and definition. Lévi-Strauss refers to these units as 'mythemes', thus implying their analogical equivalence to phonemes within linguistic structure. These mythemes may be related in a number of ways, homologous and inverted relations being two of the most important. From a consideration of mythemes found in individual variants of a myth it may be possible to reconstruct a prototype myth to which all the variants tend but which does not itself exist as an actual told myth. From an analysis of the relations between the mythemes the meaning of the myth (residing in the mythemic structure) may be extracted from the signs used to express it. The meaning resides not in the elements making up the myth but in their relations and manner of combination. Differences between individual variants may be explained by reference to infrastructural cultural determinancy which may have the effect, for example, of stressing or marking off different mythemic oppositions in a more or less pronounced way or relate to content substitution – different mythemic terms may be signifying the same thing. Such an analysis may become extremely complicated by virtue of the fact that according to the variants of the myths considered and at different stages of analysis each term can appear as a relation and each relation as a term. Consequently the phonetic analogy breaks down and the terms or units of myth have to be defined as *bundles* of terms and relations rather than singular clearly defined units between which there may be relations. These relations are considered to inhere in terms of binary oppositions such as inside–outside, day–night, male–female, nature–culture, left–right, up–down, etc.

Myth Analysis

In this section two examples will be given to illustrate the manner in which Lévi-Strauss's approach to myth operates in practice: first, the Oedipus myth (*SA1*: chapter XI), and second, a pair of myths concerning the origin of poisoned arrows and the origin of bird colour taken from *RC*.

The Oedipus myth is well known in various literary forms and this very familiarity makes it a useful vehicle for Lévi-Strauss to illustrate his approach to myth analysis. The technique used is to break down the story into the shortest possible sentences each bearing a number corresponding to the unfolding of the narrative. Such sentences are claimed to constitute the units of the myth, bundles of relations linking functions to subjects or characters. The myth can be rearranged in a tabular form which permits the discernment of underlying structure. The myth consists of strings of sentences which can be regarded mathematically:

> Say, for instance, we were confronted with a sequence of the type: 1,2,4,7,8,2,3,4,6,8,1,4,5,7,8,1,2,5,7,3,4,5,6,8 . . ., the assignment being to put all the 1's together, all the 2's, the 3's, etc.; the result is a chart:
>
> | 1 | 2 | | 4 | | | 7 | 8 |
> |---|---|---|---|---|---|---|---|
> | | 2 | 3 | 4 | | 6 | | 8 |
> | 1 | | | 4 | 5 | | 7 | 8 |
> | 1 | 2 | | | 5 | | 7 | |
> | | 2 | 3 | 4 | 5 | 6 | | 8 |
>
> We shall attempt to perform the same kind of operation on the Oedipus myth, trying out several arrangements of the mythemes until we find one which is in harmony with the principles enumerated above. (*SA1*: 213)

Following these principles Lévi-Strauss arrives at the possible arrangement of the myth shown in table 1.1 (*SA1*: 214).

Table 1.1

Column 1	Column 2	Column 3	Column 4
Cadmos seeks his sister Europa, ravished by Zeus			
		Cadmos kills the dragon	
	The Spartoi kill one another		
			Labdacos (Laios' father) = lame (?)
	Oedipus kills his father Laios		Laios (Oedipus' father) = left-sided (?)
		Oedipus kills the Sphinx	
			Oedipus = swollen foot (?)
Oedipus marries his mother, Jocasta			
	Eteocles kills his brother, Polynices		
Antigone buries her brother, Polynices, despite prohibition			

Here there are four vertical columns and ten horizontal rows. Each column consists of relations constituting an overall 'bundle'. To tell the myth all that is required is to read along the rows from left to right and top to bottom with linking narrative 'embroidery'. But to understand the meaning of the myth it is necessary to disregard one half of the diachronic dimension, that operating from top to bottom, and read instead left to right, taking each column in turn and considering such columns to be units. These columns consist of sets of relations linked to a common principle:

Column 1 overrates blood relations.
Column 2 underrates blood relations.
Column 3 refers to slaying of monsters.
Column 4 refers to difficulties in walking straight and standing upright.

At this point the meaning and structural opposition between the first two columns is clear, but that of the third and fourth remains obscure. The explanation given is as follows:

The dragon is a chthonian being which has to be killed in order that mankind be born from the Earth; the Sphinx is a monster unwilling to permit men to live. The last unit reproduces the first one, which has to do with the *autochthonous origin* of mankind. Since the monsters are overcome by men, we may thus say that the common feature of the third column is *denial of the autochthonous origin of man*.

This immediately helps us to understand the meaning of the fourth column. In mythology it is a universal characteristic of men born from the Earth that at the moment they emerge from the depth they either cannot walk or walk clumsily . . . Thus the common feature of the fourth column is *the persistence of the autochthonous origin of man*. (*SA1*: 215–16)

We are left then with a symmetrical pattern of opposition:

autochthonous origin of humanity : non-autochthonous origin of humanity : : overrating of blood relations : underrating of blood relations.

But what does this symmetrical opposition mean? Lévi-Strauss claims that the Oedipus myth, in common with other myths, tries to resolve in an imaginary manner a contradiction which is insoluble. In this case the contradiction relates to the inability of a culture which believes that mankind is autochthonous to reconcile this theory with the knowledge that people are actually born from a union of a man and a woman. The mythic 'solution' consists of a process of deflection whereby an original problem becomes translated in terms of one of secondary significance:

the Oedipus myth provides a kind of logical tool which relates the original problem — born from one or born from two? — to the derivative problem: born from different or born from same? By a correlation of this type, the overrating of blood relations is to the underrating of blood relations as the attempt to escape autochthony is to the impossibility to succeed in it. (*SA1*: 216)

The complexity of Lévi-Strauss's decoding of the Oedipus myth by means of breaking it down into bundles of mythemes and considering the relations of these bundles (the individual columns) to each other appears transparently simple when contrasted with the monumental analysis of over 800 myths in the *Mythologiques* volumes. Much of this work is concerned to demonstrate the transformative qualities of myths in relation either to common or entirely different themes. While the Oedipus analysis is concerned with demonstrating a potential to analyse the internal structure of a single myth, the bulk of Lévi-Strauss's work on mythology is concerned with what might be referred to as external structure: the relations between myths. Myths 161 and 186, analysed in *RC*, are concerned, respectively, with the origin of poison for hunting and the colour of birds, two apparently totally different themes, yet Lévi-Strauss attempts to demonstrate that the mythic structure in both is entirely symmetrical (*RC*: 326–7). Both myths are broken down into mythemic units which may then be systematically compared (see table 1.2).

Table 1.2

M161	The hero marries a monkey-woman;	he visits his parents (human);	he is abandoned at the top of a tree when he visits his parents-in-law (animal).
M186	The hero marries a vulture-woman;	he visits his parents-in-law (animal);	he is abandoned at the top of a tree on the occasion of a proposed visit to his parents (human).

≠

M161	He is able to climb down with the help of sticky lianas,	helped by birds of prey (≡ vultures);	he is adopted by the birds.
M186	He is able to climb down in spite of a thorny trunk,	helped by spiders and birds (≢ vultures);	he becomes the leader of the birds.

≠

M161	His wife has left him for good;		he destroys the monkeys with poison;	he spares one of the monkeys' sons.
M186	He does everything he can to rejoin his wife;	he is killed by his vulture-son;	he destroys the vultures by fire;	

≠

M161	By agreeing to hunt in conjunction with the eagle, man obtains curare;	origin of poison for hunting.
M186	By quarrelling over their share of the booty, the birds acquire their plumage;	origin of the colours of birds.

≠ end of myth segment
≡ homology; correspondence
≢ non-homology; non-correspondence

As with the analysis of the Oedipus myth to read the narrative line or story of myths 161 and 186 in simplified and 'mythemic' form one progresses from left to right and top to bottom along the rows. Different temporal moments in both myths are arranged in the separate blocks which follow on from each other. These culminate in the explanations for the origins of bird plumage and poison in the final block. In the previous three blocks the isolated mythemic units in the two myths can be seen to be in a relation of structured opposition or inversion. For example, in the first block we have oppositions between parents and parents-in-law in relation to whether they are human or animal which is also related to abandonment at the top of a tree. In the second block the hero climbs down the tree with the help of sticky lianas/in spite of a thorny trunk and so on. There is a logical reversal of events. The myth about the origin of bird plumage in an inverted form transforms into one about the origin of poison.

Myths 161 and 186 superficially, one might say empirically, appear to be entirely different narratives concerned to explain the origins of completely disparate phenomena. What Lévi-Strauss is concerned to show is that a recurrent *order* underlies both myths, manifesting itself in inverted form. Other superficially different myths dealt with in the *Mythologiques* volumes are shown to be in a relation of homology to each other or partial inversions or transformations of the same themes in different ways. The vast set of South and North American myths dealt with articulate human social relations in various ways to different animal or plant species, supernatural beings, categories of food and modes utilized in its preparation, sound and silence, smell and taste, types of dress, climate, bodily functions, etc. The way in which social relations are structured in relation to these other categories follows the same set of logical rules for articulation used over and over again. The claim being made is that all the myths when considered together form a synchronic set of differences. Naturally much of the material dealt with is rather fragmentary. Ethnologists have in many cases only been able to record parts of myths and there may be, of course, considerable differences between their variations. We have already seen for Lévi-Strauss that the latter does not really matter as there is no original myth. As regards the former, since it is claimed that the myths form a total set, gaps in one myth may be filled in or illuminated by material from others collected hundreds, sometimes thousands, of miles away (see e.g. *OTM*: 18–19; *JP*: chapter 4). Understanding, according to Lévi-Strauss, can only be achieved if we analyse sets of myths rather than comparing isolated examples.

On the one hand a myth for Lévi-Strauss (or one suitable for analysis) is a summation of all its different variants. On the other hand each empirical example of a myth is held to be a realization of the same essence. Now if the latter is the case we can ask whether it is in fact necessary to take all the variations of a myth into account when conducting an analysis except perhaps to elucidate fragmentary examples. An answer here is that by considering different variations it is easier to pinpoint the key mythemic units, to sort out the structural wheat from the chaff of trivial elaboration. Since Lévi-Strauss decides on *a priori* grounds that variants on a myth do share the same essence (relating to the myth's *langue*) the possible objection that variations between versions of a myth *are* significant is automatically rejected.

In *SA1* myths are held to be constituted not only by aggregates of their variants but to form 'permutation' groups for which structural laws can be formulated. Lévi-Strauss claims that every myth corresponds to a 'canonical formula' of the type:

$$Fx\ (a) : Fy(b) \cong Fx(b) : Fa{-}1(y).$$

Myths link terms to functions, the terms in the formula being a and b and the functions x and y. He suggests that:

> it is assumed that a relation of equivalence exists between two situations defined respectively by an inversion of *terms* and *relations*, under two conditions: (1) that one term can be replaced by its opposite (in the above formula, a and $a{-}1$); (2) that an inversion be made between the *function value* and the *term value* of two elements (above, y and a). (*SA1*: 228)

What is being suggested here is that the relations between versions of myths are of a *logical* rather than a social or historical character. The clearest example of the use of this canonical formula occurs in *JP*. In this book Lévi-Strauss initially considers variants on Jivaro myths concerned with the origins of pottery. He shows that women, jealousy, pottery and the goatsucker (a bird species) form part of an interrelated system in a group of myths. Pottery, women and jealousy are shown to be linked together. A woman functions to explain the origin of pottery while a goatsucker functions as a jealous bird or cause for jealousy. Potting is a jealous art and a woman is systematically linked to a goatsucker in the narrative sequences by turning into a goatsucker. The jealous function of the goatsucker in the myths is arrived at by what is termed an 'empirical deduction' (*JP*: 50). It arises from an anthropomorphic interpretation of both the appearance of the bird in the real world (i.e. the world outside myths) and its behavioural characteristics: 'its solitary life, its nocturnal habits, its lugubrious cry, and its wide beak, which allows it to swallow large victims' (*JP*: 50). a problem now arises in the analysis if the relations between the various terms and functions or signs in the myths are to be understood as a logically related permutation group. If we know that there are two functions and two terms as follows:

jealousy   :   potter   [functions]
(goatsucker)   (woman)   [terms]

then we can ask: what is the relationship between a woman and a goatsucker and a goatsucker and pottery? Application of the canonical formula gives the following result:

jealousy : potter :: jealousy : goatsucker-1
(goatsucker) (woman)   (woman)   (potter)

in which the top row consists of functions relating to a series of terms in the bottom row, the overall meaning being: the jealous function of the goatsucker is to the potter function of the woman as the jealous function of the woman is to the reversed goatsucker function of the potter (*JP*: 57). What is being suggested here is that the myths are being manipulated by an analogical logic which is encapsulated in the application of the canonical formula. This logic relates opposed functions or signs and terms. The terms are things in the real world and/or elements in the myths, units of meaning. This is all a matter of representation and the manner in which forms of representation are linked in a binary symmetrical logic of oppositions. In the first part of the formula the goatsucker and the woman are terms, their role being reversed as functions in the second part. Corresponding with this reversal the goatsucker now plays a negative role, its function being reversed. In other words the role the goatsucker plays in the myths as a function, as opposed to being a term, is the opposite of its attributes as a term (jealousy).

Lévi-Strauss claims through a rather tortuous process of manipulations that the *a priori* solution of the relation between a woman and a goatsucker and a goatsucker and pottery is to be found or is implied by consideration of the myths themselves. While the goatsucker and pottery can both be related to jealousy in various ways a problem arises as to how to link the goatsucker and pottery, such a linkage being missing in the Jivaro myths. Lévi-Strauss provides it by consideration of the role another species of bird, the ovenbird, plays in a different set of Ayoré myths. In these myths the ovenbird has all the *inverted* characteristics of the goatsucker signifying harmony as opposed to conflict and jealousy and the ovenbird can be directly linked to potting. The ovenbird can thus be claimed to be an inverted goatsucker: the final function in the canonical formula. This formula makes sense of a transformational sequence systematically linking:

woman→jealousy→pottery→goatsucker→ovenbird

in the myths acting as either terms or functions and solves an additional logical problem that while the first three are heterogeneous, the last two both being species of birds appear to be homogeneous. This redundancy disappears because the logical positions of the two birds in the system are in fact heterogeneous, the ovenbird performing the function of a reversed goatsucker. The ovenbird itself does not appear in the canonical formula because:

> it cannot be considered as a term in a relation, because it does not appear as such in the Goatsucker myths. It is present as a term only in those myths that invert the former ones. However, by using it as a function, one verifies the system of equivalencies obtained through a transformation into an empirical deduction of what started out as only a transcendental deduction (namely, that the Goatsucker may be at the origins of pottery). (*JP*: 58)

Lévi-Strauss's structural analysis of myth does not make any attempt to fix and determine once and for all the meaning of myth as reference, say, to a canonical formula might suggest. The point is that myths are 'interminable', endlessly transformable in terms of each other. There is no obvious starting-point for an analysis, and equally, no finishing-point. The analysis of myth, providing one has a rich and varied material, can go on for ever. Any mythic structure remains a transformational structure and not one involving eternally fixed oppositions between terms and functions – the mythemic 'bundles of relations'. What mythic analysis can hope to establish is common principles of relational order and transformational logic. The structural system of myth consists of an endless play of differences, fixing points of opposition only as a singular moment in an endless transformational cycle.

Myths and Mind

For Lévi-Strauss myth construction is a perfect example of acts of *bricolage*, as already mentioned. Myths seize on concrete features of the world – animals, plants, human social relations – and on previous and foreign myths to construct a logic of the world. They do not just arise out of the minds of people but in dialectical fashion aid in the very formation of these minds. The study of mythology provides a unique opportunity to study mind – conceived as a collective possession rather than an individual faculty – because they possess a great degree of autonomy from infrastructural constraint. In the world of myths anything can happen, a fabulous space is constituted for people, animals, supernatural beings, tastes, smells, colours, landscapes, sounds and heavenly bodies to inhabit. Myth performs no obvious practical function and conveys no information of immediate utilitarian use. Even ascribing to it an ethical or moral end is in most cases an exercise of dubious validity. This does not imply that myth is merely decorative, a 'myth for myth's sake' theory but rather returns us to Lévi-Strauss's own position that it is fundamentally to do with making sense of and ordering social reality, these two features being two sides of the same coin.

In *SA1* and elsewhere he notes a fundamental contradiction between the apparent total freedom of myths to do anything and everything and a definite pattern of regularity and restriction:

> It would seem that in the course of a myth anything is likely to happen. There is no logic, no continuity. Any characteristic can be attributed to any subject; every conceivable relation can be found. But . . . this apparent arbitrariness is belied by the astounding similarity between myths collected in widely different regions. Therefore the problem: If the content of myth is contingent, how are we going to explain the fact that myths throughout the world are so similar? (*SA1*: 208)

Lévi-Strauss provides two main interlinked answers to such a question. Myths do in one sense have a common purpose in solving logical contradictions (see the discussion of the Oedipus myth above). Such contradictions arise in the collective mind so that the similarity of myths collected from remote regions can be explained in terms of an intellectual determinancy arising from the nature of the human mind itself.

Nature and Culture

One primary binary opposition which myths and more broadly all other social productions articulate, Lévi-Strauss argues, is that between nature and culture. The category nature is used in two main ways: (i) that which is not cultural, i.e. everything in the perceived phenomenological world (climate, plants, animals, etc.) standing outside humanity and its productions. It is thus negatively defined, a residual category. Beyond the limits of culture there is nature. (ii) There is a human nature to which cultural codes, ways of structuring experience, are to be reduced: ultimately the physical nature of the collective human mind itself.

These two conceptions stand in a relation of considerable tension. The uniqueness of humanity resides in culture, that which is not natural but socially constructed. However the basis for this construction is ultimately to be discovered in nature: the cultural is natural. Relations existing in nature are used to produce cultural products which themselves incorporate these relations. As opposed to this, Lévi-Strauss also stresses at a number of points in his work that a contrast between nature and culture is itself a product of culture. The cultural defines and creates the natural in various forms.

One of Lévi-Strauss's most well-known discussions of the relation between nature and culture is his analysis of cooking, a major theme taken up over and over again in the *Mythologiques* volumes. All societies have language, all societies also possess foods or cook. Understanding of the significance of cooking may be illuminated by a 'culinary triangle' representing sets of binary oppositions: normal–transformed and culture–nature, found in all human societies. This relationship is illustrated in figure 1.1. All humans eat food, found in three main states: raw, cooked or rotten. In relation to cooking, raw or uncooked food represents an unmarked pole of a triangle, the other two poles being strongly marked in an oppositional form. Cooked food is a cultural transformation of the raw; rotten food is a natural transformation. The triangle formed by raw–cooked–rotten forms a semantic field which may then be related to actual cooking practices or processes transforming raw material (*OTM*: 478). Figure 1.2 shows a more advanced form of the culinary triangle developed by Lévi-Strauss to take account of different modes of cooking: roasting, boiling and smoking (*OTM*: 490). Roasting is a mode of food preparation in which the product is closest to a raw state in that the meat is directly brought into contact with an agent of cultural conversion – fire – without mediation of air or water or any other cultural apparatus. Boiling requires the mediation of water and a container. It reduces the end product to a decomposed state analagous to rotten food. Smoking requires the mediation of air and is the slowest but most complete cooking process. In roasting the amount of air utilized is reduced to a minimum whereas in smoking it is increased to a maximum. The smoked and the boiled stand in an oppositional relation in respect of the natural element utilized; the smoked and the roast are in

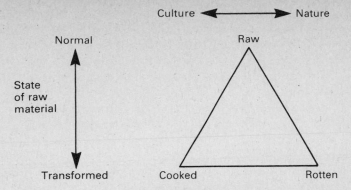

Figure 1.1 The culinary triangle

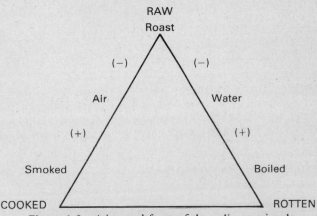

Figure 1.2 Advanced form of the culinary triangle

Source: *OTM*: 478. By kind permission, Jonathan Cape Limited and Harper and Row.

opposition in terms of the volume of air employed. The nature–culture dividing-line may be drawn parallel either to an air axis or a water axis in relation to the means of cooking utilized: roasting and smoking are natural processes whereas boiling requiring a container is cultural. However, when we consider the end products, smoked food is the most highly cultural product, boiled food belonging most closely to nature and roast food falling in between.

Lévi-Strauss does not claim that such a scheme is universal and notes that modifications are required to take account of other modes of cooking, for example grilling or frying. Further refinements might also take account of different types of unprocessed raw foodstuffs (*OTM*: 495) and so on. The fundamental point to be made, irrespective of whether or not a culinary triangle might seem a useful or plausible device, is that all humans eat culturally, as opposed to animals who do not. Various eating and cooking practices are loaded down with symbolic and cultural significance. Social practices decide what is food/non-food and link culinary arts and table manners to differing sets of social relations, categories and occasions. Leach explains this admirably:

> In that we are men, we are all a part of Nature; in that we are human beings, we are all a part of Culture. Our survival as men depends on our ingestion of food (which is part of Nature); our survival as human beings depends upon our use of social categories which are derived from cultural classifications imposed on elements of Nature ... Food is an especially appropriate 'mediator' because, when we eat, we establish, in a literal sense, a direct identity between ourselves (Culture) and our food (Nature). Cooking is thus universally a means by which Nature is transformed into Culture, and categories of cooking are always peculiarly appropriate for use as symbols of social differentiation. (Leach 1970: 34)

Cooking is a code, not just one that marks a transition from nature to culture but one that can be used to structure culture itself. The manner in which unprocessed substances may fit into a nature–culture dichotomy is both highly variable and significant. For example in *HA* Lévi-Strauss shows how both honey and tobacco transcend such a system of differentiation. Both are natural substances yet neither requires cooking. Honey, made by bees and ready for consumption by people, is naturally 'pre-cooked' requiring no cultural intervention to make it edible. Tobacco, on the other hand, must be entirely consumed by cultural means (burnt to ashes by fire) before it can be smoked. It is in a sense *beyond* cooking. Honey and tobacco represent two opposite poles, the former being over-natural, the latter over-cultural. When viewed in this light it is perhaps not surprising that both are utilized as totemic substances in rituals in which their transgression of a nature–culture divide has to be neutralized. Cooking transforms nature into culture; ritual practices transform honey from a *profane* rawness to a *sacred* rawness thus coping with its 'pre-cooked' state (*HA*: 40). This is illustrated in figure 1.3.

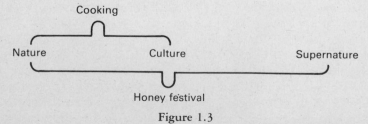

Figure 1.3

Form and Content

Contrary to formalism, structuralism refuses to set the concrete against the abstract and to recognize a privileged value in the latter. *Form* is defined by opposition to material other than itself. But *structure* has no distinctive content; it is content itself, apprehended in a logical organization conceived as a property of the real . . . If a little structuralism leads away from the concrete, a lot of structuralism leads back to it. (*SA2*: 115–16)

To what extent does a structuralist analysis sacrifice content for form as many commentators claim? Lévi-Strauss consistently claims that a structural analysis can not only take account of both form and content but actually links them. To illustrate such a claim he contrasts his own approach with Propp's formalism, or atomistic structural approach, in *SA2*.

Propp (1968) reduced all folk-tales to thirty-one fixed elements or functions (e.g. prohibition; violation; struggle; victory). Such functions are 'supported' by dramatis personae. When the functions are classified according to their supports, each dramatic character in a folk-tale brings together several functions in an 'action sphere'. So the functions 'villainy', 'struggle', 'pursuit' may form the action sphere of the villain. Propp claims that not only are the functions limited in number but so are the action spheres, their number being reducible to seven. A fairy-tale is reduced to a narrative which puts into words a limited number of functions in a regular order of succession. Differences between tales relate to choices made between the thirty-one functions and whether they are repeated or not. All fairy-tales have an identical *atomistic* structure. The elements can be completely specified without consideration of their role in a larger whole. Ultimately all the tales are of one type with regard to their structure. Lévi-Strauss comments that such a single tale:

> would be reduced to such a vague and general abstraction that nothing would be learned from it about the objective causes of a multitude of particular tales . . . Nothing can be more convincing of the inadequacy of formalism than its inability to reconstitute the very empirical content from which it was itself drawn. What then has it lost on the way? Precisely the content. (*SA1*: 134–5)

In order for a structuralist analysis to be successful taking account of this content is of vital significance. Lévi-Strauss, in the chapter on Propp, provides the example of 'plum trees' and 'apple trees'. A formalist analysis might only consider the concept 'tree' as important thus ignoring the types of tree referred to. This can only result in an inadequate analysis, for what interests a South American native is the *fecundity* of plum trees and the strength and depth of apple-tree roots:

> the one introduces a positive function, 'fecundicity', the other a negative function, 'earth–sky transition'; and both are a function of vegetation. The apple tree, in its turn, is opposed to the wild turnip (a removable plug between the two worlds), itself realizing the function: positive 'sky–earth transition'. (*SA2*: 136)

A structuralist analysis, according to Lévi-Strauss, reveals the significance or the meaning of content *in* form or structure. The meaning is included or compressed within the system (*NM*: 693). The structure generates and makes sense of the empirical richness to be found in myth in particular and cultural practices in general.

Lévi-Strauss's critique of Propp's formalism does not in fact signify a major difference between formalism and structuralism. In essence what Lévi-Strauss seems to be claiming is that Propp does not take his formalism far enough: there are still some residual elements of 'content' in his analyses. What Lévi-Strauss attempts to demonstrate is that by paying meticulous attention to the details of content it may all ultimately be reduced to and be seen to be an effect of pure form (structure): there is nothing left over or omitted. Content can be totally collapsed into the form that generates it. While Propp might consider it sufficient to put all trees into one category, Lévi-Strauss's analysis embraces and encompasses the specific varieties.

The Logic of the Concrete

Bricolage

In his major work on the logic of the 'savage' or untamed mind, *SM*, which is principally concerned with forms of classification in small-scale societies, Lévi-Strauss introduces the image of the *bricoleur*: the closest English equivalent of which is a professional do-it-yourself person who performs various patching-up and construction tasks with whatever materials happen to be at hand – a screw may be used when a nail is lacking, a hack-saw substituted for a wood-saw – a person who, in short, makes do with whatever material is at hand to achieve a given end. The set of heterogeneous instruments and materials used by the *bricoleur* to perform the task in hand is closed and he or she has to make do with that which is available, which may bear no direct relation to the current or any future project. The contingent results of the tasks engaged in by the *bricoleur* supply him or her with fresh or renewed instruments and materials from the various construction and demolition projects engaged in. Things are kept because they may be of use at a later date rather than in terms of a particular set of future tasks in view. The *bricoleur* does not possess specialized tools in relation to, say, various specific and delimited plumbing or carpentry projects; his or her means and materials are more generalized, having operational or multifunctional use in relation to different situations (*SM*: 17–18). *Bricolage* is the act of using and adapting existing elements in a fresh way. It is a vital component of the untamed mind, permitting means to be transformed into ends and vice versa. The untamed mind creates associations and meanings through repeated acts of *bricolage* that build on each other. In this activity it remains fundamentally distinct from contemporary forms of 'scientific' western consciousness in industrialized societies dependent on a high degree of differentiation utilizing specialized materials and means (calculus; abstract symbolic logic) to perform specific tasks. One primary difference between *bricolage* and Western thought is conceived by Lévi-Strauss in terms of goal orientation (*SM*: 19), itself restricted by differing forms of logic. An engineer is constrained in precisely the same manner as a *bricoleur* in that the execution of any task is dependent on prior sets of theoretical and practical knowledges, restricting possible solutions. However, the engineer will try to transcend existing constraints while the *bricoleur* is happy to work within the confines of an existing operational set. This difference arises because the engineer employs an abstract theoretical symbol set with which to approach the world whereas the *bricoleur* employs preconstituted sign systems. The fundamental opposition Lévi-Strauss proposes is that between *concepts* and *signs*. The engineer employs the former, the *bricoleur* the latter. The perspicacity of concepts inheres in their transparent relationship to the world which permit its manipulation and the extension of knowledges. Conceptual systems open up the set of possibilities and perspectives. Sign systems work by a process of reorganization which while being transformational in nature does not renew or extend the set being worked on. Such systems demand the active interposition of human culture on to reality, rather than a process of abstracted separation. The *bricoleur* communicates both with signs and through their medium. The engineer orders the world, generalizes and solves problems, through a science of the abstract. The *bricoleur*'s knowledge is a science of the concrete. These remain two different ways in which to approach the world, give sense to it, and solve problems. The relationship between these two approaches is not evolutionary or progressive. Each is equally valid in relation to differing social and historical circumstances. Furthermore, one system does not replace the other; *bricolage* is of essential importance in the constitution of day-to-day practices in all societies. For Lévi-Strauss it is a distinctively *human* quality to think in this manner, when not following a restrictive series of 'scientific' rules. Totemism and mythological thought are prime examples of intellectual *bricolage*.

Functionalism and Structuralism

The competing claims of functionalist and structuralist forms of explanation are well exemplified by consideration of various attempts to account for the phenomenon of totemism. In *T* and *SM* Lévi-Strauss demonstrates with great power and clarity the limitations of functionalist analyses and the elegance of an alternative structuralist position.

Broadly defined, totemism entails notions of special sets of relations between things existing in the natural world, most usually animals or plants, and specific social groups or individuals. These relations may involve prohibitions such as food taboos; ritual relations such as rites of increase; mythological connotations such as belief in the totem as an ancestor of the group and delimited sets of exchange relations especially involving marriage restrictions involving exogamy between totemic clans. Early anthropological work attempted to explain totemism as a primitive form of religion situated at the bottom of an evolutionary ladder and/or as irrational supersitition highlighting the rudimentary nature of the 'savage' mind. A bewildering variety of ethnological accounts of acts labelled as totemic led many anthropologists to reject it as a meaningful category altogether. In *T* Lévi-Strauss accepts this position. Whatever we might like to call totemism can itself be subsumed in terms of a much broader and universal human form of action — classification and categorization processes — and this marks a first step towards his proposed solution.

Twentieth-century functionalist anthropologies attempted to explain totemism by relating it to the practical and biological exigencies of social life. For Malinowski (1948) totemism was readily explicable. A belief system concerned with plants and animals occurs because of their economic importance. Totemism becomes a 'natural' development for any group concerned with its food supply. The rituals and prohibitions become explicable in terms of a desire to control various species and phenomena whether they are edible, inedible, benign or dangerous. From such a perspective totemism is simply explained as arising from natural socioeconomic conditions. Different types of totemism do not matter: content becomes subsumed under form. We supposedly know why it exists. The only problem becomes why it does not exist everywhere: a question deftly side-stepped by the functional-ists. Radcliffe-Brown (1929) argues that totemism plays an important role in maintaining social order, in assuring the permanence and solidarity of social units composing society. Solidarity arises from forms of individual consciousness reinforced by collective ritual conduct in terms of specific objects representing each group. Totem-ism chooses animals and plants as symbolic elements to represent groups because of their prior significance. The explanation is partly evolutionary. First, ritual relations between people and resources arise naturally amongst hunter–gatherers; later, these are extended in totemic form to promote group solidarity. An animal becomes totemic because it is 'good to eat' (T: 62).

Enormous difficulties arise from such a line of argument. There are innumerable cases of totems with no discernible use, such as the case of flies and mosquitoes. Incorporation within a functionalist framework requires considerable ingenuity. For example, totemic flies may be explained as associated with what natives desire to see at certain times of the year – rain. Alternatively their increase might benefit the local group by molesting strangers. Lévi-Strauss points out that: 'It would be difficult to find anything which, in one way or another, positively or negatively (or even because of its lack of significance?) might not be said to offer an interest, and the utilitarian and naturalist theory would thus be reduced to a series of propositions empty of any content' (T: 64).

In 1951 Radcliffe-Brown published what Lévi-Strauss refers to as his 'second theory of totemism' (T: 83) claiming that Radcliffe-Brown surreptitiously laid down the basis for a structuralist explanation, the implications of which he may have been unaware. The following basic problems are addressed:

1 Why should different groups be associated with *particular* natural species, e.g. a crow or an eagle?
2 How do the societies in question view this relation and why does it occur?

The first question demands a consideration of both form and content. Instead of just asking why birds occur as totemic emblems considera-tion shifts over to uncover specific principles which might explain why specific species of birds are utilized in terms of their *relationship* to each other within an overall system. Radcliffe-Brown attempts to answer the second question by referring to myths, finding they have a single theme: 'the resemblances and differences of animal species are trans-lated into terms of friendship and conflict, solidarity and opposition.

In other words the world of animal life is represented in terms of social relations similar to those of human society' (Radcliffe-Brown cited in *T*: 87)

This leads directly on to Lévi-Strauss's own conclusion that animals and plants are not chosen because they are good to eat but because they are good to think (*T*: 89). In other words animals and plants become manipulated as part of sign systems. They mean or connote something beyond themselves. The relationship between crow and eagle is symbolically utilized to encode relations between human groups:

crow : eagle : : Clan A : Clan B.

In other words, crow is to eagle as Clan A is to Clan B. Totemism is explained as a sign system serving to differentiate human society on either the basis of groups or individuals. But why these pairs of birds? In the case of crow and eagle it is because they have in common at least one characteristic permitting comparison. The principle underlying their differentiation, used as signs for social differentiation, is that while both are carnivorous, the eagle is a bird of prey, the crow a carrion-eater. Perceptible differences in the natural world are used to map the social world. Animal species provide a ready-made system of *differences*. They both look different and have differing behaviour patterns offering a vast set of means and techniques to contrast human groups: an ideal set of materials for intellectual *bricolage*.

SM extends this line of argument. Contemporary totemic classifications can be considered to be the results of a long process of *bricolage* using various odds and ends left over from previous historical and psychological processes. The logic of the concrete involved (playing on differences in the natural world) to create sign systems may often be an extremely complicated one involving the establishment of connections between diverse remains of pre-defined and pre-existing materials in the natural world. These materials may be used again and again for the same purpose or for a different one if the original purpose becomes historically diverted or contradicted. Various fragments are pieced together from differing sources of origin to construct a structured set or system. The patterns created actualize possibilities but these are not unlimited since meaning is a function of the overall layout, design or balance of the system affecting a finite number of incorporated elements.

Lévi-Strauss provides a concise hypothetical example (see figure 1.4). Once a series of signs is employed to differentiate a series of groups it will be synchronically coherent but may become diachronically disrupted through processes of demographic change.

In the initial stage (A) we have three clans each of which bears the

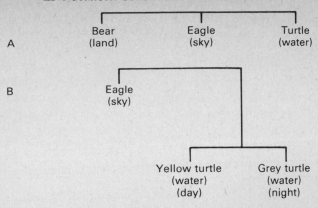

Figure 1.4
Source: *SM*: 47. By kind permission, Weidenfeld and Nicolson Ltd and University of Chicago Press.

name of an animal symbolizing a natural element. Demographic changes lead to the amalgamation or elimination of the bear clan and an increase in the population of the turtle clan, which as a result, fissures into two distinct clans. These become distinguished on the basis of colours of turtle species. The initial structure is transformed correspondingly at stage B. The original three terms involve a triple dichotomy based on natural elements. These transform into a system involving two dichotomies: sky–water and yellow–grey. If the opposition yellow–grey were to be given a further symbolic significance, e.g. by reference to day and night, then there would be an overall system involving four terms and two binary oppositions: sky–water and day–night (*SM*: 68). The latter is an example of the manner in which ideas pertaining to different levels of social reality may be converted in terms of each other and related or associated.

Various sign systems work by transforming the natural in terms of the cultural. Nature is exploited to superimpose a logical grid of meaning on the organization of social life. The logical principle at work is always to be able to oppose terms on the basis of differences. How this actually occurs is a secondary consideration. Totemic or other classificatory systems serve the purpose of *converting ideas* between different levels of social reality to create an overall structure of meaning: 'they are codes suitable for conveying messages which can be transposed into other codes, and for expressing messages received by means of different codes in terms of their own system' (*SM*: 76–7). A logic of the concrete has the primary aim of building a social logic – any set of divisions or distinctions – through the use of 'given' features of the natural world. The natural is mapped on to the cultural not just to symbolize differences between (often fairly similar) human groups, but to help to create, reproduce and reinforce these differences. In tandem with building a social logic a symbolic logic will necessarily be created and differentially incorporated into other classificatory schemes and symbol sets, based on principles of differentiation, opposition and substitution: metonymy and metaphor. These schemes and sets provide 'adjustable threads' giving social groups the intellectual means of both focusing differentially on alternative planes, from the most abstract (cultural) to the most concrete (natural) (*SM*: 136). The types of logical operations bound up in 'totemic' operations provide groups with conceptual structures or 'guides' for practice in any sphere of social life, for example kin relations, economic exchanges, eating prohibitions, pollution rites.

Now here some very interesting possibilities arise. The 'natural' distinctiveness of any particular biological species (recognized culturally) furnishes thought with potential access to a whole range of possibilities and permutations. Considered in isolation a species is a collection of individuals but in relation to other species it will form a set of definitions. Furthermore each individual animal, the theoretically indefinable collection of which makes up a species, itself forms an organism consisting of a set of functions. An animal species: 'possesses an internal dynamic: being a collection poised between two systems, the species is the operator which allows (and even makes obligatory) the passage from the unity of a multiplicity to the diversity of a unity' (*SM*: 136). Animal species form privileged entities serving to mediate between two extremes of classification: the categorical plane and the singular plane. Animals form nodes of symbolic systems structured at various levels: (i) *differentiation* of animals between species; and (ii) *similarity* between an animal and other animals between species on the basis of specific features, e.g. anatomical parts and/or behavioural characteristics. The system works, then, on two axes, one resting on differences, the other on similarities which may cross-cut each other. An 'imaginary dismembering of each species . . . progressively re-establishes the totality on another plane'. For example, five clans may adopt the totems puma, bear, eagle, deer and swan. They are thus relationally defined and differentiated at a species level. At another level each animal is decomposed into parts according to a principle of correspondence (e.g. muzzle = beak). Equivalent parts are (i) regrouped among themselves, and (ii) grouped all together in terms of some particular characteristic, e.g. as being 'charcoal animals' (see figure 1.5). Animals, in this manner, become conceptual tools with multiple possibilities for creating classificatory order, structures and

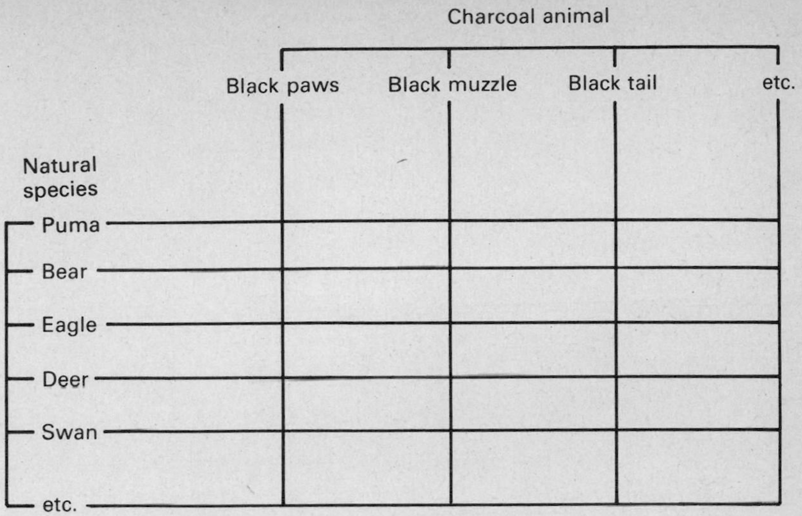

Figure 1.5

Source: after *SM*: 147. By kind permission, Weidenfeld and Nicolson Ltd and University of Chicago Press.

associations. The system creates a three-dimensional matrix *by means of* creatures constituting both objects of thought and conceptual tools:

> Thus it is never, properly speaking, the eagle which the Osage invoke. For, according to the time and circumstances, it is eagles of different species which are in question: the golden eagle, the spotted eagle, the bald eagle, etc., or eagles of different colours: red, white, spotted, etc.; or finally eagles at different stages of their life: young, old, etc. (*SM*: 149)

The different levels of species, anatomical, behavioural and ecological differentiation, furnish a treasury of signifiers which can be used to encode social relations and symbolically construct and structure both the natural and social worlds. The richness of possibilities generated is exemplified by a 'totemic operator' (figure 1.6) consisting in this case, arbitrarily of only three species with three levels of anatomical differentiation. The figure illustrates the logical possibilities (not all of which may be necessarily exploited) arising from:

1 Initial differentiation in terms of three species.
2 Detotalization of each species into individuals.
3 Detotalization of the individuals into anatomical parts: heads, necks, feet.
4 Retotalization of parts of animals within a species (e.g. all bears' necks).

34 CHRISTOPHER TILLEY

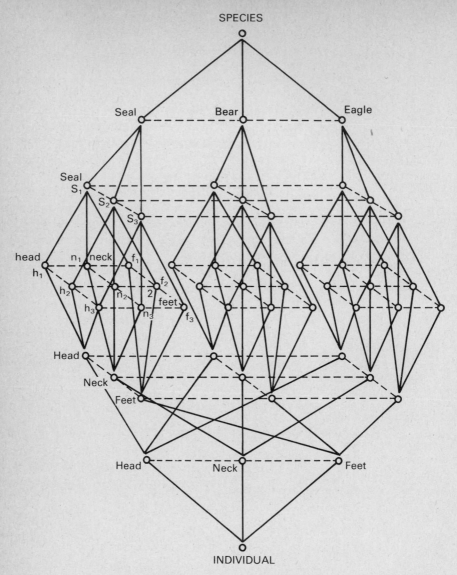

Figure 1.6   The totemic operator
Source: *SM*: figure 8, p. 152. By kind permission, Weidenfeld and Nicolson Ltd and University of Chicago Press.

5 Regrouping of classes of parts (e.g. all heads etc.)
6 Regrouping of parts to restore an individual to 'wholeness' (e.g. in the form of 'charcoal animals' — see above).

Such a system may be extended in three directions: (i) as a result of diachronic changes in social networks as in the bear–eagle–turtle example discussed above; (ii) through universalization; (iii) through particularization (*SM*: chapter 6). Universalization extends the classificatory system to domains outside the initial set. The species grid may be extended from social categories, e.g. clans, to, for example, order diseases and their cures. Each species as amongst the Indians of the south-east United States, 'possesses' a specific disease or its remedy (*SM*: 164). Alternatively, or in addition, species may serve to organize space, social territories etc. Particularization is the reverse process, narrowing the classification down to a system that just denotes or names. For example, a homology may be effected between members of groups (individual humans) and anatomical parts of animals such as limbs (*SM*: 169). If

clan A : clan B : : bear species : eagle species

then

member x of A : member y of B : : limb l of bear : limb m of eagle.

In this case particular individuals become differentiated at the level of the species grid.

Anthropology and History

History as Myth

Lévi-Strauss's most developed statements on history occur in the last two chapters of *SM* in relation to a critique of Sartre. History, he argues, is a contemporary myth to be attributed the same status in relation to the 'real world' as the American Indian myths he analyses in the *Mythologiques* volumes. Furthermore, just like myth, history, has a binary structure; it is a code for creating, maintaining and making sense of discursive objects which it creates and then sets to work on. Any historical happening such as the French Revolution has a mythic structure (*SM*: 254). As with Amazonian myths there are a plurality of different accounts using and stressing different events from varying points of view or interpretative fields. These events and their innumerable variations all supposedly relate to the same country, the same time-period, the same people. In reality the events in various accounts cut through, reduce and simplify a multilayered structural order: 'a historical fact is what really took place, but where did anything take place? Each episode in a revolution or a war resolves itself into a multitude of individual psychic movements' (*SM*: 257). The historical facts of the matter are, of course, not given but constituted. Any history, whatever its claims, can be no more than a juxtaposition of a few local histories and in even the most comprehensive account much more will be left out of the story than put in it: 'discontinuous figures, against a continuity barely good enough to be used as a backdrop' (*SM*: 257). The French Revolution conceived as a unitary event did not take place; there is not one French Revolution but an infinite multitude of them. A historical account is only possible by virtue of that evidence it ignores, not that with which it chooses to recount. The defining characteristic, then, of a successful historical text must be not so much that which it chooses to discuss, but that which it does not discuss. Absences rather than plenitudes define the essence of the telling of history.

The historian's task is to create order out of chaos. In this sense it is in principle no different an exercise than that facing an anthropologist attempting to understand a multitude of mythological fragments. The anthropologist (Lévi-Strauss) creates order by breaking myths down into constituent units composed of various types of opposition: binary structures. The historian also employs a binary structure, one which it could be argued, is consistently over-valorized. This binary structure is dependent on the constitution of a system of dates. The importance of these dates do not reside in themselves but in what they effect: a binary structure consisting of *before* and *after*. History creates it own *sign* systems which like all sign systems are essentially arbitrary, i.e. the signs do not simply mirror a fixed external reality. Histories select significant units from superimposed and arbitrary pre-established chronological systems, which themselves remain radically incompatible. All historical dates, having the effect of creating a before/after opposition are not of the same nature. Dates referring to minutes, days, years, centuries, millenia, or for that matter, C14, do not have the same status. Dates belong to different classes so dates such as 1486, 1786, 1986 belong to one class, 23 January, 26 May etc., to another and so on. Such sequences of dates have different modulations or frequencies and to make sense they must be coded in a relational series: 'The code can therefore consist only of classes of dates, where each date has meaning in as much as it stands in complex relations of correlation and opposition with other dates... In a system of this type, alleged historical continuity is secured only by dint of fraudulent outlines' (*SM:* 259–61). Notions of historical continuity, from the dawn of humanity to the present day are fraudulent because different classes of dates form discontinuous rather than continuous series, differing frames of reference based on differing processes of selection. The validity of any historical account is not found in the elements of history but their structuring, according to a code of dates, into patterns which may have greater or lesser degrees of coherence (*RC*: 13; *SM*: 261). Historical accounts code before and after sequences into differing narrative structures. There may be 'hot' histories where many dates appear to demand inclusion and 'cold' histories with fewer dates.

History, it might be said, forges 'creation' myths of various kinds, ultimately to be related to our present. The more recent the historical period being narrated, the greater the spurious solidity and immutability the account will appear to possess. History and myth are not radically opposed. They are different names for narrative accounts with similar functions in different societies. Myth in small-scale societies makes sense of social experience by ordering and structuring it. In the West histories are our myths and they serve much the same purpose. Why myth and history appear to differ is that they relate, respectively, to analogical and domesticated thought (*SM:* 263) (see pp. 26–7).

If history is merely a method for structuring reality, as Lévi-Strauss argues, then it can make no claim to providing a privileged knowledge. History conceived as events in succession is only one way of ordering human experience and not necessarily of primary significance. Furthermore historical understanding can make no claim to disclose the most fundamental features of human existence. This is the essence of his attack. It is not to claim that historical knowledge is worthless but that its hegemonic claims to superiority need to be questioned.

Other remarks on history in relation to anthropology occur in a scattered and less critical form (*SA1*: chapter 1; *SA2*: chapter 1; part IV). The two fields are sometimes regarded as simply complementary, history dealing with diversity through time, anthropology through space. Considered alone, both provide inadequate knowledge of humanity; when taken together they may begin to approach an adequate understanding of the social. It is pointless to argue for one and against the other. The major contrast drawn is between history which is argued to organize its data in relation to the 'conscious expressions of social life, while anthropology proceeds by examining its unconscious foundations' (*SA1*: 18). Marx's statement that 'men make their own history, but they do not make it just as they please' is maintained to justify history first and anthropology second (*SA1*: 23). The latter part of Marx's aphorism is used to refer to the unconscious in culture Lévi-Strauss is concerned to analyse but in order to do this successfully history must first be eliminated (*SA1*: 23). The analyst cannot combine a historical and an anthropological analysis, because the concerns of history dealing with a flux of conscious events undermine those of an anthropology concerned to unearth enduring synchronic structural patterns. For the structural anthropologist to be successful, history, both as temporal occurrence and as accounts purporting to make sense of these occurrences, must be bracketed off. However, almost despite himself, Lévi-Strauss does suggest in places that a structural analysis can contribute to history through suggesting earlier mythological forms, their associations and derivatives (*WM*: 32; cf. *SA1*: 21).

The crux of the matter is that in many statements and in virtually all the *practice* of his analyses, Lévi-Strauss while appearing to be proposing a simple division of disciplinary labour is also suggesting at the same time that the two disciplines are fundamentally incompatible. Their knowledges cannot be combined in any meaningful way; they may perhaps be placed side by side. History describes a flux of events, structural anthropology goes behind that flux to penetrate to what may be claimed to be a more fundamental and basic level of human experience: the invariant structures of the collective human mind and the manner in which they organize reality.

Time and History

A concern with history is not simply reducible to a concern with time. What Lévi-Strauss may be interpreted as arguing for is that history is not in time, rather time is in history. In other words there is no such thing as time conceived as a reference dimension but rather differing times relevant to and created by differing sociocultural realities and conditions. History, as a chronologically framed account of the past, is structurally necessary in the contemporary Western world. In other societies it has no meaning, significance or relevance. History is an imposition, not a necessity. By contrast temporality and the recognition of temporality can be argued to be an enduring feature of all societies.

Berman (1983) describes modernism, our contemporary condition – and one itself subsuming and accounting for notions of postmodernism – as:

To find ourselves in an environment that promises us adventure, power, joy, growth, transformation of ourselves and the world – and, at the same time, that threatens to destroy everything we have, everything we know, everything we are . . . a unity of disunity: it pours us all into a maelstrom of perpetual disintegration and renewal, of struggle and contradiction, of ambiguity and anguish. To be modern is to be part of a universe in which, as Marx said, 'all that is solid melts into air'. (Berman 1983: 15)

Marxism is a thoroughly modern set of beliefs, fashioned in a modern world. Forged in a society of constant change, it itself proposes to change the world, to turn it upside down to create a new social order out of the wreckage of the old. The historical code, itself forged in the modern age is packed with signs of social transformation, growth, innovation. The chronology has an internal dynamism, it is 'hot', in a thermodynamic spiral, endlessly creating diversity and forms of social differentiation. Lévi-Strauss distinguishes between the hot societies of the contemporary West and 'cold' societies in which history is both cumulative and stationary (SA2: 28ff.; C: 39). This is by no means an absolute distinction. Various societies have differing degrees of heat. The hottest are our own; by comparison the small-scale societies Lévi-Strauss studies are predominantly cold. Time is experienced differently; it has a radically different significance: 'Whereas so-called primitive societies are surrounded by the substance of history and try to remain impervious to it, modern societies interiorize history, as it were, and turn it into the motive power of their development' (C: 39). History is structurally necessary in industrial societies; it helps to fuel the fires of change. Furthermore a historical approach must be invoked in any attempt to explain them. By contrast, in cold societies, history is neither so important in their constitution, nor in their explanation. Lévi-Strauss is not denying that cold societies have a history: 'their past is as old as ours, since it goes back to the origin of the species . . . these societies seem to have developed or retained a particular wisdom which impels them to resist desperately any modification in their structure that would enable history to burst into their midst' (SA1: 28); but suggests that their conceptions of temporality are radically different. Myths are 'machines which repress time' when this time is to be conceived as irreversible, linear, empty, temporal duration. Time does not become mobilized as history. The production of history depends on a sense of historicity itself produced by the dynamism of the industrial world. It might be added that it is only when small-scale societies become thoroughly swept up in a world capitalist order that they require history. So-called development and archaeology—history go hand in hand.

For small-scale, cold, societies, history may not be necessary but this does not imply a static, frozen, atemporality. It rather suggests the operating of differing modes of temporality in terms other than a chronological code implying time as simply measurable duration.

Subjectivity and the Unconscious

> I believe the ultimate goal of the human sciences to be not to constitute, but to dissolve man. (*SM*: 247)

Lévi-Strauss postulates a homology between the structuring of language and that of other aspects of culture. Both are conceived as results or manifestations of the operation of *unconscious* processes and are to be ultimately linked back to the nature of the human mind. Linguistic structures form a system used by all speakers. This system is not discursively available and therefore is to be located as something internalized in the mind. All language-users share the same internalized patterns so that this mind is not to be reduced to an individual level but takes on the form of a collective unconscious. Lévi-Strauss assumes that the unconscious logical faculty of the mind organizes all different aspects of social life and thus permits direct linkages to be made between them from myth to kinship to culinary practices. The collective unconscious forms a basic condition of existence for the cultural and the symbolic.

Human beings no more control or operate structures than gravity. Rather they become defined by pre-existing kin and mythological systems, etc., so the structure actually defines and creates subjectivity. Intentionality or the 'I think' of human agency is quite irrelevant from such a perspective:

> there exists an 'it' who 'thinks' through me and who first causes me to doubt whether it is I who am thinking . . . To Montaigne's 'What do I know?' (from which everything stems), Descartes believed it possible to answer that 'I know that I am, since I think'. To this Rousseau retorts with a 'What am I?' without a definite solution, since the question presupposes the completion of another, more essential one: 'Am I?' Intimate experience provides only this 'it' . . . It lies in a conception of man which places the other before the self, and in a conception of mankind which places life before. men. (*SA2*: 37, modified translation)

Subjectivity is determined by structures located in the collective unconscious or the human mind. This mind constitutes the unconscious of each individual who can do no other than to act out patterns – construct culture – in accordance with its constraints. This location of determinancy in the unconscious and bracketing of the human subject is one of the most radical moves of Lévi-Strauss's structuralism. Meaning neither begins nor ends in the individual agent. The creation of meaning is itself impossible without prior location in a pre-existing structure always already in place and asserting its influence. There are no unique individuals, no singular acts, no absolute creativity: 'each man feels as a function of the way in which he is permitted or obliged to act . . . Impulses and emotions explain nothing: they are always *results*, either of the power of the body or the impotence of the mind' (*T*: 70–1). In the beginning there was the structure and this structure was the Word. Lévi-Strauss does not therefore try to explain myths in terms of putative reasons or intentions of individuals. People do not make up myths rather myths *think themselves* through people who merely form a physical support or function for their narration (*RC*: 10). Although people do tell myths, the individual nuances of content do not matter and remain contingent in comparison with the supraindividual collective characteristics of myth that Lévi-Strauss claims to be analysing.

Mind and Nature

At some stage in his analyses, and particularly when he feels pressed to ground them in some ultimate reality, Lévi-Strauss reduces his explanations either to culture, conceived as an arbitrary significative system, or to nature. As we have seen, nature performs a dual role in his work, first, as an abstract idea negatively defined — that which is not cultural; second, in the sense of a 'human nature'. This second sense involves two main aspects: persons as biological entities in many respects no different from animals and the reduction of that which is specifically human, the arbitrary symbolic construction of culture, to the human mind and its distinctive characteristics. This mind is however itself a natural (i.e. physical, biological, material) object. The mind reduces to nature because it is a natural object. In one direction the move is towards brain physiology if an ultimate cause for culture is sought: the end link in a chain. However, Lévi-Strauss has virtually nothing to say about this in its specifics apart from asserting that there are similarities between the structure of the brain and the mind. Both work in tandem to determine symbolic action setting up systems of difference and oppositions. Binary oppositions in the structuring of culture relate back to a cerebral binary mechanism (*SA1*: 92).

The human mind, then, is structural and structures. Such a conception of mind clearly has little to do with the unconscious of Freud and is argued for retrospectively on the basis of the findings of Jakobsonian linguistics. The mind or the unconscious Lévi-Strauss refers to is akin to a digital computer or any other machine programmed to structure any and every phenomenon fed into it. These materials arrive to be processed through the mind machine by virtue of the activities of people on and in the world. The end result is the structuring and classifying activity of the collective 'savage mind' which reacts to its environment and logically reconstructs it (*VA*: 110) to provide a communicative grid. The mind processes nature in a manner analogous to a potato-chipper squeezing out regularity in form from an irregular set of materials. From this perspective, then, a recourse to brain physiology may provide a causal explanation but most of Lévi-Strauss's work seeks simply to explain objects of analysis by relating them to an underlying system of distinctions, categories and principles: they are related back to culture. The mind is in a sense an empty envelope for these structures and little more: 'The unconscious . . . is always empty – or, more accurately, it is as alien to mental images as is the stomach to the foods which pass through it. As the organ of a specific function, the unconscious merely imposes structural laws upon inarticulated elements which originate elsewhere' (*SA1*: 203).

Human minds are structured in the same way everywhere so that it is possible for Lévi-Strauss to claim that if there is a final signified of myth, it resides in the mind that operates on the world to produce it. The mind produces myths and myths produce an image of the world already inherent in the structure of the mind (*RC*: 341). A logical outcome of such a tautological line of reasoning is the suggestion that it is: 'in the last resort immaterial whether in this book the thought processes of the South American Indians take shape through the medium of my thought, or whether mine take place through the medium of theirs' (*RC*: 13).

Truth and Knowledge

Lévi-Strauss claims that his anthropological studies produce objective 'scientific' knowledge of the Other. The structures he reveals are not just good, bad or indifferent interpretations but accurately represent the real. He is not dealing in a realm of possibility or plausibility but is aiming to secure or anchor knowledge in objectified forms. His structures are *the* structures. These claims of scientificity and objectivity have no doubt been a great source of attraction and interest in his work for many. What is somewhat more curious is the presence of a linked series of assertions in which the claim is made that certain knowledge is impossible to secure for our own society or its past. Scientificity is reserved for the study of the Other, a hermeneutic interpretative understanding for the study of ourselves. Why should this be the case?

This position is based on the postulation of a division between structure as a synchronic system on the one hand and history as a diachronic non-system on the other. According to Lévi-Strauss a choice has to be faced here. We can either attempt to determine the nature of the structuring of social forms in which case a historical understanding must be renounced, or we may perform a historical analysis, in which case any ambition to understand structure has to be abandoned. A structural analysis of our own society is an impossibility since the analyst participates in this society and is inevitably bound up in its historicity. Our thinking is so bound up with our own society — its self-constructed history (*parole*) and its ongoing socialization processes — that we can never achieve a significant degree of detachment to understand it scientifically; i.e. structurally (delve down to the level of *langue*). Any application of theories produced in contemporary Western industrial societies to understand their form and nature can only result in tautologies. In relation to non-Western societies exactly the opposite is true. The anthropologist is not a participant. Consequently any empathy or historical understanding is ruled out. The fact that the anthropologist is an outsider bound up with neither the society studied nor its historical understanding of itself, permits genuine detachment and hence the ability to grasp structural insight. It is impossible for the Western observer to know the history of the Other because this would require abandoning Western forms of reasoning and rationality which alone permit scientificity — structural understanding.

What the anthropologist does is to translate the Other in terms of her or his own patterns of reasoning in which structure is substituted for empirical content, while simultaneously converting the content of Western society into the form of the Other, e.g. categories such as economic, kinship, myth, etc. The result is that information flows from the Other to Us by means of the methods of structural anthropology. Scientific understanding is possible by virtue of scientific procedures of structural understanding mediating between the consciousness of the anthropologist and the Other. While it is possible to grasp the structural codes at work in the Other, the inter-subjective lifeworld which these codes relate to remains beyond comprehension, for in trying to understand that the anthropologist would inevitably impose his or her own life experiences.

Two different areas of study — that of the Other and that of ourselves — result in two different forms of knowledge; one is scientific and detached, equivalent in status to the certainty achieved in the natural sciences; the other is interpretative, political, value-loaded, since to study ourselves is also to participate in structures of historicity: the process of changing our society through working on it. Knowledge of the Other is at a scientific level of *langue*, of structure; that of ourselves is located at the constantly shifting and sliding level of *parole*. Because we are bound up with our own historicity, constantly swamped by it, and this is an ongoing process all we can do is to construct, reconstruct and deconstruct meaning and significance. History is diachrony and diachrony is both elusive and always changing. The synchronic structure of the Other, which the anthropologist can only hope to know, is not in movement or change; it is fixed, and knowledge of it can be objectively transmitted to ourselves via a structuralist methodology.

We may ask how Lévi-Strauss can be certain of obtaining a true knowledge of the Other? How is this absolute scientificity possible? What is the relationship between the anthropological observer and that studied, between subject and object? What is to count as a fact – how is knowledge to be derived? At one point he states that:

> many discussions on social structure revolve around the apparent contradiction between the concreteness and individuality of ethnological data and the abstract and formal character generally exhibited by structural studies. This contradiction disappears as one comes to realize that these two features belong to two entirely different levels, or rather two stages of the same process. On the observational level, the main – one could almost say the only – rule is that all the facts should be carefully observed and described, without allowing any theoretical preconception to decide whether some are more important than others . . . though many models may be used as convenient devices to describe and explain the phenomena, it is obvious that the best model will always be that which is *true*, that is, the simplest possible model which, while being derived exclusively from the facts under consideration, also makes it possible to account for all of them. Therefore, the first task is to ascertain what those facts are. (*SA1*: 280–1)

In this discussion Lévi-Strauss clearly falls back on a variant of standard epistemological empiricism. There apparently exists an independent world of finite facts existing in a relation of radical distanciation from the subject observer of that world. The anthropological observer constructs a theoretical model to account for *all* the facts. This model becomes true by virtue of its ability to deal with all these facts while revealing their essential and underlying (structural) nature. The facts dealt with exist prior to theory and can be understood and specified *as* facts before the application of any theory. They are not created by theory but just wait around to be discovered and incorporated within its explanatory grid. The world is already 'given' to the anthropological subject observer who only has to model it in the right way in order to proceed beyond the given facts to the structure that simultaneously serves to generate and explain them.

In his discussion of totemism and systems of classification Lévi-Strauss develops some very sophisticated and stimulating structural models in which he demonstrates the manner in which forms of animal and plant classifications can be analysed as significative sign systems used to order various aspects of social life. People recognize objective distinctions given in nature and seize upon these in their 'concrete logic' to produce sign systems. Basic patterns such as the discontinuity between species form a reality independent of thought which then operates on them. The problem is that no such distinctions, whether arrived at by the 'primitive' mind or a Western biologist, are in fact given. Any act of perception is theoretically grounded. A much more satisfactory position would be simply to say that totemic sign systems are constructions based on a reality always already socially constructed. There is no point at which we break out of the social mediation of reality. Totemic systems link socially *constituted* 'natural' categories with equally constituted 'cultural' categories. Both are theoretically *produced* as is the very division between nature and culture.

In sum: the structures Lévi-Strauss arrives at constitute an unconscious or hidden reality governing the 'superficial' world of empirically observable facts. These facts are generated by the structures but the existence of these structures can only be modelled through the empirical facts considered as relatively given and non-problematic. In a paradoxical manner Lévi-Strauss both subscribes to an empiricist view of the world (knowledge can only be based on sense-perception) while simultaneously denying its validity (knowledge cannot be based on surface appearances). This is an epistemological bind he never resolves.

Writing Structure: Myth, Music, Language

In *NM* Lévi-Strauss suggests that the field open to structural studies includes four major branches: mathematical entities, natural languages, music and myth. These areas run transversally in relation to each other along two major axes, as shown in figure 1.7. Mathematical entities constitute structures in a pure state free from any embodiment. They are entirely formal. Languages are doubly embodied in the intersection of sound and sense. A basic parallel is maintained to exist between mythic narrative and musical composition. In music the structure inheres in the sound and is detached from meaning whereas in mythology the structure is detached from sound and inheres in the meaning. Music and myth are both languages from which something

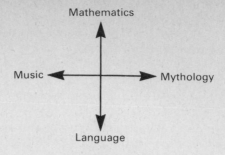

Figure 1.7

has been removed: 'by-products of a structural shift which had language as its starting point' (*NM*: 647). Music is language without meaning, myth is overloaded with meaning, becoming detached from an ordinary linguistic base. Myth uses language but is so weighed down with meaning it goes beyond it, while music only uses the sound element found in language. Myth produces structural patterns coded in images, chains of signifiers, music in sounds. Myths are, of course, recited or even chanted; a 'supplementary' sound element exists. Conversely, a listener may create 'supplementary' meaning in music (*NM*: 655). The repetitions and thematic variations of a musical piece produce responses in a listener deeply grounded in physiological rhythms themselves embedded in the human brain producing emotional as well as intellectual effects. So, too, in the performance of myth. Logical structure and emotional response are intertwined (*RC*: 16).

One of the basic contentions of the *Mythologiques* volumes is that myths only translate into each other in the same way as a melody translates into another if it retains a homologous relation, e.g. translation from a major to a minor key, or the modification of parameters to transform the rhythm, consecutive notes and so on (*NM*: 646). Neither myth nor music can be translated into anything other than themselves. To attempt to do so is to fall into the 'would-be hermeneutic verbiage characteristic of old-fashioned mythography and of too much musical criticism' (*NM*: 646). In music the melody is the diachronic, the synchronic inheres in the harmony. Myths as narrative are diachronic but beyond this there resides a synchronic harmony in the mythemes. A mytheme at the beginning of a myth may harmonize with one at the end and mythemes may harmonize between myths. One of Lévi-Strauss's main strategies for establishing the existence of

mythemic 'harmony' is a consistent pattern of synecdoche or substitut-
ing abstract qualities for persons or things: pottery becomes a
container, food a contained. Pottery manufacture and digestion
involve identical processes in reverse:

$$\left\{ \begin{array}{l} \text{clay}\rightarrow\text{extraction}\rightarrow\text{modelling}\rightarrow\text{firing}\rightarrow\text{container} \\ \text{excrement}\leftarrow\text{ejection}\leftarrow\text{digestion}\leftarrow\text{cooking}\leftarrow\text{food} \end{array} \right\}$$

Potter's clay is extracted from the earth and goes through a series of
transformations resulting in a container. Food is treated in reverse, it
is put in a container, cooked, processed in the body and ejected back
into the earth (*JP*: 175). Elsewhere a correspondence between digestion and cooking is asserted in that both have 'mediatory' functions.
During digestion the body retains and processes food before ejecting
it. Cooking suspends another natural process leading from a raw to a
rotten state. Digestion 'offers an anticipatory organic model of culture'
(*OTM*: 476).

The parallelism between mythology and music and the similarity in
their transformational structures is embodied by Lévi-Strauss in a
mythic form of presentation of the volumes themselves. They appear as
if music. *RC* begins with an 'overture', *NM* ends with a 'finale'. The
contents pages of *RC* appear as: a 'theme with variations', 'a sonata', 'a
short symphony', 'a fugue' and a 'rustic symphony in three movements'. The 'finale' is not a conclusion in any normal sense. We might
expect, for example, some kind of summation of the previous analyses
of the 800 myths in which the various structural codes are all brought
together and set out in tabular form or a series of canonical formulae.
But to expect this would be to misunderstand the interminable nature
of mythic transformations and that the *Mythologiques* itself, as linear
narrative, has a mythic status; the last chapter of *NM* could just as well
have been the first chapter of *RC*. The last movement of a symphony is
presupposed by the manner in which it begins; the end of myth is
implicit in its point of inception. Myths do not exist in chronometric
time; they are rather 'machines for suppressing time' and their
representation in the four volumes mirrors this. There are varying
passages of density in Lévi-Strauss's texts. Sometimes myth is piled
upon myth without any breaks, at other points there are varying
'melodies' of documentation, analysis and comparison.

Lévi-Strauss enters the world of myth by choosing a reference-point
within it the choice of which is necessarily arbitrary and contingent.
While the contents of the mythic music is being played in its various
transformations, Lévi-Strauss himself disappears (consistently using
the French *nous* as opposed to *je; NM*: 625 as if one of the audience. He

only intends to conduct the concert during the overture and the finale, the rest of the time dissolving himself into the mythic forms in a relation of personal distanciation, becoming, he would have us believe:

> the insubstantial place or space where anonymous thought can develop, stand back from itself, find and fulfil its true tendencies and achieve organization . . . the solidity of the self . . . does not withstand persistent application to the same object, which comes to pervade it through and through and to imbue it with an experiential awareness of its own unreality. (*NM*: 625)

The analyst of myths is a creator of them, even or perhaps especially, when referring to his own background, assumptions and influences. *TT* is supposedly autobiographical and yet it is not, a travel book and yet it is not, a series of academic ethnological accounts and yet not. He refers to geology, Marxism and psychoanalysis as three major sources of inspiration yet all this amounts to is a vague similarity — like structuralism all attempt to go beyond surface appearances in searching for explanations — and has little to do with the substantive content of his work. *TT* itself takes the literary form of a heroic quest involving a departure from ancestral shores to a distant magical Brazilian world of trials, tribulations and revelations, and a return to ordinary existence with a desire to communicate that which has been learnt (Geertz, cited in Pace 1986: 21).

Political Critique and Structuralist Anthropology

Lévi-Strauss has produced major critiques of the mass culture of the 'civilized' west, the effects of colonization and global capitalist expansion, ethnocentrism and social evolutionary schemes, racism, notions of progress and technological development, and associated environmental destruction. These critiques occur however, almost as sidelines to the main concern of his work — the production of a scientific structural anthropology — but this by no means detracts from their significance and contemporary relevance.

Culture, Nature, Landscape

Much of sections I–IV of *TT* involve a play of contrasting landscapes and peoples, in which the relationship of nature to culture is invoked constantly, from the wilderness of the South American interior to the 'semi-civilized' areas of North and South America, to Europe, to

India. The untouched forests of Brazil represent nature in its pure and pristine state: solemn, seemingly indestructible, with almost a 'geological' character, the 'shades of green suggesting the mineral rather than the vegetable kingdom' (*TT*: 113). In such a landscape nature is completely dominant over culture, it surrounds and envelops a humanity that is not opposed to it but lives in and through the forest. In other areas of South and North America cultural impact has destroyed nature, raped the land, turning it into little more than an open-air factory or systematically degraded it and then moved on leaving 'vast nondescript areas . . . a battered landscape. And on these battlefields where he grappled for several decades with an unknown land, a monotonous vegetation is slowly emerging in a confusion which is all the more deceptive since it preserves, beneath a falsely innocent exterior, memories and patterns of former conflicts' (*TT*: 117). The sparsely populated tropical and sub-tropical interiors of the Americas contrast with those on the Indian sub-continent, where nature is completely subordinate as a consequence of massive demographic pressure and social relations are dehumanized into a pressing throng characterized by poverty, misery and exploitation. In Calcutta 'daily life appears to be a permanent repudiation of the concept of human relations' (*TT*: 171). Lévi-Strauss describes the living conditions of jute workers:

> There are walls all around, and the entrance gates are guarded by armed policeman. The communal kitchens and eating-quarters are bare cement rooms, which can be swilled out and where each individual lights his fire and squats on the ground to eat in the dark . . . [in France] I had visited poultry yards specially adapted for the cramming of geese: each bird was confined to a narrow box and reduced to the status of a mere digestive tube. In this Indian setting, the situation was the same, apart from two differences: instead of geese it was men and women I was looking at, and instead of being fattened up, they were, if anything, being slimmed down. (*TT*: 161)

A European cannot live in, or understand, the tropical rain forest but can only destroy it. However, for Lévi-Strauss it is in certain areas of Europe that some kind of balance has been struck between nature, culture and populations. The landscapes are never truly wild but are rather an artifice, a human production: a harmony of mountain, field and forest, 'evidence of agreements painstakingly evolved during a long collaboration between man and the landscape' (*TT*: 116–17), a result achieved by ad hoc adjustments, interventions and interactions over centuries. It is India that provides a contemporary example of a vision of a possible European future in which both the landscape and human social relations become degraded (*TT*: 191). Mass industrial culture, as opposed to a harmonious peasant culture, seems to provide the growing impetus for such a process of degradation:

> Campers, camp in Parana. But no, on second thoughts don't. Keep your greasy papers, indestructible bottles and gaping tins for the last beauty spots of Europe! Cover European landscapes with the blight of your camping sites. But, during the short interval before their final destruction, respect the torrents plumed with virgin foam. (*TT*: 195)

'Civilization' and Diversity

For the first time in world history one cultural form, that of the industrial West, threatens to destroy or incorporate all others. This process of subsumption of cultural diversity Lévi-Strauss views as dangerous and contradictory. Cultural change and development are dependent on the interaction of differing cultural forms yet if this process is taken too far the end result will be a dissolution of diversity and a consequent stifling of future development (*SA2*: 360). Authentic sets of human social relations and an ecological harmony between people and nature can only occur where populations are of limited scale and human contacts are on a daily, face-to-face level. This is impossible in modern industrial societies with their massive impersonal bureaucracies, division of labour and huge urban areas in which people acquire an almost insect-like status, a 'swarming, microbial mass' (*TT*: 153). For Lévi-Strauss authenticity and harmony are scarcely to be found in the world today. Such relations are suffocated in the overpopulated tropics of Asia, they are being constantly eroded by mass industrial culture; a global monoculture is being substituted for cultural diversity (*TT*: 44); fragments of a past world may perhaps partially survive in a few isolated pockets of the Amazon basin interior. An underlying foundation for much of Lévi-Strauss's work is a lament for a vanished world that 'civilization' has systematically destroyed. Humanity destroys both itself and its environment.

Anthropology as a form of direct political action ought to be actively promoting heterogeneity, decentralization, the dissolution of bureaucracies and massive urban forms: promoting the small-scale and the personal from which will arise both future diversity and authenticity in human social relations. Not surprisingly, Western 'civilization', coupled with the effects of global capitalist expansion, is again and again a prime target for Lévi-Strauss's cultural critique. In 1965 he was asked which items he would like to place in a time-capsule to be opened in the year 3000:

I will put in your time-vault documents relative to the last 'primitive' societies on the verge of disappearance: specimens of vegetable and animal species soon to be destroyed by man; samples of air and water not yet polluted by industrial wastes; notices and illustrations of sites soon to be ravaged by civil or military installations. (*SA2*: 286–7)

He emphasizes the profound significance of the destruction of non-Western cultures. The Other as a cultural contrast to the West being destroyed represents a double loss; a loss of a contrastive 'mirror' for the West and a loss in itself. On the other hand the effects of colonization, missionaries, economic expansion, cultural contact situations in which the anthropologist is embroiled have already destroyed any genuine Otherness today: there are no non-Western societies in a pristine state. The anthropologist who wants to search for them must become an archaeologist of space attempting to rescue the exotic from the debris and traces that remain in the present and this is the manner in which Lévi-Strauss regards his own role (*TT*: 512ff).

Urbanism in which people are totally divorced from the natural environment constitutes a major threat to the mental health of humanity (*SA2*: 284). Far from representing progress the urban form can be regarded in many respects as a cultural loss. Lévi-Strauss notes that the development of urbanization and writing are very closely correlated and both coincide with the emergence of hierarchical stratified societies (*TT*: 392). Inventories, catalogues, mandates, the inscription of punitive rules are the real reasons for the origins of writing: it actively fosters patterns of social domination as opposed to emancipation. Lévi-Strauss claims that this insight occurred to him on witnessing an illiterate Nambikwara chief copy his practice of making field notes by producing meaningless scrawls on paper and using these as the foundation to legitimate speeches and enhance his power (*TT*: 388–9). Furthermore writing represents a loss of spontaneity: a false form of mediation between people. No longer linked to the past or the present through oral tradition we have our past and present constructed and reconstructed for us through written discourses. Contemporary communication is largely through the use of an indirect intermediary (books, newspapers, radio, TV) with a consequent loss of personal autonomy (*SA1*: 366). Naturally such media provide ideal means for use by bureaucracies and although, for example, writing may be used in a disinterested fashion for aesthetic or intellectual gratification, this is only a secondary spin-off: 'everyone must be able to read, so that the government can say: Ignorance of the law is no excuse' (*TT*: 393).

Cultural Evolution, Race, Ethnocentricism

The barbarian is first of all the man who believes in barbarism. (*SA2*: 330)

Given Lévi-Strauss's distrust of the West, in short, of modernity, it is not surprising that he should embark on a substantial critique of one of the main theoretical underpinnings provided to 'explain' its world historical success: cultural evolutionary theory. He argues in *Race and History* (*SA2*: chapter XVIII) that notions of progress are entirely misplaced, being dependent on prior forms of societal classification that merely justify an inevitable ethnocentric conclusion; the superiority of the industrial West. White's notion of an exponential increase in forms of energy capture performs such an end. An alternative ranking of societies based on adaptation to inhospitable environmental conditions would permit an entirely different conclusion: the Bedouin and the Eskimos would walk off with the laurels (*SA2*: 342). Progress is 'nothing but the maximum of progress, predetermined, in a sense, by everyone's taste' (*SA2*: 354). Vague analogies between Darwinian biological evolution and cultural evolution are inadequate and logically suspect: one tool form does not mutate to permit the creation of another. Material culture is mediated by determinate sets of social relations. Stadial notions of change and development from bands to states only work by subsuming or ignoring manifest variability. That variability documented in ethnology and archaeology remains the mere tip of an enormous iceberg (*SA2*: 326). Furthermore no societies can be considered to be in their infancy. All have an equally long history and thus to use certain social forms such as the Australian Aborigines to provide direct analogies for prehistoric social organization is entirely ill-founded. The only major difference is that some societies keep diaries of their adolescence while others do not (*SA2*: 335). All societies have lived, endured and changed for equally long periods. A 'simple' society today may merely be a relic of a more 'complex' one. The apparent eagerness of other societies to 'develop' to an equivalent economic status to the industrial West and adopt its cultural forms has nothing to do with superiority; it is in fact fostered by structures of global domination: the workings of global capitalism (*SA2*: 344ff.). Lévi-Strauss questions a distinction between static and cumulative history or societies that appear to stay the same as opposed to those that develop. Such an opposition is itself founded on particular conceptual structures that create significance and meaning within a particular cultural context. In the West any culture which appears analogous to ours appears cumulative. Other societies may not because they simply do not fit into our preconceived frame of reference.

While suggesting a total abandonment of cultural evolutionism

Lévi-Strauss has only a few remarks as to what might replace it. Sociocultural change is regarded as a contingent process. He substitutes notions of gradual cumulative development with one of stochastic combination based on rather vague analogies to game theory. Societies are analogous to gamblers playing on the roulette wheel of history. In roulette a combination of two different numbers, e.g. seven and eight, is fairly common, sequences of three numbers rarer and so on. A single player betting on long cumulative sequences would soon lose all his or her money. Players who co-operate will have more chance of achieving a long sequence, i.e. a significant structural change. The purpose of Lévi-Strauss's analogy is to suggest that differing forms of human culture may be regarded as structured permutations of a finite series of human potentialities. Completely isolated societies (players) will not cumulatively develop; such development only comes through mutual influence and contact. To compare cultures positively or negatively is ridiculous since they contribute to each other's development. Since virtually no known human societies have been in complete isolation when and where significant change takes place is a matter of chance, of a lucky 'throw' and set of conjunctural circumstances existing between societal players: 'in human history, a combination (to the degree n) has taken a time of duration (t) to emerge; it could have happened much earlier or later . . . The fact is no more significant than the number of throws a player must wait for to see a given combination occur' (SA2: 355). From such a perspective the Industrial Revolution could not at all be regarded as a unique product of the West but rests ultimately on the throws of thousands of societies on the global roulette wheel. Its location in a European space and historical date of occurrence have no inevitability and could easily have been otherwise (SA2: 359).

In an article entitled 'The anthropologist and the human condition' (VA: chapter 2) Lévi-Strauss has also cogently criticized sociobiological theories, recently advocated as possible candidates for the replacement of cultural evolutionism in archaeology, as naively reductionist: the discursive production of a *Homo geneticus* (VA: 34), with exorbitant claims for there being a genetic source for particular cultural characteristics:

> Sociobiologists reason as if the human condition obeyed only two kinds of motivation: one kind unconscious and determined by genetic heritage; the other deriving from rational thought. However, even in sociobiological terms, it is hard to understand why the second type cannot be reduced to the first. Indeed, we are told, the man who does not know what he is doing has a genetic advantage over one who does know; for the former benefits if his selfish motive is viewed by both others and himself as altruism. (VA: 33–4)

Such reductive frameworks can be used to accommodate any observations, providing simultaneously their advantage and their manifest inadequacy. The essence of humanity resides in culture, not in genetics.

II

Critiques of Lévi-Strauss

The Political Critique

Under this label I refer to a number of critiques of the work of Lévi-Strauss (e.g. Diamond 1974; Fabian 1983: 52–69; Scholte 1974; 1978) stemming from what can be broadly understood as a critical tradition within Marxist theory, distancing itself from the scientism evident in a considerable body of Marxist work, which perhaps reaches its apotheosis in that of Althusser (1970; 1977) whose 'structural-Marxism' has attempted to tie structuralism and Marxism together.

Lévi-Strauss has noted that anthropology, with its colonial roots,

> is the daughter of this era of violence; its capacity to assess more objectively the facts pertaining to the human condition reflects, on the epistemological level, a state of affairs in which one part of humanity treated the others as an object . . . Exotic cultures, treated by us as mere things, could be studied accordingly, as things. (Lévi-Strauss, cited in Scholte 1981: 153)

The irony is that Lévi-Strauss's structuralism embraces precisely this epistemology. His entire emphasis on 'savage thought' as an alternative logic to scientific rationality, the critiques of ethnocentricism and cultural evolutionism seem to suggest the reverse. But there is a central contradiction in Lévi-Strauss's work. It is relativist in all but the most critical sense; the relativism does not extend to himself. Lévi-Strauss has no way of reflecting on how his own work arises – its status, its effects, its relation to social and political conditions. While Lévi-Strauss's science can explain myth, myth cannot explain science. thus the 'absolute superiority of science cannot be denied' (NM: 636). He thus rationalizes myth and mystifies rationality (Diamond 1974: 303). While Lévi-Strauss is able to describe writing, art and other cultural products of Western civilization as fostering patterns of inequality and dominance, science, or at least his version of it, apparently remains pure and untainted knowledge divorced from social value systems. While denying the superiority of the West in some of his work he then proceeds to reintroduce it in another form: that of science.

Why should we wish to understand and appropriate the Other in the first place? Does not this very act presuppose a whole set of social and personal values intimately related to the appropriation and analysis of mythic or other 'facts'? What consequences does this appropriation have on the Other — is it not part and parcel of its systematic destruction? Or neutralization? We might ask, with Scholte, if thought and reality are both continuous because both can be reduced in the final analysis to an unconscious infrastructure, why is scientific analysis discontinuous and irreducible? (Scholte 1978: 32). Lévi-Strauss has no acceptable answer to such a question and usually makes a quick retreat into cerebral reductionism. This provides no acceptable solution and Lévi-Strauss's position, lacking in any critical relation between existential experience of the Other and scientific conceptualization, moves inexorably towards an impasse:

> as an explicit product of conscious thought, scientific discourse can only stand in a metaphorical, not metonymical, relation to that silent and unconscious Being which is its privileged subject-matter and to which, in principle, it too is reducible. The integration between form and essence, method and reality, to which structuralist discourse explicitly aspires would paradoxically reach its 'logical' fulfilment in the inexplicable domain of unconscious silence. (Scholte 1978: 33)

Ultimately structural anthropology renders the experiences of humanity as inexplicable because its explanatory framework totally dissolves and dispenses with either concrete men and women or concrete social forms. Humanity is dissolved and so is cultural difference. Just as there is no original myth, there is no original culture because the latter are always already created by others in space and time. Any specificity is denied and this also includes Lévi-Strauss, who would have us believe that he does not actually *write* (i.e. make active interpretative choices) the *Mythologiques* but rather 'orchestrates' their progression. What might appear superficially as conscious and creative production on the part of Lévi-Strauss is in fact itself produced by a determinate and determining underlying unconscious.

To what extent is Lévi-Strauss's Other a product of the unreflective imposition of Western categories? Does a binary mythemic logic have any reality outside an active interpretative process? Is it not forged and created by the analyst? It is highly significant that when Lévi-Strauss sets out a series of analogies between myth and music, it is only *a particular type* of music he is referring to; it is not indigenous tribal music, which might seem most appropriate, but a 'cultured' Western classical musical tradition. Debussy, Ravel and Wagner appear to be his models.

Are the lessons to be learned from the 'savage mind' merely to confirm a set of beliefs (such as the superiority of science, of classical music) engrained in the West? The effect of Lévi-Strauss's work is perhaps, after all, to rationalize the world rather than to question or challenge it. In this respect it should not be forgotten that structural anthropology appears to have little or no place for human suffering, power, domination, alienation, exploitation. These are either ignored or filtered out of the accounts. Similarly, Lévi-Strauss's discussions of ideology do not so much relate to power as logical contradictions within mythic thought, which in turn relate to a collective mind. He invokes the unconscious in order to neatly by-pass both society and consciousness.

Lévi-Strauss is a classic anthropologist of the post-colonial era, sifting through the fragments of myths and anthropological accounts to create discourses striking in their icy 'infrastructural' detachment. In the face of global capitalist expansion, he has 'mourned' and 'lamented' the loss of small-scale indigenous communities (to professional audiences) but done nothing to preserve them or intervene. The difference of the Other is something to be respected. It also serves as a structural laboratory rat.

Pace (1986: chapter 9) describing Lévi-Strauss as a 'half-hearted prophet', has noted that he could very well, with the ideas set out in *TT* and elsewhere (see p. 48ff.) and given his international prestige, have played an active role in the development of the kind of oppositional politics embraced by the 'green movement'. Or equally it could have been Lévi-Strauss in the late 1950s as opposed to Schumacher in the late 1960s, promoting the notion that 'small is beautiful'. However, in a typically positivist mould Lévi-Strauss has continually asserted a division between his professional work as an anthropologist and his personal views made outside the arena of academic anthropological discourse; he has, in effect, defused these views from the outset by regarding them as insignificant personal opinions. Lévi-Strauss is indeed a 'universal intellectual' (in subject-matter) but he can hardly be described as one in Sartre's terms nor as a 'specific intellectual' in Foucault's (see chapter 6 of this volume). What are the effects of all this? Diamond puts it well;

> He is mandated to understand everything but himself and that, in turn,
> relieves his colleagues of the need to engage in a serious critique of

themselves or of their society ... he exemplifies how the Western intelligentsia can make imposing careers out of their alienation. And we can understand why a distinguished *anthropologist*, a member of the most alienated profession, should now occupy a central position in the intellectual life of the West. (Diamond 1974: 304)

Structural anthropology, posing as a universal and comparative science in some respects, appears as an ethnocentric ideology rationalizing the Other in its own terms and ignoring itself as a form of reductionist and essentialist Western academic imperialism. There is no reflexive relation between theory, practice and society. Humanity is dissolved and so is any aspiration to change rather than merely document the world. With satisfaction Lévi-Strauss tells us in the 'finale' to the *Mythologiques* that only those who practise structuralism know: 'what a sensation of fulfilment it can bring, through making the mind feel itself to be truly in communion with the body' (*NM*: 692). Lévi-Strauss has also remarked that 'history may lead to anything — providing you get out of it' (*SM*: 262). The same could be said for structuralism. Two ways of 'getting out' of structuralism will now be briefly reviewed. The first is to substitute a hermeneutic position, as with Geertz (see chapter 3 of this volume), or to attempt actively to link aspects of structuralism with a hermeneutic position, as in the work of Ricoeur (discussed in detail in chapter 2 of this volume). The second is to transcend some of the limitations of structuralism in various forms of post-structuralist critical practice as manifested in the later work of Barthes and Foucault, and in that of Derrida (discussed in chapters 4–6 of this volume).

The Hermeneutic Critique: Ricoeur

In a number of important texts Ricoeur has set out elements of a critique of Lévi-Strauss's structuralism and attempted to integrate a structuralist methodology within a wider hermeneutic philosophical tradition (Ricoeur 1974: section I; 1981: chapter 5). This critical encounter is important because it attempts to positively incorporate aspects of Lévi-Strauss's work rather than negatively dismiss it as irrelevant and fundamentally misguided — the form in which empiricist critiques usually realize themselves.

Ricoeur argues that what occurs in *SM* and elsewhere is an illegitimate extension of structuralism from a methodological series of operations into a philosophy and it is this more than anything else that sets up a whole series of problems. The putative solution is a structural hermeneutics. The major problems with structuralism are:

1   A lack of self-reflexivity. Structuralism puts everything at a distance and embraces a subject–object dichotomy. It separates out the person doing the investigation from that being investigated. In so doing it establishes a non-historical relationship between subject and object: 'understanding is not seen here as the recovery of meaning . . . there is no hermeneutic circle . . . no historicity to the relation of understanding' (Ricoeur 1974: 33–4). Lévi-Strauss cannot reflect on the origins of his theories nor relate them to the sets of historical and social circumstances in which he finds himself.

2   Diachrony is subordinated to synchrony. Within Ricoeur's hermeneutics the inverse holds true: diachrony is only meaningful through its relation to synchrony. Ricoeur is far too astute a commentator to simply accuse Lévi-Strauss of denying history altogether. The major point of contention is that of the relation of structure to historical event and for Ricoeur the latter must be primary. History – diachrony – is not simply a passage from one structural synchronic state to another, but involves human praxis. Humanity produces itself through linguistic and other productions.

3   Lévi-Strauss's position on mind is described as a 'Kantianism without a transcendental subject' (Ricoeur 1974: 54) (a description which Lévi-Strauss accepts; *RC*: 11). A structural homology underlies all human thought but without a transcendental subject. The concomitant of such a position is that there can be no privileged access to the meaning of myth either by the natives who transmit them or the anthropological observer. Such a position seems to set up very real difficulties as to how we acquire knowledge: 'an order posited as unconscious can never, to my mind, be more than a stage abstractly separated from an understanding of the self by itself; order in itself is thought located outside itself' (Ricoeur 1974: 51).

4   Many of these problems arise from the use of a Saussurian linguistic model in which there is a systematic neglect of acts of situated speech (*parole*). Ricoeur poses a rhetorical question: 'Would it not be just as much in keeping with the teachings of linguistics if one held that language, and all the mediations for which it serves as a model, was the unconscious instrument by means of which a speaking subject can attempt to understand being, beings, and himself? (1974: 54). What structuralism does not take into account is language as a medium for expression and self-reflection. Although the act of speaking is structurally determined by an unconscious grammar, people speak with a purpose: they wish to make statements about something. Humanity speaks in order to be able to *say* (Ricoeur 1974: 84). For Ricoeur the understanding of myth or any other meaning tradition must take place through the *conscious* appropriation of

symbolic content by an active interpreter entering directly into the semantic field of that which is to be understood. To do this one inevitably enters a hermeneutic circle involving a productive dialogue with the Other.

Ricoeur suggests that it is simply not possible to generalize from a study of totemic systems to constitute a 'savage' or undomesticated mind as in *SM*. It is precisely at this point that structuralism transforms itself from being a highly effective analysis into a dubious philosophy. So-called totemic systems do seem to fit a structural—synchronic model perfectly because in them the structural arrangements do appear more important than the specificity of the contents, and the thought contained in them does seem to resemble a process of *bricolage*. Ricoeur contrasts another thought tradition, the mythical base of Semitic, Hellenistic and Indo-European traditions, claiming that a structuralist perspective applied here would result in a much greater loss of meaning content. In understanding the core of meaning in the Old Testament it is not nomenclatures or classifications that are important but founding events. In the theology of the Hexateuch, the signifying content is a kerygma, the sign of the action of Jahweh is constituted by a series of events providing Israel with a historical self-interpretation. Theological interpretative work on these events in effect produces an ordered history, an interpreting tradition which itself becomes reinterpreted for each generation and used in different ways, for example to foster unity. Rather than being an exemplar of 'savage thought', totemism could very well be regarded as an exceptional case (Ricoeur 1974: 41) at one end of a spectrum, the historicity of the 'kerygmatic' case representing another pole. As regards the latter a structuralist account cannot exhaust a surplus of meaning so easily as in the former, but might represent a useful strategy to approach meaning while never being self-sufficient.

Even in the case of understanding totemic systems a hermeneutic comprehension is required. For example, on what basis can a homology be considered to be present between marriage rules and food prohibitions (*SM*: 114ff.)? Ricoeur suggests that it is because the apprehension of similitude precedes structural formalization and founds it (cf. the discussion of synedoche, p. 47). This apprehension of similitude is a matter of a hermeneutic process of active appropriation of the content of the Other. Hermeneutics fills a gap, or radical lack, in structuralism. It clothes structuralism in more viable philosophical garments stripping away its objectionable wolf's clothing.

If hermeneutics fills a gap or replaces a lack in structuralism then, for Ricoeur, the reverse is also true — structuralism extends hermeneutics in a fresh direction. The relationship between the two is complementary rather than antagonistic, on the understanding that structuralism is understood as a productive methodology inhering within a hermeneutic philosophy. Ricoeur briefly discusses Lévi-Strauss's analysis of the Oedipus myth in terms of the derivation of mythemes as bundles of relations that possess a signifying function relating to the structure of the myth as opposed to any existential significance (see pp. 13–16) and concludes that Lévi-Strauss has satisfactorily *explained* the myth but that he has failed to *interpret* it (Ricoeur 1981: 155). In other words Lévi-Strauss has failed to go outside the myth; he simply exposes its structural form from within. Interpretation for Ricoeur requires a form of active appropriation on the part of the interpreting subject; it relates that studied to the self. Interpretation overcomes distance; in the process of interpretation the subject makes his or her *own* that which was initially *alien* (1981: 159). Ricoeur notes that the mythemic contrasts identified by Lévi-Strauss are not just an interplay of oppositions but crucially involve meaning, e.g. the underrating or overrating of blood relations, and can still be written in the form of sentences: 'the blood relation is the highest of all' and so on. Furthermore, Lévi-Strauss's explanation of the myth as an imaginary resolution of fundamental contradictions also involves meaning, which he more or less admits despite himself. There could be no question of contradictions if there were no significant questions about the nature of humanity and its existential situation. Myth simply is not a logical operator between *any* set of propositions. What structuralist analysis does with singular power is to impugn the surface semantics of the myth to reveal a depth semantics which is *simultaneously* the real living semantics of the myth. Structural analysis, then, represents a vital stage between a naive and a critical interpretation, between a superficial understanding and a depth interpretation. Explanation and interpretation take place along a 'hermeneutical arc' integrating and linking them together (Ricoeur 1981: 161).

Gone, then, are any claims to an independent existence for structuralism as involving a fundamentally different form of philosophy. Instead it forms an invaluable tool in the hermeneutic grasping and appropriation of experience channelled back into the concerns of the self. Structuralism constitutes one moment in a much wider process, the apex of an arc that begins with the self, leads to an in-depth constitution and appropriation of the Other and finally returns to the self a fresh plenitude.

The Post-Structuralist Critique: Derrida

The hermeneutic practices of Ricoeur, who allies himself with aspects of structuralism, and Geertz, who searches for depth-meaning, which is itself dependent on historical and social context, are bound up with the self and problems of translation. Real flesh and blood; real men and women; real meaning to be grasped; a productive fusion between persons and persons; persons and things; persons, things, history and context. In short, while aware of human fallibility in the interpretative endeavour, we nevertheless find ourselves a cosy and secure, recognizable, and human world to inhabit. Interpretation 'gets' somewhere, linking past, present, and future. If we never actually reach the inner core or hidden essence of meaning in a literary work, in prehistoric artifact patterning, in painting, etc., we perhaps approach it. Meaning is restricted by virtue that meaning can only be present because other meanings are manifestly impossible. Meaning depends on convention and convention is not infinitely expansive.

Post-structuralist practice upsets this comfortable picture in various ways by calling into question the very possibility of a subject-centred discursive strategy, of a world ready and waiting to be 'read', its essential meanings grasped. In the brief notes that follow I will confine my comments to Derrida's major critical engagement with Lévi-Strauss's work (Derrida 1976: 101–40; 1978).

Characteristically, Derrida uses Lévi-Strauss to deconstruct Lévi-Strauss. He portrays Lévi-Strauss as tottering on the outer edge of the precipice of a logocentric tradition of thought going back to Plato and Aristotle. In fact he has one foot over the edge, but the other remains firmly rooted on the ground of a foundational philosophy Derrida wishes to debunk. Key concepts in Derrida's position – logocentricism, phonocentricism, writing, the trace – are exemplified in his critique of Lévi-Strauss. Since these are all discussed at length by Yates (chapter 5 of this volume) the exposition here will deliberately be skeletal.

A logocentric tradition, or a metaphysics of presence, assigns both truth and spontaneity to the spoken word. This phonocentricism means that writing becomes regarded as something supplementary, a parasitic expression of speech, of oral form. Such a brief is readily apparent in Lévi-Strauss's discussion of the effects of writing on the Nambikwara (*TT*: 385–99; see p. 51). Writing becomes portrayed as intimately linked with violence, evil, the development of structures of social domination. The 'natural goodness' of the Nambikwara is very strongly related by Lévi-Strauss to the fact that this is a face-to-face community of 'spontaneous' orality. Derrida does not deny a link between writing and domination. What he is much more concerned to demonstrate is the phonocentric privileging of speech in Lévi-Strauss's discussion. Derrida asserts a priority of writing rather than speech in

a theory of language. Although empirically (as, say, in child development or the history of the human species) the spoken word comes first,
the concept of speech is preceded by the concept of writing. Writing is
not impure, secondary or derivative but embodies in a primordial
sense that which language is all about. Writing spawns speech: 'text',
the graphic trace, comes before the book. It is not in fact writing that
is secondary to language but speech. But in a logocentric tradition a
supposedly full and immediate presence of the voice is elevated over
the mute signs of writing which, especially in phonetic script, attempt
to imitate an originary utterance. Writing becomes collapsed as
secondary speech. Writing, for Derrida, has to be understood in the
special sense of an *arche*-writing: any practice of spacing, differentiation, constituting units. In this sense writing inaugurates not only
language but consciousness and social being. These all emerge out of
silence: the unconscious, non-being, writing. The Nambikwara, to be
sure, do not write books but writing is present in the form of naming
systems and tracks traversing the landscape they inhabit, in calabash
decoration.

The Nambikwara outlaw a system of spoken proper names as a basis
for differentiating between individuals. Lévi-Strauss describes an
incident in which children displayed their private animosity to each
other by revealing to him, the anthropologist, the names of their
rivals. He recalls that 'from then on, it was easy, although rather
unscrupulous, to incite the children against each other and get to
know all their names' (*TT*: 365). For Derrida this incident is symbolic
of the inherent violence of *arche*-writing. There is no pure authenticity,
no pure system of verbal 'presences' to be destroyed by writing.
The violence of *arche*-writing inaugurates social discourse. The violence of phonetic writing described by Lévi-Strauss has its foundation
in the:

> violence of arche-writing, the violence of difference, of classification, of the
> system of appellations . . . There was in fact a first violence to be named.
> To name, to give names that it will on occasion be forbidden to
> pronounce, such is the originary violence of language which consists in
> ascribing within a difference, in classifying, in suspending the vocative
> absolute. To think the unique *within* the system, to inscribe it there, such
> is the gesture of arche-writing: arche-violence, loss of the proper, of
> absolute proximity, of self-presence, in truth the loss of what has never
> taken place, of a self-presence which has never been given but only
> dreamed. (Derrida 1976: 110–12)

What Derrida is doing here is to reverse the terms of Lévi-Strauss's
argument. *Arche*-writing, a silence, is the origin of violence, a

foundation for speech in which that violence first manifests itself as a presence, a form. The violence of speech in systems of naming and appellation, precedes, is the fount and origin for, that violence induced by phonetic writing. Writing (*écriture*), a non-being or absence of the voice, induces being, the entry into language which differentiates. This strategy of reversal, of undoing privileged oppositions such as speech–writing, in which the former is valued and privileged in relation to the latter, forms the core of a *deconstructive* critical strategy.

Western metaphysics from Plato onwards is, according to Derrida, constituted as a logocentric system, a series of oppositions in which the first term always has privileged status and is valued at the expense of the second:

spoken word (*logos*) : graphic mark
being : non-being
conscious : unconscious
thing : sign
presence : absence
essence : appearance
innocence : corruption
nature : culture

and so on. A deconstructive reading shows how such value-loaded oppositions undo themselves in texts. The nature–culture opposition is employed over and over again by Lévi-Strauss who regularly privileges the former in relation to the latter. In *TT* the Nambikwara (a South American hunter–gatherer group) are consistently portrayed as existing in an almost natural and untainted state approaching as far as is possible in a world system destroyed by the products of civilization a state of innocence, natural goodness, 'animality', tenderness, authenticity. To escape culture is to escape violence and repression. Lévi-Strauss puts forward a powerful and explicitly Rousseauesque nostalgic dream of innocent and natural human societies, a Garden of Eden before the Fall, Nature is full human presence, is speech; is opposed to culture, differentiation, writing. Yet nature cannot exist on its own as a pure presence to itself. Derrida points out that throughout his work, from *ESK* onwards, Lévi-Strauss simultaneously uses a nature–culture opposition, while being unable to accept it (1978: 284).

Derrida claims that although logocentric oppositions pervade Lévi-Strauss's thought he also initiates the possibility of their deconstruction and this is vividly portrayed in the 'overture' to and subsequent form of the *Mythologiques*. What a logocentric tradition effects is to set up a vision of humanity as a subjective individual presence in the world endlessly searching for absolutely solid foundations on which thought can rest, primary truths, origins, presences: a fixing of humanity and a fixing of the world. In overthrowing a logocentric tradition a search for ultimate origins, essences and truths is necessarily abandoned in an endless play of signification and interpretation. Lévi-Strauss's structuralism takes a number of steps in this direction (Derrida 1978). A traditional view of humanity is dissolved and in the *Mythologiques* there simply is no central core of essential meanings. The books are myths about myths whose lack of singularity and endless signification and transformational qualities are repeatedly displayed. The initial 'reference' myth in *RC*, Lévi-Strauss admits, neither merits this name or treatment; there is no unity or absolute source to a myth. Any notion of a total originary set of myths which analysis should attempt exhaustively to explain is rejected both as useless and an impossibility. The 'structural' technique employed by Lévi-Strauss, however, attempts to arrest the endless play of the myths. It imposes itself, posits limits, creates form, fixes a centre, establishes a structural core.

Derrida notes that there are two interpretations of interpretation:

> The one seeks to decipher, dreams of deciphering a truth or an origin which escapes play and the order of the sign, and which lives the necessity of interpretation as an exile. The other, which is no longer turned toward the origin, affirms play and tries to pass beyond man and humanism, the name of man being the name of that being who, throughout the history of metaphysics or of ontotheology – in other words, throughout his entire history – has dreamed of full presence, the reassuring foundation, the origin and end of play. (Derrida 1978: 292)

Both of these, to a certain extent, coexist in Lévi-Strauss's work. The logocentric interpretation, to which Lévi-Strauss ultimately resorts (while also simultaneously mapping out the ground for its own dissolution) seeks to establish a stable centre or truth; Derrida's 'grammatological' interpretation seeks to transgress this entire process neither demanding nor providing essential truths, essential centres. There are no logocentric myths, only logocentric readings.

III

In this section I wish to indicate some of the implications of Lévi-Strauss's work for material-culture studies commenting on three main areas: (i) the structural analysis of material culture; (ii) the question of history and its relation to the social construction of meaning; (iii) relations between structuralism, knowledge and a theory of subjectivity.

Structure and Material-Culture Analysis

A considerable body of literature now exists in which some form of structural analysis has been employed in relation to archaeological, historical and ethnoarchaeological studies (e.g. Hodder 1982 a and b; 1987; Leroi-Gourhan 1965; Miller and Tilley eds 1984; Shanks and Tilley 1987a; Washburn 1983). A number of general reviews and critical assessments also exist (Hodder 1986: chapter 3; Shanks and Tilley 1987b: chapter 4; Tilley 1989). I do not intend to rehearse arguments 'for' and 'against' these studies here other than to note that such work has been principally concerned with the delimitation of *determinate historical contextually situated structures* rather than with the universal structures Lévi-Strauss claims to isolate. This has involved regarding material culture as a significative system forming a communicative 'text', structured in a manner analagous to a language, to be 'read' by the archaeologist. The search has been for recurrent generative principles ordering and giving meaning to the observed and contextually situated artifacts and features of the archaeological record. For example, attempts have been made to recover underlying principles which can be shown to generate pottery design structure, sequences of mortuary practices, relationships between distinctive attributes of material-culture patterning in settlement and burial and so on. Different aspects of the archaeological record may be regarded, from this perspective, as embodying a series of transformational homologies or inversions of the same structured system of relations of difference, a system which may very well encompass contradiction rather than being regarded as a neatly dove-tailed unity.

The use of a structuralist approach in material-culture studies has been both methodological and epistemological. It has existed both as a method of substantive analysis of particular sets of materials and as a critique of empiricist archaeologies. Structuralism has been regarded as an invaluable key to the recognition of patterns of meaning in the archaeological record. But the meaning of the structures recovered have primarily been interpreted through grafting various Marxist, hermeneutic and post-structuralist perspectives (principally those post-structuralist perspectives concerned to link a theory of structure with one of agency and praxis as found, for example, in the work of

Bourdieu (1977) and Giddens (1979) and differing in certain significant respects from the forms of post-structuralist theory discussed in this volume associated with Barthes, Derrida and Foucault) to structuralist forms of analysis. This has usefully led to a dialectical theory of material-culture production in relation to social practices: that it is not only structured but actively *structures*.

I believe that some type of structuralist analysis, loosely related to the kinds of work on myth and classification that Lévi-Strauss has undertaken, to be absolutely essential to an active interpretative understanding of the archaeological record. However, such a structuralist approach marks only the beginning of a fresh perspective on material culture studies: it is something to be transcended. Possible means of accomplishing this are discussed in the other chapters forming this book.

In what follows I want to discuss some of Lévi-Strauss's own contributions to material-culture analysis, in which a theory of structure is linked to one of ideology, and then provide a brief example of structural analysis in a 'purely' archaeological study. What is of interest in Lévi-Strauss's own studies of material culture is that in some senses he is less concerned with the delimitation of pan-universal structures than with the linkage of structure to determinate sets of sociocultural relations involving power strategies, dominance, ideology and social contradiction. In these studies we can clearly see the potentiality of extending a structural approach in a dialectical materialist direction.

Ideology and Material Culture

Lévi-Strauss's work provides a series of fascinating insights by means of which it is possible to understand the ideological nature of material production and use in small-scale societies. The concern here is the manner in which ideological practices may work to reproduce asymmetrical relations of power and dominance operating through the medium of everyday material forms such as village plans and artefact form and decoration. In a number of texts Lévi-Strauss argues that material forms play an active role in resolving social contradictions in an imaginary way. In some respects the analyses are similar to those put forward as an explanation for the function of myths (see section II) but with the important difference that Lévi-Strauss locates the contradictions in determinate and material social realities as opposed to those postulated to arise simply in a collective unconscious.

The Bororo village (*SA1*: chapter VIII) (figure 1.8) appears super-

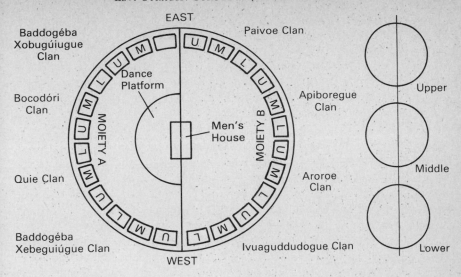

Figure 1.8   The Bororo village: apparent and real structure
Source: after *SA1*: figure 9, p. 141; *TT*: figure 4.3, p. 319.
By kind permission Jonathan Cape Limited and Atheneum.

ficially to have a simple concentric structure. Individual houses are arranged in a circle with a central men's house, to which women are forbidden access, adjoined to which is a dancing platform. The village area consists essentially of a clearing in the forest with the houses placed on the periphery at the forest edge. Descent in Bororo society is matrilineal and residence matrilocal. The houses at the periphery therefore 'belong' to the women and are opposed to the central men's house. The ground-plan directly symbolizes male–female relations: men at the centre and women on the periphery. A direct reflection of this occurs during ritual ceremonies such as death rites: women passively watch as spectators while men perform. Another opposition is thus brought into play: that between the profane houses on the periphery, arena for domestic activities, and the men's house at the centre, the domain of the sacred. A classic structural opposition comes into play involving relations between the following:

men : women : : centre : periphery : : sacred : profane.

This concentric village structure may be easily seen as a direct reflection of male–female relations in Bororo society. But it also coexists with other dualisms which contradict it. The Bororo village is separated into two moieties by an east–west axis dividing eight clans into two groups of four units practising exogamy. Another north–south axis splits up the eight clans into two other groups of four, termed 'upper' and 'lower' (or when the village is situated on a river referred to as 'upstream' and 'downstream' – i.e. these terms do not refer to a status division). The concentric village structure is thus cross-cut by two cardinal axes marking out two symmetrical diametric structures. Again, a dualism appears to be expressed:

west : east : : moiety A : moiety B and north : south : : upper : lower.

In addition to these three spatial dual structures there coexists a triadic structure. Each of the eight clans is further subdivided into three classes, upper, middle and lower, relating to wealth and prestige; marriage may only take place within each of these classes, i.e. a man from the upper division may only marry a woman from the same division and so on. This practice has the effect of converting the apparently dual exogamous system into a triadic pattern. Bororo society consists of three intermarrying classes with no kin ties between them. The reality of this triadic system associated with differential status between groups becomes represented sociologically as a binary moiety system and materially in terms of a simple diametric and symmetrical village organization. The apparent dualistic spatial organization of the village misrepresents sociological reality but, according to Lévi-Strauss, this is nevertheless a real rather than an imaginary reality to the Bororo: they live out their lives in terms of the concentric dualisms of the village plan and the cardinal axes. The native informants describe a 'ballet in which two village moieties strive to live and breathe each through and for the other; exchanging women, possessions and services in fervent reciprocity; intermarrying their children, burying each other's dead, each providing the other with a guarantee that life is eternal, the world full of help and society just' (*TT*: 318). Such a situation might exist between the three intermarrying clans but has no reality at the level of the two moieties. The concentric and diametric divisions physically embodied in the village ground-plan act ideologically to misrepresent sociological reality. A contradiction between a principle of total social reciprocity and another involving restricted exchange of goods and services between clans in asymmetrical relationship to each other becomes displaced and 'resolved' in an emphasis on dual spatial organization. This need not automatically suggest, as Lévi-Strauss implies, that the Bororo possess a false consciousness of social reality. Rather material culture – the spatial arrangement of the village – lends legitimating force to a society that might otherwise be torn apart if sociological reality were to find direct expression in a material form (spatial patterning) directly experienced (as inter-clan exchange is not) on a day-by-day, hour-by-hour basis.

Lévi-Strauss analyses a similar situation in relation to Caduveo artistic practice (*TT*: 229–56). This is characterized by a male–female dualism. The men are sculptors, producing figurative and representational designs, the women are painters, employing purely abstract designs in forms occurring both on ceramics and body-painting. Two styles are employed either separately or, more usually, together: one angular and geometric, the other curvilinear and free-flowing. In the case of pottery a geometric or curvilinear pattern may be specifically related to spatial divisions such as that between the neck and the belly. Similarly, the two different styles are applied to the face or the body. Lévi-Strauss argues that this distinction between angular and curvilinear patterns is related to others: symmetry and asymmetry, line and surface, border and motif, piece and field, pattern and background. These 'static' oppositions become fused in the dynamic 'movement' of the art itself: 'the primary themes are first decomposed, then reconstituted as secondary themes which use fragments taken from the first as elements of a provisional unity, and then these secondary themes are juxtaposed in such a way that the original unity re-emerges' (*TT*: 249). Lévi-Strauss argues that the meaning of such a pattern is related to and 'resolves' contradictions in Caduveo society. Caduveo society is hierarchical, being organized by various relations of dominance, and is characterized by a division into three endogamous castes. Details of the facial paintings of the women vary in relationship to caste or group membership. Such an endogamous marriage system and ever-increasing hierarchical gradations in Caduveo society make it more and more difficult to have marriages actually corresponding to social necessity, the biological reproduction of the social group as opposed to the social reproduction of hierarchy. In other words the basis for the maintenance of the social order becomes increasingly contradictory. The graphic art of the Caduveo women 'is to be interpreted . . . as the phantasm of a society ardently and insatiably seeking a means of expressing symbolically the institutions it might have, if its interests . . . did not stand in the way' (*TT*: 256).

What Lévi-Strauss is doing here is identifying a purely formal series of oppositions and contradictions within Caduveo art. These are then related to an underlying social contradiction. The manner in which the patterns are put together — juxtaposed and interwoven — in the art are held to provide a symbolic resolution of the social contradictions found in Caduveo society. Yet we can ask: is this merely a play on words? Can a difference and claimed tension between two purely visual patterns amount to a contradiction? What is the precise relation between such a contradiction (if we can consider it as such) and social contradiction? Is a pattern and a linkage simply being imposed? Might not the Caduveo simply produce patterns appropriate to them with none of the connotations Lévi-Strauss, as external observer, ascribes?

Dowling (1984: 120) suggests that Lévi-Strauss's claim has to rest 'on the further claim that aesthetic objects project their own norms; this is the context in which we want to say, objectively speaking, that a landscape painting hung upside down has been hung wrong'. If, then, an internal tension between elements can be demonstrated, this cannot be written-off as something that just happens. It demands an explanation. If a tension or contradiction between graphic elements or their organization occurs then its meaning requires investigation in relation to social context. We could begin, like Lévi-Strauss, by asking what real contradiction the designs 'resolve'. Such an analysis is, of course, necessarily predicated on the assumption that graphic form and social organization are linked together at an underlying *structural* level, i.e. by the same series of relational principles, and should not be conceived as autonomous entities with no necessary relation (for an archaeological analysis of ceramic design as ideological 'resolution' of contradiction, undertaken partly along the lines discussed above, see Shanks and Tilley (1987a: chapter 7).

Identifying and Interpreting Structure in Prehistoric Rock Carvings

In this section I want to make some remarks about the manner in which some form of structural analysis can be taken to be indispensable to studies of prehistoric material culture. The discussion is taken from a larger study in preparation (Tilley n.d.). The data set is the rock-carving site at Nämforsen, Northern Sweden, documented by Hallström (1960). Nämforsen is one of the largest, and almost certainly one of the most dramatic, rock-carving sites known in Europe. The carvings were produced sometime during the period c.3,500 BC and 2,000 BC. We have no evidence for a more precise date or for the length of the actual carving phase. What is clear is that whether the carvings were produced over a longer or a shorter period the same limited number of motifs were employed over and over again. These rock-carving surfaces appear to be very definitely 'cold'. There is very little evidence for dynamism or significant stylistic change. Rather they appear to be portraying a quality of timelessness involving an endless series of repetitions.

Around 1,700 designs have been documented along a 500 metre stretch of both banks of the Ångerman river and on two central islands in the river course. At precisely the point where the carvings occur there is a series of violent rapids. Torrents of water swirl round the islands and along the river banks on which the designs occur. All identifiable designs are representational in nature, and seven distinct classes occur: elks, boats, humans, fish, birds, shoe-soles and tools. Of these the first two make up, respectively, about 55 and 27 per cent of the total number of designs.

The huge accumulation of designs at Nämforsen, its northerly location (just below the Arctic Circle) and isolation from other major carving sites, coupled with the fact that the designs were produced in the context of a hunter–fisher–gatherer economy with a neolithic technology, has aroused much archaeological interest. Explanations have centred principally on two classes of the designs: the elks and the boats. The former have been accounted for in terms of hunting magic and functionalist notions of animal totemism (see pp. 28–35), while the boats, it has been suggested, imply the importance of exchange links between the hunter–gatherers at Nämforsen and prosperous Bronze Age farming communities in southern Scandinavia: a classic case of centre–periphery relations. It is appreciated that this must have been an important ritual centre and suggestions have been made that the rapids might have provided an ideal natural elk-trap or an important salmon-fishing location. So, the animal species have been accounted for as representing basically a prehistoric menu that has to be magically controlled, other designs as symbolizing cultural contacts. These are, of course, valuable insights but such explanations lack specificity and detail. All we know is why elks and boats might have been important to depict rather than, say, wombats or spacecraft. The great stumbling-block in interpretation has been to concentrate on the designs themselves rather than the relations between the designs. This latter emphasis is, of course, the hallmark of any structuralist approach.

Identifiable designs occur on 234 separate carving surfaces. Each of these carving surfaces can be considered to be an individual structural unit. Superpositioning of designs is not common at Nämforsen. Where it occurs this might be regarded not as a lack of concern for previous carvings but as a way of drawing attention to particular symbolic associations. The prehistoric act of carving any particular motif in a specific place on a rock surface might be considered to be an act of *parole* governed by an underlying *langue* of rock-carving in general.

What is of interest in a structural analysis is not quantities of design classes but their *difference*. Consequently a rock-carving surface on which one elk and twenty boats occur is identical, for the purposes of the analysis, to a carving surface with one elk and one boat. What is important is the fact that two different classes of design occur together. By means of a careful analysis of the carving surfaces at Nämforsen it has been possible to construct a relational design grammar, i.e. the delimitation of rules for the association of different classes of design on the same carving surfaces. For example: of the carving surfaces on which only one of the seven different design classes (elks, boats, fish, etc.) occurs it is of interest to note that human beings (ninety-two separate depictions in the rock-carving area as a whole) never occur on their own. they have a *purely relational* significance, i.e. they can only occur in association with other different design classes. There is only one rock-carving surface at Nämforsen on which all seven different design classes occur together. What is of interest here is that on precisely this carving surface a unique design occurs (a circle with an internal cross). This carving surface is also right at the centre of the rock-carving area, on the most inaccessible island in the river. The unique design, which is the only abstract or non-representational design in the carving area, occurs at a central point in the carving area. It is also the only point where all other designs occur together. It would seem to mark the coalescence of a relational structure.

We can, then, work out a design grammar for the site on the basis of differences and relations between designs and define a central carving surface. Knowing which designs can and cannot occur in an associational series when we consider carving surfaces with one, two, three or more different designs occurring together brings us closer to meaning but can we go further? One step forward is to concentrate on the relations between different design classes. Here I have space to consider only one such relation: that between elks and boats. It can be demonstrated that these two designs occur in a definite series of associations, including linearity (arrangement in rows); opposition (they face each other); overlap, merging or superpositioning; relational displacement in relation to other design classes (e.g. in some cases a carving surface may have elks and humans in a central position while boats occur in marginal areas or vice versa). Virtually all the boats are depicted with elk heads on the prows. Elk heads on poles also occur in the boats on some carving surfaces. But what is the meaning? In order to investigate this further we can consider design content in more detail. What is striking about the elks is that they all lack antlers apart from six possible exceptions. This has nothing to do with technical incompetence but represents a definite decision. In the few cases in which antlers occur they bear a striking resemblance to boats. An ambiguous elk–boat association is being created in these cases. But what of the 99.9 per cent of elks lacking antlers? The most reasonable assumption seems to be that it is female elks (which lack antlers) that are being depicted. Here we have a clue as to meaning which can be extended in relation to the series of elk–boat associations and ambiguous antler/boat depictions. Elks represent a female principle; boats a male principle. So the relationship is

elk : boat : : female : male.

Elks and boats are connotative signs. Their significance goes beyond themselves. It should immediately be apparent how such an interpretation connects up with Lévi-Strauss's discussion of systems of classification (see pp. 28–35). But we can go much further by suggesting that the elk–boat relation is not simply reducible to an oppositional male–female principle by setting up the following chain of links:

elk : boat : : Group A : Group B : : wife/husband-givers : wife/husband-takers.

In this case we have a transformational significative system in which elks and boats are being used as signs for different social groups taking part in a definite series of exchange relations involving circuits of marriage exchange in which wife/husband-givers are 'female'; wife/husband-takers, 'male'. The rock-carving surfaces at Nämforsen represent a process of *bricolage* in which species differentiation is actively used to map out and *create* difference in the social world. Other symbolic relations are immediately suggested such as:

elk : boat : : land : water : : nature : culture,

and these can be further explored by consideration of relations between the other motif categories (shoe-soles; fish; birds; tools; humans). Spatial relations between rock-carving surfaces with particular types of design combinations can also be examined and structural relations betwee variations in the depiction of individual types of motifs (e.g. different types of boat forms, elk forms, etc.). By means of an analysis of this type it may be possible to capture the design variability and relations apparent at Nämforsen in terms of an overall structured and structural system. The form, nature and reality of such a system can, of course, be further investigated by considering other types of archaeological evidence not mentioned up to this point, e.g. the contextual distributions of faunal and artefactual remains on contemporaneous archaeological sites; types of designs on mobiliary art. similar structural analyses could be undertaken on other rock-carving sites to see to what extent similar design grammars and associations emerge. The possibilities are endless (interpretation has no end) and the prospects exciting.

The above is an extremely compressed example from a much larger study. The purpose has been to demonstrate the manner in which a structural analysis generating an underlying grammar of design relations can be a powerful aid to approaching meaning in what otherwise appears to be an incoherent mass of random depictions. Archaeologists have generally considered rock-carving sites such as Nämforsen in just this manner: as a gradual accretion of unrelated designs with no meaningful relation between them. If one starts with this assumption then naturally the question of meaning is ruled out from the start. The designs remain inexplicable and incomprehensible.

But structuralist analysis can take us only a limited distance in our *appropriation* of the meaning of Nämforsen or the archaeological record in general. In view of the political, hermeneutic and post-structuralist critiques of Lévi-Strauss outlined in section II it is necessary to employ structuralism while also going beyond it. In relation to Nämforsen, for example, it is necessary to consider: (i) the particular socioeconomic context of the production of the carvings; (ii) alliance relationships, exchange, power and ideology in the context of this hunter–fisher–gatherer society; and (iii) text and meaning creation. What is involved in the creation of meaning out of the visual 'text' of the rock carvings? What is implied in this besides an analysis simply inspired by the work of Lévi-Strauss? Does the analysis in some sense redouble or duplicate original meaning? How could such a claim be made? Was there *an* original meaning to the carvings? Or are there just meanings that change over time, including the archaeologist's (Tilley's) ascribed meaning, none necessarily better or worse than the others? Is this important in any case, or is it an irrelevant epistemological distraction? In what manner is Nämforsen to be *written* into the present by the archaeologist? To answer such questions requires awareness of the structures of archaeological discourse into which the account fits; consideration of the transformational nature of language use; self-reflexivity: why is the study being produced and to what end?; consideration of general problems such as the relation between subjectivity and objectivity and what it means to produce history. These are some of the central issues considered in the other chapters in this book. Two general problem areas will be examined in the following section through further consideration of the implications of Lévi-Strauss's contribution to the human sciences.

History and the Construction of Meaning

Lévi-Strauss's critique of history cannot easily be dismissed for it has a strong normative and political element. Evolutionary theories, for example, are not only radically underdetermined by empirical culture sequences but in addition no longer appear *desirable* as accounts aspiring to explain the genesis of our social reality. The latter more than anything else has contributed to their demise within the social sciences as a whole and, much more belatedly, in archaeology. No one has pointed out more forcefully than Lévi-Strauss that history is a Western preoccupation of recent date. This historical sense, cumulatively building on itself since the Enlightenment, has led to an unparalleled intensity of detailed empirical research to reconstruct the past of individual nation-states and, more recently, is being channelled to create a notion of a distinctive 'European' past. The local temporal and cultural scales of the West have always acted as measures of world historical significance. It is, therefore, *necessary* to know precisely why the Industrial Revolution first occurred in Europe and not Africa. Such an event must be shown to have unique roots in European social developments from the Neolithic onwards so that it can be seen to be historically and culturally determined rather than a matter of historical conjuncture and contingency.

The anthropological and historical constitution of the Other has always been a double-edged ideological weapon. It may strengthen the ethnocentric priority and superiority the West has always granted to itself or systematically serve to demolish these beliefs. Lévi-Strauss's work in its various manifestations, and in a highly ambiguous manner, has served both ends. The enormous cultural diversity documented in the ethnographic, historical and archaeological literature can be conceptualized in evolutionary or (more weakly) in developmental terms only by means of a conjuring trick in which the cards have been already pre-sorted according to criteria which determine a favoured value-judgement. Our historical consciousness has indeed intended to produce 'fradulent outlines' quite remarkable in their degree of insensitivity to empirical richness and variety, no sooner lavishly documented than dismissed or forgotten.

It is Lévi-Strauss's emphasis on a particular conception of scientific rationality that undermines his project. How is he (or we?) to account for the fact that 'structural anthropology' explains myth but myth adds nothing to an understanding of this 'science'. Why does this knowledge flow in only one direction? The point is that it doesn't, and in places Lévi-Strauss almost admits as much.

History, it might be said, forges 'creation' myths of various kinds, ultimately to be related to our present. the more recent the historical period being narrated, the greater the spurious solidity and immutability the account will appear to possess. History, archaeology and myth are not radically opposed. They are different names for narrative accounts with similar functions in different societies. Myth in small-scale societies makes sense of social experience by ordering and structuring it. In the West histories are our myths and they serve very much the same purpose. Why myth and history appear to differ is that they relate, respectively, to analogical and domesticated thought. In myth the events are imaginatively created; in history they are actively produced out of disparate archival and material fragments that do not speak for themselves but out of which a meaningful narrative structure is created. This is not to diminish the status of historical investigation. It is rather to assert its indispensability. Our 'hot' socieites require histories just as much as 'cold' societies need myth. The question of what kind of histories these should be is one that can be reflexively addressed only by considering the status of archaeological and historical investigation itself, providing a *leitmotif* for this book.

Lévi-Strauss's concept of *bricolage* provides a powerful way of understanding the nature, not just of 'savage' thought but of our own. We are all *bricoleurs* constructing arguments out of fragments of life-experiences, books, conversations, material remains. In terms of Western academic activity archaeology perhaps provides the most vivid illustration of the *bricoleur* at work. The past is reconstructed by means of the use of whatever fragments are to hand: potsherds, rock carvings, post-holes, skeletal remains, stone monuments and so on. The meaning of these traces is mobilized by means of the development of conceptual structures derived principally with reference to the fragments of living societies collected by ethnography, and the question of their social significance addressed. This process is in its essentials no different from one in which non-identity in the natural world, such as species differentiation, may be used to order social relations in small-scale societies. In both cases whatever comes to hand is, and must be, utilized. The archaeological *bricoleur* maps social relations on to material objects in precisely the same way as the aboriginal *bricoleur*. In this sense archaeological cultures, or whatever, can be seen to be truly totemic constructions. Their significance is constructed by the *bricoleur* archaeologist in an active process of attempting to make sense out of the past, itself being derived from a Western 'will to interpret'. Such a will to interpret is clearly manifested in the Nämforsen example discussed above and in all archaeological investigations. Meaning *had* to be found, *had* to be created. This does not imply that such activity is unreal or a fantasy. For any archaeologist this remains a self-imposed burden of responsibility. Archaeology is a process by means of which material evidence becomes encoded in discursive structures. This process of encodification produces the meaning. A series of broken potsherds recovered in a wooden framed structure remain value-neutral and meaningless evidence. Through discursive encodification this evidence becomes both meaningful and value-loaded. Archaeology–history, through its interpretative will, has created and is creating, in a very positive sense, cultural richness to a Western sense of self-understanding and identity in which the social constitution of past and present are dialectically drawn together and integrated. Nothing more can be expected. The Nämforsen example did not aim transparently to convey a real past. What was attempted was a fresh inscription of surviving fragments of that past into the present, into text.

Meaning is something we create for our own times. It is something we typically tend to create out of the past and may actively use in forging the future. It is perhaps not so much the results of archaeological or historical investigation that matter but their practice and the nature of their effects.

Structure, Knowledge, Subjectivity

There is one important difference between the 'savage' and the archaeological *bricoleur* in the construction of mythic histories and historic myths. The former may use his or her imagination constrained only by the limits of conscious and unconscious thought. The latter is additionally limited by virtue of Western rationality, or 'science', requiring that the production of statements about the past be empirically or factually constrained. This system of constraint aims to set up certain limits as to the manner in which the past may be worked upon through the consciousness of the present. Such limits are traditionally explored through epistemologies and ontologies aiming to ground discourse in various ways by means of the exploration of the logics of subject–object and object–subject relations. Aspects of Lévi-Strauss's work aspire to explode traditional empiricist epistemologies in which the knowledge of the subject is purely grounded in sensory experience of the object: meaning resides in the surfaces of things.

Structural anthropology attempts to demonstrate to the contrary that knowledge is grounded in that which is non-observable. Structures are real although they may not be seen and they serve to generate that which we do observe. No amount of empirical description and sensory observation will ever enable us adequately to understand or explain the social world. Knowledge does not reside in the surfaces of things but in underlying realities. It cannot, as in positivism, be derived simply on the basis of prediction and hypothesis-testing in relation to observations but must involve the construction of conceptual schemes that both account for and render the observations intelligible. As Ricoeur notes, this may be regarded as a shift from a naive to a depth interpretation of texts, social relations and material remains. The question of any absolute ontological and epistemological grounding of such an approach in my view needs to be set aside. A structuralist analysis cannot claim to be a process in which essential characteristics of the real are captured and grounded for once and for all. It remains a valuable interpretative approach which, rather than attempting to evade a theory of human subjectivity, through recourse to a collective biological mind, needs to be related to it.

Post-structuralism, and the late hermeneutics explored in this volume, in the most general sense, may be regarded as taking seriously both some notion of structure − principles underlying human action − and an exploration of the manner in which subjects and subjectivity are constituted, i.e. how and why we interpret and the manner in which this interpretation is part and parcel of a process of social and individual constitution. This might be called the exploration of a politics of subjective identity and it is one followed up in the other chapters in this volume.

BIBLIOGRAPHY

Virtually all the work of Lévi-Strauss published to date of major significance has been translated into English. For more complete bibliographies refer to: Lapointe and Lapointe (1977), Pace (1986) and Rossi (1974).

1 Books by Lévi-Strauss

Abbreviations used are given after the titles. Original date of publication in the French is given in square brackets.

The Elementary Structures of Kinship (ESK) [1949] (1969) Eyre & Spottiswoode, London. Trans. J. Bell, J. von Sturmer and R. Needham.
Introduction to the Work of Marcel Mauss (IMM) [1950] (1987) Routledge & Kegan Paul, London. Trans. F. Baker.
Tristes Tropiques (TT) [1955] (1973) Jonathan Cape, London, Trans. J. and D. Weightman.

Totemism (*T*) [1962] (1964) Merlin Press, London. Trans. R. Needham.
The Savage Mind (*SM*) [1962] (1966) Weidenfeld & Nicolson, London.
  Trans. anonymous.
Mythologiques (Introduction to a Science of Mythology) 4 volumes:
The Raw and the Cooked (*RC*) [1964] (1969) Jonathan Cape, London.
  Trans. J. and D. Weightman.
From Honey to Ashes (*HA*) [1966] (1973) Jonathan Cape, London.
  Trans. J. and D. Weightman.
The Origin of Table Manners (*OTM*) [1968] (1978) Jonathan Cape,
  London. Trans. J. and D. Weightman.
The Naked Man (*NM*) [1971] (1981) Jonathan Cape, London. Trans.
  J. and D. Weightman.
The Way of the Masks (*WM*) [1975] (1982) University of Washington
  Press, Seattle. Trans. S. Modelski.
The Jealous Potter (*JP*) [1985] (1988) University of Chicago Press,
  Chicago. Trans. B. Chorier.

2 Collections of writings and lectures

These have all been complied by Lévi-Strauss.
Structural Anthropology 1 (*SA1*) [1958] (1968) Penguin, London.
  Trans. C. Jacobson and B. Grundfest Schoep.
Structural Anthropology 2 (*SA2*) [1973] (1977) Penguin, London.
  Trans. M. Layton.
The View from Afar (*VA*) [1983] (1985) Penguin London. Trans. J.
  Neugroschel and P. Hoss.
Anthropology and Myth (*AM*) [1984] (1987) Basil Blackwell, Oxford.
  Trans. R. Willis.

3 Interviews

Conversations with Claude Lévi-Strauss (*C*) [1961] (1969) Jonathan Cape,
  London. Ed. G. Charbonnier; trans. J. and D. Weightman.

4 Works on or discussing Lévi-Strauss and other works referred to in the text

Althusser, L. (1977) *For Marx*, Verso, London. Trans. B. Brewster.
Althusser, L. and Balibar, E. (1970) *Reading Capital*, New Left Books,
  London. Trans. B. Brewster.
Badcock, C. (1975) *Lévi-Strauss: Structuralism and Sociological Theory*,
  Hutchinson, London.
Berman, M. (1983) *All That is Solid Melts into Air: The Experience of
  Modernity*, Verso, London.

Bourdieu, P. (1977) *Outline of a Theory of Practice*, Cambridge University Press, Cambridge.

Derrida, J. (1976) *Of Grammatology*, Johns Hopkins University Press, Baltimore. Trans. G. Chakravorty Spivak.

Derrida, J. (1978) 'Structure, sign, and play in the discourse of the human sciences' in *Writing and Difference*, Routledge & Kegan Paul, London, Trans. A. Bass.

Diamond, S. (1974) 'The myth of structuralism' in I. Rossi (ed.) *The Unconscious in culture: The Structuralism of Claude Lévi-Strauss in Perspective*, Dutton, New York.

Dowling, W. (1984) *Jameson, Althusser, Marx*, Methuen, London.

Fabian, J. (1983) *Time and the Other*, Columbia University Press, New York.

Giddens, A. (1979) *Central Problems in Social Theory*, Macmillan, London.

Glucksmann, M. (1974) *Structuralist Analysis in Contemporary Social Thought*, Routledge & Kegan Paul, London.

Hallström,, G. (1960) *The Monumental Art of Northern Sweden from the Stone Age*, Almqvist & Wiksell, Stockholm.

Hayes, E. and Hayes, T. (eds) (1970) *Claude Lévi-Strauss: The Anthropologist as Hero*, MIT Press, Massachusetts.

Hodder, I. (1982a) *Symbols in Action*, Cambridge University Press, Cambridge.

Hodder, I. (ed.) (1982b) *Symbolic and Structural Archaeology*, Cambridge University Press, Cambridge.

Hodder, I. (1986) *Reading the Past*, Cambridge University Press, Cambridge.

Hodder, I. (ed.) (1987) *The Archaeology of Contextual Meanings*, Cambridge University Press, Cambridge.

Jenkins, A. (1979) *The Social Theory of Claude Lévi-Strauss*, Macmillan, London.

Lapointe, F. and Lapointe, C. (1977) *Claude Lévi-Strauss and his Critics*, Garland, New York.

Leach, E. (1970) *Lévi-Strauss*, Fontana, London.

Leroi-Gourhan, A. (1965) *Lévi-Strauss*, Fontana, London.

Malinowski, B. (1948) *Magic, Science and Religion*, Anchor Books, New York.

Miller, D. and Tilley, C. (eds) (1984) *Ideology, Power and Prehistory*, Cambridge University Press, Cambridge.

Pace, D. (1986) *Claude Lévi-Strauss: The Bearer of Ashes*, Ark, London.

Propp, V. (1968) *The Morphology of the Folk Tale*, Indiana University Press, Austin, Texas.

Radcliffe-Brown, A. (1929) 'The sociological theory of totemism' reprinted in *Structure and Function in Primitive Society*, Cohen & West, London (1952).

Radcliffe-Brown, A. (1951) 'The comparative method in social anthropology', *Journal of the Royal Anthroplogical Institute*, 81: 15–22.

Ricoeur, P. (1974) *The Conflict of Interpretations*, Northwestern University Press, Evanston. Ed. D. Ihde.

Ricoeur, P. (1981) *Hermeneutics and the Human Sciences*, Cambridge University Press, Cambridge. Ed. and trans. J. Thompson.

Rossi, I. (ed.) (1974) *The Unconscious in Culture: The Structuralism of Claude Lévi-Strauss in Perspective*, Dutton, New York.

Scholte, B. (1974) 'Structural anthropology as an ethno-logic' in I. Rossi (ed.) *The Unconscious in Culture: The Structuralism of Claude Lévi-Strauss in Perspective*, Dutton, New York.

Scholte, B. (1978) 'From discourse to silence: the structuralist impasse' in S. Diamond (ed.) *Towards a Marxist Anthropology*, Mouton, The Hague.

Scholte, B. (1981) 'Critical anthropology since its reinvention' in J. Kahn and J. Llobera (eds) *The Anthropology of Pre-Capitalist Societies*, Macmillan, London.

Shanks, M. and Tilley, C. (1987a) *Re-Constructing Archaeology*, Cambridge University Press, Cambridge.

Shanks, M. and Tilley, C. (1987b) *Social Theory and Archaeology*, Polity Press, Cambridge.

Sperber, D. (1979) 'Claude Lévi-Strauss' in J. Sturrock (ed.) *Structuralism and Since*, Oxford University Press, Oxford.

Tilley, C. (1989) 'Interpreting material culture' in I. Hodder (ed.) *The Meaning of Things*, Unwin Hyman, London.

Tilley, C. (n.d.) *The Art of Ambiguity: Material Culture and Text*, Routledge, London (forthcoming).

Washburn, D. (ed.) (1983) *Structure and Cognition in Art*, Cambridge University Press, Cambridge.

Part II
Hermeneutics

2

Paul Ricoeur: Action, Meaning and Text

Henrietta Moore

> There never was nor will there ever be any man who has certain knowledge about the gods and about all the things that I tell of. And even if he does happen to get most things right, still he himself is not aware of this. Yet all may have shadows of the truth. (Xenophanes, cited in *FM*: 14)

It is peculiarly appropriate to discuss the scholarship of Paul Ricoeur in relation to material culture because of the emphasis his work places on the theory and practice of interpretation. Material culture, like all other social phenomena, poses problems of interpretation. These problems arise, in part, because of a need to discover what material culture represents, what it means and what it says. Ricoeur's work deals in elegant and wide-ranging fashion with the issues of language and meaning, action and interpretation, subjectivity and the will, and history and narrative. This chapter does not attempt to represent or synthesize the writings of a lifetime, but rather to reflect on those aspects of Ricoeur's work which might be of direct use in developing our understanding of the textual characteristics of material culture.

The Work of Paul Ricoeur

Language, Symbolism and the Philosophy of Reflection

Ricoeur's concept of text has grown out of his work on language which he has been developing since the early 1960s. However, in order to demonstrate the ideas which underlie Ricoeur's theory of text it is necessary to begin by tracing the origins of certain of the theoretical preoccupations which emerge in his work.*

---

* It is impossible to provide any overview of the work of Paul Ricoeur without reference to the work of his outstanding 'interpreter' in the English-speaking world, John

85

Ricoeur's early work is concerned in a variety of ways with the nature of the subject, and with the relations between subject and language. The guiding principle of Ricoeur's work is hermeneutics, or interpretation, and in *Freedom and Nature*, and the two volumes of *Finitude and Guilt*, he begins to develop his distinctive understanding of the human subject as something which requires hermeneutic analysis. In *FN* he discusses the essential structure of the human will, the voluntary and the involuntary. He argues that the relationship between the voluntary and the involuntary is one of fundamental reciprocity. While the expression 'I will' involves a decision which lies within the actor's power, the actual decision itself is based on motive, any action consequent on that decision is mediated through the body, and the very act of willing must be conditioned by factors, such as life and the unconscious, which are beyond the actor's control. The relationship between freedom and necessity for the human subject is thus one of reciprocity. Ricoeur continues his investigations into the nature of the subject in the two volumes of *Finitude and Guilt: FM* and *SE*; in these two texts he moves away from a consideration of essential structures towards an investigation of the language in which human experience is expressed. The issues of human fallibility and evil which are addressed in these works draw Ricoeur towards an analysis of symbols and their interpretation. In *SE* Ricoeur makes a semantic study of the avowal of evil, in which he argues that there is no direct discourse of avowal, and thus evil is confessed through indirect expressions which are taken from the experience of everyday life, but which have the ability to refer analogously to another experience. One example of this is the image of the stain or spot which the sinner has to wash away. Lady Macbeth's anguished cry 'Out, damned spot!' carries the force which Ricoeur wishes to impute to these archaic forms of avowal, but interestingly he makes it clear that it is only in language that these images take on a symbolic dimension. Symbolism and language are thus coextensive, and this is the argument Ricoeur takes up and develops in the first part of his book Freud and Philosophy. 'There is no symbolism prior to man who speaks, even though the power of symbols is rooted more deeply, in the expressiveness of the cosmos, in what desire wants to say, in the varied image-contents that men have' (*FP*: 16). Symbolism arises when language produces composite signs, so that one meaning designates a further meaning which is only attainable in and through the first. Ricoeur argues that

Thompson. I have decided not to cite Thompson's work in the text, but I would like to record here that my understanding of Ricoeur's work is heavily indebted to his own, and that I have drawn freely on his work in writing this article.

the function of symbols is to mean something other than what is said. The relationship between symbol and interpretation is itself given in the double-meaning of symbols. Symbols require interpretation precisely because they are made up of a primary meaning, which refers beyond itself to a secondary meaning, which is never directly revealed, and which always requires interpretation. 'Thus a symbol is a double-meaning linguistic expression that requires an interpretation, and interpretation is a work of understanding that aims at deciphering symbols' (*FP*: 9). However, according to Ricoeur, symbols call for philosophical reflection as well as for interpretation. Symbols are meaningful in themselves, but they are also the material from which cultural myths are constructed. Ricoeur analyses four cycles of such myths: the myths of primal chaos, the myths of the wicked god, the myths of the soul exiled in an evil body and the myths concerning the historical fault of an individual who is both an ancestor and a prototype of humanity (*SE*). Ricoeur argues that in myth new features of the symbol appear. These new traits are connected to three aspects of myth. First, the myths introduce 'exemplary personages' – Adam, Prometheus – who provide ways of generalizing human experience on the level of a universal paradigm in which we can 'read our condition and destiny'. Second, because of the narrative structure of the myth – the sequence of events which make a story – our experience receives a temporal orientation. Third, myths recount a transhistorical moment when the innocence of being gives way to the guilt of history: the paradigmatic Fall. On the level of myth, symbols are not only expressive, but they also confer universality, temporality and ontological import upon our self-understanding'. Ricoeur thus argues that interpretation is not simply a matter of uncovering the double-meaning of symbols, because it also consists of a process through which the universal, temporal and ontological features of human existence which are implied in myth are theorized and thematized. Reflection is a necessary part of the interpretation of symbols (*FP*: 38–9). This is most particularly the case since any interpretation of specific symbols must involve some reflection on the place of those symbols in the totality of the symbolic universe.

The reflection to which Ricoeur refers is, of course, self-reflection. The positing of self which is based on the thought operation 'I am, I think: I exist in so much as I think', is an unverifiable proposition. The only way in which this reflection on the existence of self can be grasped is indirectly through the mirror, so-to-speak, of the objects, acts, works and signs which the self produces and wherein the self is disclosed (*FP*: 43). Reflection is thus the effort to recapture the subject or self in the 'mirror' of its objects.

Reflection is the appropriation of our effort to exist and of our desire to be, through the works which bear witness to that effort and desire . . . the positing or emergence of this effort or desire . . . is evidenced only by works whose meaning remains doubtful and revocable. This is where reflection calls for an interpretation and tends to move into hermeneutics. The ultimate root of our problem lies in this primitive connection between the act of existing and the signs we deploy in our works; reflection must become interpretation because I cannot grasp the act of existing except in signs scattered in the world. (FP: 46)

Ricoeur's allegiance to the tradition of hermeneutic phenomenology is demonstrated by his treatment of the interpretation of self, dealing as it does with both existence and interpretation.* Under hermeneutic analysis, the human subject becomes 'like' a text, because its existence can only be grasped through its works and signs, and as such it calls for a work of decipherment or interpretation.

The Displaced Subject: The Distinction between Semiotics and Semantics

The emphasis on the human subject and on language as a medium of expression in Ricoeur's work has brought him into direct conflict with structuralism. Ricoeur's main disagreement with structuralism is that, like psychoanalysis, it effects a displacement of the subject (CI: 250). This displacement is the result of a series of assumptions which underlie the structuralist approach. The dichotomy of language (langue) and speech (parole), the subordination of diachronic to synchronic analysis, and the emphasis on language as a system of signs, where meaning is given through relations of opposition and difference, all function so as to bracket off the speaking individual whose linguistic utterances refer to the world of lived reality. 'How does an autonomous system of signs, postulated without a speaking subject, enter into operations, evolve toward new states, or lend itself to usage and to history? Can a system exist anywhere but in the act of speech?' (CI: 249). Ricoeur argues that because of its underlying assumptions structuralism excludes from consideration a number of important factors. The act of speaking is excluded both as a form of communication 'exterior' to the closed system of signs and as a creative activity. History is excluded, not only as the change from one system state to another, but as 'the production of culture and of man in the production of his language' (use of the generic in the original). Finally,

* Hermeneutic phenomenology is a synthesis of two continental philosophical traditions. In addition to Ricoeur, the key figures in this synthesis are Martin Heidegger and Hans-Georg Gadamer.

Ricoeur argues that structuralism excludes the 'primary intention of language, which is to say something about something': the referential dimension of language (*CI*: 83–4). Following the French linguist, Emile Benveniste (1971) Ricoeur develops his own theory of language in response to the insufficiencies of structuralism (*IT*: 7; *HHS*: 133). This theory rests on a distinction between semiotics and semantics, that is between the sign and the sentence.

Semiotics is a science of signs, and while it is a legitimate form of enquiry, investigating phonological, lexical, even 'mythological' signs –as in the work of Lévi-Strauss – it cannot form the basis for the study of speech utterances or sentences (*RM*: 66–9; *HHS*: 152–7). The sentence, as Ricoeur sees it, is the basic unit of discourse and as such it has features which are quite distinct from those of the sign. The sentence is a 'synthetic construction' and is therefore something more than merely a combination of discrete entities or words. As Ricoeur says, the sentence is not a larger or more complex word. It is certainly true that it can be broken down into words, but these words cannot themselves be treated as if they were simply short sentences. Thus, while a sentence is composed of signs, it is not itself a sign, and we cannot understand a sentence merely by analysing the words or signs which make it up. For Ricoeur, this also means that sentences cannot be analysed using the methodology appropriate to the analysis of signs. 'There is . . . no linear progression from the phoneme to the lexeme and then on to the sentence and to linguistic wholes larger than the sentence. Each stage requires new structures and a new description' (*IT*: 7). Signs and sentences constitute different levels of language and the relationship between them is hierarchical. However, these different levels cannot be studied in isolation from each other because the relationship between semiotics and semantics is a necessary as well as a complicated one. This is demonstrated by the intermediary role of the word. A word is a sign in place within a sentence, and a sign can only be said to become a word when someone speaks and produces a sentence. But, a word is more than this because it outlives the transitory nature of its usage in a single utterance, and as part of the system of signs (*langue*) which speakers draw on when they speak, it has a history of used-meanings which accounts for the existence of polysemy – that is, for the fact that words can have more than one meaning. As Ricoeur says, the word is 'a trader between the system and the act, between the structure and the event' (*CI*: 92).

While Ricoeur acknowledges the interdependence of semiotics and semantics, he nevertheless wishes to privilege the study of sentences and discourse over the study of signs and language systems. Ricoeur argues that the analysis of discourse brings back into consideration those features which structuralism specifically excluded. Discourse is an event; it is realized in the here and now, and this distinguishes it from the system of language which is virtual and outside time. Whereas language has no subject, because the question of who speaks is not relevant to the structuralist problematic, discourse, on the other hand, refers back to the speaker through a variety of indicators, including personal pronouns (*IT*: 13). Ricoeur thus argues that discourse is self-referential because the event of saying is now linked to the person who speaks. Discourse also has a further referential dimension. While the signs of a language system refer only to other signs within the closed system, discourse says something about something, and as such it refers to a world outside the language system. The final distinction between language system and discourse is that although language has to exist before communication can take place, it is through discourse that messages are actually exchanged. Thus discourse, unlike language, has an interlocutor, another person to whom it is addressed. This further underscores the temporal nature of discourse, because it emphasizes the eventful nature of a communication or dialogue which can be started, continued or interrupted (*CI*: 88; *HHS*: 133–4). Ricoeur thus identifies discourse as involving those features which structuralism 'brackets out': time, a subject, the world and an interlocutor. The subject who is displaced by semiotics takes up a central position in semantics.

Meaning, Reference and Metaphor: the Creativity of Language

Ricoeur makes it clear, however, that the eventful character of discourse is only one of its constitutive poles; the other is that of meaning. While a speech utterance or sentence is a fleeting and transitory phenomenon, the meaning of what is said has a different character. This is because sentences may be re-identified as the same on subsequent occasions, and thus the meaning of what is said does not pass away with the speech event.

> An act of discourse is not merely transitory and vanishing . . . It may be identified and reidentified as the same so that we may say it again or in other words. We may even say it in another language or translate it from one language into another. Through all these transformations it preserves an identity of its own which can be called the propositional content, the 'said as such'. (*IT*: 9)

Ricoeur thus argues that while all discourse is realized as event, it is understood as meaning. The notion of meaning here has two dimensions. On the one hand, there is the 'objective' dimension, or what the sentence means, and on the other, there is the 'subjective' dimension, or what the speaker means (*IT*: 12–19). Following Frege (1970) Ricoeur distinguishes between the two aspects of the 'objective' dimension of meaning, and he argues that the sentence has both an ideal sense and a real reference (*RM*: 73–4; 216–21). 'The "objective" side of discourse . . . may be taken in two different ways. We may mean the "what" of discourse or the "about what" of discourse. The "what" of discourse is its "sense", the "about what" is its "reference"' (*IT*: 19). This distinction between sense and reference is directly connected to the distinction between semiotics and semantics. In the system of language, there is no problem of reference; signs refer only to other signs within the system. In discourse, however, language is used to refer to the world. The ability of an utterance to refer to the world is, of course, predicated on the existence of a language system. In a speech event, someone refers to something at a certain time, but this event receives its structure from the sense meaning of what is said. In fact, the speaker can only refer to something through the ideal structure of the sense of the sentence, and thus an ability to refer is dependent upon the ability to make sense. However, the sense of the sentence is always surpassed by the referential aspect of what is said. Semiotics and semantics have a necessary relationship to one another. Ricoeur uses this point to show that the dialectic of event and meaning is connected to the dialectic of sense and reference (*IT*: 20).

The referential dimension of discourse is further linked both to the creativity inherent in ordinary language and to the necessity for interpretation. At the root of the basic creativity of language is the intrinsic polysemy of words. Words in a natural language have more than one meaning, and these meanings can be gathered together and codified in a lexical system (*HHS*: 107). However, Ricoeur contends that the phenomenon of polysemy can only really be grasped at the level of the sentence because words have meaning in the context of sentences, and not merely by virtue of being lexical entities (*HHS*: 169). Ricoeur argues that the semantic potential of words is never exhausted by any particular usage, and that because of their polysemic character words provide sentences with a 'surplus' of meaning which must be screened out. This screening-out is effected by the context of use, where a univocal or single meaning is produced from a polysemic word through a process of filtering or sifting. It is this process of filtration or selection which demands an act of interpretation. 'It is with [the] selective function of context that interpretation, in the most primitive sense of the word, is connected. Interpretation is the process by which, in the interplay of question and answer, the interlocutors collectively determine the contextual values which structure their conversation' (*HHS*: 107). Ricoeur sees this spontaneous process of interpretation as part of the basic exercise of understanding in all situations of dialogic exchange. However, the polysemic character of words is linked not only to a process where ambiguity is reduced through interpretation, but also to a creative process where meaning is expanded through metaphor (*HHS*: 169). Ricoeur challenges the traditional idea that metaphor is simply a type of trope or rhetorical device in which a figurative word is substituted for a literal one. Instead, he argues that metaphor is a semantic innovation which takes place at the level of the sentence. Metaphor arises as the result of a contextual action – a speech utterance – which places the semantic fields of several words in interaction. Through this process, new meaning is created by metaphorical extension. Ricoeur retains a certain emphasis on the distinction between metaphorical and literal meaning because he agrees that the metaphorical meaning of a word cannot be codified in dictionaries. However, he makes it clear that by the term 'literal meaning', he does not wish to imply the 'original' or 'proper' meaning of a word on the lexical plane, but rather to imply the totality of the semantic field, that is, the set of possible contextual uses which constitute the polysemy of a word. In Ricoeur's view, therefore, a metaphorical meaning is something other than the actualization of one of the possible meanings of a polysemic word. While metaphor certainly depends on the creative potential of polysemy, new metaphorical meanings are produced in the context of sentences and they thus go beyond the known polysemy of words. It is the conjunction of several polysemic words in the context of language use which produces what Ricoeur terms the 'semantic impertinence' or metaphor.*

In the context of a speech act, metaphorical meaning is emergent and it can be grasped only through an act of interpretation which seeks to make sense of the sentence as a whole. This act of interpretation is linked to the referential dimension of metaphor, that is, to its power to redescribe reality. To speak of the Attorney-General as a jellyfish is to refer to contexts outside the context of utterance in which the qualities of Attorney-Generals and jellyfish are known, but it is also to create a new meaning which quite literally redescribes reality (Moore 1986: 79).

It is clear from the above discussion that Ricoeur's semantics,

---

* Ricoeur develops his ideas on metaphor in relation to the work of a number of other writers who have also argued that metaphor operates primarily at the level of the sentence (Black 1962; Richards 1936).

premised on the fundamental creativity of language use, involve complex and very specific ideas about meaning, reference and metaphor. However, the full implications of Ricoeur's arguments on these issues only become apparent in the context of his work on the theory of the text.

The Concept of the Text

With his work on the concept of the text, Ricoeur makes the move from semantics to hermeneutics in the proper sense. Language can be analysed not simply as systems of signs or as types of sentences, but also as extended sequences of written discourse, that is, as texts. However, the move from semantics to hermeneutics, from speech to written discourse, involves a consideration of a number of new theoretical issues.

The first of these issues concerns the concept of work. Ricoeur maintains that there are three distinctive features of discourse considered as a work. First, the work is a structured totality composed of more than one sentence. According to Ricoeur, the irreducible nature of this totality raises a new problem of understanding which cannot be dealt with merely by analysing or comprehending the individual sentences which constitute the work. Second, every work has a codified form which characterizes its composition, and which transforms it into a poem, a play, an essay, etc. Each work is thus produced in accordance with a series of rules or codes which define its literary genre. Third, a work is produced as a unique configuration which expresses its individual character and which may be called its style (*HHS*: 136). Each work is therefore a structured totality of a certain genre and style.

Ricoeur arrives at the notion of work because he sees the composition of discourse, with its particular genre and individual style, as a form of production or labour. 'To impose a form upon material, to submit production to genres, to produce an individual: these are so many ways of treating language as a material to be worked upon and formed' (*HHS*: 136). Thus the notion of discourse as a form of practice, which takes place within a particular context of production, is further strengthened and elaborated by the concept of work.

However, the text is more than a work of discourse, it is also a written work. In confronting this fact, Ricoeur emphasizes that the text is not simply speech written down, because speaking and writing are alternative and equally fundamental modes of the realization of discourse. But the inscription of discourse through writing does involve a series of transformations which Ricoeur embraces in the concept of distanciation. Distanciation, as developed by Ricoeur, has four principle forms. The first form of distanciation concerns the fact that what writing preserves is the meaning of discourse in such a way as to transcend the passing moment of the instance of discourse itself. Thus the event of saying is surpassed by the meaning of what is said. Ricoeur argues that the various parts of the speech act — the locutionary, illocutionary and perlocutionary acts as described by Austin (1976) — are exteriorized and can be realized in writing through the use of grammatical and other devices (*HHS*: 134–5; 198–200). The second form of distanciation concerns the relationship between the intention of the author and the meaning of the text. In spoken discourse, the sentence designates the speaker through various indicators, and thus it is assumed that the subjective intention of the speaking subject and the meaning of the discourse overlap. In written discourse, the author's intention and the meaning of the text cease to coincide: 'the text's career escapes the finite horizon lived by its author. What the text says now matters more than what the author meant to say, and every exegesis unfolds its procedures within the circumference of a meaning that has broken its moorings to the psychology of its author' (*HHS*: 201). The third form of distanciation concerns the gap between the text and the conditions of its production. Unlike spoken discourse, which is addressed to a hearer, the written text is addressed to an unknown audience, and, in theory, to anyone who can read. To a certain extent then, we can argue that the text frees itself from the social and historical conditions of its production, and becomes open to an unlimited number of readers or series of readings. The fourth form of distanciation designates the emancipation of the text from the limits of 'ostensive reference'. In spoken discourse, the dialogue ultimately refers to the situation common to the interlocutors, and there is always the possibility of indicating or clarifying the import of what is said through gesture and so on. In the written text, this link between discourse and ostensive reference no longer exists. A text does not refer to the situation of its production, but to the world. According to Ricoeur, it opens up a world and outlines a way of being-in-the-world for the subject who is engaged with the text (*HHS*: 201–3). To understand how this is so, it is necessary to turn to Ricoeur's theory of interpretation.

Explanation and Interpretation

Hermeneutics, as a philosophical tradition, analyses the text as the medium which links human subjects to their world and to their past. One of the charges levelled against this tradition is that a concern with the relationship of subject to life-world produces explanations which are basically 'romantic' or 'psychologistic'. Critics see the role of interpretation in hermeneutic analysis as little more than a kind of empathy which, because it involves identification with the intentions and situation of the subject, is necessarily individualizing and lacking in rigour. However, Ricoeur's approach to the analysis of the text allows him to avoid the criticisms of 'psychologism' and 'romanticism'. He argues that the paradigm of text-interpretation offers a fresh approach to the question of the relationship between explanation (*Erklären*) and understanding (*Verstehen*) in the human sciences (*HHS*: 209).

According to Ricoeur, this paradigm or theory of interpretation, draws its main features from the autonomous status of the written text. This autonomy is encapsulated in the four forms of distanciation: (i) the fixation of the meaning as opposed to the event of saying; (ii) the dissociation of meaning from the mental intention of the author; (iii) the non-ostensive nature of the text's references; and (iv) the universal range of the text's audience. Together these four traits constitute the 'objectivity' of the text (*HHS*: 210).

Ricoeur maintains that the disjunction between the meaning of the text and the intentions of the author produces 'an absolutely original situation' which creates a dialectic between explanation and understanding. He develops this notion by clarifying how this dialectic is involved in the process of text interpretation. 'If the objective meaning is something other than the subjective intention of the author, it may be constructed in various ways. The problem of the right understanding can no longer be solved by a simple return to the alleged intention of the author' (*HHS*: 211). Ricoeur thus argues that there is more than one way of construing a text, and that a construction based on authorial intention cannot be privileged over other interpretations. The emphasis on construction arises from the fact that a text must be treated as a whole, and its status as a structured totality irreducible to its constituent sentences must be maintained. A construction is, of course, an interpretation, and a text is always open to a variety of different interpretations. However, Ricoeur makes it clear that the plurivocity of texts as texts is something other than the polysemy of individual words in ordinary language and/or the ambiguity of individual sentences. The plurivocity of texts arises because the text as a whole is open to a variety of readings and thereby to several constructions (*HHS*: 211–12). This means that the interpretation of texts is an open process, it does not mean that all interpretations are valid, or that there is no way of judging which of the several interpretations is the more plausible. The validity of an interpretation is not, however, a matter of empirical verification and proof, but rather the result of a rational process of argumentation and debate (*HHS*: 175–6). 'It is always possible to argue for or against an interpretation, to confront interpretations, to arbitrate between them and to seek agreement, even if this agreement remains beyond our immediate reach' (*IT*: 79). In order to argue for or against an interpretation, it is necessary to produce reasons and coherent arguments based on what is contained in the text itself.

The third and fourth forms of distanciation are equally important for Ricoeur's theory of interpretation and for the argument concerning the relationship between explanation and understanding. The freeing of the text from the interlocutors and from the circumstances of the speech situation makes it possible to approach the text in two ways. First, the reader can suspend judgement regarding the referential dimension of the text, and treat the text as a 'worldless' and closed entity. This first approach is that adopted by structuralist approaches to the study of texts. Such approaches attempt to provide an *explanation* of the text on the basis of the objective science of linguistics. Ricoeur uses Lévi-Strauss's classic analysis of the Oedipus myth (see chapter 1 of this volume) as a paradigmatic example of the strengths and weaknesses of the structuralist approach (*HHS*: 160–1). Ricoeur acknowledges that, within limits, this approach is a valid one, and he argues that in essence what it seeks to uncover is the *sense* of the text. This sense is disclosed through an analysis of the elements of the text and their arrangement, considered in the light of the text's narrative form and the protagonists involved (*IT*: 84–5).

In the second approach to the analysis of the text, however, the reader abandons the notion of the closed, 'worldless' text, and attempts instead to disclose the non-ostensive references of the text. Ricoeur makes it clear that this second approach produces a form of understanding which cannot be reduced to structural explanation, but which is none the less dependent upon it. The aim of this second approach to the text is to understand the world projected by the text; that is, what it refers to, what it speaks about. Conceived in this way, understanding a text has even less to do with the author and the author's situation, because the purpose of understanding is to grasp the 'world propositions' opened up by the referential dimensions of the text. 'To understand a text is to follow its movement from sense to reference: from what it says, to what it talks about' (*IT*: 87–8). Ricoeur thus maintains that texts should be subject to a depth interpretation. This interpretation is one mediated by structural analysis, in which the reader moves from the sense to the reference of the text, from the closed system of the text to the world which it projects. (For further discussion of this point see chapter 1, section II of this volume.) However, the consequence of this movement from sense to reference is that the readers situate themselves within the world of the text, and comes thereby to have a deeper understanding of themselves and of others. Ricoeur terms this apprehension of the world brought about by insertion into the text 'appropriation'. This act of appropriation does not reduce the objectivity of the text to the subjectivity of the individual, because appropriation, as Ricoeur sees it, has nothing to do with the empathetic understanding of an agent's intentions or the process of identifying with another psychic life. To appropriate is to expand one's sense of self, one's consciousness, through the understanding and incorporation of worlds which were formerly unknown or alien or distant:

> appropriation is the process by which the revelation of new modes of being
> . . . *gives* the subject new capacities for knowing himself. If the reference of
> a text is the projection of a world, then it is not in the first instance the
> reader who projects himself. The reader is rather broadened in his capacity
> to project himself by receiving a new mode of being from the text itself.
> (*HHS*: 192; emphasis and use of the generic in the original)

Appropriation is thus a form of taking hold of the world projected by the text in such a way as to effect a kind of dispossession of the self. This dispossession of self is an essential prerequisite of self-understanding, and, as Ricoeur sees it, self-understanding is an essential part of understanding human phenomena in general (*HHS*: chapter 7). Ricoeur is thus at great pains to point out that the objective meaning of the text is not compromised by the particular form of understanding which appropriation involves, and in so doing, he is able to claim that explanation and understanding, including self-understanding, are phases in the process of depth interpretation, a process of interpretation which avoids subjectivity, but still manages to take account of the acting subject (*HHS*: 161–2).

Meaningful Action Considered as a Text*

Ricoeur's theory of interpretation may be extended beyond the written text to encompass other human phenomena which can be said to have textual characteristics. One such phenomenon is meaningful action, but in order for it to become an object of study it must undergo an objectification which is equivalent to the fixation of discourse by

---

* This is taken from the title of Ricoeur's own article on the subject, see *HHS*: chapter 8.

writing (*HHS*: 203). This process of objectification is encapsulated in the four forms of distanciation.

First, just as the event of saying is surpassed by the meaning of what is said, the event of doing is eclipsed by the significance of what is done. Second, Ricoeur maintains that the action-event has the features of a speech act because it has both a propositional content (the act of doing), which allows it to be re-identified as the same action, and an illocutionary force (actions can be threats, warnings, expressions of regret, etc.). Taken together, the propositional content and the illocutionary force of the action constitute its 'sense-content'. Thus Ricoeur argues: 'Like the speech-act, the action-event (if we may use this analogical expression) develops a similar dialectic between its temporal status as an appearing and disappearing event, and its logical status as having such-and-such identifiable meaning or "sense-content"' (*HHS*: 205). The meaning or 'sense-content' of an action can acquire an autonomy which is comparable to the autonomy of textual meaning. Action can become detached from the agent and develop consequences of its own. Ricoeur asserts that the meaning of an action is freed from the intentions of the acting subject and thus leaves a trace – or puts a mark – on the course of events which is human history (*HHS*: 206–7). This autonomy has further consequences because just as written discourse is freed from the dialogical situation, so action is freed from the situation of performance. An action, like a text, is an 'open work'; it can be interpreted and judged by an indefinite range of possible 'readers'. The interpretation of action by contemporaries has no particular privilege. 'The judges are not the contemporaries, . . . but history itself' (*HHS*: 208–9). Thus, action, like text, transcends the social conditions of its production. Human action, like a written work, is freed from the restrictions of ostensive reference. Action, like text, opens up a world (*HHS*: 208).

In so far as meaningful action can be considered as a text, it can be analysed using Ricoeur's theory of interpretation. The advantages of this, as Ricoeur sees them, relate once again to the question of the relationship between explanation (*Erklären*) and understanding (*Verstehen*) in the human sciences. The analogy of 'reading' human action allows for a dialectic between explanation and understanding through the process of interpretation which transcends the traditional dichotomy established in the human sciences between objective explanation and empathetic understanding. In order to demonstrate that his theory of interpretation provides a suitable methodology for the study of human phenomena other than written texts. Ricoeur has to set down how this theory can be applied to the study of action.

First, Ricoeur argues that human action, like texts, has a plurivocity, and, as such, it must be considered as a structured totality which can be read in several ways.

> That the meaning of human actions, of historical events, and of social phenomena may be construed in several different ways is well known by all experts in the human sciences. What is less known and understood is that this methodological perplexity is founded in the nature of the object itself and, moreover, that it does not condemn the scientist to oscillate between dogmatism and scepticism. As the logic of text-interpretation suggests, there is a specific plurivocity belonging to the meaning of human action. Human action, too, is a limited field of possible constructions. (*HHS*: 213; emphasis in original)

An action is understood when it can be explained why the individual acted as they did, and this can only be explained when a reason or motive for the action can be adduced. Consequently, an individual can make his or her action intelligible by explaining that it was done out of compassion or sorrow or revenge. However, Ricoeur makes it clear that there is nothing definite about such an explanation. It is always possible to argue about the meaning of an action, to argue for or against a particular interpretation (*HHS*: 213–4). Actions, like texts, are thus open to competing interpretations, and these interpretations must be supported or refuted through argumentation.

The same dialectic between explanation and understanding is evident with regard to the analysis of the referential dimensions of human action. Ricoeur agrees that structuralist analysis can be extended beyond linguistics to all the forms of social phenomena which can be characterized as systems of signs (*HHS*: 218). This is, of course, precisely the way in which social anthropology has used structuralist analysis. Ricoeur maintains, however, that structuralist explanation is only a preliminary step in the depth interpretation of social phenomena, and that this is so because those phenomena characterized by objectified action have a reference as well as a structure or sense dimension. Human actions exceed the situations in which they are performed, and as such they have non-ostensive references, they project a world. Thus to analyse human action is to move from sense to reference, from what it does to what it says about the world. This movement which characterizes the process of interpretation is based on a dialectic between explanation and understanding.

Ideology and Social Integration

The discussion of meaningful action as a text which discloses a world and which is open to a variety of competing interpretations, brings

Ricoeur to a consideration of the question of ideology. Ricoeur begins by dismissing the narrow view of ideology as falsehood and illusion, and instead he asserts that what ideology is actually concerned with is the broader phenomenon of social integration (*HHS*: 223). Ideology, Ricoeur argues, is linked to the self-representation of social groups as historical entities.

> Ideology is a function of the distance that separates the social meaning from an inaugural event which must nevertheless be repeated. Its role is not only to diffuse the conviction beyond the circle of the founding fathers, so as to make it the creed of the entire group; its role is also to perpetuate the initial energy beyond the period of effervescence. (*HHS*: 225)

The inevitable gap between the inaugural events of a group and its contemporary situation demands a set of images and symbols, a set of interpretations, which will mediate between the past and present of the group, and provide the mechanisms for social integration.

However, ideology is also a dynamic theory of social motivation. The founding act of the group, if it is to be relevant to changing, contemporary circumstances, must be revived and reactualized through representation and interpretation. This process will involve not only consensus among the members of the group, but also convention and rationalization. Consequently, ideology becomes something which justifies the way the world is. Ideology cannot be reduced to justification alone, however, because it is not just a reflection of the founding ideas of the group. Ricoeur makes it clear that ideology also constitutes a project; it carries the group forward; it has a generative character.

While recognizing this generative character, Ricoeur is equally well aware that although, in some sense, ideology carries the group forward because it functions as a motivation, it also has countervailing tendencies. For example, ideology easily becomes a simplifying schema which persuades the members of the group that they are correct to think as they do. 'Hence ideology is readily expressed in maxims, in slogans, in lapidary formulas' (*HHS*: 226). It also acquires an inertia, a lag, which arises from the sedimentation of social experience, but which is resistant to change and intolerant of marginality.

The recognition of these negative features of ideology leads Ricoeur to reflect on the particular function of domination which ideology performs, and which is linked to the hierarchical aspects of social organization 'What ideology interprets and justifies is, above all, the relation to the system of authority' (*HHS*: 228). Ricoeur develops a wayward notion of surplus-value here, because he asserts that every system of authority seeks to legitimate itself in the eyes of the individuals whom it subjects, but that in so doing it claims a legitimacy which exceeds the belief individuals are prepared to accord to it. Surplus-value is thus the excess of demand for legitimation in relation to the offer of belief. Ideology is the bearer of this surplus-value, as it mediates between demand and supply (*HHS*: 228).

Ricoeur considers the Marxist concept of ideology and is critical of it. However, he does agree that the notion of ideology as serving the interests of the dominant class is a useful and necessary addition to his own analysis of the form and function of ideology which stresses both the relationship of ideology to authority and its role in social integration ('the symbolic construction of the social bond'; *HHS*: 229–31). Ricoeur's consideration of ideology leads him to the conclusion that: 'ideology is an unsurpassable phenomenon of social existence, in so far as social reality always has a symbolic constitution and incorporates an interpretation, in images and representations, of the social bond itself' (*HHS*: 231). This view of ideology raises the question as to whether it is ever possible to stand outside ideology and analyse it. Ricoeur maintains that it is not possible because a non-ideological discourse on ideology will always come up against the impossibility of reaching a social reality prior to symbolization (*HHS*: 237). Ricoeur argues that all objectifying knowledge about our position in society, in a social class, in a cultural tradition and in history is preceded by a relation of *belonging* upon which we can never entirely reflect. We belong to a history, a class, a nation, a culture, to one or several traditions, before we can manage to have any critical distance from these groups or traditions. This belonging is sustained by ideology – in the sense of ideology as image and self-representation – as a medium of social integration. None the less, even if all objectifying knowledge is preceded by a relation of belonging, it can nevertheless acquire a 'relative autonomy'. This autonomy is a consequence of the distance we must create between ourselves and history in order to understand that we belong, that we are historical beings. Distanciation is thus an essential part of understanding ourselves as historically constructed beings (*HHS*: 243–4). Distanciation is involved in the fixation of discourse by writing and in other comparable processes of objectification – as in the case, for example, of social action considered as a text. The interpretation of texts and text-analogues is therefore the route both to self-understanding and to an understanding of our world through an objectified medium and in a critical way (*HHS*: 110–11). The dialectical relationship between distanciation and belonging thus creates the possibility for a critique

of ideology and of historical understanding. However, although the critique of ideology can partially free itself (distanciation) from its initial anchorage, it can never do so completely because it is constrained by the relation of belonging which is the counterpart of distanciation. The critique of ideology is condemned to remain partial, fragmentary and insular; 'its *non-completeness* is hermeneutically founded in the original and unsurpassable condition which makes distanciation itself a moment of belonging' (*HHS*: 244–5).

History, Time and Narrative

The recognition that the critique of ideology can never be conducted from a position outside the history or the society to which we belong brings us to a consideration of Ricoeur's views on history, time and narrative as they are developed in the three volumes of *Time and Narrative*. The work contained in these volumes is an extension of the arguments put forward in *RM*. According to Ricoeur, both metaphor and narrative belong to the realm of semantic innovation produced in discourse; that is, at the level of acts of language equal to or greater than the sentence (*TNI*: ix). In the case of metaphor, a new meaning is created through an 'impertinent attribution': 'The Attorney-General is a jellyfish'. With narrative, the innovation involves the creation of a new work of synthesis: a plot. Plots mimic action, and they do so through a poetic refiguring of action. The experience of time and the temporal experience of action are both involved in this process of refiguration. 'I see in the plots we invent the privileged means by which we re-configure our confused, unformed, and at the limit mute temporal experience' (*TNI*: xi). It is the plot, or rather, the dynamic of emplotment, which is crucial to understanding the relation between time and narrative. The connection which Ricoeur wishes to establish between time and narrative is a close one, and is, in fact, squarely within the framework of his hermeneutic phenomenology, which continues to manifest itself through an enduring concern with the nature of being and of being human in a socially constructed world:

> my basic hypothesis [is] that between the activity of narrating a story and the temporal character of human experience there exists a correlation that is not merely accidental but that presents a transcultural form of necessity. To put it another way, time becomes human to the extent that it is articulated through a narrative mode, and narrative attains its full meaning when it becomes a condition of temporal existence. (*TNI*: 52)

Ricoeur elaborates on this point by investigating the ways in which the relation between time and narrative is mediated through the dynamic of emplotment. Emplotment consists of three moments of mimesis, which Ricoeur terms mimesis$_1$, mimesis$_2$ and mimesis$_3$. Mimesis$_1$ is concerned with the fact that the making of a plot presupposes a prior or pre-understanding of the world of action, its meaningful structures, symbolic resources and temporal character. If it is true that plot imitates action, then some preliminary ability to recognize action by its structural features is required. It must be possible, for example, to distinguish action from mere physical movement. Actions involve such things as goals, motives, agents and consequences, both intended and unintended. Ricoeur thus argues that every narrative presupposes a familiarity with such terms as agent, goal, means, conflict, success, failure, etc., both on the part of the narrator and on the part of the listener. Such terms are part of a conceptual network the utilization and recognition of which involves a competence which can be designated as 'practical understanding' (*TNI*: 54–5). However, narrative has a reference as well as a sense component. In other words, it has discursive features which distinguish it from simple sequences of action sentences.

In addition to an ability to identify the structural features of action, emplotment will also involve a capacity for identifying the symbolic resources implicit in the world of action. Ricoeur draws on the work of Cassirer and Geertz here (see chapter 3 of this volume), as he speaks of a symbolic system or framework necessary to understand action in a particular context.

> A symbolic system thus furnishes a descriptive context for particular actions. In other words, it is 'as a function of' such a symbolic convention that we can interpret this gesture as meaning this or that. The same gesture of raising one's arm, depending on the context, may be understood as a way of greeting someone, of hailing a taxi, or of voting. Before being submitted to interpretation, symbols are interpretants internally related to some action. (*TNI*: 58)

In this regard, symbolism confers an initial readability on action. Action is a 'quasi-text' because symbols, understood as interpretants, supply the rules of meaning as a function of which behaviour can be interpreted. The idea of a symbol in this context is connected, for Ricoeur, to the notion of a rule, not just in the sense of rules for description and interpretation, but also in the Winchian sense of a norm. As a function of the norms immanent in culture, actions can be evaluated or judged according to sets of moral precepts. The values thus attributed to actions are extended to the perpetrators of such

actions. Ricoeur concludes from this that actions can never be ethically
neutral, and that the ethical nature of action is a corollary of the fact
that it is always symbolically mediated (*TNI*: 58–9).

However, understanding action is not confined to being familiar
with the conceptual network of action and its symbolic mediations; it
also involves the recognition of temporal structures. Action is
something which takes place in time. Everyday praxis orders the
present, past and future in terms of one another. This question of
being 'within' time is irreducible to the representation of linear time
(*TNI*: 59–63).

Mimesis₁ thus involves the realization that to imitate or represent
action is first to pre-understand what human action is, in its
semantics, its symbolic system and its temporality (*TNI*: 64).

Mimesis₂, according to Ricoeur, has a mediating function which
derives from the dynamic character of the configuring operation
known as emplotment. This dynamism arises because a plot exercises
an integrating function, which permits it to bring about a mediation
between the pre-understanding of the order of action and its temporal
features, and the post-understanding which subsequently arises
through the process of emplotment. A plot is mediating in three ways.
First, it mediates between the individual events and the story taken as
a whole. It therefore transforms events and incidents into a story.
Second, plot brings together a large number of heterogeneous factors,
such as agents, goals, means, circumstances, intended and unintended
consequences of action. As a result, it exercises a complex, configuring
role and is much more than a mere setting-down of the order of events.
Third, plot is mediating because it combines, in variable proportions,
two temporal dimensions, one chronological and the other not. There
is the chronological, or episodic, dimension of narrative, and, in
addition, there is the single unity of the temporal whole which is
created through the 'grasping together' of events to constitute a story.
The fact that a succession of events is 'grasped together' and
transformed into a meaningful whole is what makes the story
followable. Ricoeur suggests that to follow a story is to move through
events, contingencies and so on under an expectation which will find
its fulfilment in the 'conclusion' of the story. This 'end-point' provides
the point of view from which the story can be perceived as forming a
whole. To understand a story is therefore to understand how and why
successive episodes lead to this point. According to Ricoeur, a new
quality of time emerges from this understanding. Furthermore, the
repetition of a story, governed as a whole by its way of ending,
constitutes an alternative to the representation of time as flowing from
past to future. Recollection inverts the apparently natural order of

time (*TNI*: 64–7). 'In reading the ending in the beginning and the beginning in the ending, we also learn to read time itself backwards, as the recapitulation of the initial conditions of a course of action in its terminal consequences' (*TNI*: 67–8). The 'grasping together' characteristic of plot produces a configurational act which Ricoeur likens to the work of the productive imagination. Following Kant, Ricoeur argues that the productive imagination constitutes a generative matrix of rules, in so far as the categories of understanding must first be schematized by the productive imagination. The schematic function of the productive imagination is a synthetic one; it connects understanding and intuition through synthesis. Emplotment also synthesizes the intellectual point of a story with an intuitive presentation of circumstances, characters, reversals of fortune, etc., which go to make up the story. This schematization of the narrative function is constituted within a history which may be termed a tradition. Tradition consists of an interplay between innovation and sedimentation. Sedimentation derives from the fact that a typology of plots exist, both at the level of the formal features of plots and at the level of literary genres. Innovation arises because, in the last analysis, every work is a singular work. Ricoeur likens the relationship between sedimentation and innovation in plot to the relationship between grammar and speech in language. However, he stresses here that innovation remains governed by the rules of the tradition's paradigms, although it is true that the 'range of solutions is vast' (*TNI*: 69). Innovation is thus a form of 'rule-governed deformation'.

Mimesis$_3$ marks the intersection of the world of the text and the world of the reader; that is, the world configured by the plot and the world in which real action occurs and unfolds its specific temporality (*TNI*: 71). The transition between mimesis$_2$ and mimesis$_3$ is brought about by the act of reading. The two features which characterize the plot at the stage of mimesis$_2$, schematization and traditionality, are involved in the interaction between writing and reading. The received paradigms structure the expectations of readers and help them to recognize formal rules and the genre or type exemplified by the story. In so far as they provide guidelines for the 'encounter' between text and reader, they govern a story's capacity to be followed. However, it is only in the act of reading that a narrative's capacity to be followed is actualized. 'To follow a story is to actualize it by reading it' (*TNI*: 76). It is also the act of reading which accompanies the interplay of innovation and sedimentation within emplotment. Through reading, the reader plays with narrative constraints and creates gaps. In this sense, it is the reader who completes the work of emplotment. The written work is a 'sketch for reading', and it is the reader who works with the absences, holes and lacunae of the text to carry forward the burden of emplotment.

Ricoeur completes his linking of writing and reading by returning to the question of reference. What is communicated in the end is beyond the sense of a work. 'What a reader receives is not just the sense of the work, but, through its sense, its reference, that is, the experience it brings to language and, in the last analysis, the world and the temporality it unfolds in the face of this experience' (*TNI*: 78–9).

Ricoeur's purpose in discussing at length the three-fold mimetic relationship between the order of narrative, the order of action and the order of life is not to develop a theory of mimesis, but to set the context for his reflections on the relationship between time and narrative. Both history and fiction as forms of narrative refigure time, or, rather, refigure our experience of time. Ricoeur inserts himself into the debate about the relations between lived experience, historical time and fictional time with a breadth of scholarship and wealth of detail which is impossible to summarize. He draws on a list of scholars and thinkers from Aristotle to Michel De Certeau, and on a range of disciplines from philosophy and philosophical linguistics to social anthropology with a verve and understanding which is quite breath-taking. There are, however, a few points which are worth drawing attention to here because of their relevance to the question of understanding material culture and to our efforts to write and read about the past.

In *TNI*, Ricoeur begins his discussion of the relationship between history and narrative by examining French historiography and the writings of the Annales school. He emphasizes, amongst other things, the utility of distinguishing between the history of events, the history of social groups, their political institutions, their *mentalités* and the history of human–environment relations. These different histories involve different sorts of time, different temporalities. There is an awareness of the plurality of social times. The concept of a long time-span (*la longue durée*) is opposed to the concept of the event, and the history of civilizations is opposed to the brief history of the lives of contemporaries (*TNI*: 96–111). In *TNIII*, Ricoeur extends his reflections on the variable nature of temporality, and puts forward an argument that historical time is on the fracture-line between pheno-menological time and astronomical, physical and biological time (*TNIII*: 95). He points out here that the notion of a single scale of time introduces an abstract and misleading idea that the different tempor-alities involved are commensurable with regard to comparative chronology. 'The fact that this alignment along a single scale of time is ultimately misleading is attested to by the following paradox. The length of time of a human life, compared to the range of cosmic time-spans, appears insignificant, whereas it is the very place from which every question of significance arises' (*TNIII*: 90). Ricoeur argues that, strictly speaking, these different forms of temporality are not commensurable because what physical time and the sphere of nature lack is narrative, and the understanding of being-within-time which narrative refigures. There are, however, overlappings of meaning which compensate, to a certain extent, for this epistemological break between the two forms of temporality. There is, for example, an obvious overlap between the phenomena of datability, the passing of time and the nature of public time as they are lived and the astronomical considerations which govern the construction of calendars and clocks. According to Ricoeur, history – historical time – is the place where these overlappings find their meaning. Historical time is thus set between mortal time and cosmological time. It is through narrative, the process of emplotment, that history refigures praxis and therefore refigures time. Both historical and fictional narratives have the power to refigure time and praxis in this way, and they do so through a mutual borrowing.

> These borrowings . . . lie in the fact that historical intentionality only becomes effective by incorporating into its intended object the resources of fictionalization stemming from the narrative form of imagination, while the intentionality of fiction produces its effects of detecting and transforming acting and suffering only by symmetrically assuming the resources of historicization presented it by attempts to reconstruct the actual past. (*TNIII*: 102)

Ricoeur draws attention here to the semantics of the term 'history', which designates, in a number of languages, and particularly in French, both the totality of the course of events and the totality of narratives referring to this course of events. Ricoeur is anxious to join these two meanings to indicate the process of totalization underway at the level of historical narrative and at the level of actual history, which can be referred to as 'historical consciousness'. The question of historical consciousness or the historical condition is what is at stake in the refiguration of time by narrative.

The wider question which Ricoeur has to address as a consequence of the relationship he establishes between history, fiction and time, and to which he returns in all three volumes of *TN*, is that of how we are to deal with the reality of the past, with the fact that history purports to say something about something which really happened.

This issue has been extensively debated, of course, by a very large number of scholars, and Ricoeur discusses the work of many of them and the solutions they propose in *TNIII*. Ricoeur himself proposes that we can say something meaningful about the past by thinking about it in terms of the Same, the Other and the Analogous. Under the heading of the Same, Ricoeur places those ways of thinking about the past which see it as rethought or re-enacted in the present. The temporal distance of the past is dulled, and what is re-enacted is the past in the mind of the historian. Under the heading of the Other, Ricoeur considers those ways of looking at the past which see it as strange to us, as other than what exists in the present; sometimes to the extent of denying the survival of the past in the present. With the term Analogous, Ricoeur joins sameness, otherness and similarity together, and characterizes the relationship of history to the past as a 'taking the place of' or a 'standing for'. It is with this return to 'standing for', to tropology, that we begin to see why Ricoeur himself considers the three volumes of *TN* to be an extension of *RM*. The role of the trope, as Ricoeur argues in *RM*, is one of redescription, a redescription which is brought about through a process of 'standing for'. 'That is why, between a narrative and a course of events, there is not a relation of reproduction, reduplication, or equivalence but a metaphorical relation' (*TNIII*: 154).

However, unlike certain scholars, such as Hayden White, Ricoeur does not want to argue that history's relationship to the past is primarily metaphorical. He insists that our relation to the reality of the past has to 'pass successively through the filters of the Same, the Other, and the Analogous' (*TNIII*: 154).

> In the hunt for what has been, analogy does not operate alone but in connection with identity and otherness. The past is indeed what, in the first place, has to be reenacted in the mode of identity, but it is no less true, for all that, that it is also what is absent from all our constructions. The Analogous, precisely, is what retains in itself the force of reenactment and of taking a distance, to the extent that being-as is both to be and not to be. (*TNIII*: 155)

The claim that history is and is not the past is Ricoeur's answer – in so far as there can be said to be a solution – to this question. However, Ricoeur does not leave the debate there; he returns once again to the question of the relationship between text and reader, and, to a certain extent, resumes the theme of his earlier work. The role of reading is crucial to Ricoeur, who claims that the configuring work of the text must be accompanied by a reader; without a reader plots configure and refigure nothing. Similarly, without a reader to appropriate it, there is no world unfolded before the text (*TNIII*: 164). The relationship envisaged is a dialectical one because the structure of the text is brought to light through an interpretation which is a reading, and the reading itself is constrained by the limits which the text sets; the reader is thus constructed, in a way, in and through the text. Ricoeur is striving here to establish some sort of understanding about the balance between the expectations created by the text and those contributed by the reading (*TNIII*: 178). However, Ricoeur has also to confront the problem that reading itself, like writing, is a form of action. He addresses this issue glancingly, and he asserts that reading appears by turns as an interruption in the course of action and as an impetus to action. This is because it is through reading that the confrontation and the connection between the imaginary world of the text and the actual world of the reader comes about.

One point which Ricoeur does stress is that theories of reading are primarily about the reception of literary texts, and he makes the simple point that we are readers of history just as much as we are readers of novels. All forms of writing, including historiography, must take their place within an extended theory of reading, and therefore the mutually encompassing nature of historical and fictional narratives which Ricoeur earlier posits must, in fact, be rooted in reading itself.

Perhaps, in the long run, Ricoeur is not particularly interested in the question of how we come to know the past, and what exactly we can claim to know about it, although he is certainly interested in certain philosophical and methodological aspects of the historian's craft. To put it another way, he is ultimately rather more engaged with the ontological than the epistemological meditations on historicity.

> As regards the reality of the past, no one can, I think, really go beyond, by way of any direct approach, the . . . interplay of broken-off perspectives arising from the reactualization of the Same, the recognition of Otherness, and the assumption of the Analogous. To go any further, we have to take up the problem from the other end and to explore the idea that these broken-off perspectives come together in a sort of pluralistic unity if we bring them together under the idea of a reception of the past, pushed to the point of becoming a 'being-affected' by the past. (*TNIII*: 207)

Ricoeur wishes to establish the basic historicity of human experience, and to emphasize that this historicity can only be brought to language as narrativity. In addition, narrativity itself can only be articulated by the crossed interplay of the two narrative modes: history and fiction. This must necessarily be so since historicity comes to language only in so far as we tell stories or tell history. Our historical condition requires the conjunction of history and fiction as narrative genres because this is implied in the nature of our experience of being historical, the three-fold nature of which is that we make history, we are immersed in history and we are historical beings. In the experience of being historical, that is, in being an historical being, the subject–object relation is undermined, and this is because of the fundamental nature of belonging which characterizes our relationship with our world. 'We are members of the field of historicity as story tellers, as novelists, as historians. We belong to history before telling stories or writing history. The game of telling is included in the reality told' (*HHS*: 294). There is, therefore, an intimate involvement of the act of narrating in the historical experience itself. When we examine the historian's interest in 'facts' about the past, we discern a more deeply sedimented interest in communication. The ultimate interest in doing history is to enlarge our sphere of communication, and this interest expresses the situation of the historian as belonging to her world, her time, her field of study. The historian retains from the past what appears to be memorable, significant, valuable and so on. According to Ricoeur, this resurrecting of the forgotten requires as its counter-part the capacity to suspend our own prejudices, our own convictions, 'to put into parentheses our own desires'. As a consequence of this *epoché*, the Otherness of the Other is preserved in its difference. A dialectic is thus established between the alien and the familiar, the far and the near. This dialectic brings history within the purview of fiction because to recognize the difference between the values of the past and the values of the present is to 'open up the real towards the possible'.

> The 'true' histories of the past uncover the buried potentialities of the present . . . History, in this sense, explores the field of 'imaginative' variations which surround the present and the real that we take for granted in everyday life. Such is the way in which history, precisely because it seeks to be objective, partakes of fiction'. (*HHS*: 295)

However, fictional narrative also shares something of the realist intention of history. Everything Ricoeur argues about the mimetic dimension of fictional narrative emphasizes that 'the world of fiction leads us to the heart of the real world of action'. For Ricoeur, this is an ontological issue; it is about the nature of being in the world. Through opening us to difference, history opens us to the possible, while fiction, by opening us to the unreal, directs us to what is essential in reality (*HHS*: 296).

Critical Reflections

Paul Ricoeur's philosophy is very rich and very productive. Taken as a whole — in so far as this is possible with such a prolific author — his writings work and rework a series of themes. Most notable in this regard are the themes of meaning, action and being-in-the-world. While Ricoeur's earlier work was concerned with phenomenology, his later work shows a marked shift towards hermeneutics. An initial concern with the intentional objects of subjective processes and with the symbolic expression of subjective experience has given way to a concern with written discourse, with the interpretation of texts and text-analogues. The wide-ranging nature of Ricoeur's thought defies easy generalization, but in the light of an emphasis on material culture, it is perhaps possible to draw out, and critically comment on, some of the issues his work raises.

In all his work, Ricoeur emphasizes that social relations and the social world are symbolically constituted. He attempts in his theory of interpretation to develop an approach to the study of human phenomena which will encompass meaning and action, subject and social relations, structure and event in a single analytical framework. The problem of analysing meaningful action, or, rather, the problem of the relation between action and social structure, is at the centre of social theory and of much philosophical speculation in the social sciences.*
In the hermeneutic tradition which Ricoeur represents, this problematic is approached through the understanding that the social world is made up of individuals who speak and act in meaningful ways; these individuals create the social world which gives them their identity and being, and their creations can only be understood through a process of interpretation.

All human phenomena which may be deemed to have textual characteristics — that is, all those capable of undergoing an objectification comparable to the fixation of discourse by writing — are susceptible to interpretation. This view offers us the possibility of applying Ricoeur's theory of interpretation to material culture provided it can be demonstrated that material culture undergoes the necessary process of objectification. I have argued elsewhere that

* Marx, Weber and Durkheim all tackled this problem. Notable recent contributions include: Bhaskar (1979); Bourdieu, (1977; 1980); and Giddens (1979; 1984).

material culture can be considered as a text precisely because it is the product of the inscription of meaning and meaningful action on the material world (Moore 1986). The sheer physicality of material culture lends tremendous weight to this argument, whether we are talking about transformations of the landscape, domestic architecture, textile design, vessel form or the plastic arts. Material culture embodies meaning, it is the product of meaningful action, and it is involved in the reproduction of meaningful action in determinate social and historical contexts. However, Ricoeur's emphasis on objectification, which is encompassed in the notion of distanciation, provides us with the means to analyse material culture without reducing our explanation of the meaning of material culture to the mental intentions of its producers or to an empathetic understanding of the psychology of 'other' cultures, whether contemporary or in the past. Following the four forms of distanciation, it can be argued that what is inscribed in material culture is not the actuality of past actions, but their meaning; that what material culture signifies does not coincide with the intentions of individual producers/actors; that its signification is not addressed to a particular individual/audience; and that it is freed from the ostensive references of the shared situation of production. The emancipation of the material text from the intentions of its producers and from the sociohistorical conditions of its production open it to an unlimited series of interpretations, that is, to a multiplicity of readings. The freeing of the material text from the limits of ostensive reference which apply in the context of production means that the text possesses non-situational references which outlive the immediacy of contextual reference and which can only be recovered through interpretation. These non-situational references offer possible representations or orientations in the world; they proffer a symbolic dimension to understanding, a play on form. To interpret a text in this way is to enlarge our understanding of our position in the world.

To analyse material culture as a text is to begin with the assumed interdependence of meaning with action, of structure with event, and of sense with reference. This assumption permits a text to be approached in two ways. It can either be analysed and explained in terms of its internal relations (*langue*, sense), or it may be interpreted as a process, as the actualized product of social actors in a particular context (*parole*, reference). Both approaches are valid and, according to Ricoeur, both belong to the activity of reading, which must be understood as a dialectic between them (*HHS*: 152). The distinction between sense and reference is very helpful with regard to the analysis of material culture. First, it maintains the validity and importance of the structuralist approach, and Ricoeur emphasizes that the referential dimensions of a text can be disclosed only through an analysis of its internal relations or sense. In this regard we could say that Ricoeur's work is genuinely post-structuralist. Second, it provides a single framework in which to analyse the different levels or units of the discourse inscribed in the material text. We could take, for example, the problem of decorative designs on a pot. On the 'first' level we have the individual motif (word), on a 'second' level we can identify design sequences (sentences) and on a 'third' level we should consider the decorated pot as a whole (text). It is at this final level that we are also able to make use of Ricoeur's comments on style and genre with regard to the execution of the final product. The arguments about sense and reference stress the interdependence of these levels of analysis, but the theory of interpretation also emphasizes that what the text as a whole (the pot, in this instance) refers to, what it means, what it 'talks about' cannot be reduced to or adjuced from the structural analysis of its internal relations of meaning alone. The ability of a text to refer to a 'world outside itself', through an act of interpretation, is linked to the issue of polysemy. According to Ricoeur, all the words in a natural language are polysemic, that is, they have more than one meaning, and all these meanings can be collected and codified in a lexical system. Following Ricoeur's own theory, the same must be true, by analogic extension, of individual actions. However, the actual polysemic functioning of a word can only be grasped within the context of the sentence. The context of the speech utterance functions to screen out some of the word's surplus-meaning, and a single meaning is thereby produced from a basically polysemic word. It is this screening which Ricoeur takes to be the first act of interpretation because it is on the basis of the meaning of the word as it is established in the sentence that the hearer is able to understand what the sentence refers to. The referential dimension of individual sentences is similarly constrained by their placement within the text. There is, therefore, as Ricoeur suggests, a hierarchy of contextualization.

However, in his work, Ricoeur makes it clear that the polysemic character of words is linked not only to a process whereby ambiguity is reduced through interpretation, but also to a creative process where meaning is expanded through metaphor. Metaphor arises as a result of a contextual action – speech utterance – which places the semantic fields of several words in interaction. Through this process, new meaning is created. While metaphor certainly depends on the creative potential of polysemy, new metaphorical meanings are produced in the context of sentences and they go beyond the known polysemy of words. New metaphorical meanings are emergent within their context of use and can only be grasped through an act of interpretation. This act of interpretation discloses the referential dimensions of metaphor, that is, its power to redescribe reality, to project a world.

Ricoeur's work on metaphor is useful for the analysis of material culture because it describes how new meanings can emerge through the context of use, that is, through social action. The distinction between sense and reference helps us to grasp how this process actually works because it emphasizes that while the new metaphorical meaning is contextually produced, it refers none the less to an understanding outside that context. This is precisely why Ricoeur has described metaphor as a 'work in miniature', and it is also why he argues that we construct the meaning of a text in a way which is very similar to that in which we make sense of a metaphorical statement.

The fundamental point of Ricoeur's work is that things (words, actions) find their meaning in their context of use, and that it is also in this context that new meanings may be created through metaphorical extension. In summary form, this may not seem a very bold statement, but its value lies in the way it integrates meaning and action within a single analytical frame. However, perhaps the most insightful and innovative part of Ricoeur's work concerns the relationship between reference and interpretation. The referential dimensions of texts can only be revealed through an act of interpretation, but the question is through whose interpretation? Ricoeur's position is quite distinct from that of structuralist scholars. While structuralism 'brackets out' the individual actor, and gives no space to their actions or interpretations, Ricoeur moves in the other direction and privileges the actions and interpretations of knowledgeable social actors in determinate historical and social circumstances. Because individual social actors use discourse, make texts and construct interpretations new meanings are created, new understandings reached and innovations made.

So far I have concentrated on the positive aspects of Ricoeur's work and on how it can help us to construct and interpret material culture as a text, I now want to turn to some of the difficulties with Ricoeur's theory of interpretation. One of the first difficulties concerns the way in which the possibility for treating action and other human phenomena (e.g. material culture) as texts depends upon the emancipation of these phenomena from the circumstances of their production and from their producers. Ricoeur contends that just as a text is autonomous from its author, from the social conditions of its production and from the limits of ostensive reference, so too is action. Action becomes detached from its agent, has a relevance beyond the situation in which it is performed, and is open to a variety of interpretations, that is, to anyone who can read. There are a number of problems with these arguments. First, it seems contradictory on the one hand to emphasize the construction of meaning in context and on the other to suggest that the meaning of the text is the product of its emancipation from the social and historical conditions of its production. It could be argued here that Ricoeur is merely making the very reasonable point that the meaning of human phenomena cannot be reduced to the intended meanings of their producers. This is clearly a perfectly sound argument, and can be defended simply with reference to the number of authors who are at pains to explain that the meanings imputed to their novels by critics are not of their own making. Likewise with social action, it is clear that the unintended consequences of actions are often the result of the unintended meanings of those actions. However, it is still the case that Ricoeur's emphasis on the emancipation of the text leads him to neglect what might be termed the 'conditions of meaning'. Ricoeur does not actually provide us with any understanding of the social and historical conditions of meaning production, and this is, at least in part, because his work is philosophical rather than anthropological or sociological. It refers to the human condition rather than to any known society. Texts are not produced in a vacuum; they are always the product of determinate sociocultural and politicoeconomic conditions, and while they can refer to a world outside the circumstances of their production, we still need some theory of how and in what degree they are determined by the actual historical circumstances of their production.

Second, Ricoeur's emphasis on the emancipation of the text from the dialogic situation, so that it ceases to be addressed to any particular individual or audience means that he neglects certain aspects of enquiry concerned with the reception of texts, particularly in his early work. While Ricoeur's theory of interpretation provides the basis for a theory of text reception of some sort, there is still the problem of the 'conditions of reception' and of how they relate to the conditions for the production of texts. It is quite clear that texts are actually produced for an audience. This is particularly true for material-culture texts, many of which are actually consumer items, and are thus acquired through a variety of exchange mechanisms in human society, including market relations. This being so, it is equally clear that the expectations and wishes of the audience have a determining effect both on the text and on its production. This can be most dramatically demonstrated in modern industrial society by such things as the market in 'video nasties', 'snuff movies', Mills-and-Boon-type novels and the rest. Cultural convention and social and historical conditions determine the horizons of expectations within which a text becomes intelligible. If a White Paper on Reproductive Technologies fails to take a certain form, if it fails to produce certain evidence and/or to make certain arguments, it quite simply ceases to be a White Paper. If a text does not conform to the expectation of its audience, it simply ceases to be a text. It becomes meaningless.

Third, Ricoeur's contention that when a text is freed from the limits of ostensive reference, it becomes open to a variety of interpretations, and thereby to anyone who can read, is insufficient because it fails to take account of the way in which the production of meaning is always involved in the production and maintenance of power relations. Ricoeur acknowledges that if it is true that there is always more than one way of interpreting a text, it is not true that all interpretations are equal. However, Ricoeur is referring here to the analytical strengths of differing interpretations, and not to inequalities which produce and are produced by social inequalities of various sorts. In human societies, it is simply not true to say that all those who can read may provide interpretations. Interpretation — as Ricoeur himself argues — always has symbolic significance, and often it may have economic and political consequences as well. Interpretation is always bound up with social inequality and with domination. Discrimination in society prevents many groups from making an interpretation, either because they are directly denied a platform or because they are debarred from access to the resources — notably education — which would equip them to make interpretations. In many instances, even when they make interpretations they are not heard, they lack an audience.

Ricoeur does try to deal with issues of power, coercion, authority and control in society through his discussions on ideology. Here again, however, he seems to lack an understanding of the real basis of social and symbolic power. He suggests that ideology functions to integrate groups by means of images and/or representations which are collectively shared. This view of ideology is well suited to his discussion of the symbolic constitution of society and to his image of social authority, but it is insufficient with regard to a consideration of issues of domination, discrimination and conflict. It is a highly contentious point as to whether members of a society do share a significant number of beliefs. Feminists have been arguing for some time that women do not share many dominant social beliefs, but that in male-dominated social formations, they are not in a position to voice their dissent and/ or that where dissent is made public it is ignored or trivialized.

The above discussion makes it clear that Ricoeur's theory of interpretation is applicable to material culture considered as a text, and that his method of analysis, which seeks to combine meaning and action within a single analytical frame has much to offer. However, as the above summary makes equally clear, there are serious difficulties in

Ricoeur's work with regard to the treatment of the social and historical conditions of text production and reception.

In the final volume of *TN*, Ricoeur does take up a discussion about reading and the reception of texts. This discussion takes as its starting-point the position he elaborated in his earlier work on metaphor and on social action considered as a text. In other words, that texts have a referential dimension as well as a sense-meaning and that it is through reading as an act of interpretation that the text is opened to a world beyond itself. In *TNIII*, he stresses that considered apart from reading, the world of the text, its referential dimension, remains a transcendence in immanence only. It is only through reading that the dynamism of emplotment or configuration is completed, and it is beyond reading, in the effective action which is informed through reflection on the world revealed by the text, that the configuration of the text is transformed into the refiguration of life (*TNIII*: 158–9). It is very hard to assess the real force of this argument, particularly when we move from ontological considerations to the more epistemological issues which confront anthropologists and archaeologists as they strive to interpret both material culture and the past. On the one hand, it could be argued that Ricoeur is effectively saying little more than the literary critics of various generations who have argued that literature is concerned with the great issues of human existence and its value is that it allows us to reflect on our human condition and possibly gain some insight into that condition. To go beyond this kind of argument, Ricoeur would have to specify how it is that the interpretations arising from reading actually give rise to further action. While Ricoeur himself does not provide answers, it is clear that in the analysis of material culture there is a great potential for actually elaborating on this connection, and in my discussion of Marakwet domestic space considered as a text, I discussed the ways in which interpretations of space inform subsequent actions, and how those actions provide a historical context in which further interpretations and actions take place (Moore, 1986). The ability to do this depends, of course, on having a very detailed and well-specified social context in which it is possible to establish the chronological order of interpretations and actions. This in turn raises the question of how to treat the time dimensions involved in the production–interpretation–consumption– production sequences in which material culture is involved in the context of social praxis. Ricoeur himself recognizes a similar problem with regard to the interpretation of historical events. He points out that to say that a given event reported by a historian was observable by witnesses in the past solves nothing because it merely shifts the problem of 'pastness' from the event reported to the testimony which reports it (*TNIII*: 157). The issue in both cases then is that in order to demonstrate the interdependence of interpretation and action, at least as a social scientist, one is drawn back time and time again to models which have various combinations of causal and chronological features. In other words, it is difficult to demonstrate effect without presupposing sequence. This might not be such a stumbling-block were it not for the argument about whether the sequences implied and/or demonstrated in the relevant models can actually be said to exist or to have existed in the past. These sequences and the models constructed from them are provided by observers and it matters little whether these observers are interpreting contemporary social praxis or past social praxis.

Various solutions to this difficulty have been proposed by a number of authors. One type of solution, and one to which Ricoeur subscribes to a very large extent, is that it is important to realize that the writing and interpretation of the past is a project which takes place in the present and in the future, and, to that extent, it is not actually about the past *per se*. What is at stake for Ricoeur in arguments about the past is not how accurately we describe what took place, but the fact that a reflection on the historicality of being and on the temporal nature of that experience of being, a reflection configured and refigured through narrative, is at the base of what it is to be human in the world. We cannot help but tell stories about ourselves.

Ricoeur's work is enormously wide-ranging and stimulating. It is also, at times, very difficult to comprehend in its full significance. The potential contribution of his work to the interpretation of material culture is clear, but because his work lacks a properly sociological and materialist dimension it cannot provide a framework for the interpretation of social phenomena without being refined and supplemented by other theoretical perspectives. While Ricoeur draws extensively on the work of sociologists and anthropologists, he often makes the point that he is not a sociologist, and emphasizes his ignorance with regard to these matters. This is undoubtedly false modesty, but the implied distinction between philosophy and social science is perhaps worth heeding, if only because it may goad us into employing these powerful and insightful ideas more fruitfully and more critically in the interpretation of archaeological and anthropological data.

There never was nor will there ever be any man who has certain knowledge about the gods and about all the things that I tell of. And even if he does happen to get most things right, still he himself is not aware of this. Yet all may have shadows of the truth.

BIBLIOGRAPHY

For a full list of Ricoeur's writings up to 1972 see:
Vansina, D. F. (1962) 'Bibliographie de Paul Ricoeur (jusqu'à 30 juin 1962)', *Revue Philosophique de Louvain*, 60: 394–413.
Vansina, D. F. (1968) 'Bibliographie de Paul Ricoeur, compléments (jusqu'à la fin de 1967)', *Revue Philosophique de Louvain*, 66: 85–101.
Vansina, D. F. (1974) 'Bibliographie de Paul Ricoeur, compléments (jusqu'à la fin de 1972)', *Revue Philosophique de Louvain*, 72: 156–81.
For an updated version of this bibliography, see:
Regan C. (1979) *Studies in the Philosophy of Paul Ricoeur*, Ohio University Press, Athens, Ohio.

1 *Books by Ricoeur*

Abbreviations used are given after titles. Original date of publication in the French is given in square brackets, where applicable.

Freedom and Nature: The Voluntary and the Involuntary (FN) [1950] (1966) Northwestern University Press, Evanston. Trans. E. V. Kohák.
Fallible Man (FM) [1960] (1965) Henry Regnery, Chicago. Trans. C. A. Kelbley.
The Symbolism of Evil (SE) [1960] (1967) Harper Row, New York. Trans. E. Buchanan.
Freud and Philosophy: An essay on Interpretation (FP) [1965] (1970) Yale University Press, New Haven. Trans. D. Savage.
The Conflict of Interpretations: essays in Hermeneutics (CI) [1969] (1974) Northwestern University Press, Evanston. Ed. D. Ihde, trans. W. Domingo *et al.*
The Rule of Metaphor: Multi-Disciplinary Studies of the Creation of Meaning in Language (RM) [1975] (1978) Routledge & Kegan Paul, London. Trans. R. Czerny.
Interpretation Theory: Discourse and the Surplus of Meaning (IT) (1976) Christian University Press, Forth Worth, Texas.
Hermeneutics and the Human Sciences (HHS) (1981) Cambridge University Press, Cambridge. Ed. and trans. J. Thompson.
Time and Narrative. Vol. I *(TNI)* [1983] (1984) Chicago University Press, Chicago. Trans. K. McLaughlin and D. Pellauer.
Time and Narrative, Vol. II *(TNII)* [1984] (1985) Chicago University Press, Chicago. Trans. K. McLaughlin and D. Pellauer.
Time and Narrative, Vol. III *(TNIII)* [1985] (1988) Chicago University Press, Chicago. Trans. K. Blamey and D. Pellauer.

2 *Books on or discussing Ricoeur, and other works referred to in the text*

Austin, J. (1976) *How to do Things with Words*, Oxford University Press, Oxford.

Benveniste, E. (1971) *Problems in General Linguistics*, University of Miami Press, Fla. Trans. M. E. Meek.

Bhaskar, R. (1979) *The Possibility of Naturalism*, Harvester Prerss, Sussex.

Black, M. (1962) *Models and Metaphors*, Cornell University Press, Ithaca.

Bourdieu, P. (1977) *Outline of a Theory of Practice*, Cambridge University Press, Cambridge.

Bourdieu, P. (1980) *Le Sens pratique*, Minuit, Paris.

Bourgeois, P. (1973) *Extension of Ricoeur's Hermeneutic*, Martinus Nijhoff, The Hague.

Frege, G. (1970) 'On sense and reference' in P. Geach and M. Black (eds) *Translations from the Philosophical Writings of Gottlob Frege*, Basil Blackwell, Oxford.

Giddens, A. (1979) *Central Problems in Social Theory*, Macmillan, London.

Giddens, A. (1984) *The Constitution of Society*, Polity Press, Cambridge.

Ihde, D. (1971) *Hermeneutic Phenomenology: The Philosophy of Paul Ricoeur*, Northwestern University Press, Evanston.

Madison, G. B. (1975) *Sens et existence: en hommage à Paul Ricoeur*, Seuil, Paris.

Moore, H. L. (1986) *Space, Text and Gender: An Anthropological Study of the Marakwet of Kenya*, Cambridge University Press, Cambridge.

Philibert, M. (1971) *Paul Ricoeur ou la liberté selon l'espérance*, Seghers, Paris.

Rasmussen, D. (1971) *Mythic–Symbolic Language and Philosophical Anthropology*, Martinus Nijhoff, The Hague.

Regan, C. (1979) *Studies in the Philosophy of Paul Ricoeur*, Ohio University Press, Athens, Ohio.

Richards, I. (1936) *The Philosophy of Rhetoric*, Oxford University Press, Oxford.

Thompson, J. B. (1981) *Critical Hermeneutics: A Study in the Thought of Paul Ricoeur and Jurgen Habermas*, Cambridge University Press, Cambridge.

Thompson, J. B. (1984) *Studies in the Theory of Ideology*, Polity Press, Cambridge: chapter 5.

3

Clifford Geertz: Towards a More 'Thick' Understanding?

Eric Kline Silverman

Spurred by a heightened awareness of affinities across the disciplines and a sense of methodological impasse, social scientists are turning to literary theory and notions of the literary text as models or metaphors of culture. Clifford Geertz has been the leading proponent of this interpretivist school and its textual metaphor in American cultural anthropology. His widespread influence derives from such distinguished essays as 'Thick Description: Toward an Interpretive Theory of Culture' (*IC*: 3–30), 'Deep Play: Notes on the Balinese Cockfight' (*IC*: 412–53), and 'Blurred Genres: The Refiguration of Social Thought' (*LK*: 19–35).

Geertz belongs to a broad American anthropological tradition predicated on 'the unfrightened acceptance of human diversity; the passion for ethnographic circumstantiality; and the view that culture is an imaginative form' (*F*: vii). But Geertz reworks this tradition into a novel approach to cultural anthropology. He was the first American anthropologist to employ a textual metaphor for understanding culture. In Geertz's writings, however, we do not find a single, clearly articulated, elaborate theory of the text. We find instead several recurrent statements to the effect that we can analogously or metaphorically understand certain features of culture and social action like literary texts. His textual metaphor emerges from a series of conceptual themes — it is not one notion but a composite of several orientations. Thus, this chapter attempts to explicate the general parameters of Geertz's textual metaphor — it is not a comprehensive analysis of Geertz's work.

I also hint throughout at alternative orientations, ones which build on Geertz's work. My own view draws on post-structuralist ideas in what are recently acknowledged to be two closely related disciplines: literary theory and post-modern cultural anthropology. Geertz's texts,

I will argue, fix public meaning and dissolve individuals into anonymity. Moreover, he reduces social practices to a homogeneous society and construes culture without contradictions and ambiguities. These are problematic orientations. This chapter not only discusses Geertz's textual metaphor, but in doing so, represents an attempt to overcome these facets of his interpretivism.

Geertz did not begin his anthropological career with an interpretivist posture. His early monographs adhered to the normative expectations for American ethnographic thought in the 1950s and 1960s (e.g. *DJE, RJ, SH, IO*). His particular interest was Third World socioeconomic and agricultural development (e.g. *PP*), to which he often returns (*IC*: 142–69, 234–54, 255–310, CSC). Geertz's pre-interpretivist work was highly successful. His innovative 'involution' thesis for Indonesia (*AI*) – one of his enduring achievements – continues to generate considerable research, debate and criticism (see CSC).

Despite the notoriety of Geertz's 'involution' thesis and his conventional ethnographic accounts, his interpretivist works have the greatest impact on contemporary anthropological and social thought. But I do not wish to polarize Geertz's work as many others, to his dismay (CSC: 515–16), have done. Continuities aside, I nevertheless concentrate on works he predominantly orients around interpretivist themes: mainly, two collections of essays (*IC* and *LK*), assorted papers (BE, AAR and UD), a historical narrative (*N*), and a recent account of anthropological authorship (*WL*).

Geertz's prolific interpretivism appeals to anthropologists interested in the meaning of culture. It remains a refreshing alternative to the still-dominant ethnographic genres in American anthropology. He stimulated, moreover, recent developments in post-modern ethnographic theory, although not always to his satisfaction (*WL: passim*). Many post-modern ethnographers, in a sense, are in fact post-Geertzian interpretivists.

Regardless of Geertz's achievements, however, he occupies a historically perplexing position in the discipline. He forms part of both the centre and the periphery of anthropology. In the early 1970s, Geertz appeared – and still does to traditional cultural anthropologists – ethnographically *avant garde*; recently, he often reads too conservative. Geertz is one of the more adept literary stylists in cultural anthropology. Frequently, he writes for a broader audience than do most of his colleagues. Among others, his essays appeal to historians (Walters 1980) and theologians (Morgan 1977). As one of the pre-eminent anthropological interdisciplinarians, Geertz prefigured many developments in recent social thought. But his critics (e.g. Shankman 1984;

Walters 1980) often demur his failure to publish a systematic methodological statement. (I address this misconstrued criticism on pp. 129–131.) To add to his disciplinary alienation, Geertz remains widely unknown (see Kuper 1983: 189) or derided (e.g. Leach 1981; but see Moore 1986) in British social anthropology, and while British archaeologists (e.g. Hodder 1985) now cite him, their American counterparts still largely ignore his work.

For all the above reasons, Geertz receives abundant criticism. But his critics generally misunderstand why he advocates certain, typically controversial, positions. By selectively exploring aspects of his interpretive *oeuvre*, Geertz's work can appear eclectic and puzzling. Instead, and in order to present a more rounded understanding of Geertz, I heuristically isolate the major orientations of his interpretivist thought. This thematic approach highlights the contours of his anthropology. Since we cannot delineate interpretivism into axioms and theorems, I am unable to reconstruct a formal logic out of Geertz's anthropology and his textual metaphor. I therefore begin by enumerating six recurrent orientations in his interpretivism.

Geertz

(1) During the 1950s, Geertz studied with Talcott Parsons in the Department of Social Relations, Harvard University. Parsons was instrumental in integrating Weber's thought into American social science. Parsonian sociology (e.g. 1937) revolves around Weber's anti-materialist and anti-Marxist approach to social action. It also exhibits a strong, albeit perhaps indirect, debt to Durkheimian functionalism and a systemic rather than person-centred approach to social analysis.

As Weber partitioned sociocultural life into discrete and autonomous realms, so did Parsons and, consequently, Geertz. In an authoritative alliance, Kroeber and Parsons (1958) defended the culture and society dichotomy which still permeates Anglo-American social thought. Culture, they argue, refers to values, ideas and symbols rather than social interaction. Along with other cultural anthropologists who studied with Parsons (e.g. Schneider 1976; 1984), Geertz assumed these orientations (see Peacock 1981).

Aspects of the Weberian tradition assimilated into Geertz's interpretivism include the analysis of social action from the standpoint of cultural beliefs and values. Weber (1958), specifically attacking Marxist materialism, rejected causal explanations of human action that were rooted in social organization, material and economic interests, and modes of production. Weber (1949) also repudiated psychological explanations of social phenomena. Instead, he argued that culture determines or shapes the significance of social action, although he recognized the importance of economics and other factors.

Most notably, Weber (1958) traced the origins of European capitalism to the rationality, morality and work ethic that emerged from Calvinism and the Reformation. Weber based the sociological explanation of capitalism, therefore, on religious beliefs as much as on economic behaviour. But Weber's individuals, much like Durkheim's, are collective and anonymous. He investigated how culture directs action rather than how persons integrate cultural idioms into meaningful experience. In a textual perspective, particularly Geertz's, this view obscures the active role of the individual.

Through Parsons, Weber influences Geertz's work in two broad respects. First, Geertz focuses on actors rather than persons and individuals or subjects. Actors behave according to pre-determined scripts. Individuals, by contrast, possess subjectivity, a sense of self, and biographical uniqueness. Individuals become persons when they acquire social roles, expectations and jural status. Geertz's actors are driven by the larger cultural totality and its public meanings. Geertz focuses on culture as a whole, devoid of actual subjects, exemplified in ideal-type cultural texts. 'Collective experience', he declares, 'far transcends' the individual (*LK*: 108). This view informs all Geertz's interpretations, especially his celebrated essays on the Balinese cockfight (*IC*: 412–53) and the classic Balinese negara (*N*).

After Bourdieu (1977), Giddens (1979) and other similarly minded post-structuralists, Geertz's Weberian conception of actors and meaning can be challenged through a focus on what is variously termed practice, praxis and structuration. In this view, structures or culture guide the individual's actions, but only through action do structures and culture become real; this is a major recognition, and a methodological challenge, for contemporary social thought (see Ortner 1984; Hodder 1985; 1986). Geertz begins with culture and then descends to actors' behaviour. By abstracting cultural idioms from experience and practice, he does not explore the dialectic between culture and the individual's agency, choices and strategies. For Geertz, culture determines social action and its meanings. Although he admonishes structuralism (see *IC*: 345–59), he is not, for this reason, a post-structuralist thinker.

In the second and more significant instance of Weber's influence on Geertz, the meaningful dimensions of social action are explored in relation to culture and ethos rather than materialist considerations. Without culture, Geertz writes, our lives would be 'a mere chaos of pointless acts and exploding emotions . . . experience virtually shapeless' (*IC*: 46). Culture is the medium through which lives acquire meaning, both locally and for outsiders (*IC*: 14).

Weber and Parsons argued that culture was one of several autonomous realms, *equal* to social, psychological and adaptive systems. Yet many of Parsons' students, such as Geertz and Schneider, refigure culture into a *primary* force which directs, and even determines, social existence. Geertz stops short of maintaining that culture is the cause of society, behaviour or economics (e.g. *IC*: 125). Rather, culture infuses social activities with significance and meaning. This culturological outlook stands as an alternative to techno-environmental, social-structural, materialist and psychodynamic approaches to cultural phenomena.

Geertz displays his Weberian orientation perhaps most prominently in his reconstruction of the classic Balinese negara, a 'theatre state' (*N*). Geertz investigates the 'power' of the negara in terms of cultural idioms that were foregrounded during Balinese dramatic displays. Power did not emerge from socioeconomic factors and inequities in wealth. Instead, power was ethos, pomp and a 'poetics . . . not a mechanics' or economics (*N*: 123). In the negara, 'statecraft is a thespian art' (*N*: 120).

We read a similar view elsewhere: 'What makes Balinese cock-fighting deep is thus not money in itself, but what, the more of it that is involved the more so, money causes to happen: the migration of the Balinese status hierarchy into the body of the cockfight' (*IC*: 436). In the Balinese cockfight, money, like power in the negara, represents culture or ethos rather than a fundamental economic or psychological reality. Power and money — understood via Western economics — are not universal forces which cause the particularities of social formations everywhere. They are local cultural constructions which encode local meanings.

(2) Geertz approaches cultural meaning through a symbolic or semiotic framework. He was particularly influenced by Susan Langer (1960 [1942]; see also Austin 1979), a student of Cassirer. In a classic and widely discussed essay (e.g. Asad 1983; Munson 1986), Geertz defines cultural symbols as models *of* and models *for* social reality. A symbol is: 'any object, act, event, quality, or relation which serves as a vehicle for a conception — the conception is the symbol's "meaning" . . . [symbols] are tangible formulations of notions, abstractions from experience fixed in perceptible forms, concrete embodiments of ideas, attitudes, judgments, longings, or beliefs . . . they are as public as marriage and as observable as agriculture' (*IC*: 91). Geertz's symbols become vehicles by which public conceptions constitute and represent

cultural reality. In his concern with collective cultural meaning that is 'stored' (*IC*: 127) in public symbols or texts, Geertz implies the existence of a unified and unchanging reality for any particular society. Moreover, 'the symbolic dimension of social events is, like the psychological, itself theoretically *abstractable* from those events as *empirical totalities*' (*IC*: 91; emphasis my own). This view, which I term 'representational abstractionism', can be challenged by a more individual-centred, fluid and dynamic textual metaphor.

Victor Turner (1975: 155) understands symbols to emit 'multivocality, complexity of associations, ambiguity, [and] open-endedness'. This view of symbolic meaning contrasts with Geertz's orientation. Geertz seemingly rejects the notion that symbolic meanings are fluid, polysemic constructions. Instead, he opts for a static and dual view: models *of* and *for* reality. For Geertz, meaning – and the autonomous symbolic forms or texts in which meaning is fixed – reference specific cultural ideals and a single public reality.

(3) Geertz's third orientation amounts to a general, often inarticulate, hermeneutic approach to cultural anthropology. We should understand culture, he argues, in terms of actor-oriented meanings since culture cannot be explained on the basis of causal sequences of events and situations. 'My anthropology', Geertz said recently (cited in Silk 1987: 56), 'raise[s] serious questions for traditional notions of causality.'

Interpretivism rests on the emphatic denial that we can understand cultural phenomena in causal terms. To use a spatial metaphor, any alleged explanation of how cultural phenomena become generated inevitably positions culture in a secondary and peripheral space. This is a fallacy of scientism in anthropology. If we argue that antecedent conditions or forces give rise to cultural values and institutions, then we argue that culture is an epiphenomenal factor in human affairs, driven by something more basic. Instead, Geertz argues that culture is a primary force, one responsible for instilling significance and meaning into our social existence. In addition, Geertz's hermeneutic assumptions, like most contemporary conceptions of the 'text', lie outside the methodological grasps of standardized data-collection, classification, and the formation, testing and prediction of hypotheses (see p. 129ff.).

Yet Geertz's hermeneutics centre on collectivities rather than agents. Geertz thereby diverges from Dilthey's 'empathy' tradition. He advocates that we see things 'from the native's point of view' but maintains that:

> accounts of other peoples' subjectivities can be built up without recourse to
> pretensions to more-than-normal capacities for ego effacement and fellow

feeling . . . Understanding the form and pressure of, to use the dangerous word one more time, natives; inner lives is more like grasping a proverb, catching an allusion, seeing a joke – or, as I have suggested, reading a poem – than it is like achieving communion. (*LK*: 70).

Geertz suggests that the hermeneutic reading of cultural texts is accomplished less by trying to enter someone else's head than by trying to comprehend the public significance of an event or value (see NPT: 202–3).

In the above passage, we can detect Geertz's latent disciplinary fear of interpretivist extremism, of embracing complete personal subjectivity. Geertz retains the telling realist ambition for something real and unyielding on which to hang conclusions. Although he now reports (Bernstein 1988) that he views his interpretations with lessening confidence, Geertz never questions his basic assumption that something called culture exists in the world, in a coherent and determinable fashion.

(4) Through his hermeneutic and culturological orientations, Geertz assails structuralism and other theories which account for culture through reductionistic explanations, purported prime movers and supposed bottom-line realities. Relativism forms the fourth theme in his thought (discussed on p. 150ff.). Geertz's relativism typically materializes in an attack on Lévi-Straussian structuralism, which, as he writes:

is an infernal culture machine. It annuls history, reduces sentiment to a shadow of the intellect, and replaces the particular minds of particular savages in particular jungles with the Savage Mind immanent in us all . . . Like Rousseau, Lévi-Strauss is not after all for men, whom he doesn't much care for, but for Man, with whom he is enthralled. (*IC*: 355–6)

Geertz vehemently repudiates all anthropological attempts at uncovering the essential nature of human societies and thought – a 'basic, sticker-price *homo* and essential, no additives *sapiens*'.

(5) In his interpretations, Geertz employs a textual model for understanding culture. Nevertheless, his model is overly formalized and restrained. This stems from his belief that cultural texts reference fixed public meanings which are external to interlocutors and persist despite the temporality of the immediate context of social discourse. We can most directly trace Geertz's textual metaphor (e.g. *IC*: 19) to a noted essay by Ricoeur. Ricoeur writes:

> What has to be understood is not the initial situation of discourse ...
> Understanding has less than ever to do with the author and his situation.
> It wants to grasp the proposed worlds opened up by the references of the
> text. To understand a text is to follow its movement from sense to
> reference, from what it says to what it talks about. (1971: 557–8)

In Geertz's reading, Ricoeur argues that texts freeze meanings which
arise out of specific social contexts yet draw their significance from
something other than the immediacy of their creation. Geertz's
assumption that cultural meaning can be fixed, in lasting forms, seems
to be his way of grappling with the evanescence of social discourse. It
also provides the object for anthropological study.

Ricoeur (1971: 546) defines texts as fixing meaning, dissociating
from authors and their intentions, entailing 'non-ostensive' reference,
and becoming involved with unbounded readerships and audiences
(see chapter 2 of this volume). These characteristics constitute textual
objectivity. Drawing on Ricoeur's formulation, Geertz writes:

> The key to the transition from text to text analogue, from writing as
> discourse to action as discourse, is, as Paul Ricoeur has pointed out, the
> concept of 'inscription': the fixation of meaning ... The great virtue of the
> extension of the notion of text beyond things written on paper or carved
> into stone is that it trains attention on precisely this phenomenon: on how
> the inscription of action is brought about, what its vehicles are and how
> they work, and on what the fixation of meaning from the flow of events –
> history from what happened, thought from thinking, culture from
> behavior – implies for sociological interpretation. (LK: 31)

Geertz's notion of cultural texts is similar to his conception of
symbols. Both are representational, public, and contain durable
meaning. But as Fernandez (1985: 25) claims, Ricoeur's text
metaphor – like Geertz's – 'takes us back into a world ... with its
concerns for distance, invariance, truth value'. Geertz's texts do not
engender multiple, typically ambiguous or conflicting readings. They
seem to reach unitary and satisfying resolutions.

(6) Geertz's interpretivism includes a self-conscious aesthetic quality
and an emphasis on anthropological writing. He believes that an
identifiable and overarching texture or mood colours social lives and
local cultures. Because cultures inherently possess unique aesthetic
tones, Geertz tries to evoke the particularity of each cultural ethos
through his literary style. As Ortner (1984: 129) suggests, 'Geertz's
heart has always been, more with the "ethos" side of culture than with
the "worldview", more with the affective and stylistic dimensions than

with the cognitive'. This orientation permeates Geertz's writing and is often said to recall the work of Benedict (1934; see Ortner 1984: 129; Munson 1986: 23 n. 28). He does not strive to uncover the organization of cultural thought in an ethnoscience or structuralist sense. Instead, he investigates the tones and stresses of culture, public sentiment and emotion. Narrowly defined, Geertz does not write descriptive prose. Instead, he writes to evoke, on the part of the reader, a sense of being an imaginary and competent cultural interlocutor.

These six reconstructed themes in Geertz's interpretivist thought — Weberian, symbolic, hermeneutic, relativist, textual, aesthetic–literary — coalesce into a 'blurred genre'. As a prominent motif in contemporary social thought, 'blurred genres' are 'not just another redrawing of the cultural map . . . but an alteration of the principles of mapping' (LK: 20).

An important conceptual tension emerges from Geertz's blurred framework, however: his belief that cultural texts and symbols fix public meanings. Geertz founders on this tension, one that can be traced perhaps to the opposed Enlightenment and Romanticist views of the mind and culture (see Shweder 1984b). Geertz aims to unpack cultural meanings, but he does so through an essentialist perspective: Janus-like, Geertz the interpretivist is also an 'essentialist' (M. Penn, personal communication). A great paradox in Geertz's interpretivism is that he restrains his textual metaphor by a moderate yet unmistakable ethnographic realism and an exclusive focus on the public as a single social mind. If we are going to develop interpretivism and the textual metaphor into responsible and insightful frameworks for understanding cultures as we begin to turn towards the final decade of this century and the next, we will need to expunge essentialism from our theories.

Explanation and Understanding

Social scientists often confront a difficult conceptual choice between two opposed research methodologies. Typically, this dilemma is phrased in terms of the dichotomy between explanation and understanding. I propose here a slightly different reading of this dichotomy, one centring on the efficacy of classifications.

For the sake of simplicity, we can trace the first approach, which Geertz adamantly rejects, to the Enlightenment. This tradition primarily characterizes the physical and biological sciences. In it, scientists study phenomena as objects, exclusive of such qualities as emotion, complex symbolic thought, awareness and experience. Furthermore, scientists investigate phenomena through comparative schemes, particularly taxonomic inclusion and exclusion. The Linnean biological classification is the best-known instance of this scientific paradigm. Knowledge arises from the characteristics of the class rather than from the individual entity. Diversity is consolidated into a single or a few typically developmental or evolutionary schemes.

The romanticist tradition, in which we can situate Geertz's textual metaphor for culture, opposes the scientistic view of knowledge and inquiry in two respects. First, the locus of study is unique sociocultural phenomena rather than non-human natural occurrences. For Geertz, this means that we investigate localized inter-subjective meanings. Second, this tradition rejects the view that we can taxonomically analyse human actions as objects and explain them through reference to classes and categories.

In what is by now a familiar scenario, American archaelogists during the 1960s rebelled against the previous generation of prehistorians. They embraced an Enlightenment perspective for scientific inquiry and aimed to subsume context and local cultures under nomothetic laws of societal development. New archaeologists turned to philosophers of science such as Hempel, Popper and Salmon for models, guidance and legitimation. The New Archaeology represents an anthropological antithesis to Geertzian interpretivism.

There was a widespread belief in the positivist goal of a unified methodology for science. Many archaeologists passionately argued for the existence of an abstract deductive logic to archaeological and cultural inquiry, a logic that could be isolated outside its applications and formally articulated. Definitions, explanatory parsimony and typologies were widely emphasized. Most contemporary archaeologists continue to operate in this scientistic tradition. The New Archaeology has a counterpart in sociocultural anthropology, mainly the linguistically influenced New Ethnology, ethnoscience and componential analysis. Yet most ethnographers do not retain their positivist aspirations with the tenacity of processual archaeologists.

Geertz and interpretivism rebel against the positivistic constellation referred to above and the methodological analogy of the physical sciences. Instead of seeking legitimation from philosophers of science, Geertz looks to such humanistic thinkers as Burke, Langer, Ricoeur and Wittgenstein, as well as theorists in the social sciences and the humanities. Geertz writes: 'to see social institutions, social customs, social changes in some sense "readable" is to alter our whole sense of what such interpretation is and shift it toward modes of thought rather more familiar to the translator, the exegete, or the iconographer than to the test giver, the factor analyst, or the pollster' (*LK*: 31). Geertz's interpretivism and its textual metaphor resist formal classification, the derivation of nomological laws, hypothesis formation and the abstract construction of a logic to social science. Contrary to the claims of his critics (e.g. Shankman 1984), Geertz's textual perspective categorically defies interpretive evaluations based on formal verification, replicability, prediction and similar scientistic tenets.

The Enlightenment approach to science inherently embodies comparative schemes. Geertz has not forsaken comparative anthropology (e.g. *N*). Yet classifications have never moved to the forefront of his concerns. Initially, though by no means exclusively or predominantly, Geertz investigated anthropologically universal typologies (FV). But even in his early, pre-interpretivist work, we can see his emphasis on sociocultural variation rather than on a single essential pattern from which individual cases might deviate. Geertz consistently seeks to understand the unique aspects of local cultural phenomena and how they compare with other examples – in order to further our understanding of cultural diversity rather than reducing diversity to a primordial cause or essential template. Explanation theorists, by contrast, often begin with a general scheme and then explain how a unique situation arose.

In Geertz's textual metaphor, ethnographic content cannot be divorced from the process of inquiry. Geertz investigates local cultures and local knowledges rather than the structure of anthropological knowledge. If we expel the ethnographic–historical information from *Negara*, only three or so pages of text, including the preface, remain. Likewise, we find little method, abstractly conceived, in Geertz's analysis of the cockfight. As he writes, 'we are reduced to insinuating theories because we lack the power to state them' (*IC*: 24).

Geertz rejects 'testing' modes of verification since ethnographic data result from 'our own constructions of other people's constructions of what they and their compatriots are up to' (*IC*: 9). This is a paramount idea in his interpretivist outlook. There is no stationary datum in culture and social action from which, once discovered, we can cease our anthropological analysis and measure the accuracy of our interpretation. Broadly speaking, Geertz roots his notion of interpretivist evaluation in discourse. Successful interpretive anthropology allows us to 'converse' with cultural others (*IC*: 13), to enter into social discourse as competent and creative interlocutors. 'Looked at in this way, the aim of anthropology is the enlargement of the universe of human discourse' (*IC*: 14).

Geertz's Cultural Texts

From his blend of Weberian, textual and symbolic orientations, Geertz believes that cultural texts and their meanings exist, somewhat autonomously, in the public world. This is his representational realism. He closes his account of the Balinese negara by writing: 'the dramas of the theatre state, mimetic of themselves, were, in the end, neither illusions nor lies, neither sleight of hand nor make-believe. They were what there was' (N: 136). For Geertz, cultural texts are specific, ultimately unambiguous, public configurations; this guarantees objectivity. Indeed, Geertz states that 'the culture concept to which I adhere has neither multiple referents nor, so far as I can see, any unusual ambiguity'(IC: 89).

But Geertz is neither a naive realist nor a representational realist after the manner of an earlier generation of ethnographers (see Marcus and Cushman1982: 29–38). He does not, for example, partition societies into universal and mutually exclusive, formally defined, categories called kinship, economy, religion and politics. But Geertz consistently presents a 'common denominator people' perspective, conveys the unspecified indigenous point of view and generalizes from particular ethnographic instances, three common strategies in realist ethnography. At the same time, Geertz recognizes the mediation of interpretation, whether informant's or ethnographer's, and challenges the structural constraints of conventional ethnographic narrative. He therefore stands at the crossing of traditional and recent experimental ethnographies.

Geertz views cultural texts akin to public webs of meaning, 'thus accessible to overt and corrigible *plein air* explication' (N: 135). Following Weber, Geertz (IC: 5) suspends actors in 'webs of significance' they themselves have spun. His cultural texts are the public moments when actors spin these webs into recognizable and highly visible public displays. They fix meaning which is woven from and references localized cultural themes. Geertz's cultural texts are not inconspicuous. Meaning may be screened or cryptic, but it usually lurks near the surface of public discourse and activity.

In Geertz's cultural texts, meaning does not internally unravel in a deconstruction sense. It does not emerge structurally or formally, psychoanalytically, or through the reader's reception. Instead, the meaning of the text is an enduring aspect of culture which expands beyond the text proper but to which the text semantically points. Geertz argues, therefore, that the meaning of the Balinese cockfight references not the cockfight itself but rather the fixed, overarching cultural idioms that permeate all of Balinese life. The cockfight is merely a single, albeit salient, manifestation of these cultural themes.

Geertz's theory of the text, and therefore his style of reading, takes root in a form of realism which has lately fallen into disrepute among literary theorists and post-Geertzian interpretivists. Few, if any, anthropologists would deny the existence of real sociocultural phenomena, Geertz most certainly included. But Geertz's textual realism bespeaks essentialism because he not only sees sociocultural phenomena and cultural texts in unambiguous and fixed forms, but understands meaning to inhere within the text.

Geertz's methodology, fashioned under the influence of Gilbert Ryle, suggests that the meaning of cultural texts is multifarious. The ethnographic 'object' is a 'stratified hierarchy of meaningful structures' (*IC*: 7) and culture itself is a 'deep' construction. Geertz writes:

> There is an Indian story — at least I heard it as an Indian story — about an Englishman who, having been told that the world rested on a platform which rested on the back of an elephant which rested in turn on the back of a turtle, asked (perhaps he was an ethnographer; it is the way they behave), what did the turtle rest on? Another turtle. And that turtle? 'Ah, Sahib, after that it is turtles all the way down.' (*IC*: 28–9)

This parable reflects at least four important themes in Geertz's cultural texts. First, it encapsulates Geertz's fundamental belief in the autonomy of culture. Although he understands cultural texts to be multilayered constructions, he emphatically indicates, in an explicit refutation of Lévi-Straussian structuralism (see *IC*: 345–59), that no single level causes or generates all the others.

The second theme arises from Geertz's layered conception of culture. He believes in a stratigraphy of textual meaning, a hierarchy of levels in which some appear more insightful. In his attempt at clarifying cultural meaning, Geertz thereby diminishes the multidimensional quality of cultural texts. There has always been a tendency for him to expose what he deems are the more prevailing and influential themes of societies and cultures, those which direct more aspects of social life and import greater significance to behaviour. At first, these themes were sociological (e.g. T); in his interpretivist work, they tend towards ethos, sentiment and culture more generally.

Third, Geertz's parable is an Indian tale, one told to an Englishman, in a distant discourse that is far removed from either Geertz's experiences or doubtless most of our own. Geertz reads relativistic, local and context-bound texts. But the meaning of cultural texts — not their initial discourse — can be communicated and understood by people living in different and unrelated cultures. Textual meanings transcend the vicissitudes of momentary discourse. Geertz maintains that the Balinese cockfight enables the Balinese, like Macbeth enables us, to read their own subjectivity. He does not suggest that the cockfight and Macbeth communicate the same message; this would violate his cultural relativism. Both are local texts, engendering local meanings. Geertz nevertheless understands the cockfight presumably; the Balinese, after appropriate instruction and literary exposure, could understand Macbeth.

Finally, the story concerns an infinite number of turtles who, along with an elephant, support the world. Like all cosmologies – turtles and elephants, Atlas and Brahma, strings and gluons alike – this is a local myth. If the Balinese believe it, we can reasonably assume that Geertz, like ourselves, does not. The turtles stand as a metaphor, a common literary figure in Geertz's cultural texts along with rhythm, irony and pun. His cultural texts are not literal. They are meta-phorical, figurative, symbolic or semiotic – in a word, aesthetic – not descriptive.

Geertz (*IC*: 412–53) reads a diversity of localized cultural themes in the Balinese cockfight: secrecy and defiance, social psychodynamic associations between men and cocks, fetishism, a reversal of normal Balinese revulsion towards animality, blood sacrifice, masculinity, 'hatred, cruelty, violence, and death', nature versus culture, wagers and money, honour and dignity, and kinship. Yet it is not to the polyvocality of the cockfight that Geertz attributes either its signi-ficance or its effectiveness. He does not explore the cockfight to see how a single momentary event can meaningfully ramify throughout different apparent and masked aspects of Balinese life. Instead, and having descended through a hierarchy of referent levels, Geertz attri-butes the meaning of the Balinese cockfight to imagined status: 'the slaughter in the cock ring is not a depiction of how things literally are among men, but what is almost worse, of how, from a particular angle, they imaginatively are. The angle, of course, is stratificatory. What, as we have already seen, the cockfight talks most forcibly about is status relationships' (*IC*: 446–7). This passage illustrates the public nature of Geertz's cultural texts and, through a reduction of polysemy, his belief that they contain an essential meaning. It also expresses Geertz's aesthetic outlook.

Geertz's cultural texts express multiple cultural idioms, but these expressions mainly reference dominant ideologies and their construc-tions of public reality. Paradoxically, Geertz sometimes thins the 'thickness' of cultural meaning. As Roseberry (1982) recognizes, Geertz's interpretations silence oppositional and alternative voices.

His cultural texts often seem hegemonic since they reference 'the central, effective and dominant system of meanings and values' (Williams 1973: 9).

Through his thinning of meaning, Geertz's cultural texts are also microcosms. They funnel the idioms and ethos of particular cultures into public events: single, intensive, univocal expressions, lacking ambiguity and polyphony. It is in this manner that he interprets the Balinese cockfight (*IC*: 412–53), the Balinese negara (*N*) and the Moroccan suq (BE; *MO*). These texts of social self-affirmation, what Munson (1986: 29) calls 'personality writ large', are like kaleidoscopes, with society peering through one end at a cultural mirror. As Geertz writes, the cockfight 'is a Balinese reading of Balinese experience, a story they tell to themselves about themselves' (*IC*: 448).

Not surprisingly, many reviewers trace Geertz's microcosmic view and his ideal-type theme to Weber and Parsons. The cockfight essay purports to analyse a cockfight. Yet as Boon (1977: 33) suggests, it reads more like a prescription of how cockfights ideally should be rather than an interpretation of how any particular cockfight actually seemed. This type of analysis not only derives from Weber, but also from Geertz's literary claim that his interpretations are 'fictions' (Lat. *fictio*), scenarios fashioned and created but not necessarily false (*IC*: 15).

Geertz's cultural texts, I have argued, are always public. Often, they revolve around ritual and ceremony. For this reason, Bloch (1977: 286) contends that Geertz, like Radcliffe-Brown, vitiates his methodology by avoiding a 'long conversation view of society'. Because Geertz concentrates exclusively on ritual discourse, Bloch argues, he neglects the equally important realms of non-ritualized and quotidian communication. 'Unlike Malinowski,' Bloch writes, 'when the magician had stopped incanting his spells, they did not stay to watch the canoe building'. In other words, Geertz interprets only selected aspects of cultures rather than their entirety.

As Bloch recognizes, social discourse and cultural constructions vary in accordance with immediate context and social strategies. True, this premise is often wanting in Geertz's work. But Bloch misunderstands Geertz's Weberian, textual and symbolic frameworks. Since Geertz reads cultural texts as microcosmic metaphors for a whole cultural ethos, any single text will encapsulate the meaningful dimensions of both ritualized and mundane activities. This type of cultural text is thus a 'totalizing cultural performance' (Clifford 1983: 129). Like a Maussian 'total social fact', it serves as a nexus for the entire local cultural universe.

Reading and Writing

In a controversial claim – one perhaps even scandalous to some – Geertz suggests that ethnographers primarily inscribe social discourse (*IC*: 3–30). If ethnographers are writers, then ethnography is inherently literary. Geertz reads cultures as if they were literary texts. He translates and transcribes sociocultural events into literary prose.

Unlike the previous generation of descriptive ethnographers, however, Geertz does not presume that he translucently views sociocultural events in all their holistic reality. The current 'crisis of representation' (Marcus and Fischer 1986) resulted from a collapse of anthropological confidence in literal rendition, unfiltered representation and naive description. Since Geertz recognized these issues in the early 1970s, he not only preceded but precipitated the present 'crisis'. Geertz continues to debase models of naive anthropological realism, recently by deconstructing Evans-Pritchard's ethnographic 'transparencies' (*WL*: 49–78).

Geertz reads cultural texts by 'tracing the curve of a social discourse'; he then writes it down, 'fixing it into an inspectable form' (*IC*: 19). It is not the discourse itself which he reads, and certainly not what he writes down. Discourse acts soon dissipate. Instead, Geertz reads the essential reference of the discourse – its meaning.

Geertz's view of ethnographic writing too, like his vision of texts, draws on Ricoeur (1971). Geertz (*IC*: 3–30) argues that ethnographic writing fixes the reference of specific moments of cultural discourse – their exteriorization or objectification – rather than the acts themselves: 'the *said*, not the *saying*' (*LK*: 31).

This orientation, it is often noted (e.g. Roseberry 1982; Marcus 1986: 179), tends to reify cultural meaning. But 'to see culture as an ensemble of texts' does not inevitably, contrary to Roseberry's (1982: 1022) polemic, 'remove culture from the process of its creators'. Roseberry's materialistic condemnation of Geertz's textual metaphor prevents him from realizing the obvious – that Geertz's formulation is not the only one available. A more dynamic view is possible. Whereas Geertz strives toward textual integration and the translation of fluid discourse into fixed texts, post-modern ethnographers (e.g. Tyler 1988), for example, strive toward fragmentation and a retention of discourse.

In a different view from that of Geertz, reading occurs intertextually. We read texts against a background of anticipations, intentions and other texts we have already read. Prior readings and experiences compose the basic toolkit for textual exegesis. Cultural texts are not interpreted by 'innocent' readers since we all bring to the task our own psychological, social, political, economic and cultural states. This recognition, however, is often missing from Geertz's accounts; he is wary, perhaps unjustifiably so, lest the locus of ethnography encompass only the individual.

But Geertz recognizes a second aspect of intertextuality: 'hopping back and forth between the whole conceived through the parts that actualize it and the parts conceived through the whole that motivates them, we seek to turn them, by a sort of intellectual perpetual motion, into explications of one another' (*LK*: 69). Cultural anthropologists, Geertz suggests, 'tack' between 'global' and 'local' forms of knowledge, between what he calls, after the psychoanalyst Heinz Kohut, 'experience-near' and 'experience-distant' concepts. On this point, Geertz also acknowledges his debt to Dilthey's hermeneutic circle (*LK*: 69). Reading cultural texts therefore becomes a conceptual or actual interpersonal negotiation, sometimes among ourselves, at other times with the culturally unfamiliar. In this manner, we avoid both solipsism and nihilism (*LK*: 181–2) since interpretivism is fundamentally a collaborative or dialogic enterprise.

Until recent post-modern ethnographic thought, Geertz's writing style stood almost alone in the discipline. It displays true literary, aesthetic and experimental merits. Prior to Geertz, there were few intentional deviations from conventional ethnographic genres. His interpretivist writing seeks to expand the canons of ethnographic literature by attempting to re-animate local experience rather than merely describe or explain objectified sociocultural institutions. For these reasons, Geertz's writing is often criticized. Typically, critics reject his prose outright. They consider it to be anti-scientific and consequently ill-suited to academic discourse. They argue that his primary goal is to impress rather than inform the reader. These claims are naive and unsupportable.

Lately, more sophisticated literary studies of Geertz's writings have appeared. In fact, remarks about Geertz's prose seem common in the rhetoric of contemporary interpretivism, this essay included. Literary-minded anthropologists frequently deconstruct Geertz's manner of establishing textual authority – in no small measure as an attempt to assert their own – sustained through such devices as pronoun shifting and seductive sentencing (e.g. Clifford 1983; Crapanzano 1986; Rabinow 1986).

The Balinese cockfight essay (*IC*: 412–53) is the typical target. In the opening passage, we read about the Geertzes' arrival in Bali, 'malarial and diffident'. Shortly thereafter, the police raid an illegal

cockfight which they were observing. But since the ethnographic
distinction between observation and participation is itself a blurred
genre of sorts, the Geertzes, like everyone else, fled.

This anecdote establishes Geertz's presence in the text, lending
credence to his ethnographic account and demonstrating his rapport
with the Balinese who subsequently accepted the Geertzes as 'persons'
rather than non-persons after the raid. Geertz initially sustains his
interpretive legitimacy by moving his self into the focus of the passage
in the conventional 'I was there so that's the way it was' manner of
establishing ethnographic veracity. Several pages later, Geertz disappears from the text in an equally common mode of ethnographic
authority, one that transforms a dialogic encounter into outsider
omniscience (Clifford 1983).

Geertz's essays repeatedly begin with an appeal to himself or to
some notion of 'we', 'you', social scientists or the reader. He often asks
a question which, as a literary strategy, actively engages us with his
text. Geertz claims that the author's signature, 'the construction of a
writerly identity', forms a major textual persuasion in anthropological
writing (*WL*: 8–9). In his recent book, *WL*, he reasons that the
persuasive force of classic ethnographies lies not so much in their 'raw
data', a vacuous phrase in his anthropological lexicon, but in the
rhetorical power of the prose. The force of his own signature generally
arises either by gradually fading through the writing or by appealing
to his self or to readers. Geertz's texts are alluring. They provoke
readers, stimulate their imagination and cause them to engage in a
dialogue with the page.

Ethnographic texts are currently receiving unprecedented critical
attention (see esp. Clifford and Marcus 1986), with Geertz figuring on
both sides of the issue. By contrast, archaeological texts, as literary
creations, remain almost completely neglected. I know of no published experiments with archaeological writing. Archaeologists typically model their accounts after natural science works. Site reports and
journal articles abound with diagrams, charts, statistics, weights and
measures, all drawn from Western science, which have little or
no relation to sociocultural practices and symbolic conceptions in other
traditions.

Sanctioned forms of archaeological writing do not 'aid us in gaining
access to the conceptual world in which our subjects live', the goal,
according to Geertz (*IC*: 24), of cultural interpretation and anthropological writing. I am not arguing that archaeologists should do
what Geertz does. Obviously, they are not ethnographers. But I am
suggesting that Geertz's work and interpretivism can encourage
archaeologists — all social scientists — to explore alternative modes of

interpretation, writing and presentation. The imaginative quality of cultural texts – not their only quality, of course – should be retained, undiminished, in the standards of disciplinary writing. If those standards prove inadequate, then one should take Geertz's cue and rewrite them. At the same time, we must not push writing *per se* to the forefront of cultural studies. Admittedly, this is a constant contemporary danger.

Geertz's writing is aesthetically motivated, but not to the point of over indulgence. The aesthetic quality of his prose stems from his view of local cultural configurations and ethos. It also represents an attempt, deliberate or not, to forge a non-objectivist claim to legitimacy and authority since Western epistemology separates the aesthetic experience from scientific, logical and linear thought. Hence Geertz precludes traditional and scientistic modes of ethnographic evaluation.

For his interpretivist writings, Geertz selects the essay as his literary genre, not the standard academic article or book. He even formats his historical 'monograph' (*N*) as a lengthy non-specialist essay. In fact, we must read the endnotes of *N*, which are purposely set off from the narrative and comprise nearly half the text, to find the types of information that satisfy normative standards for social scientific scholarship.

The modern essay, Marcus (1986: 191) notes, evolved as a critique of realist writing. It attempts to evoke rather than represent the world. Several aspects of Marcus's characterization of the modernist essay read like a summary of Geertz's writing style: 'It opposes conventional systemic analysis, absolves the writer from having to develop the broader implications of his thought (while nonetheless indicating that there are such implications) or of having to tie loose ends together . . . It is finally a hedge on the holistic commitments of anthropological ethnography.' Geertz's essays are neither systematic nor holistic, like classic realist ethnography. He refuses to develop his ideas according to the tradition of social science Grand Theory, despite his training under Parsons. As Geertz repeatedly emphasizes throughout his classic paradigmatic essay, 'Thick description: toward an interpretive theory of culture' (*IC*: 3–30), Grand Theory paradigms inhibit understanding local knowledges by shrouding local idioms.

But in spite of Geertz's anti-holism and open-ended essays, he retains the confidence of Grand Theory and ethnographic realism. His writings express little of the subjective epistemological doubt that often emerges from many contemporary ethnographies (e.g. Crapanzano 1980). Geertz's moderate interpretive uncertainty is evident at the beginning of the ethnographic encounter (e.g. *IC*: 412 ff.) – by the end of the cockfight, his interpretive confidence is assuredly restored: the cultural expressions he interprets exist, for all actors, in specific forms invested with fixed meanings.

For an anthropologist, Geertz's essays contain an unexpected variety of literary allusions and invocations: Burke, Goodman, Nabokov, Keats, Yeats, Faulkner, even Hunter Thompson. Geertz obviously reads anthropologists. Still, his primarily interest lies not in writing solely for them. He only rarely addresses ethnographers exclusively. He writes almost all his interpretivist essays for the liberal-arts interdisciplinarian. The items of ethnographic information contained in most of Geertz's essays serve as examples rather than foci. His arguments often weave through rather than centre on his fieldwork. The types of journals which have published his work reflect this orientation: the *Antioch Review*, the *American Scholar, Bulletin of the American Academy of Arts and Science*, *Daedalus*, *Encounter*, the *Georgia Review* and *Modern Language Notes*.

Geertz writes in meandering, seductive, melodic prose. His literary sensibility echoes the polymorphic quality of culture and the nature of ethnographic understanding. Geertz sees subtle congruencies between anthropological writing and lived cultural texts. Those who do not share Geertz's vision read his prose as a mystification (e.g. Shankman 1984; Walters 1980) and fail to address his insightful claim that 'the line between mode of representation and substantive context is as undrawable in cultural analysis as it is in painting' (*IC*: 16). Geertz encourages the use of literary devices such as metaphor, irony, paradox and metonymy (e.g. *IC*: 209, 213 n. 30) because cultural texts and social discourse include these tones, nuances and moods.

Regardless of Geertz's commendable literary sophistication, he clings to an earlier generation's literary–political outlook. Geertz generally strives to remain apolitical, at least within the accepted boundaries of progressive liberal thought, which is a common outlook among anthropologist of his generation (see p. 148). But Geertz's writings reveal unintended meanings, paradoxes and ironies – themselves favoured post-modern tropes – which cause us to question his straightforward views of culture and cultural texts. Crapanzano (1986), for example, uncovers an erotic pun in the Balinese cockfight essay (*IC*: 412–53).

Whether or not the pun was intentional is of little consequence – Geertz was probably shocked by the suggestion. The point is, despite intentions, anthropological writing occurs within the larger issues of the day. It entails values, morals and strategies, sometimes overt, not infrequently veiled and allegorical (see Clifford 1986a). As Geertz

(*WL*: 50) declares, 'let him who writes free of his time's imaginings cast the first stone'.

The erotic pun and its unravelling by Crapanzano, an ethnographer of astute psychoanalytic sensibility, further deconstructs Geertz's claim that the cockfight is best interpreted in cultural rather than psychodynamic and sexual terms. In a similarly ironic twist, Fernandez (1986: 235) suggests that Geertz's methodology and the title of his book *The Interpretation of Cultures* were directly influenced by Freud's *The Interpretation of Dreams*. And Geertz's most recent book, can be read as a chapter in anthroplogy's latest re-enacting of the primal crime. Geertz's sons (gender intended), the post-modern ethnographers, attempt to slay their father and thereby establish their own hegemony and authority. Geertz — and can we fault him? — is reluctant to go.

The Subject and Subjectivity

As I indicated above, unique persons neither constitute nor read Geertz's cultural texts. Individual agency and experience dissolve. The individual and her readings are governed, or even overdetermined, by the larger cultural web. Motivation for social action arises from public cultural values rather than from personal strategies and desire. Geertz unequivocally writes that 'culture is public because meaning is' (*IC*: 12) and that 'human thought is consummately social: social in its origins, social in its functions, social in its forms, and social in its applications' (*IC*: 360; see also 53–83).

Geertz reads the Balinese cockfight from the perspective of the collective, although largely unconscious, experience of all Balinese. The cockfight is publicly constituted, publicly read and publicly infused with meaning. Geertz appears bothered by, or perhaps ashamed of, our inner, personal worlds in which we are antisocial beings. I allude here to psychodynamic constructs, and Oedipal rivalry and sexuality, themes which frequently surface in Geertz's writings and belie his view of subjectivity and motivation. Public perception and cultural cohesion far overshadow the occasional recognition of individual subjectivity and cultural disjunction (e.g. *IC*: 17–19; 134).

Geertz's perspective not only denies the active and creative role of the subject — defined, of course, through local idioms — but also assumes sociocultural homogeneity and even, at times, politico-economic hegemony. In Geertz's interpretations, cultural texts seem to belong to everyone. But certainly the Balinese cockfight is a cultural text only for specific Balinese individuals. From whose perspective, then, does Geertz profess to interpret?

The conspicuous absence of active persons in Geertz's texts contravenes the two principles of intertextuality discussed earlier. Because of this interpretive lacuna, Geertz is incapable of encompassing either what readers desire, a topic he consistently avoids, or what readers know from past experiences. At the same time, his textual metaphor disregards the importance of the negotiations that occur between interlocutors, whether indigenous, anthropological or both. These omissions undermine his interpretivism by creating cultural objects.

As Geertz acknowledges (e.g. *IC*: 449), compassion, affect and emotion are instrumental for cultural interpretation. Geertz stresses the ethnographic importance of sentiment, not as a peripheral issue but as a central theme in cultural anthropology (e.g. *IC*: 135). (Of course, he upholds a public view of sentiment.) Geertz's textual metaphor thus challenges vulgar materialist views of human behaviour, those which analyse sociocultural events without reference to intentions, beliefs, ideals and values.

In line with Geertz's focus on public sentiment is his refutation of psychological and psychoanalytic approaches to understanding cultural meaning, what he terms the 'cognitivist fallacy' (*IC*: 12). This is a long-standing theme in his thought, from his pre-interpretivist days (e.g. *IO*: 95) to more recent works (*LK*: 94–120; *AAR*: 8). Geertz labels 'psychologism' as well as 'logicism', by which he refers to structuralism – a 'great saboteur of cultural analysis' (*IC*: 405). He prefers instead, we have seen, shared public texts and interpersonal webs of meaning. When Geertz, in a characteristically Weberian mode, writes that cultural analyses should be 'actor-oriented' (*IC*: 14), he does not mean persons who possess psychodynamic motivations. The issue, of course, is a long-standing one within American cultural anthropology, one that harks back to Kroeber and Sapir.

Yet Geertz's actors are not completely anonymous. He is not compiling something on the order of the Human Relations Area Files. His work stands at a midpoint between the ethnographic slide-shows of unknown voiceless actors and a focus on unique subjects who negotiate cultural texts and therefore create multiple readings.

Yet an emphasis on subjectivity and sentiment, whether public in Geertz's view or individual from an alternative perspective, and the argument that we can interpret culture as a text, do not imply a fundamental blindness to materialist considerations. Geertz and interpretivism do not uncritically adhere to idealism. According to Geertz, ideas are not 'unobservable mental stuff' (*N*: 135). They are meanings – envehicled in symbols, signs and texts – which form the substance of public discourse. Moreover, Geertz uses the text as a metaphor or a model of culture. As a means and not an end to cultural analysis, a textual metaphor should not obscure lives. Geertz does not allow his textual metaphor to become the focus of his analysis.

History, Temporality and Context

Of the many trends in contemporary cultural anthropology, the rise of historical consciousness is one of the most important. Geertz too now explicitly embraces history. Geertz's narrative of the nineteenth-century Balinese state, *N*, is an attempt at synthesizing and highlighting, through his interpretivist framework, the cultural idioms of a complex royal state. The study is noteworthy but at the same time enigmatic. It is a work of fine erudition and accomplishment. But it is also an unsatisfactory work, especially when gauged by the standards of Geertz's ethnographic essays and the theoretical sophistication of many recent historical works within anthropology. History continues to vex Geertz and, alas, interpretivism.

Geertz's current historical vision was foreshadowed in a much earlier work, *DJE*, and this I find disappointing. It shows that Geertz either fails to take the issue seriously – which I strongly doubt – or else has not fundamentally altered his interpretivist notion of anthropological history. Geertz rejects two common constructions of history: the 'period approach' and the 'developmental approach'. In the period approach, history is a series of events. The second approach depicts history as a continuous development of sociocultural stages. One parcels time into discrete moments along a continuum while the other views it continuously. In Geertz's words, time is 'the thread along which specific happenings are strung' or the 'medium through which certain abstract processes move' (*N*: 5). Both views employ linear concepts of temporality, the dominant historical vision in western intellectual discourse. Furthermore, these two approaches to history are universal frameworks and thus obscure – and deny the validity of – local knowledges.

After having rejected these two approaches to history, Geertz sketches his own view, but he does so in such a brief fashion that one wonders about his footing on the topic. Geertz uses comparative material written about both past and present Balinese societies and politics, and joins them to a modified Weberian ideal-type paradigm. Neither move seems very novel. What is new, however, is that Geertz writes an ethnographic history, one based on his interpretivist outlook. But Geertz offers us no theory of history. Apart from a few theoretical ruminations, the book concentrates on social structure, land tenure, irrigation and the hierarchy of Balinese political integrations. For the most part, the book seems decidedly traditional.

Geertz creates an abstract model of the classic Balinese state, paying close attention to its royal symbolic displays and their intended public meanings. He examines the past Balinese analogue of the twentieth-century cockfight. Geertz attempts to unpack the cultural ideals of Balinese society that were enshrined in the public displays of the nineteenth-century 'theatre state'. He centres his analysis on the dramas of the negara as enactments of ideas which dispersed throughout the state.

To be certain, N is a particularistic account in the tradition of Boas and Weber. At the same time, as an ideal account, the negara state can be compared with other local polities, most usefully in island South-East Asia. Geertz's view of historical scholarship combines the unique exegesis of local constructs with general models. His is not an Annalistic account. Being an interpretation, it is 'a conceptual entity, not an historical one' — has Geertz truly confronted the issue of history and temporality or merely sublimated it through his largely synchronic interpretive methodology?

When he explored contemporary Balinese constructions of 'person, time, and conduct', Geertz concluded that 'Balinese social life . . . takes place in a motionless present, a vectorless now' (*IC*: 404). The nature of time, history and context in his own interpretations, however, is often not quite as lucid, apparently, as that of the Balinese. One might posit, however, that Geertz's interpretations always revolve around context and that, indeed, this is what 'thick description' is all about. Without a sense of contextual framing, it is impossible to sort out winks from twitches, and from parodies of both — what Geertz figuratively maintains he has been doing all along (*IC*: 3–30).

Nevertheless, Geertz himself dismantles these claims through his use of symbolic essences, fixed public meanings and ideal cultural models. Since Geertz reads meaning from cultural action with respect to an idealized symbol invested with fixed referentiality, he ultimately dispels context, temporality and historicity. Moreover, while he characterizes culture as 'an historically transmitted pattern of meanings' (*IC*: 89), he has yet to explore either the process of transmission or, following Asad (1983), 'processes of formation'.

The scope of contextual considerations necessary for reading cultural texts is a key issue, especially if we define context as a significant matrix of interacting relationships, persons, things and events from which meanings arise. In reading the material expressions of the

Iatmul ceremonial house of Papua New Guinea, a contemporary example drawn from my own fieldwork, do the contextual boundaries terminate with the men who frequent the structure or perhaps the entire village? Or, must we extend context to the range of Iatmul social discourse, a region of interacting cultural groups, the entire Sepik river, the island of New Guinea, Melanesia or the modern world system? At each of these contextual frontiers, moreover, time and history, whether locally or globally conceived, vary for anthropological analysis and indigenous meaning.

Geertz reads context largely in terms of local cultural idioms rather than global forces and interaction. Because his contexts often exclude issues of political power, colonialism, domination and the modern world system, his interpretive readings seem constrained. It is Geertz alone who discerns the relevant parameters for reading and constituting cultural texts. The parameters Moroccan traders employ while imparting significance into their activities and into their readings of their own lives remain unclear. Local experiences are not, in Geertz's essays, apparently locally defined.

Anthropologists often impose western constructions of time, history and context on to other cultures and unknowingly augment unspoken ideologies (*pace* Fabian 1983; Said 1978). Geertz recognizes this imposition. He writes about how the west reads Bali as a paragon of the primitive, savage, quaint and idyllic, South Pacific island setting, resplendent with horror and passion (*LK*: 36–54). But is Geertz innocent of such constructions? Perhaps not. He too has etched on the minds of Western social scientists examples of exotica, especially cockfights and North African bazaars. But what are the locally conceived visions of exemplary cultural texts? Again, it is not in Geertz's writings that we learn the answer. It is axiomatic, at least within an interpretivist framework, that in order to read cultural texts one must consider history and context. But sensitivity can be trained on constructions of these dimensions and how they colour our understanding of other cultures.

Geertz and Functionalism: Change and Discontinuity

Earlier, I situated Geertz's interpretivism against the traditions of Weber, Parsons and Durkheim. In different ways, it is well known, these three social thinkers initiated and developed aspects of functionalist theory. Functionalism, especially the Parsonian variant, is frequently accused of over-emphasizing systemic equilibrium at the analytical expense of discontinuity and change. Moreover, functionalism seems predicated on the notion that stability is the norm and ideal for sociocultural systems. This view of funtionalist theory is admittedly simplistic (see Lipset 1975). Nevertheless, it helped shape Anglo-American anthropology, social thought and archaeology during this century.

Geertz's interpretivism includes elements of a functionalist outlook. They are, however, best illuminated with respect to the Weberian–Parsonian and Durkheimian traditions rather than that of Radcliffe-Brown, Malinowski and British structural-functionalism. Indeed, as a consummately American cultural anthropologist, Geertz has little in common with the British tradition and he rarely refers to its contemporary practitioners. In this section I address Geertz's functionalism by concentrating on his views of sociocultural change, cultural integration, homogeneity and hegemony.

In large measure due to the historic–geographic situation of his fieldwork, Geertz grapples with the ability of interpretivism effectively to make sense of extensive sociocultural transformation (see esp. *IC*: 142–69; 234–54; 255–310; CSC). During sociocultural change, 'the moral substance of a sort of existence . . . social mind' most profoundly alters (CSC: 524). Following Weber, Geertz directs his initial attention to cultural transformation and typically interprets change from the perspective of the society *in toto* rather than with respect to specific groups.

Geertz analyses sociocultural change and discontinuity in terms of the division between culture as the system of meanings and society (social structure) as the patterning of interaction. Society, being more malleable, often alters at a faster pace than culture. Upon analysing a Javanese funeral that he witnessed during his fieldwork in 1954, Geertz concluded that there was 'an incongruity due to the persistence in an urban environment of a religious symbol system adjusted to peasant social structure' (*IC*: 169).

Through a similar dichotomy, Geertz characterizes an obstacle encountered by emerging nation-states. On the one hand, these polities remain enveloped in resilient 'primordial sentiments'. On the other hand, emerging nation-states strive toward civil order. This dichotomous view, common in Anglo-American anthropology and sociology, derives from Parsonian functionalism and, ultimately, Weber. The overwhelming problem, according to Geertz, is one of integrating these two systems. In both the Javanese funeral and emerging nation-states, Geertz interprets sociocultural changes as a dynamic reconciliation between the need to import meaning and significance into our lives with the equally pressing need to maintain a viable social order. Geertz insists on the eventual systemic integration of society and culture into a viable, disencumbered, organic unity. The inertia of change inevitably leads to stability.

A variation of this conceptual theme can be read in Geertz's interpretation of the Balinese negara. Sociologically, the negara was a loosely connected system, an unglued amalgam rent by constantly fighting political units which caused a persistent breakdown of the state. Culturally, however, the divisive negara was held together by dramatic displays in the royal cities. The chronic violence and internal strife cohered in a systemic web of symbols and meanings which expressed the ideal Balinese society according to a presumably elite ideology. Social structural appearances notwithstanding, the negara was maintained through cultural essences. Society failed; culture triumphed.

Conflict, politico-economic power, hierarchy, social dissonance and cultural ambiguity largely dissolve in Geertz's interpretations. In the 1950s, Geertz worked in Indonesia. Within a decade of his fieldwork, the region exploded into violence, revolt and class struggle, especially after Sukarno's fall in 1965. Yet we read little about these events and their forewarnings in his interpretivist essays. As Walters (1980: 553; see also Roseberry 1982) writes, 'it would be easy to read a conservative bias in Geertz', particularly through his alliances with Parsons (e.g. *IC*: 234–54) and Shils (e.g. *IC*: 255–310), and 'their plea for a civil, temperate, unheroic politics'. One need not be a Marxist or a materialist – and I am neither – to agree.

It is true that Geertz's interpretations often neglect economic inequities, brute power, social hierarchy, class formations and incongruities between ideology and social practice. It is equally true, we have seen, that he interprets the Balinese negara in terms of 'a poetics of power, not a mechanics' (*N*: 123). Yet Geertz (*CSC*: 527 n. 11) disagrees with the criticism that he views the Javanese peasantry, for example, 'as an undifferentiated lump'. More important, however, is his interpretivist assertion that universal glosses such as 'class formation' are inappropriate for deriving local knowledges. Nevertheless, Geertz's interpretivism infrequently addresses societal differentiation, whether couched in universal concepts or framed in local idioms, whether materialist or cultural.

Moreover, it seems important to note Geertz's affiliations with three of the most powerful institutions in American higher education – the Department of Social Relations at Harvard University, the Department of Anthropology at Chicago University, and currently, the noted Institute for Advanced Studies in Princeton. These centres of academe not only set the pace of much American intellectual life but also rest on vast private, rather than public, endowments. They are not accountable to the general populace – and hence society – in the same manner as public institutions.

Such loaded comments aside, I cannot definitively speak about Geertz's politics or what sometimes appears as a conservative subtext in his interpretations. But all Geertz's works can be read as a challenge to racism and ethnocentrism through their focus on local idioms rather than on universal criteria from which to evaluate all societies. Geertz also cannot be accused of neglecting issues of power. He is almost obsessed, even seduced, by power, but by cultural not economic power. Cultural power is a central concern in many of his essays (e.g. *IC*: 412–53; *N*; *UD*). Hence, Geertz's work displays two of the greater tasks for interpretivism and post-modern ethnography: given the demise of realism, how can we assert moral judgements – for it is impossible to avoid them in today's world – and how do we balance global vision with local knowledges?

Although Geertz claims to focus on local knowledges, he espouses certain universal values and sees a global role for interpretivist anthropology. In a tone reminiscent of earlier claims (*IC*: 3–30) but with a renewed sense of ethical and contemporary imperative, Geertz writes that interpretive anthropology can: 'enlarge the possibility of intelligible discourse between people quite different from one another in interest, outlook, wealth, and power, and yet contained in a world where, tumbled as they are into endless connection, it is increasingly difficult to get out of each other's way' (*WL*: 147).

In UD Geertz challenges Lévi-Strauss's defence of ethnocentrism. In this rare, overtly ethical mode, Geertz argues that ethnographic relativism can serve as a responsible perspective for effectively coping with the cultural and moral diversity that now constitute the reality of Western industrialized nations. Geertz's cultural anthropology revolves around the traditional ideals of American liberal thought. His acknowledgements in *RJ*, the published version of his 1956 doctoral thesis, echo a prevailing concern of ethnographic research during that era. He hopes that his study will contribute to Indonesia's 'aspirations to build a strong, stable, prosperous, and democratic "New Indonesia"'. He similarly ends the book: despite Java's religious pluralism and divisiveness, he looks forward to an organic Javanese society, one of 'cultural unity and continuing social process'. Although not as explicit as these earlier calls, his interpretivist works all resonate with the same sentiment.

I would argue that lapses and omissions in Geertz's thought result more from his methodological pedigree than his overt politics, although the two, of course, are inseparable. Like Parsons, Weber, Durkheim and functionalists, Geertz's conceptual apparatus is not constructed, first and foremost, to encompass cultural discontinuity and social contradiction. His interpretations thus largely reproduce the relationships between dominated and dominant — most noticeably in his Balinese and Indonesian studies — because his focus on public meanings often amounts to a tacit acceptance of ruling and elite ideology.

Geertz rarely — and never explicitly — voices dissatisfaction with what he has seen. Ideology and cultural reality become conflated. At times, Geertz (esp. in *IC*: 3–30) equates culture with normative prescriptions for action, hence, social control mechanisms (Rosaldo 1985). He typically omits unanticipated results, uncertainties and 'contingent happenings' from his analyses. They are included only as deviations from cultural norms.

Although these considerations traditionally lie within Marxist concerns, the cultural focus of interpretivism is adequately, indeed uniquely, competent to deal with them. In a textual or discursive view of society, Parkin (1982: xlvi) notes, power does not solely inhere in economic possession and control — a materialist fallacy. It also, and often more significantly, involves 'unequal access to semantic creativity, including the capacity to nominate others as equal or unequal, animate or inanimate, memorable or abject, dicusser or discussed'. Vocal critics of Geertz, such as Roseberry (1982) and Keesing (1987), incorrectly assume that all textual metaphors are inherently opaque with respect to illuminating oppression and exploitation, a view which can be persuasively countered with the aid of literary theorists such as Eagleton (1976) and Williams (1977). But it remains a political and ethical imperative for interpretivist social scientists to grapple with these issues.

Geertz's cultures are fundamentally, if not always coherently, interconnected through ultimately logical, localized patterns of meanings and symbols. Culture, for Geertz, whether expressed through religion (*IC*: 87–125), ideology (*IC*: 193–233), common sense (*LK*: 73–93) or art (*LK*: 94–120), is a *system*, a term deliberately and repeatedly chosen, and one which connotes a particular image when placed in the history of anthropology.

In a particularly illuminating instance, Geertz (*IC*: 407–8) images culture after an octopus, an organic metaphor which envisions connectedness and integrated movement. What gaps we find arise more from our own interpretive oversights than from the cultures themselves (Geertz, cited in Shweder 1984a: 19). Geertz's texts are unified systems of meaning. In the final analysis, they hold together. Discontinuity results from flawed interpretation or the disruption of sociocultural systems which eventually, or hopefully in Geertz's

sentiment, disappear. This is not a necessary outcome of a text
metaphor since texts, like cultures, possess gaps, discontinuities and
ambiguities which resist resolution on any level. I am not arguing for a
neo-hyperdiffusionist, threads-and-patches view of culture. Instead,
and following one of Geertz's students, Meeker (1979; 1980), social
scientists need to reorient the basic premise or 'moral vision' that
cultures are fundamentally integrated and coherently unified. The
textual metaphor should not gloss over social and cultural hierarchies.
Indeed, by virtue of its inherent pluralism, the text metaphor can aid
in discerning difference.

Relativism

The world, according to Geertz, is composed of diverse cultures and,
more to the point, different local ways of life. Every society exists
within a unique constellation of cultural constructions. In so far as we
know, universal concepts such as personhood and time do indeed exist.
Cultural difference does not imply incommensurability. But in a
universal view, common concepts are manifestly vacuous since their
cultural detail varies across the globe. Thus, through such experience-
distant — at least to us — practices as teknonyms and a ten-cycle
'permutational' calendar, the Balinese comport themselves and think
about their world in a rather different, experience-near way than do we
(IC: 360–411). Given this assumption of non-reducible cultural
diversity, the interpretivist task is to understand local knowledges.
This is the strong thesis of Geertz's paradigmatic essays, 'Thick
description' (IC: 3–30) and 'From the native's point of view' (LK: 55–
70), from which stems his cultural relativism. Recently, this aspect of
his thought assumes the form of an anti anti-relativism, or rather, a
refutation of anthropologists who question the validity and insight of
relativism (Spiro 1986).

We can partially situate Geertz's cultural relativism in the wider
American tradition which recognizes, accepts and extols the benefits of
cultural pluralism. This tradition, moreover, rests on a moral foundation, evident in Geertz's recent essay on 'The uses of diversity'. It
stands as his first overtly ethical piece and represents an attempt to
explode the myth that cultural relativism inextricably leads to
nihilism and solipsism (but see Rabinow 1985).

Geertz's relativism draws on Wittgenstein's 'forms of life' philosophy. Each way of life must be understood in terms of its own
constructions, that is to say, with reference to its localized systems of
meanings, values and symbols. Indeed, complex symbolic thought is

the very essence of human societies and social thought (NPT). We cannot, according to Geertz, adequately understand local forms of life and the specific aspects of local knowledges through the application of universal models and the search for global sociocultural traits. The goal of interpretation is neither to reduce cultural phenomena to the commonality nor to explain them in causal terms. Relativism, therefore, assumes no rock-bottoms to cultural life. Since our data consist of interpretations of interpretations, we lack fixed cultural elements from which to 'objectively' cease interpretation and latch on to a universal property. The nature of ethnographic inquiry, according to Geertz, as well as the nature of cultural life, prohibit any other position.

Geertz, however, is an 'ethnographic relativist' (M. Penn, personal communication). He does not enter into the wider and copious philosophical discussion of relativism (Brown 1984; Hatch 1983; Hollis and Lukes 1982; Jarvie 1984). Although he maintains that cultures are different, he does not imply that cultures are inherently incommensurate. From Geertz's perspective, cultural relativism does not amount to cultural isolationism; cross-cultural knowledge is possible, we can converse with others. Relativism does not impede knowledge.

Culture as Text: The Contemporary Critique

A material culture as text metaphor rests on the basic premise that humans are 'symbolizing, conceptualizing, meaning-seeking animal[s]' (*IC*: 140). Geertz's interpretive anthropology attempts to understand, through the broad methodological perspective I outline above, the local ways in which cultures are meaningfully constituted. But at least four of his interpretivist themes can be critiqued from the perspective of contemporary thought viz. post-structuralism, deconstruction and post-modern ethnography. When we join these critiques to Geertz's own formulations, we can begin to forge a viable contemporary textual metaphor. Geertz's interpretivist insights germinated at least twenty years ago. They are in need of emendation.

The four troublesome orientations in Geertz's work are: (i) cultural texts 'fix' essentialistic meaning and are ultimately unambiguous; (ii) cultural and textual meaning is consummately public; (iii) cultures and cultural texts are homogeneous, cultural ideation often amounts to dominant ideology; (iv) cultures and cultural texts are integrated wholes, largely devoid of conflict, disjunction and pluralism. The momentum of sociocultural change leads to stability.

We can contest Geertz's notion that cultural texts 'fix' meaning, for as Barthes (1977: 159) writes, 'the Text is plural . . . an *irreducible* (and not merely an acceptable) plural'. Texts engender a multiplicity of readings and interpretations. Any alleged mimesis dissolves. In Geertz's view – an essentialistic view – a text has a real, true and objective existence. As an object, this text is constituted somewhat independently of its readers. It is created at a specific historical moment and continues to reference that moment as well as the author's intentions, regardless of the conditions surrounding its subsequent readings. Geertz's texts have unity: they exhibit closure and self-contained meaning.

In a different view, a text exists only as a specific sociocultural creation, tied to events occurring at the time of reading. From this perspective, the text is constituted by both its authors and specific readers. It is therefore an individual-centred, subjective creation, not an objective external entity. This text is open-ended yet historically framed, and its meaning is fashioned, as opposed to self-contained. The text has no unity and no essential meaning. Different readers see different texts and derive different meanings. Difference and plurality, not a unified single meaning, inhere in the text.

The first notion of text, Geertz's perspective, almost represents a unit of reality – a literary snapshot that records life in its actuality. This is an older view which is challenged by the second, deconstructionist, view of texts (see Butler 1984; Culler 1982; Norris 1982). In the latter interpretation, the text is a fluid construct. It refers to sociocultural events at which persons read and interpret meaning. As meaningful social expressions, social texts are negotiated and fashioned encounters. Meaning is created or interpreted *with* the text rather than extracted *from* something inherent in it. These cultural texts are 'in a state of continual production' (Boon 1985).

This is the perspective of reader-response criticism (see Freund 1987). Yet, again, this is not to suggest that meaning, as a product of the reader's reception, emerges in a sociohistorical vacuum. The alternative to essentialism is not 'anything goes'. Texts, meanings and interpretations are open-ended. Nevertheless, they are situated in specific sociocultural and historico-economic fields, and arise from individual action and social practice. The recognition that specific persons interpret within history mitigates the fears of Keesing (1987) and Harris (cited in Sass 1986), among others, that disciplinary nihilism and solipsism might run adrift from adopting a textual metaphor. It also counters the argument that a textual perspective prevents anthropologists from assuming moral judgements.

We can also challenge Geertz's view that meaning is solely

constituted and read at the level of a single public discourse. Societies, after all, comprise different groups and persons. The meanings of culture texts often arise from personal responses to the text, and, in turn, these are significantly affected by biography, gender, age, religion, kinship, education and other 'horizons of expectation' (Culler 1981: 13). In addition, ideology, power relations, the control of knowledge, material inequalities, strategies for social action and history colour interpretations. But I am not arguing that culture can be reduced to individuals as transcendent egos and subjects, an ever-present fallacy in post-modern ethnographic thought. Rather, individuals, as understood according to local cultural constructs and idioms, are an important locus for cultural analysis.

If we acknowledge that persons read and contribute to the constitution of cultural texts through their participation in cultural fields or 'discursive space', we can avoid what Culler (1981: 12) terms a 'bizarre fiction', namely, 'a self-contained encounter between innocent reader and autonomous text'. Intertextuality simultaneously creates the open-endedness of the text's meaning and obstructs solipsism.

As I argued earlier, societies are not fundamentally integrated totalities and, moreover, the object of textual interpretation need not always be dominant ideology. A contrary view glosses over internal contradictions, class struggles, the control of power and knowledge and its differential allocation, and the presence of alternative ideologies. In this sense, feminist theory is helpful since it centres on the idea that to read culture is to interpret meanings that diverge from conventional, seemingly 'natural', accounts. Texts are a form of difference and plurality.

Yet difference and plurality imply politics, broadly construed. In reading cultural texts, therefore, it is necessary to explore aspects surrounding both text production and interpretation. This, we have seen, is largely absent from Geertz's accounts. But a political recognition also challenges the crude deconstructionist assumption that nothing exists outside the text. Indeed, the recent revelation that Paul de Man, the late leading American proponent of literary deconstruction, wrote anti-Semitic apologetics for the Nazi regime during the Holocaust lends powerful credence to the idea that texts and interpretations are, first and foremost, sociocultural and historical phenomena and that they must be understood in those terms.

American cultural anthropology and especially ethnography is at a moment of profound crisis. As Geertz recognizes, in a book borne out of this crisis and directly stimulated by his immediate interpretivist successors, the current mood is one of disquiet and malaise, 'estrangement, hypocrisy, helplessness, domination, disillusion' (WL: 97).

The expansion of interpretivism and its textual metaphors in cultural anthropology have not been greeted with welcome glances and open arms. Suspicion, anger and acrimonious debate everywhere linger. Interpretivists on the offensive, non-interpretivists on the defensive, nobody within American anthropology seems very pleased with where they are or anything within the discipline. Geertz was the first interpretivist ethnographer, but perhaps the last to have any deep confidence in what he was doing and in how ethnography ought to be done.

But Geertz observes that of all the 'blurred genres' currently employed in social science, the text is 'the most venturesome, and the least well developed' (*LK*: 30). To this, we may attribute much of its appeal; at the same time, we can anticipate the work to come. There is interpretivist light at the end of our disciplinary tunnel. Although Geertz has made great strides towards a viable interpretivist theory of cultural texts, he has only walked half the distance: the other half remains to be explored.

ACKNOWLEDGEMENTS

Thanks to Julie Benz, David Lipset and Larry Shillock for commenting on earlier drafts, and the University of Minnesota for a Shevlin Fellowship. John Ingham stimulated many of my psychodynamic allusions. I am especially grateful to Mischa Penn and his willingness to help me develop many of the ideas in this essay. I alone, however, assume full responsibility for all shortcomings and omissions.

BIBLIOGRAPHY

This is a select list.

1 Books by Geertz

The Development of the Javanese Economy: A Sociocultural Approach (DJE) (1956) MIT Center for International Studies, Cambridge, Mass.
The Religion of Java (*RJ*) (1960) Free Press, Glencoe.
Agricultural Involution: The Process of Ecological Change in Indonesia (AI) (1963) University of California, Berkeley.
Peddlers and Princes: Social Developments and Economic Chance in Two Indonesian Towns (PP) (1963) University of Chicago Press, Chicago.

The Social History of an Indonesian Town (*SH*) (1965) MIT Press, Cambridge, Mass.
Islam Observed: Religious Development in Morocco and Indonesia (*IO*) (1968) Yale University Press, New Haven.
Meaning and Order in Moroccan Society (*MO*) (1979) with H. Geertz and L. Rosen. Cambridge University Press, Cambridge.
Negara: The Theatre State in Nineteenth Century Bali (*N*) (1980) Princeton University Press, Princeton.
Works and Lives: The Anthropologist as Author (*WL*) (1988) Stanford University Press, Stanford.

2 Collections of writings

The Interpretation of Cultures (*IC*) (1973) Basic Books, New York.
Local Knowledge: Further Essays in Interpretive Anthropology (*LK*) (1983) Basic Books, New York.

3 Articles by Geertz

'Form and variation in a Balinese village structure' (FV) (1959) *American Anthropologist*, 61: 991–1012.
'Tihingan: a Balinese village' (T) (1964) *Bijdragen Tot de Taal-, Land-en Volkendunde*, 120: 1–33.
'Foreword' (F) (1977) in G. Witherspoon, *Language and Art in the Navajo Universe*, University of Michigan Press, Ann Arbor.
'The bazaar economy: information and search in peasant marketing' (BE) (1978) *American Economic Review*, 68: 28–32.
'Notions of primitive thought' (NPT) (1983) Inverview in J. Miller (ed.) *States of Mind*, Pantheon, New York.
'Anti anti-relativism' (AAR) (1984) *American Anthropologist*, 86: 263–78.
'Culture and social change: the Indonesian case' (CSC) (1984) *Man* (n.s.), 19: 511–32.
'The uses of diversity' (UD) (1986) *Michigan Quarterly Review*, Winter: 105–23.

4 Other works referred to in the text

Asad, T. (1983) 'Anthropological conceptions of religion: reflections on Geertz', *Man* (n.s.), 18: 237–50.
Austin, D. J. (1979) 'Symbols and culture: some philosophical assumptions in the work of Clifford Geertz', *Social Analysis*, 3: 45–86.

Barthes, R. (1977) 'From work to text' in *Image – Music – Text*. Hill & Wang, New York.

Benedict, R. (1934) *Patterns of Culture*, Houghton Mifflin, New York.

Bernstein, R. (1988) 'Anthropologist, retracing steps after three decades, is shocked by change', *New York Times*, 11 May, p. 23.

Bloch, M. (1977) 'The past and the present in the present', *Man* (n.s.), 12: 278–92.

Boon, J. (1977) *The Anthropological Romance of Bali, 1597–1972: Dynamic Perspectives in Marriage and Caste, Politics and Religion*, Cambridge University Press, Cambridge.

Boon, J. (1985) 'Mead's mediations: some semiotics from the Sepik, by way of Bateson, on to Bali' in E. Meitz and R. Parmentier (eds) *Semiotic Mediation*, Academic Press, New York.

Bourdieu, P. (1977) *Outline of a Theory of Practice*, Cambridge University Press, Cambridge.

Brown, S. C. (ed.) (1984) *Objectivity and Cultural Divergence*, Cambridge University Press, Cambridge.

Butler, C. (1984) *Interpretation, Deconstruction, and Ideology*, Clarendon Press, Oxford.

Clifford, J. (1983) 'On ethnographic authority', *Representations 2*, Spring 1983: 132–43.

Clifford, J. (1986a) 'On ethnographic allegory' in J. Clifford and G. E. Marcus (eds) *Writing Culture: The Poetics and Politics of Ethnography*, University of California Press, Berkeley.

Clifford, J. and Marcus, G. E. (eds) (1986b) *Writing Culture: The Poetics and Politics of Ethnography*, University of California Press, Berkeley.

Crapanzano, V. (1980) *Tuhami: Portrait of a Moroccan*, University of Chicago Press, Chicago.

Crapanzano, V. (1986) 'Hermes' dilemma: the masking of ethnographic subversion in ethnographic description' in J. Clifford and G. E. Marcus, (eds) *Writing Culture: The Poetics and Politics of Ethnography*, University of California Press, Berkeley.

Culler, J. (1981) *The Pursuit of Signs: Semiotics, Literature, Deconstruction*, Cornell University Press, Ithaca.

Culler, J. (1982) *On Deconstruction: Theory and Criticism After Structuralism*, Cornell University Press, Ithaca.

Eagleton, T. (1976) *Marxism and Literary Criticism*, University of California Press, Berkeley.

Fabian, J. (1983) *Time and the Other: How Anthropology Makes its Object*, Columbia University Press, New York.

Fernandez, J. W. (1985) 'Exploded worlds – text as a metaphor for ethnography (and vice versa)', *Dialectical Anthropology*, 10: 15–26.

Fernandez, J. W. (1986) *Persuasions and Performances: The Play of Tropes in Culture*, Indiana University Press, Bloomington.

Freund, E. (1987) *The Return of the Reader: Reader-Response Criticism*, Methuen, New York.

Giddens, A. (1979) *Central Problems in Social Theory: Action, Structure and Contradiction in Social Analysis*, University of California Press, Berkeley.

Hatch, E. (1983) *Culture and Morality: The Relativity of Values in Anthropology*, Columbia University Press, New York.

Hodder, I. (1985) 'Postprocessual archaeology', *Advances in Archaeological Method and Theory*, 8: 1–26.

Hodder, I. (1986) *Reading the Past: Current Approaches to Interpretation in Archaeology*, Cambridge University Press, Cambridge.

Hollis, M. and Lukes, S. (eds) (1982) *Rationality and Relativism*, Basil Blackwell, Oxford.

Jarvie, I. C. (1984) *Rationality and Relativism: In Search of a Philosophy and History of Anthropology*, Routledge & Kegan Paul, London.

Keesing, R. M. (1987) 'Anthropology as interpretive quest', *Current Anthropology*, 28: 161–76.

Kroeber, A. L. and Parsons, T. (1958) 'The concept of culture and of social systems', *American Sociological Review* 23: 582–3.

Kuper, A. (1983) *Anthropology and Anthropologists: The Modern British School*, Routledge & Kegan Paul, London.

Langer, S (1960) *Philosophy in a New Key*, 4th edn, Harvard University Press, Cambridge, Mass.

Leach, E. (1981) 'A poetics of power: a review of "Negara: The Theatre State in Nineteenth Century Bali", by C. Geertz', *New Republic*, 4 April 1981, pp. 30–3.

Lipset, S. M. (1975) 'Social structure and social change' in P. Blau (ed.) *Approaches to the Study of Social Structures*, Free Press, New York.

Marcus, G. E. (1986) 'Contemporary problems of ethnography in the modern world system', in J. Clifford and G. E. Marcus (eds) *Writing Culture: The Poetics and Politics of Ethnography*, University of California Press, Berkeley.

Marcus, G. E. and Cushman D. (1982) 'Ethnographies as texts', *Annual Review of Anthropology*, 11: 25–69.

Marcus, G. E. and Fischer, M. M. J. (1986) *Anthropology as Cultural Critique: An Experimental Moment in the Human Sciences*, University of Chicago Press, Chicago.

Meeker, M. E. (1979) *Literature and Violence in North Africa*, Cambridge University Press, Cambridge.

Meeker, M. E. (1980) 'The twilight of a South Asian heroic age: a rereading of Barth's study of Swat', *Man* (n.s.), 15: 682–701.

Moore, H. L. (1986) *Space, Text and Gender: An Anthropological Study of the Marakwet of Kenya*, Cambridge University Press, Cambridge.

Morgan, J. (1977) 'Religion and culture as meaning systems: a dialogue between Geertz and Tillich', *Journal of Religion*, 57: 363–75.

Munson, H. Jr (1986) 'Geertz on religion: the theory and practice', *Religion*, 16: 19–32.

Norris, C. (1982) *Deconstruction: Theory and Practice*, Methuen, New York.

Ortner, S. B. (1984) 'Theory in anthropology since the sixties', *Comparative Studies in Society and History*, 26: 126–66.

Parkin, D. (1982) 'Introduction' in D. Parkin (ed.) *Semantic Anthropology*, Academic Press, New York.

Parsons, T. (1937) *The Structure of Social Action*, McGraw-Hill, New York.

Peacock, J. L. (1981) ' The third stream: Weber, Parsons, Geertz', *Journal of the Anthropological Society of Oxford*, 7: 122–9.

Rabinow, P. (1985) 'Humanism as nihilism: the bracketing of truth and seriousness in American cultural anthropology' in N. Haan et al. (eds) *Social Science as Moral Inquiry*, Columbia University Press, New York.

Rabinow, P. (1986) 'Representations are social facts: modernity and post modernity in anthropology' in J. Clifford and G. E. Marcus (eds) *Writing Culture: The Poetics and Politics of Ethnography*, University of California Press, Berkeley.

Ricoeur, P. (1971) 'The model of the text: meaningful action considered as a text', *Social Research*, 38: 529–62.

Rosaldo, R. (1985) 'While making other plans', *Southern California Law Review*, 58: 19–28.

Roseberry, W. (1982) 'Balinese cockfights and the seduction of anthropology', *Social Research*, 49: 1013–28.

Said, E. W. (1978) *Orientalism*, Pantheon, New York.

Sass, L. A. (1986) 'Anthropology's native problems: revisionism in the field', *Harper's*, May 1986, pp. 49–57.

Schneider, D. M. (1976) 'Notes toward a theory of culture' in K. Basso and H. Selby (eds) *Meaning in Anthropology*, University of New Mexico Press, Albuquerque.

Schneider, D. M. (1984) *A Critique of the Study of Kinship*, University of Michigan Press, Ann Arbor.

Shankman, P. (1984) 'The thick and the thin: on the interpretive theoretical program of Clifford Geertz', *Current Anthropology*, 25: 261–79.

Shweder, R. A. (1984a) 'Preview: a colloquy of culture theorists' in

R. A. Shweder and R. A. LeVine (eds) *Culture Theory: Essays on Mind, Self, and Emotion*, Cambridge University Press, Cambridge.

Shweder, R. A. (1984b) 'Anthropology's romantic rebellion against the Enlightenment, or there's more to thinking than reason and evidence' in R. A. Shweder and R. A. LeVine (eds) *Culture Theory: Essays on Mind, Self, and Emotion*, Cambridge University Press, Cambridge.

Silk, M. (1987) 'The hot history department; Princeton's influential faculty', *New York Times Magazine*, 19 April 1987, p. 42.

Spiro, M. E. (1986) 'Cultural relativism and the future of anthropology', *Cultural Anthropology*, 1: 259–86.

Turner, V. (1975) 'Symbolic studies', *Annual Review of Anthropology*, 4: 145–61.

Tyler, S. A. (1988) *The Unspeakable*, University of Wisconsin Press, Madison.

Walters, R. G. (1980) 'Signs of the times: Clifford Geertz and historians', *Social Research*, 47: 537–56.

Weber, M. (1949) *The Methodology of the Social Sciences*, Free Press, Glencoe.

Weber, M. (1958) *The Protestant Ethic and the Spirit of Capitalism*, Scribner's, New York.

Williams, R. (1973) 'Base and superstructure in Marxist cultural theory', *New Left Review*, 82: 3–16.

Williams, R. (1977) *Marxism and Literature*, Oxford University Press, Oxford.

Part III
Post-Structuralism

4

Roland Barthes: From Sign to Text

Bjørnar Olsen

Recently we have witnessed a steadily increasing influence of post-structuralism in works concerned with the interpretation of cultural production. While formerly being restricted to the domain of philosophy and literary theory and criticism, it now seems to have transgressed the border of its normal site, literary texts, and concepts such as 'inter-text', *'différance'*, 'deconstruction', etc., appear today frequently in other areas of cultural production as well. This expansion is undoubtedly related to the blurring of the boundaries of the textual itself, as we approach today the 'limitless text' of architecture, food, film, paintings, culture, time and social action.

Roland Barthes was central to the post-structuralist project, as he was to the semiological and structuralist projects preceding it. As a writer largely on the margin of the academic scene he played an important role in introducing the theoretical approaches of semiology and post-structuralism to a wider audience through an impressive number of articles and essays in newspapers and magazines. He was also a pioneer in applying these theories to cultural objects outside linguistics and literary texts, through his studies of the semiotics of food, photographs and fashion, the myths of mass culture, the 'rhetoric' of love, etc. He became famous for his demystification of the 'naturalness' and 'universality' with which newspapers, literature and common sense constantly dressed up a socially and historically determined reality. It is when history is denied, he says, that it is most unmistakably at work. By a radical integration of the reader in the production of the text, his literary criticism opposed the traditional notion of authors as producers and readers as consumers. He proclaimed 'the death of the author', and questioned the mimetic function of writing as a representation of reality or a 'dress to thought'.

Despite his various projects Roland Barthes was first and foremost a literary critic, and most of his work was articulated around writing and the literary text. This urges the sceptical question of why something taking place within a field so distant from archaeology as literary criticism should be worth considering by someone who mainly deals with an object world, i.e. the material culture of the past. To me there seem to be several parallels between literary criticism and archaeology, as well as between their 'subject-matters':

1   Both the literary critic and the archaeologist aim at an interpretation of 'texts', and both have a certain prerogative in conducting this task (the archaeologist is of course in a far more privileged position than the critic because archaeologists generally read each other's criticisms while literary criticism is, at best, a supplement to the ordinary reader).

2   Material culture can be seen as analogous to text, or, rather, it can read as text. As a literary text it is separated from the context of production, and like the most plural text it has an openness to signification which cannot be tied down to the intention of its 'author'.

3   Although archaeologists study an object world, this world only becomes archaeologically conceivable by the use of language (or meta-language). To make objects intelligible we transfer them into words, and this inescapable fact of textualization includes all analysis, description, observation and teaching. In short, archaeology *is* text, and to realize that we participate in the same structure as the epic, the novel and the drama is to let our own practice as producer of this text be examined by the same procedures as those applied to literary texts. It should itself be a target for criticism, i.e. a meta-archaeology.

In this chapter I will first draw a rough section of the stratigraphy of Barthes's writings, before I attempt a more detailed description and analysis of the various layers (mythology, semiology, writing, subjectivity, text and history). Finally, I will discuss the implications of Barthes's work for our contemporary practice of archaeology and for reading material culture and the past.

The Archaeology of Roland Barthes: Chronology and Typology

It is common to divide the works of Roland Barthes into an 'early' (and structuralist) phase and a 'late' (and post-structuralist) phase. However, a more detailed evaluation of his writing as it develops from the early 1950s until his death in 1980 suggests a more complex stratigraphy entailing the following four – partly overlapping – phases:

1   The first of these phases is marked by his 'committed' writings in the 1950s, which were clearly influenced by Marxism and Sartrean existentialism, as well as the phenomenology of Merleau-Ponty. This phase includes his two earliest works, *WDZ*, and *MPL*, which consider the relationship between writing, history and society, as well as his penetrating study of modern myths, *M*. The latter is one of the most effective critiques of bourgeois culture and ideology ever written, and contributed greatly to his fame outside the French intellectual scene.

2   At the same time as *M* brought to the fore his committed writing, conforming to the ideology critique formulated by the young Marx, it also initiated the next phase in the Barthes opus; the semiological and structuralist project of the 1960s. This project, which he later described as a 'euphoric dream of scientificity' (1971), was partly manifested in his works on literary criticism, *OR*, *CV* and *CE*, where he proposed a structuralist science of literature based on discoveries in structural linguistics from Saussure onwards. However, it is probably most clear in his semiological studies of non-linguistic sign systems, *EOS* and *FS*. The latter study represents the culmination of the semiological project initiated in *M*. It is his most technical and 'scientific' study, but it provides a brilliant analysis of the rhetoric of bourgeois society as exemplified by fashion.

3   What is considered as his shift from structuralism to post-structuralism denotes the third phase, of which *SZ* is regarded as diagnostic. This shift was clearly influenced by *Tel Quel* textualism and the writings of Derrida and Kristeva. *SZ* rejects parts of the structuralist project by proposing discourse formation to be the product of a structuration according to various codes rather than a manifestation of an underlying structure or grammar. More ambiguous representatives of this phase are *PT*, where he undertakes to write a theory of textual pleasure, and *SFL*, where he develops the psychoanalytic approach initiated in *OR*. However, in both of these works he develops his concern with textual plurality by showing how meaning explodes by integrating the reader and the moment of reading in the text being read.

4   His travel account on Japan, *ES*, his rather unorthodox autobiog-
     raphy *RB*, his rhetoric of love, *LD*, and his last book, *CL*, present
     Barthes as more a commentator than an analytical and critical
     writer. *LD* exemplifies the pleasure of reading discussed theoretically
     in *PT*. *CL* is described as his only novel (Lavers 1982: 214), and
     can be read both as a love story to his mother and as a series of
     theoretical reflections on photographs and history. This last phase,
     marked by his writings from the 1970s until his death in 1980, is
     often referred to as his 'hedonist' period. Gone is the technical
     complexity which characterized his writings of the 1960s, and
     which was even present in *SZ*. Commenting on his own develop-
     ment in this phase he wrote in *RB*: 'He had also worked
     successively under the aegis of a great system (Marx, Sartre,
     Brecht, Semiology, the Text). Today it seems to him that he
     writes more openly, more unprotected.' In his inaugural lecture at
     the Collège de France he foresaw the age of a new experience
     (replacing research): that of unlearning or forgetting. He called
     this experience 'Sapientia': 'no power, a little knowledge, a little
     wisdom, and as much flavour as possible' (*BR*: 478).

Those who dig for a lasting commitment to particular projects in the
writings of Roland Barthes are likely to be disappointed. Although
there are elements of continuity, as a result of his consistent denial of
the ideas of the transcendency of language and of human essence, his
writing conforms more to a perpetual movement. His refusal to be tied
down is articulated in his repeated shifts and by his mocking his own
previous procedures. Thus there is no distinctive 'Barthesian' approach
but rather many (semiology, structuralism, mythology, post-
structuralism, pleasure, etc.) to which his name has been attached.

Myth Production and the Political Creation of Meaning

It was *M* that brought Roland Barthes to the fore as a leading French
writer and intellectual, and it is probably the most frequently read of
his books. It consists of a collection of brief articles which appeared in
Les Lettres nouvelles between 1954 and 1956, to which is added a
lengthy theoretical essay called 'Myth today'. In *M* he undertakes to
show how modern society applies myths to naturalize socially determined meanings and thereby to eternalize the present state of the
world in the interests of the bourgeois. Everything which claims to be
universal and natural turns out to be cultural and historical. Myth is to
be found everywhere: in striptease, wrestling, the new Citroën car,

BARTHES: FROM SIGN TO TEXT

soap-powder and in the brain of Einstein. By social usage the most innocent, natural and utilitarian object achieves a *second-order* meaning. Wine is not only good to drink, it is also 'good to think' as a totem drink to the French, 'corresponding to the milk of the Dutch cow or the tea ceremonially taken by the British Royal Family' (*M*: 58).

Barthes's notion of 'myth' is closely related to the Marxist notion of ideology: a camera obscura which turned the world upside down, and made bourgeois reality appear as 'rational' and 'universal' (*M*: 141). Myth universalizes the world as immediate, self-evident and without contradictions, whereby the dominant order is presented as the natural order. Differences and social conflicts are just superficial features which, when torn away, reveal an essential human nature: Essential Man. This ideological content of myth is well displayed in one of Barthes's essays on an exhibition of photographs entitled 'The Great Family of Man', which aims at showing the 'universality of human action in the daily life of all the countries of the world: birth, death, work, knowledge, play, always impose the same types of behaviour' (*M*: 100). The exhibition proclaims that all humanity should be conceived as one great family where diversity is restricted to exterior features of human morphology. Like any classic humanism it postulates that by 'scratching the history of men a little, the relativity of their institutions or the superficial diversity of their skins (but why not ask the parents of Emmet Till, the young Negro assassinated by the Whites what *they* think of *The Great Family of Man*), one very quickly reaches the solid rock of a univeral human nature' (*M*: 101). To create this image of the unity of humanity the exhibition utilizes universal features such as birth, death and work. However, what is there to be said about these universal facts if history is removed from them?

> True, children are *always* born: but in the whole mass of the human problem, what does the 'essence' of this process matter to us, compared to its modes which, as for them, are perfectly historical? Whether or not the child is born with ease or difficulty, whether or not his birth causes suffering to his mother, whether or not he is threatened by a high mortality rate, whether or not such and such a type of future is open to him: this is what your Exhibition should be telling people, instead of an eternal lyricism of birth. (*M*: 102)

As it stands, the mythical function of this exhibition is to mask the shocking differences in social and economic conditions under which people are born, live and die, and eventually the political causes of these conditions, beneath the smooth surface of humanism.

A progressive humanism, on the contrary, aims at showing nature itself as historical. Because the very principle of the myth is that it has emptied reality of history ('for it is well known that History is not a good bourgeois') and has filled it with nature, 'it has removed from things their human meaning so as to make them signify human insignificance' (*M*: 142–3). The *Blue Guide* presents Spain as constructed for the tourists. It presents a picturesque landscape of monuments denuded of history. The guide rejects both explanations and phenomenology of a countryside which is real and which exists in time – Franco-time: 'To select only monuments suppresses at one stroke the reality of the land and of its people, it accounts for nothing of the present, that is, nothing historical, and as a consequence, the monuments themselves become undecipherable, therefore senseless' (*M*: 75–6). The landscape, the monuments and Spain itself appear as objectified and out of history; all one has to do is to enjoy these beautiful objects from which all soiling trace of origin or choice has been removed (*M*: 151). By removing history from the historical the innocent travel-guide latently supports the existing Fascist regime.

In the theoretical postscript to *M* Barthes defined myth as part of that project Saussure had termed 'semiology', a general science of signs, and this text is the first one where Barthes in an explicit manner makes use of concepts drawn from structural linguistics. Reflecting upon this change in an interview with *Tel Quel*, published in *CE*, he said:

> I have always been interested in what might be called the responsibility of form. But it was only at the end of my book *Mythologies* that I realized that this problem must be raised in terms of signification ... ever since the final fifty page essay of *Mythologies*, ideas and terms interest me less than the way society take possession of them in order to make them substance of a certain number of signifying systems. (*CE*: 150)

Thus myth was conceived as a semiological system, a system of signs with their signifiers and signifieds. According to Saussure the sign is a symbolic representation of a referent (e.g. the conceptualization of an object in language). It consists of an expressive level (signifier) and a content level (signified). The latter is a mental (or ideological) construction of the referent and must not be confused with the 'real object'. An essential point in the Saussurian notion of the sign is, moreover, that the relationship between the signifier and the signified is arbitrary (or, rather, unmotivated).

Although regarding myth as a semiological system, Barthes claimed that it was a peculiar one in that 'it is constructed from a semiological chain which existed before it: *it is a second-order semiological system*. That which is the sign in the first system, becomes a mere signifier in the second' (*M*: 114; emphasis in original). In semiological terms, myth is what Hjelmslev has called a connotative or second-order language. *Connotation* is defined as secondary meaning, whose signifier is itself constituted by the sign of the primary system of signification, which is *denotation* (*SZ*: 7; cf. *EOS*: 149–50) (figure 4.1). To put it simply, denotation is the direct or literal meaning, while connotation is the mythical or symbolic meaning.

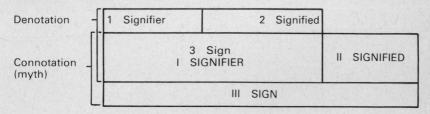

Figure 4.1
Source: after *M*: 115. By kind permission, Jonathan Cape Limited and Hill and Wang.

As an example Barthes cites the cover illustration of a French magazine: a picture of a young black soldier saluting the French flag. The direct, denotative meaning of this sign is just this reproduction of a black soldier and a French flag. But this denotative and perfectly justified meaning is taken over by a second-order system of meaning:

> whether naively or not, I see very well what it signifies to me: that France is a great Empire, that all her sons without colour discrimination, faithfully serve under her flag, and that there is no better answer to the detractors of an alleged colonialism than the zeal shown by this Negro in serving his so called oppressors. I am therefore again faced with a greater semiological system: there is a signifier, itself formed with a previous system (a black soldier is giving the French salute); there is a signified (it is here a purposeful mixture of Frenchness and militariness); finally there is a presence of the signified through the signifier'. (*M*: 115)

However, the defender of myth could always claim that the picture simply is showing a black soldier in French uniform, nothing more. Because when attacked myth always has an emergency exit: the denotative or first-order level of meaning.

Mythical production is characterized by the insistent imposition of given connotations upon denotative signs, what Lavers (1982: 104) has called a 'semantic overkill': a superimposition of a 'natural' layer on to what is already justified culturally. When nine out of ten advertisements for washing-powder or cooking utensils show women washing and cooking, this naturalizes the location of women at home.

The effect is to make the arbitrary relation between expression and ideological content into a 'natural' unity, something obvious beyond human explanation and interpretation. As Barthes notes, myth makes things 'go without saying', it gives them

> a natural and eternal justification . . . a clarity which is not that of an explanation but that of a statement of fact . . . it organizes a world which is without contradictions because it is without depth, a world wide open and wallowing in the evident, it establishes a blissful clarity: things appear to mean something by themselves. (M: 143)

And this is a common and subtle principle of all myths: they hide nothing, their function is to distort, not to make things disappear (M: 121). Thus, advertising does not hide or deny women's location in society. Quite the contrary, it exhibits this location as natural and given. Forced between a lie and a confession, myth finds a third way out: it naturalizes the social and historical determined appearance (M: 129). The function of this principle of 'that's the way it must be' is to legitimate and preserve the status quo of present-day society in favour of the ruling interests. Therefore, 'statistically, myth is on the right' (M: 148).

What allows the reader to consume myth innocently? According to Barthes the reason is that he or she does not see it as a semiological system but as an inductive one. Where there is only equivalence, he or she sees a kind of causal process: the signifier and the signified have, in his or her eyes, a natural relationship (M: 131). Thus, myth is read as reason. It is this confusion of a semiological system for an inductive or causal one which is at work when people see a causal elationship between capitalism and democracy, between private property and freedom, between Reagan and justice, and between human nature and profit maximization.

The Semiology of the World

Barthes's semiological project was brought to the fore by the publication of EOS. This book was a systematic presentation of some central concepts acquired from Ferdinand de Saussure (langue/parole, signifier/signified, syntagmatic/paradigmatic and diachrony/synchrony) and Louis Hjelmslev (denotation/connotation/metalanguage). These concepts from structural linguistics were applied to non-linguistic sign systems such as garments, food, furniture and architecture:

Semiology — aims to take in any system of signs, whatever their substance and limits; images, gestures, musical sounds, objects, and the complex associations of all these, which form the content of ritual, convention or public entertainment; these constitute, if not languages, at least systems of signification. (*EOS*: 77)

In the food system, for example, the *parole* consists of all events and variations of cooking and eating, while the *langue* is the systems of rules underlying their actual realization, such as rules of exclusion (edible/non-edible), rules of association, either simultaneous (at the level of a dish) or successive (at the level of a meal) and rituals of use (*EOS*: 94). A restaurant menu is a kind of 'food grammar': here we find syntagmatic slots (e.g. appetizers, soups, main course, desserts) and paradigmatic variations within each slot (e.g. the soups among which one chooses). We also clearly recognize the conventions governing the syntagmatic order of a meal: soup followed by main course then dessert is correct, whereas dessert followed by soup then main course is 'ungrammatical' (Culler 1983: 72–3), although there is nothing in the nature of these dishes which prevents such a combination. A main premise of semiology is that it denies the singular object any ontological quality; e.g. in language there are only differences without positive terms. Meaning is generated only through the oppositions and differences between objects, not by any given quality immanent in the object itself. 'Hot' only gets its meaning because there is an opposite term 'cold', as with 'good'/'bad', 'male'/'female', etc.

EOS was a methodological preface to Barthes's comprehensive study of the semiology of fashion advertising, *FS*. In these works he distinguishes between linguistics as the science of verbal signs and semiology as the science of object signs, i.e. the term semiology is reserved for non-linguistic signs (cf. *FS*: x). The difference between the linguistic sign and the semiological sign he locates in the relationship between signifier and signified. In the linguistic sign the relation between the signifier and signified is unmotivated (if not arbitrary), while many non-linguistic signs (objects, gestures, images) are at least partly motivated (*FS*: 215–16).

According to Barthes many semiological systems have a substance of expression whose essence is not to signify: clothes are used for protection and food for nourishment even if they also are used as signs. He proposes to call these semiological signs, whose origin is utilitarian and functional, 'sign-functions'. The sign-function is the very site where the technical and the significant are woven together: a fur-coat protects from the cold (denotation) while simultaneously signifying high social status (connotation) (*EOS*: 106–7). It is marked by an interplay between denotation and connotation, a double movement, which Barthes termed a 'semiological paradox': on the one hand it seems that all societies deploy a tireless activity of semantization 'by converting objects into signs ... on the other hand, once these systems are constituted ... human beings display an equal activity in masking their systematic nature, reconverting the semantic relation into a natural and rational one; therein lies a double process, simultaneously contradictory and complementary: of signification and of rationalization' (*FS*: 285). This transformation of sign into reason is the rhetoric of ideology (or myth) which gives it an emergency exit: the denotative level into which it can escape when named. Myth always has its alibi ready. People wear mink to keep them warm, not for its signification. The referent and the signified seems to unite, whereby the semiological sign naturalizes itself.

Even if *EOS* and *FS* deal with non-linguistic sign systems there is a clear privilege to language and speech in these studies:

> It is true that objects, images and patterns of behaviour can signify ... but never autonomously; every semiological system has its linguistic admixture ... to perceive what a substance signifies is inevitably to fall back on the individuation of language: there is no meaning which is not designated, and the world of signifieds is none other than that of language. (*EOS*: 78)

Thus Barthes inverted Saussure's classical formulation that linguistics was a part of a general science of signs (semiology), 'it is semiology which is part of linguistics' (*FS*: 79). Consequently, he chose to write only on fashion *writing* in *FS*, not on clothing itself, because in present-day society he found that objects as clothes only signified through their written or spoken *meta-languages* (see below). As he said in an interview: 'fashion exists only through the discourse of it' (Sontag 1982: xxiii).

> The reason is, of course, an economic one. Calculating, industrial society is obliged to form consumers who don't calculate; if clothing producers and consumers had the same consciousness, clothing would be bought (and produced) only at the very slow rate of its dilapidation ... In order to blunt the buyer's calculating consciousness, a veil must be drawn around the object – a veil of images, of reasons, of meanings ... in short a simulacrum of the real object must be created, substituting for the slow time of wear a sovereign time free to destroy itself by an act of annual potlatch. (*FS*: xi–xii)

It is not the object but the name that creates desire.

The concept of meta-language is of central concern to Barthes in these semiotic studies. Like denotation and connotation it was acquired from the works of Louis Hjelmslev. While the primary language (denotation) constitutes the plane of expression (signifier) of the second-order language (connotation), it constitutes the plane of content (signified) in the meta-language (figure 4.2) (*EOS*: 150–1; *FS*: 27–8). The meta-language speaks *about* another language or system. Archaeology, for example, is a meta-language of the past (while a study of archaeology itself would be a meta-archaeology).

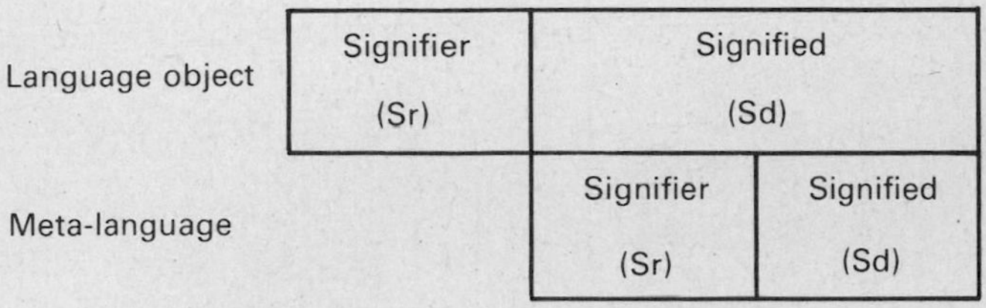

Language object	Signifier (Sr)	Signified (Sd)	
Meta-language		Signifier (Sr)	Signified (Sd)

Figure 4.2   Meta-language

Hjelmslev saw the meta-language as a neutral and scientific language beyond and opposed to connotations (Egebak 1972: 83). Barthes rejected this neutrality by showing how a meta-language itself signifies by at least connotating 'science', thus opposing the split between ideology and science latent in the task of demythification. Although it is evident that the political purpose of semiology at this stage was to unmask the signifying world of the bourgeois, Barthes never conceived it as an innocent science.

In his analysis of fashion as a rhetorical system (figure 4.3) he starts with the 'real' world (clothing/fashion/objects) with its signifiers and signifieds. This object world is taken over by a meta-language (fashion writing) which creates a simulacrum of the 'real' object. However, this meta-language itself becomes the denotative level of a con-notative (second-order or mythical) system, making it into the rhetorical expression (signifier) of its ideological content (signified). On top of this the analyst (e.g. the semiologist) constructs a meta-language in which (fashion as a rhetorical and mythical system is analysed.

If we ended here the analyst would be in the privileged position of having the objective function of deciphering and unmasking the alien truth of fashion mythology. However, this level can be taken over by another level (e.g. the myth of demythification), urging another meta-language, and so on (*FS*: 293–4). There is no truth to be recovered from this 'archaeology', only further and opposed levels of meanings.

Contrary to the various positivist conceptions of the critic's or

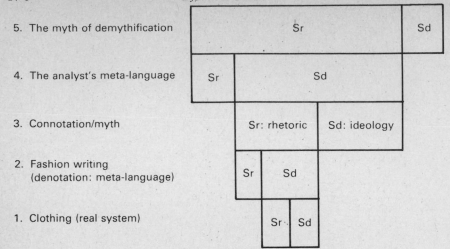

5. The myth of demythification

4. The analyst's meta-language

3. Connotation/myth

2. Fashion writing
   (denotation: meta-language)

1. Clothing (real system)

Figure 4.3   The rhetoric of fashion
Source: after *FS*: figure 3.9, p. 37. By kind permission, Jonathan Cape Limited
and Editions du Seuil.

scientist's role, Barthes argues against any external position of
certainty that is beyond history and society:

> The relation between the system-object and the analyst's metalanguage
> does not therefore imply any 'real' substance to be credited to the analyst,
> but only a formal validity; it is a relation at once ephemeral and necessary,
> for human knowledge cannot participate in the World's becoming except
> through a series of successive metalanguages, each of which is alienated in
> the moment which determines it ... the semiologist is a man who
> expresses his future death in the very terms in which he has named and
> understood the world (*FS*: 293–294).

Barthes consistently rejected the idea of transcendency, i.e. that which
can be taken to be the most real is in fact latent, submerged. However,
he eventually realized that his advocacy of a structuralist and
semiological science during the 1960s, in fact was contradictory to
this project. Also structuralism (*pace* Saussure), implying a priority to
an underlying model or grammar, of which all other signs were just a
secondary expression, was affected by what Derrida has termed a
'metaphysic of presence' (see chapter 5 of this volume). This transcendency was immanent in the concept of the sign itself because of the
distinction between signifier (expression) and signified (hidden content). The awareness of the ideological implications of the concept of
the sign led Barthes to abandon his 'scientific dream' and to join
Derrida and Kristeva in the critique of the sign. Referring to his
earlier strategy of 'demythification' (*M*) he now proposed a 'semio-

clasm': 'it is no longer the myths which need to be unmasked . . . it is
the sign itself which must be shaken; the problem is not to reveal the
(latent) meaning . . . to change or purify the symbols but to challenge
the symbolic itself' (*IMT*: 167). Later, in his inaugural lecture, he
proposed a 'negative semiology', 'not in that it repudiates the sign,
but in that it denies that it is possible to attribute to the sign traits
that are positive, fixed, ahistoric, acorporal, in short, scientific' (*BR*:
473). *ES*, his travel account on Japan, might be seen as an example of
this new semiology. In this work he gives his immediate reflections on
different aspects of Japanese culture such as puppet theatres (bunraku),
haiku, faces, food and gift-wrapping. In Japan he finds his utopia of a
culture which denies transcendence and celebrates the surface, the
signifiers. Like the Japanese practice of elaborate gift-wrapping it is
not what is inside, the content, which counts, but the wrapping.
Thus, in Japanese culture he found the ideal of 'the absence of all sign'
imagined already in *WDZ* (cf. *WDZ*: 6).

Writing the World

Like Sartre, Barthes devoted much effort to the task of defining the
role of the writer (the term defined in a very broad way); how a writer
relates to historical moment, what a writer's tasks are, and what a
writer can do in order to be assured of a place in history. In the conclusion of *M* he isolated the choice regarding the writer's (and
mythologist's) relation to society as being between 'ideologizing' and
'poeticizing' (*M*: 158–9). By 'ideologizing' he meant perpetuating the
ties among objects and things already assumed within a given culture;
to posit a reality which is entirely preamble to history; 'poeticizing'
breaks down our assumptions and posits a reality which is ultimately
impenetrable and irreducible. The latter causes readers to think and
act creatively, while ideologizing passifies and makes them redundant
(cf. Champagne 1984: 106–7).

Barthes's first published book, *WDZ*, was an attempt to write a
modern, Marxian history of French literature by investigating the
ideological implications of literary form. Five years earlier Jean-Paul
Sartre had published his influential book *What is Literature?*, claiming
that literature essentially should take up a position in the world, and
make it self a site for social and political commitment. Although
Barthes at this point clearly saw himself as a 'committed' writer, and
wanted to join Sartre's project, he opposed the simplicity in the
Sartrean idea that writers should 'bear witness to the world' by 'calling
things by their names' in an efficient, transparent langue (*WDZ*:

23–4). Contrary to Sartre, Barthes saw 'clarity' as the main ideological attribute of classical bourgeois writings: 'In actual fact', he argued, 'clarity is a purely rhetorical attribute, not a quality of language in general, which is possible at all times and in all places, but only the ideal appendage to a certain type of discourse, that which is given over to a permanent intention to persuade' (*WDZ*: 49).

WDZ traces the bourgeois style of writing and the responses to the crisis it ran into around the middle of the nineteenth century. The writers of the classical period (1650–1850) regarded themselves as 'witnesses to universal truth' and saw their own writing as an innocent reflection of reality. The realist or classical style was not conceived as a style at all, but as the only right and rational way of formulating written discourse, suitable for all times and places. However, after the moment of the third French Revolution in 1848, writers found themselves confronted with a new situation which made them unhappily aware of their historical and social location. Writers were no longer objective witnesses above and beyond history, but rather voices for different social and political alternatives. There was no universal, transparent mode of writing, and writers had to become self-conscious about style. As Culler notes (1983: 29), 'writing had to reflect upon itself as writing'. At this point Barthes clearly saw this change from classical to modern texts as epiphenomenal to major historical changes in the socio-economical sphere, mirroring the determinate role of base over superstructure in orthodox Marxism (cf. *WDZ*: 51, 53). The replacement of the transparent, classical '*écriture*', by a self-conscious, problematical and 'poetic' writing formed the basis for Barthes's ideal of a 'zero degree' writing, a style of 'absence' which denied transcendency and resisted ideological signification.

In an essay called 'Authors and writers' (reprinted in *CE*), Barthes asserts that language is neither an instrument nor a vehicle, but a structure (*CE*: 145). He makes a division between those writers who use language as an instrument to write something (*écrivants*/writers), what Sartre meant by a writer ('who calls a spade a spade'), and those who rather write (*écrivains*/authors). The writer mystifies the production of meaning, making it something finished, preconceived and objectified, rather than a product of intellectual labour. The text becomes the object of a fetishization, in the Marxist sense of the term, whereby the production is masked or mystified as a communication of fixed meanings.

> The writer is a transitive man . . . of which language is merely a means. For him language supports a praxis — it does not constitute one . . . For what defines the writer is the fact that his project of communication is

naive: he does not admit that his message is reflexive, that it closes over itself, and that we can read in it, diacritically, anything else but what he means. (*CE*: 147)

For the author (*écrivain*), on the other hand, to write is an intransitive verb. He or she does not aim to take us to any world or signified beyond the text, but concentrates on its signifiers. The only field of the author is writing itself, not as the 'pure' form conceived by an aesthetic of art for art's sake, but much more radically, as the only area for the one who writes (*CE*: 144–6).

Barthes is here confronting the problematic of the structure of language versus the structure of reality. To him these structures are totally different and to write is to lose the structure of the world in the structure of language. As soon as one sits down to write one becomes dislocated, made into a plaything of language. Instead of looking through language as a window to the world, Barthes urges us to look at language itself. Barthes's complaint against Sartre's committed writing is that it conceives language from the outside (*CE*: 98). 'By identifying himself with language', he notes, 'the author loses all claim to truth . . . This is why it is absurd to ask an author for "commitment": a "committed" author claims simultaneous participation in two structures' (*CE*: 146).

This clearly is of relevance also for a discussion of scientific texts and their relation to the structure they are realized in. The normal conception of language in science has been that

language is merely an instrument, which it chooses to make as transparent, as neutral as possible, subjugated to scientific matters (operations, hypothesis, results), which are said to exist outside it and to precede it: on one side and *first of all*, the contents of the scientific message, which are everything; and on the other and *afterwards*, the verbal form entrusted with expressing these contents, which is nothing. (*ROL*: 4)

For science then, language is only a means to create a simulacrum of its real object. Its main interest is said to be in its content, what it speaks *about*, not the act of speaking, hence the opposition between language objects and their meta-languages. This conception is clearly misconceived as it rests on the paternal model of 'science without language' (*ROL*: 10), that scientific truth exists as a kind of 'transcendental signified' outside and beyond the play of textual signification. Science can be examined like any other discourse since science, as meta-language, can only present itself in language; there is no exterior or neutral space on which it can inscribe itself (Ekebak 1972: 95). In this sense science cannot be opposed to literature as science exists only in a literary moment – all scientific knowledge is stored in writing (*BR*: 463).

The distinction which Hjelmslev originally drew between meta-language as neutral and scientific language, and connotative language as distorted and committed language cannot be accepted. Nothing – except silence – can prevent scientific discourse from connotation, from being made into the denotative level for a second-order system of signification. Because there is no possibility of closing the list of these levels (*ROL*: 35; cf. figure 4.3), science cannot escape the situation of simultaneously being meta-language and connotative language. Clearly this is of relevance for a deconstruction of the science–ideology split upheld in positivist epistemology and in certain Marxist approaches to ideology. The latter seem to assume that Marxist science will unmask false consciousness and recover true social reality. Such a positivist notion of science cannot be defended as it asserts the existency of universal understanding beyond society and history, i.e. beyond signification. Even the meta-language of the critical analyst who undertakes to decipher the myth of science as objective and neutral, cannot escape connotation (e.g. the myth of demythification) (*FS*: 293–4).

Scientific discourse tries to obviate this connotation and to objectify itself as innocent and neutral by applying rhetorical devices. The most typical is probably the way the writer tries to 'absent' him- or herself from the discourse through a systematic attempt to remove any sign referring to the sender of the scientific message. The effect of this attempt is to create a *referential illusion* whereby the referent (e.g. history or reality) seems to speak for itself (*ROL*: 132). However, this trick does not remove the writing subject from the text, it is rather a matter of how this subject constitutes him- or herself in discourse. As Barthes writes:

> what is excluded is never anything but the 'person' (psychological, emotional, biographical), not the subject; moreover, this subject is filled, so to speak, with the very exclusion it so spectacularly imposes upon its person, so that objectivity, on the level of discourse – an inevitable level, we must not forget – is an image-repertoire like any other. (*ROL*: 8)

The effect of this image is to assert authority on part of the writer and thereby to eliminate any dialogue with the readers. It is rhetorical in that it tries to persuade the reader by pretending to have an unchallenged access to reality. The fact that this 'realism' in scientific discourse is obtained by employing literary conventions (style, rhetoric) illustrates the power of language in the production of reality.

Subjectivity and Authorship

The writings of Roland Barthes express a strong distaste for the subject-centred Cartesian philosophy which dominated the French intellectual tradition, in which the self was identified with consciousness. Throughout his career this was manifested through his repeated attacks on the essentialist notion of the author as an autonomous ego, separated off from the text, and merely using it as an instrument for communicating a preconceived meaning. This also includes his own writings, to which he denies any authorial authority, 'it is not "me" who wrote *S/Z*: it's "us": all those "readings" rather than "authors" that I have directly cited and recalled' (1971: 102, translated in Champagne 1984: 33). Crucial in his rejection of individualism is the replacement of the idealist notion of self with the term 'body', referring to a transindividual (sub)consciousness: 'Whenever I attempt to analyze a text that has given me pleasure, it is not my subjectivity I encounter but . . . my enjoying body' (*SFL*: 7). His strangely arranged account of his own life and works, *RB*, exemplifies the way he de-centres the *person* Roland Barthes from his works. (This distance from his works is also manifested in the fact that he even reviewed this book for a magazine.) 'I abandon the exhausting pursuit of an old piece of myself, I do not try to restore myself (as we say of a monument). I do not say: "I am going to describe myself"; but: "I am writing a text, and I call it R. B."' (*RB*: 56). He thereby denies this text any authority as a main entrance to himself and his book is 'nothing but a further text' (*RB*: 120). A similar attempt at deconstructing his own authorial authority is manifested in *LD*, where he constantly refers to writers, composers and friends by noting their names in the margins, thereby suggesting other entrances to the text.

Barthes's insistent de-centring of the author from textual production is in some ways consistent with the project of the Anglo-American 'New Criticism' of the post-war years. However, while the New Critics assigned a superior role to the critic in the interpretation of texts (cf. Norris 1982: 2–3, Barthes de-centres the critic as well (cf. *IMT*: 147; *SZ*: 174). No privilege can be attached to the critic, and any attempt to authorize certain interpretations is to be rejected.

Barthes opposed the idea of human integrity or unity and professed instead a philosophy of disintegration, 'whereby the presumed unity of any individual is dissolved into a plurality and we each of us turn out to be many instead of one' (Sturrock 1979: 53). He regarded the idealist notion of 'human essence' as one of the big myths of bourgeois society, produced by the linked forces of protestantism and capitalism. This myth presents society as consisting of 'free' and 'independent' participants with 'individual' rights and 'individual' personality, and whose social fate results from their pre-given essence as 'clever', 'gifted', 'lazy', etc. This myth also created the image of the author's individuality and originality. Literature (due to its presumed trans- parency) was conceived as the subject's 'expression' of the self, a translation of personality into style: Ronsard had a sincere and profound Catholic faith; Villon, a cry from the heart, etc. (*ROL*: 27). This metaphysic considered meaning as prior to the appearance of the ego and knowable by it, 'but never calling into doubt the unity of the ego — precisely the guarantee of such knowledge' (Kristeva 1975, quoted in Coward and Ellis 1977: 124).

Barthes was highly critical of contemporary academic literary criticism. He saw it as a worshipping of the author, that this figure and his (*sic*!) doings was the only key to a qualified interpretation of the texts. In his work on the nineteenth-century historian Jules Michelet (*MPL*) he opens with the warning that 'In this little book the reader will not find either a history or Michelet's ideas, or a history of his life, still less an explanation of one by the other' (Sturrock 1979: 57). He dismisses Michelet's intention in favour of his own readings of grouped fragments from the texts, and the meanings this produces in the present context of reading. A similar lack of interest in the author is manifested in another early work, *OR*, which caused great antagonism from leading academic critics. The author himself is totally missing in Barthes's analysis of Racine's works, as are all those facts about his life and doings which critics normally bring in to interpret his play. He saw the plays of Racine not as filled with any pre-given meaning, but as 'an empty site eternally open to signification . . . Let us try out on Racine, in virtue of his very silence, all the languages our century suggest' (*OR*: ix–x).

In traditional literary criticism the author is regarded as the father and owner of the work, whose declared intentions are to be respected by those who read it. This centring of the author in textual production obviously implies a theme of *authority*:

> The author, it is believed, has certain rights over the reader, he constrains him to a certain meaning of the work, and this meaning is of course the right one, the real meaning: whence a critical morality of the right meaning (and of its defect, 'misreading'): we try to establish *what the author meant*, and not at all *what the reader understands*. (*ROL*: 30; emphasis in original)

The author is the only entrance to a qualified interpretation of the text, and the discovery of this figure 'beneath' the work becomes the important task of the critic: once the author is found, the text is explained (*IMT*: 147). Interpretation rests on the ability to grasp the author's intention behind the work. This can only happen through a careful reconstruction of 'the world of the author', the society he or she lived in, his or her immediate historical situation, personality, etc. In short, the text is explained by facts outside the text.

This contextual approach to the interpretation of texts was of course not solely an invention of literary criticism. It finds its philosophical heritage in the early hermeneutic conception of understanding developed by Schleiermacher and Dilthey, whereby to grasp the full meaning of a text one had to be able to put oneself into the place of its author. Historical distance was something one had to overcome by thinking oneself into the categories of past societies. This version of hermeneutics embedded two fundamental philosophical positions, on the one side the *Aufklärung* (Enlightenment) and its struggle against prejudices, and on the other romanticism and its nostalgia for the past (Ricoeur 1981a: 66). The 'openness of mind' of romantic hermeneutics was restored in Collingwood's idealist conception of historical understanding (1939; 1946), and the influence of the latter on the recent revival of 'contextualism' in archaeology (e.g. Hodder 1982; 1986) clarifies the philosophical heritage of this approach.

To desacralize the image of the author, to remove the author from the text, becomes a necessary operation to a new epistemology of reading: 'To give a text an Author is to impose a limit on that text, to furnish it with a final signified, to close the writing' (*IMT*: 147). Thus the birth of the reader has to be at the cost of the death of the author.

This deconstructs the notion of writing as a communication of the author's preconceived meaning, and of interpretation as an attempt to recover this meaning. Even the most self-conscious and critical writer can only circumscribe a small area of meaning. The reader who reads the text brings to it other voices and reads into it textual material which transforms this area of meaning far beyond the author's intention. It would be absurd to say that a text by Childe, for example, should have the same meaning today as it had in the moment of production, or that this meaning should conform to Childe's intention. We translate into the text the intervening history of theoretical and sociocultural development, we read into it things the author did not know about, and transform it to a product in the present. We 'try out' the text against our former readings, and explore the meanings it produces in the present moment.

Barthes's decentring of the subject in social and cultural production radically opposes the bourgeois myth of human beings as free and rational entities. This idealist conception of the subject as something

sacred which has to be restored, can even be traced far into critical
studies and aids at universalizing this late historical invention of
capitalism. The decentring of the subject in Barthes's writing is
closely related to his conception of power and of language as the site of
this power. In his inaugural lecture at the Collège de France, Barthes
opposes what he calls our modern innocence, which considers power as
a single thing: on the one hand those who have power, on the other
hand those who do not. Contrary to this opinion he finds power to be
present everywhere, even in the liberating movements which try to
counteract it. The reason for this is that power is inscribed in
language. As the subjects are totally imprisoned in language, we
cannot escape power without escaping language: 'If we call freedom
not only the capacity to ecape power but also and especially the
capacity to subjugate no one, the freedom can exist only outside
language. Unfortunately, human language has no exterior; there is no
exit' (BR: 461). The only solution to this dilemma is to 'cheat speech'
in the practice of writing. In the plural, writerly text (see p. 184) he
finds the very index of non-power: 'The Text contains in itself the
strength to elude gregorious speech, even when that speech seeks to
reconstitute itself in the Text' (BR: 473).

Approaches to Texts: From Grammar to Difference

What is a text? To clarify this we have to separate the linguistic level
(and structuralist theory) from the textual level (and post-structuralist
theory), two levels which often are confused in the recent celebration
of the 'textual metaphor' (e.g. Patrik 1985). Barthes's approach
shifted from the former to the latter level, and his notions of the text
can be conceived from both of these. Very briefly we might say that
the linguistic approach stops at the sentence, its object is the grammar
of sentence formation. Structuralists hold that there is a homological
relation between sentence formation and the formation of discourse,
that the sentence is perfectly and wholly representative of discourse.
The relationship between the sentence and the text is like that between
the flower and the bouquet: beyond the sentence are only more
sentences (IMT: 82–3). The textual approach within post-
structuralism (as within hermeneutics) rejects this linguistic reductionism; 'beyond the sentence', Barthes writes (ROL: 95), 'there is no
linguistics, for here discourse begins'. A text is conceived as totally
irreducible to the sentences of which it is composed, and discourse
formation cannot be modelled on linguistic grammar. A text, in short,
is what is going beyond the sentence and which resists the domination

of any preconceived system. However, Barthes's approaches cannot be reduced to such simplistic statements, and a more detailed consideration is needed, focusing on Barthes's shifting approaches to literary texts.

In a similar manner to which he had advocated semiology as the 'science of signs', *CV* proposed a structuralist 'science of literature' based upon the linguistic discoveries of Saussure, Jakobson, Greimas, Benveniste and Hjelmslev. At the core of this structuralist position was the Saussurian notion of *langue*, an underlying and unconscious structure of which *parole* was just a secondary expression. Originally *parole* was a linguistic concept, referring to speech, but later and especially due to the structuralism of Lévi-Strauss and the semiology of Barthes, any human manifestation could be analysed as governed by an underlying *langue*, 'insofar as it is likely that a similar formal organisation orders all semiotic systems' (*IMT*: 83). Hence a structuralist science of literature. This science could not be a science of content, but rather a science of the conditions of content, i.e. a science of forms (*CV*: 57). In *OR* Barthes undertakes to show how certain thematic oppositions 'moved' the plays of Racine and essentially contribute to generate meanings unintended by the author. This approach to literary texts is close to that applied by Lévi-Strauss in his structural studies of tribal myths.

The proposal of a 'literary science' led Barthes into a search for the universal nature of narratives, i.e. an underlying grammar or *langue* from which all of them are generated. In the article 'Introduction to the structural analysis of narratives' he defined as the aim of structuralism 'to master the infinity of utterances [*paroles*] by describing the 'language' [*langue*] of which they are produced and from which they can be generated' (*IMT*: 80). He modelled his ambition of a scientific approach to all the world's narratives on the deductive procedure of linguistics: 'Linguistics itself, with only some three thousand languages to embrace . . . has wisely turned deductive, a step which in fact marked its veritable constitution as a science and the beginning of its spectacular progress, it even succeeding in anticipating facts prior to their discovery' (*IMT*: 81). According to this scheme, narrative analysis was obliged first to work out a hypothetical model of description and then gradually to work down from this model towards the different narrative species (*IMT*: 81). It is far from clear what status he assigned to this model. In *CE* he defined it as 'a veritable fabrication of the world which resembles the primary one, not in order to copy it but to render it intelligible' (*CE*: 215), i.e. some kind of 'methodological structuralism'. However, in the next sentence he still talks about structuralism as 'essentially an activity of imitation' (*CE*:

215), giving such models an 'ontological' status. However, Barthes's
search for a 'grammar' of narrative that functions by drawing up
deductive models of their systematicity, such that any expression
could be predicted by their operation, clearly had positivistic over-
tones, as prediction is the basic requirement of a positivist notion of
science.

In *SZ* Barthes undertakes to show how certain discourse-formative
strategies produce the realist text as natural, and simultaneously to
deconstruct this dominant mode of writing, where the reader is
'reduced to a consumer, left with no more than the poor freedom to
accept or reject the text' (*SZ*: 4). Contrary to his former approach,
textual formation is now regarded as a process of structuration
according to various codes, rather than a generation of an underlying
structure or grammar as in sentence formation. Moreover, this
structuration is related to the reader's integration in the text, which
produces a basic typology of texts. This typology is based on the
distinction between those texts which give the reader a role, a
contribution to make, and those which render the reader idle or
redundant, as passive consumer. He used the term 'readerly' (*lisible*) to
refer to the latter type of texts, while the term 'writerly' (*scriptible*) was
used to refer to the former. This distinction corresponds dialectically
to the division he had made earlier between a writer (*écrivant*) and an
author (*écrivain*): a writer produces readerly texts (or 'works', cf. *IMT*:
155–64), an author produces writerly texts.

The readerly text, whose typical form is the realist or classical text,
is characterized by the unity between form (signifier) and content
(signified). It pretends to be an innocent representation, a mimesis, of
reality. The passage from signifier to signified is clear, established and
without contradictions. The readerly text is controlled by this
principle of non-contradiction (*SZ*: 156). It has a narrative structure
which makes us read horizontally from start to finish, revealing a
single, unified meaning. It employs rhetorical devices to tie together
the writer and reader in the production of meaning. It makes the
reader an inert consumer of the author's production. The readerly text
is always assigned an origin (an author, a character, a culture).
However, as Barthes was to show, it might happen that the voice gets
lost, and a certain polyvalence is revealed.

Contrary to the readerly text, the writerly text admits no easy
passage between signifier and signified. The writerly text is open to
the free play of signifiers and of difference; it is unconstrained by
representative consideration, and transgressive of any desire for a
unified, totalized meaning (Johnson 1980: 7). The writerly text is
ourselves writing, ourselves producing meaning; it is not a finished

product ready for consumption. Such texts invite the reader to 'join in', and offer us some kind of 'co-authorship'. In the writerly text, Barthes writes: 'the networks are many and interact, without any of them being able to surpass the rest, this text is a galaxy of signifiers, not a structure of signifieds, it has no beginning, it is reversible, we gain access to it by several entrances, none of which can be authoritatively claimed to be the main one' (SZ: 5). The reason why Barthes makes the writerly text his ideal is that it makes the reader no longer a consumer, but a producer of the text (SZ: 4). However, through a deconstructive reading of the readerly text it is possible to demonstrate that even this has a certain, limited, plurality, and it is exactly this plurality which SZ aims to demonstrate in *Sarrasine*, a typical realist novella by Balzac.

The reading technique consists of a slow-motion reading provided by cutting the story into 561 reading units ('lexias'), and the identification of the codes or voices on which each of them relies. Barthes singles out five such codes in terms of which each of the 561 lexias are analysed. Of these codes, the hermeneutic code and the action code produce the readerly texts. The hermeneutic code governs mystery and suspense, it constitutes the way which a narrative enigma can be distinguished, formulated, held in suspense and finally disclosed, while the action code is a series of actions which make the reader place details in plot sequences (SZ: 19). These establish permutable and reversible relations both within the text and exterior to it, as they operate outside the constraint of linear time (SZ: 30). Instead of manifesting a structure, these codes are producing a structuration by creating a network through which the entire text passes ('or rather, in passing becomes a text') (SZ: 20). The purpose of this 'dismantling' of the text is to destroy its 'naturalness', its smooth, readerly surface, and to pluralize the reader's reaction to it. Through this procedure the text loses any claim to unequivocal domination of one signifying system over another, and even the readerly text appears as an intertextual product of prior cultural discourses.

SZ was a turning-point in Barthes's career. Several commentators claimed that it reflected a shift from a structuralist to a post-structuralist mode of textual engagement, involving a shift of focus from sign to text, and from signified to signifier. It provocatively starts off with an attack on the structuralist procedure he once had proposed himself, by describing it as an attempt 'to see all the world's stories within a single structure: we shall, they thought, extract from each tale its model, then out of these models we shall make a great narrative structure, which we shall reapply (for verification) to any one narrative: a task as exhaustive as it is ultimately undesirable, because the text thereby loses its difference' (*SZ*: 3). Instead of treating the work as the manifestation of an underlying structure or system, the ultimate task for Barthes in *SZ* is to explore the text's 'difference'. The concept of 'difference' is crucial in constituting the plurality of the text (cf. Derrida's notion of *différance*; see chapter 5 of this volume). A text's 'difference' does not refer to its uniqueness of individuality (its difference from other texts), but to the difference existing within the text itself (*SZ*: 3, 6). It refers to the text's own fragmentation as a product woven of quotation from other texts, other languages, which traverse it through and through (*ROL*: 60). 'Difference' is what makes the totality and closure of a text impossible. As noted by Johnson (1980: 4):

> Difference, in other words, is not what distinguishes an identity from another. It is not a difference between, but a difference within. Far from constituting the text's unique identity, it is that which subverts the very idea of identity, infinitely deferring the possibility of adding up the sum of a text's parts or meanings and reaching a totalized intergrated whole.

The notion of 'inter-text', which Barthes adopted from Kristeva, is another way of expressing the plurality of the text. Inter-textuality refers to the transportation of one text into another within the matrix of all texts (not only written ones) (Kristeva 1986: 111). Every text is thus itself the intertext of another text, and cannot be identified with an origin or source: 'We know now that a text is not a line releasing a single "theological" meaning (the "message" of the Author–God) but a multi-dimensional space in which a variety of writings, none of them original blend and clash. The text is a tissue of quotations drawn from the innumerable centers of culture' (*IMT*: 146). Inter-textuality brings about a radical integration of the readers in the production of the text. The readers count for a considerable degree of transportation of textual material between various signifying systems. They translae their lives and experiences (former readings) into the text they read, and as they do this they establish legions of ties to other texts (cf. Drummond 1983). As noted by Champagne, 'parts of the reader's past enters into the present reading and gives it a physically present character' (1984: 108).

All texts, even those constrained by readerly codes, have a certain plurality. This textual plurality could only be perceived in the act of *re-reading*, an operation contrary to the commercial and ideological habits of our society, which would have us 'throw away' the story once it has been consumed (*SZ*: 15). Re-reading makes possible the discovery of textual plurality; each word or group of words reverberates with other and similar uses, opening on to limitless 'perspectives of fragments, of voices from other texts, other codes' (*SZ*: 12). Re-reading is a way of deconstructing the text's unity, to reveal its *jouissance* beneath the layer of readerly pleasure:

> reading, in short, is the permanent haemorrhage by which structure — patiently and usefully described by Structural Analysis — collapses, opens, is lost, thereby consonant with any logical system which ultimately nothing can close — leaving intact what we must call the movement of the subject and history: reading is the site where structure is made hysterical. (*ROL*: 43)

Deconstructive reading does not aim at destroying the text. If it destroys anything it is the text's unity and 'naturalness', and the claim to be the single voice of an author–god. Such reading does not consist of finding a hidden original meaning, but of revealing the polyvalence of the text. To read a text is like peeling an onion, Barthes writes, 'a superimposed construction of skins (of layers, of levels, of systems) whose volume contains, finally, no heart, no core, no secret, no irreducible principle, nothing but the very infinity of its envelopes — which envelop nothing other than the totality of its surfaces' (*ROL*: 99). Barthes is thereby reversing the traditional task of interpretation. 'In the multiplicity of writing', he notes (*IMT*: 147), 'everything is to be disentangled, nothing deciphered.'

The importance of the act of reading itself led Barthes to develop the ties between reading and physical desire. In *PT* he distinguishes between two forms of pleasure, that between 'normal' pleasure (*plaisir*) and delight or bliss ('*jouissance*'), and which refer to the opposite sensations to be had from reading a text. While pleasure is associated with the homely, cosy comfort of reading readerly texts, delight 'imposes a state of loss that discomforts (perhaps to the point of a certain boredom), unsettles the reader's historical, cultural, psychological assumptions, the consistency of his tastes, values, memories, brings to a crisis his relation with language' (*PT*: 14). Delight or *jouissance* (the connotations of *jouissance* in French are sexual) is the feeling of unsettledness we get from reading writerly texts (or at climactic moments of readerly ones).

Such 'hedonist' conceptions of reading, like pleasure and erotics (cf. *SFL* and *LD*), may seem to be simplistic and idealist, but on the contrary: 'the whole effort consists in materalizing the pleasure of the text, in making the text an object of pleasure like any other . . . to abolish the false opposition of practical and contemplative life. The pleasure of the text is just that: a claim lodged against the separation of the text' (*PT*: 58–9). Rather there is nothing outside the text, and this is precisely the inter-text: the impossibility of living outside the infinite text (*PT*).

Narrative and History

Barthes's (temporal) reputation as a leading structuralist made his works victims of the superficial critique directed towards structuralism as 'ahistoric' and 'static'. To cite a rather extreme opponent (Sumner 1979: 147): 'structuralism could be said to have taken the history out of history and left it with the rotting skeletons of form which act as signposts or monuments to an elusive, never-present reality. It is no wonder structuralists talk of "archaeology" '. I want to argue that this critique is misconceived, even for the period when Barthes wished to inscribe his work within the field of a structuralist science. Contrary to denying history, his projects challenge a linear and singular conception of history in favour of plural histories. As he responded himself to the critique of 'ahistoricism':

> But we are not outside of history. This must be explained . . . we are proposing the theory of a historical pluralism. Until now, we have had a purely linear, deterministic, and even a somewhat monistic history. Structuralism has helped to instigate the consciousness of a historical pluralism. We are not trying to abandon history. On the contrary, we try to complicate history. (1970: 11, translated in Champagne 1984: 119)

Barthes's distaste for linear history is manifested already in *WDZ*. He regards this linearity as an effect produced by the most common type of discourse formation, narrative writing, which he identified with an ideological representation of reality. According to Barthes, narration reduces a curved and plural world into a plane projection, 'the exploded reality to a slim and pure logos, without density, without volume, without spread, and whose sole function is to unite as rapidly as possible a cause and an end' (*WDZ*: 26–7). Narrative organizes past events as a pure linear serial of happenings ranked according to its internal chronology. The 'paper time' of narrative discourse breaks down the plural time of history, and presents historical time as linear duration. This temporal hierarchy between past events produces a logical link of unspoken causality: earlier events cause later events. Thus, narrative duration becomes simultaneously the representation and explanation of history. (Cf. Ricoeur 1981b for a strong counter-argument to this view, cf. chapter 2, this volume.)

Barthes finds that our entire civilization possesses an incessant need to authenticate the 'real', exemplified by the photograph, the realistic novel, documentary literature, museums, exhibitions of ancient artifacts, tourism to monuments and historical sites (*ROL*: 139, 146). All this aims at showing the 'real' as self-sufficient: 'To be simply true, to be what things are and nothing more than that, and nothing except that' (*ROL*: 148). Narrative history, which constituted itself as genre in the nineteenth century, instituted narration as a privileged signifier of the real. The 'pure and simple' relation between facts constituted by this discursive architecture, became the best proof of these facts (*ROL*: 140). It just related things 'as they really happened'. This presupposes, as White writes (1981: 6), 'a notion of reality in which "the true" is identified with "the real" only insofar as it can be shown to possess the character of narrative'. It is verified by its very structure without appeal to the substance of the content. The ordered sequence of events with well-marked beginning, middle and end phases thus becomes the signifier of history *per se*. The referent (history) seems to enter into a direct relation with the signifier, 'and the discourse, meant only to *express* the real, believes it elides the fundamental term of imaginary structures, which is the signified' (*ROL*: 138–9; emphasis in original). This produces what Barthes has termed the 'reality effect':

> in 'objective' history, the 'real' is never anything but an unformulated signified, sheltered behind the apparent omnipotence of the referent. This situation defines what we might call the *reality effect*. The extrusion of the signified outside the 'objective' discourse, letting the 'real' and its expression apparently confront each other, does not fail to produce a new meaning, so true is it, once more, that within a system any absence of an element is itself a signification. This new meaning – extensive to all historical discourse and ultimately defining its pertinence – is reality itself, surreptitiously transformed into a 'shamefaced' signifier: historical discourse does not follow the real, it merely signifies it, constantly repeating *this happened*. (*ROL*: 139; emphasis in original)

In other words, by the very absence of the signified, to the advantage of the referent which it merely pretends to describe, narrative becomes the signifier of reality. It creates a simulacrum of the structure of historical events, a meta-language which pretends to be an imitation of historical duration. This produces what Barthes termed a 'referential illusion' typical of 'objective' history: the historian claims to let history speak for itself (*ROL*: 132). This illusion is of course not proper to historical discourse. As mentioned earlier, in realist literature the text was regarded as transparent, a means to reflect or represent reality based on the idea that the highest art conceals art in the hope of being mistaken for reality (Sturrock 1979: 55). 'What is "imaginary" about any *narrative* representation', Hayden White writes (1984: 14), 'is the illusion of a centred consciousness capable of looking out on the world, apprehending its structure and process, and representing them to itself as having all of the formal coherency of narrativity itself.'

A considerable part of Barthes's writing from *WDZ* onwards was devoted to the deconstruction of this mimetic image of narratives. Regarding past events, these have their only existence in the present though their various meta-languages, of which the writing of history is the most prominent. This intervention of language creates the paradox of historical discourse: facts never have anything but a linguistic existence, 'yet everything happens as if this linguistic existence were merely a pure and simple "copy" of *another* existence, situated in the extra-structural field, the "real"' (*ROL*: 138). Since a multidimensional order (the real) cannot be made to coincide with a unidimensional order (language) this causes a contradiction between the 'representative reality' and the 'real reality' (*BR*: 465). As the discourse of history never has anything but a linguistic existence, the opposition between fictive narrative and historical narrative is false (*ROL*: 127). This also challenges the too-readily-accepted division between 'historical' (or 'hot') and 'non-historical' (or 'cold') people, since the ordering principle of narration is common to both 'savage myths' and Western 'historical knowledge' (White 1984: 11–12, 31–3; cf. Lévi-Strauss 1966: 248–62; *IMT*: 79).

Barthes's critique against narrative history is in some way consistent with the objections raised by the Annales school, and in his early phase he clearly admired Febvre and Braudel for constructing a new history which abandoned the narrative of events in favour of the analysis of structures. However, he was clearly opposed to the Annales's project of a 'total history' (cf. Braudel 1980) and their positivist aspiration to make historical studies into a kind of science. Their realism consists in a desire to show how the past reality was, irrespective of how it was seen by those who lived in it. This reality was largely constructed on 'hard structures' outside human signification, such as climate, ecology and demography (Clark 1985: 189–90).

In the passage quoted earlier Barthes said he wanted to 'complicate' history through a 'historical pluralism'. He is far from formulating any programme for what such a history should look like, rather it is to be indicated from his own inquiries in literary history. As has already been stated, this entailed a deconstruction of the notions of textual origin and mimesis. He made us aware of how interpretation is overdetermined by society through its various forms of censorship on the ways in which we can read past texts. For example, a certain number of key doctrines were used to individualize different periods and to unify the meaning of the texts produced within each of them, such as classicism or the Renaissance (*ROL*: 22–8; Champagne 1984: 103). This is a 'centred' history which would, as Lentricchia writes (1980: xiv), 'generate itself as a unity and a totality while resisting forces of heterogeneity, contradiction, fragmentation, and difference: a "history", in short, which would deny "histories"'.

Contrary to this singular and coherent conception of history Barthes opted for a pluralization of history: 'Each historical moment may think that it has isolated the canonical meaning of a work, but we only need to expand one's view of history a bit to transform this singular meaning into plural meanings and the closed work into an open work' (*CV*: 50, translated in Champagne 1984: 72). In *SFL* Barthes shows how the texts of Sade, Fourier and Loyola resist being tied down to their own historical moment of creation. Rather they establish a 'paradigmatic relationship' to society and writing. Such a paradigmatic relationship allows the text to form ties to any historical moment. As he did on the texts of Michelet (*MPL*) and Racine (*OR*) he wants to 'try out' the effects and shock-value (the *jouissance*) produced by texts when they exceed the univocal expectations of a certain culture at a particular historical moment. This entails an expansion of our understanding of a text's historical connections by establishing a dialogue of the text with other texts in other historical moments (Champagne 1984: 119–20). An essential link in this dialogue is the reader, 'who holds together in a single field all the traces by which the written text is constituted' (*IMT*: 148). By re-writing a reading the reader (or the reader–writer) incorporates into it his or her own historical moment and readings from other texts, linking them together in one signifying practice. Historical reading becomes an inter-textual activity forming ties to a vast corpus of past and present texts which breaks down the linearity and coherence of history. We read, we remember, we intersect – no origin, no end, no authoritative version, only fragments in the enormous grid of history. History itself – as any other text – is a plural composition, a system without end or centre, which can only be understood in terms of its difference.

Archaeology and Material Culture as Texts

In the final part of this paper I shall discuss how Barthes's projects as outlined above may affect our understanding of material culture and of our contemporary practice of archaeology. This will be done in relation to three areas. The first considers archaeology as written discourse, and problems of writing the past and material culture; the second contains a brief exposure of writing and the mythical production of the past; and the third focuses on material culture as text and considers a new epistemology for reading these texts and the past.

Archaeology as Written Discourse

Archaeology is discourse of the past in the present. It is a meta-language which has ancient objects and the past as its language object. Archaeology exists only as text. Every analysis, teaching, observation, classification and description is formulated, transmitted and stored in language. A material object is an archaeological object only in so far as it is realized as text (site reports, catalogues, etc.). Even a photographed or exhibited item gets its identity from the sub-text (or meta-text) which always accompanies it. Thus, the existence and identity of archaeology consists in the inescapable fact of textualization.

While textualization has attracted considerable attention in ethnography (e.g. Clifford and Marcus 1986) and history (e.g. White 1981; 1984), few – if any – archaeologists have seriously considered the implication of the transformation from real objects to meta-language. Most archaeologists regard language only as a means for communication and representation, and the only celebrated genre or style of writing is clarity. 'Write so that people can understand you!' Writing is conceived as transparent both to the past and to the mind of the archaeologist. The archaeologist is an *écrivant*, a writer, who first conceives the signified and then finds for it, according to the chance of his (gender intentional!) imagination, 'good' signifiers. We are always supposed to go from signified to signifier, from content to form, from idea to text. Not only do the signifier and the signified seem to unite in archaeological texts, but 'the signifier seems to erase itself or to become transparent, in order to allow the concept to present itself as what it is, referring to nothing other than its presence' (Derrida 1978: 22).

Barthes's works urge us to adopt a critical stance to the writing of archaeological texts, and to be aware of the implications of textualization, i.e. the movement from our language object to our meta-language. It is necessary to advance our awareness of the fictional quality of archaeological writings and the way literary conventions produce effects such as 'realism' and authorial authority. Although it constitutes a very rare example in archaeology, Flannery's *The Golden Marshalltown* (1982), is illuminating for the image and persuasive power created by a certain style of writing. In this novel the author places himself within the story, not as an active participant but mainly as an observer of the other characters who play the roles as advocates of opposing views on archaeology. The stereotyped script soon makes us sympathize with the 'Oldtimer', whose view on the practice of archaeology makes up the concluding moral to the story: stop the speculative theorizing and go back to digging. The rhetoric of this message is strong because of the literary form applied: it is the characters who are speaking, the author only reproduces it 'just as it happened'. The writer has 'absented' himself from the story, which seems to tell itself. The archaeological world appears as already narrated, 'speaking for itself' in the form of a well-made story. This referential illusion does not remove Flannery from the text, it is rather a matter of *how* he constitutes himself in the text, applying rhetorical devices to tie the reading to the writer's intentions.

In archaeological narratives experiential images are often used to create the authority of the writer, for example through a detailed introductory description of the site, its environment, etc., creating an 'I-was-there-so-I-know-it'-image, which aims at quieting all critical voices. This image can be further strengthened by a simultaneous careful selection of personal nouns, either by omitting self-referential signs and thereby absenting the archaeologist from the story, letting the site or the past 'speak for itself', or by universalizing the author's experiences by applying signs of collective references ('As *we* can see from this'), making the reader into a hostage of the author's intention. The effect of these referential illusions is to produce archaeological data as given and beyond signification, whereby the signifiers of the (meta-)text enter into a seemingly direct relationship with the referent, eliding the mental construction, i.e. the signified. However, the 'reality effect' produced by this archaeological realism is an ideological or mythical construction, because of the attempt to mask an imaginary constructed signified as immediate and universal reality. A critical stand to archaeological writing urges us to deconstruct this mimetic myth of realism, and to show it as a rhetorical device used to assert authority on behalf of the writer. Such a demystification of archaeological realism does not aim to take us to a more true or real level of writing the past, but to expose the fictional quality embedded in all writing.

In this connection it is also worth considering the *readerly* element in archaeological writing. On the discourse-formative level archaeological realism is a product of readerly codes. These codes force an irreversible and linear order on archaeological texts. We read from beginning to end, and 'the end' achieves a connotation which goes beyond the actual termination of the text being read. In a relation of simultaneity the readerly text offers a destination, the end of the text, it also offers one intention, one overall meaning. Most archaeological narratives start off by posing a question which conforms to the formulation of the enigma in a detective story. As in the latter, the hermeneutic code structures the archaeological enigma, holds it in suspense while the story unfolds, creates expectations by arranging details as possible contributions to its solution, and finally discloses it in the last chapter after being delayed and suppressed in all the former chapters. Then, as in other narratives, expectation becomes the basic condition for truth; 'Truth is what is at the end of the expectation. Truth is what completes, what closes' (SZ: 76). Writing 'the end' or 'conclusion' dissolves the tension and re-establishes harmony in the archaeological reader.

A critical attitude toward archaeological texts also implies a questioning of the role assigned to the archaeologist as central to archaeological discourse, and to deconstruct the positivist notion of the scientist as an essentialist subject who is separated off from the text, and uses it only as an instrument of communication. All texts – even readerly scientific texts – are products of multitudes of codes and voices related to history and textual production itself. Language, which archaeology has as its only space to unfold its meta-language, is never innocent or neutral. This space is characterized more by what it compels us to say, than what it permits us to say. We are not free to choose our way of expression. Language carries with it a considerable number of presuppositions of all types. Every word and formulation have been written earlier and have been loaded with a seemingly 'natural' layer of signification from history and culture (such as expressions having gender connotations). Writing is a meaning-constitutive action. This signification is largely outside our control.

All this questions the validity of any strict division between archaeology and fiction. Archaeology as discourse participates in the same structure as the epic, the novel and the drama, and we are in no privileged position to make authorized truth claims about a world outside this structure. Archaeological facts never have any but a linguistic existence. This breaks down the naive assumption of archaeological writing as a pure reflection or representation of its language object. Archaeology as text makes up a unidimensional structure which cannot be made to coincide with reality. The inescapable fact of textualization implies constraints both on sentence and discourse formation which forces the 'representative reality' to be different from the 'real reality'. The 'real world' has no preface, introduction, analysis, conclusion or any other arrangements of plots similar to archaeological texts. According to the later Barthes it has no grammar either.

Writing and the Ideological Construction of the Past

Our activities as archaeologists consist in dismantling an object (the past, material culture) and reconstructing a simulacrum of it in our meta-language. This urges the question of the ideological function of textualization, and what we do in terms of signification when we transfer objects into words.

Material objects are polysemeous. Underlying their signifiers is, as Barthes noted for the image, 'a "floating chain" of signifieds' (*IMT*: 39). This polysemy creates uncertainty, disquieting in a civilization which likes signs but likes them to be clear (*IMT*: 29). The lack of control over the signifieds urges a means to channel them, to tie the signifier and signified together, in order to impose a certain meaning on the object: 'Hence in every society various techniques are developed intended to *fix* the floating chain of signifieds in such a way as to counter the terror of uncertain signs; the linguistic message is one of these techniques' (*IMT*: 39; emphasis in original). The past appears as chaotic and out of control, prehistoric objects may signify anything. The construction of a simulacrum of it in language is a way of coping with this worrying plurality. This transformation can be seen as turning the writerly and plural into the readerly and singular. We recognize it in the prehistoric exhibits in museums and in archaeological textbooks, everywhere it is the (meta-)text which imposes the signifieds. The transformation from a material object (i.e. a piece of burnt clay with ornamentation) to meta-language ('This is a beaker'), involves a dramatic reduction of the object's possible signification. The intervention of the linguistic message loads the object with a preconceived signified, burdens it with a culture, a moral, an interpretation (*IMT*: 26): 'the text *directs* the reader through the signifieds of the image, causing him to avoid some and receive others; by means of an often subtle *dispatching*, it remote-controls him towards a meaning chosen in advance . . . With the respect to the liberty of the signifieds of the image, the text has thus a *repressive* value' (*IMT*: 40; emphasis in original). The meta-text is rhetorical, it persuades the reader of the material object to accept a predetermined interpretation. It urges a closure of signification, makes the past into a readerly narrative, and thereby reaffirms our power over it. This closure of signification through the meta-text is a necessary presupposition for myth-production, since 'it is at this level the morality and ideology of a society are above all invested' (*IMT*: 40).

What are the morality and ideology invested in archaeology as written discourse in the present? To most people there is nothing ideological at all in archaeology and this of course makes it a perfect site for myth. Mainstream Western archaeology, dealing only with the distant past, has achieved a presumed innocence and a daydream-like image. Reading archaeological texts or visiting the museum entails a mystery of readerly, comforting pleasure without any distorting moments. The prehistoric monument is fetishized, as an object of pleasure out of time and place. Surrounded by descriptions such as 'majestic', 'magnificent', 'glorious' or 'elegant' it seems to conform to the universal aesthetic of the bourgeois: 'all that is left for one to do is to enjoy this beautiful object without wondering where it comes from. Or even better: it can only come from eternity: since the beginning of time, it has been made for bourgeois man' (M: 151). It is exactly a presumed innocence which has made archaeology into an ideal supplier of familiar bourgeois myths about human essence, individuality and rationality. What archaeology supplies these myths with is historical 'reality', and what myth gives in return is a *natural* image of this reality (M: 142). Thus, paradoxically, the supply of historical reality to myth contributes to the process of depriving the object of which it speaks of all history, and turning it into nature. When myth has finished there is nothing historical or cultural about rational calculation, individualism or humanism; these are all values embedded in human nature. From palaeolithic flakes, neolithic potsherds and Bronze Age burials only one figure rises: Essential Man. The past has been turned into a story of homely, comforting pleasure, well suited to confirm the bourgeois experience. The favourite story of the bourgeoisie must be the very familiar one about palaeolithic society where the hunter appears in the role of the rational decision-maker who conducts a cost—benefit analysis ('minimizing costs, maximizing profit') in advance of any hunting trip. The second-order meaning of this story is simple and unambiguous: profit maximization and rational calculation is part of human nature. Thus, on the connotative level it universalizes bourgeois experience by silently saying 'That's the way it must be. Look, it has always been like this.'

By imposing present sectional values, images and attitudes on the past, their present appearance becomes naturalized and universalized. The arbitrary relations between people, objects and actions on the one hand, and their historical and social connotations on the other, are in myth tied together in a natural and obvious unity. Myth has turned history itself into a sign, where the political and cultural present becomes the connotative level of the (denotative) past.

Reading Material Culture

Regarding the problem of material culture as text in the light of the writings of Barthes, we have to start with a few considerations of the relationship between material culture and language. In those texts where Barthes most extensively worked with non-linguistic sign systems, *EOS* and *FS*, he clearly regarded material culture as subordinate to language. Even if objects and images can signify, they never do this autonomously, 'every semiological system has its linguistic admixture' (*EOS*: 78); further, 'Is not speech the inevitable relay of any signifying system?' (*FS*: xi). Even if I think that this question is not as straightforward as many archaeologists seem to think, and that language plays an extremely important role in the production of signification from material culture, I still think Barthes in this 'scientific' phase treated material culture in very much the same way as writing has been distrusted in western tradition. This tradition of 'logocentrism' has privileged speech as being the undistorted reflections of the mind and the only reliable access to meaning, writing being unreliable because it operates without the presence of its producer (Derrida 1978: 10–11, 22; cf. chapter 5 of this volume). In the light of the later writings of Barthes I think we rather should regard material culture as a plural text and as a space where speech can be 'cheated'; it contains in itself the strength to elude speech, even when that speech seeks to reconstitute itself in the text (*BR*: 473). In the same way as we have started to think of material culture as a space where power can be inscribed, I think it also should be conceived as a possible space outside the power of language.

The work of Roland Barthes suggests a new epistemology for reading past material texts because it strongly challenges the authority of origin which dominates archaeological epistemology. This obsession with origin has constituted archaeology as a practice of unravelling, a search for an ultimate meaning somewhere in the past, of which ancient objects were just secondary expressions. Within this epistemology any meaning assigned to material culture has to be legitimized as the original meaning, preconceived in the minds of those who produced it. This reflects the 'logocentric' tradition of western metaphysics, where meaning is regarded as preconceived, existing before and outside the text. Using the metaphor of reading texts and regarding ourselves as critics, our practice is characterized by our trying 'to establish *what the author meant*, and not at all *what the reader understands*' (*ROL*: 30). Hence the prototype archaeological questions: what was the meaning or idea *behind* the monument or object? This desire for the origin of meaning appears in its archaeologically most sophisticated form in the so-called 'contextual archaeology' (Hodder 1982; 1986). Founded on the heritage of the hermeneutics of the romantic period, and consistent with the framework of traditional literary criticism, this approach attempts the impossible task of putting oneself in the place of the prehistoric 'authors'. A new epistemology of reading material culture goes beyond the nostalgia of this origin-centred contextualism, and proposes instead a 'decontextualized' approach.

The archaeological discipline aims at a closure of the troubling plurality of the past; it aims at an interpretation, fixing a meaning, finding a source (the author) and an ending (the truth) (Coward and Ellis 1977: 45). It is interesting to ask why we do have this desire for the true signified of the past, and why we fear the pluralism of meaning as suggested by Barthes (soon to be condemned as 'extreme relativism', 'anarchism', etc.). I think the answer is to be found, at least partly, in a fear of losing power as privileged speakers of the past. As we have learnt from Nietzsche and Foucault, truth has always been in the service of power. Power appears in the discourse of knowledge as 'rules of exclusion'; rules which distinguish the true from the untrue, reason from unreason, and determines who has the right to speak on a given subject (see Chapter 6 of this volume). Every discourse produces certain criteria to verify whether a statement is 'within the true', and archaeological discourse legitimizes its truths as being original, preconceived and only recovered from the past. This is to distinguish them from 'untrue superstitions' produced by non-archaeologists in the present. The desire for power in the present is masked as the desire for knowledge of the past. Thus the tyranny of the past serves the power of the present. The pluralism suggested by Barthes is a threat to any authoritative and disciplined version of the past. It liberates the reader and dismantles the privilege of the archaeologist to decipher the past.

This approach does not aim at closing the reading of a material text around any ultimate signified, origin or truth, but to appreciate the text as open and plural. What is 'new' to this approach is that it radically incorporates the reader in the production of meaning, and regards both the text and the reader as inter-textual constructs. Rather than attempting the impossible task of recovering a lost origin it points to the necessity of creative interpretation without looking to the past for legitimation and confirmation. Barthes has created 'a case for a new epistemology whereby the signifier constantly generates new knowledge without returning to the past merely to confirm its existence and to close the realm of human understanding' (Champagne 1984: 75). The meanings of things are not hidden at a depth where an original signified can be recovered, but are produced by repeated confrontation with the readers. This new 'vision' is formulated in the following manner by Barthes:

> a text is made of multiple writings, drawn from many cultures and entering into mutual relations of dialogue, parody and contestation, but there is one place where this multiplicity is focused and that place is the reader, not, as was hitherto said, the author. The reader is the space on which all the quotations that make up a writing are inscribed without any of them being lost; a text unity lies not in its origin but in its destination. (*IMT*: 148).

How do we read material culture? If we consider well-known archaeological monuments, such as megaliths, we will find that most approaches to these texts have been characterized by logocentric questions, such as: what was the idea behind their creation? Few have asked *how* megaliths meant, what thoughts they stimulated, or about the plurality of meanings obtained through 6,000 years of reading into them the ever-changing experiences and former readings of neolithic women, Bronze Age men, medieval priests, not to mention the tourists and archaeologists of our own time.

Rather than regarding megaliths as filled with a pre-given meaning which has to be thawed out, we should, as Barthes suggested for the plays of Racine (*OR:* ix–x), regard them as an 'empty site' eternally open to signification. This openness creates a paradigmatic relationship to society, which allows megaliths to establish ties to any historical moment and culture (cf. Champagne 1984: 19). A material text, such as a megalith, is in many ways more open, more radically plural, carnivalesque and out of authorial control, than any literary text. Even if we imagine the megalith-builders as rational Cartesian subjects who wanted to translate a certain preconceived meaning into a megalith design, the monument soon became separated from the context of meaning controlled by these 'authors'. It became 'decontextualized' (or liberated) from the historical moment of creation, and committed to new readers and the future. Due to its veritable duration this material text opens itself to infinite readings as it continuously confronts new readers in altered historical situations. Its origin became lost in its own creation. Only the material signifier remains constant, the signifieds are repeatedly created and lost through the historical act of re-reading.

It is exactly this process of re-reading which makes possible the 'opening' of the polyvalence of the text. This reading is matter of translation rather than recovering. We read into the text, rather than out of it. Confronting these material texts as readers we translate into them our former readings, establishing a multitude of connections to a vast body of past and present texts. By creating ties to both preceding and succeeding texts we are reversing the linear conception of historical communication into a kind of zigzag history. These multitudes of ties and quotations drawn from innumerable sources are gathered in one place only, the reader, who carries in herself all alone the megalithic 'difference'. Because the reader who confronts the megalith in ever-changing historical and cultural circumstances is not an empty space, but an inter-textual construct of other and already-read texts (*SZ*: 10). These texts may consist of different signifying materials: written, material, memories, emotions, etc. Thus we not only establish links with other material texts drawn from 'objective' history (e.g. prehistoric burials, henges and houses), but also translate into it signifying material from the 'subjective' history of our own bodies and present circumstances. Inter-textuality as defined by Kristeva (1986: 111) 'denotes this transportation of one (or several) sign-system(s) into another'. The denoted object – in this case the megalith – is never 'single, complete and identical to itself, but always plural, shattered, capable of being tabulated' (Kristeva 1986: 111).

Our logocentric attitude towards material culture has made us think that the process of signification has travelled from meaning to objects, from content to expression. Rather than regarding the prehistoric producers of megaliths as *écrivants*, who knew what they wanted to express and then decided *how* to express it, it might be better to conceive them as *écrivains*, who first decided how to express it and then found out what it was. As a consequence we should stop hunting for a preconceived signified before and outside the text, and concentrate more on the signifiers – the megaliths themselves – and how these have stimulated thinking on various subjects. If megaliths, through their inter-textual ties to other texts, have stimulated thinking on, let us say, control over nature or linear time – or even on present-day tourism – this has not come through as preconceived ideas to which megaliths only were illustrations, but as the result of the 'free play' of these signifiers themselves.

What then is the truth about megaliths? Have not we as modern and reflective archaeologists made sufficient progress that we can claim our interpretations as better or 'closer' than previous ones? Such questions are obviously misplaced. Even if we by chance should come across ideas close to those held by the prehistoric producer (how should we know?), nothing says that these can be privileged as the 'right' ones. The plurality of meanings obtained through the historical process of re-reading can hardly be ranked according to their presumed veracity. Each and all of these readings are in a sense 'true', even if arguments, rhetoric or power in different contexts may favour one reading over others. First and foremost we have to learn to appreciate our own historically situated understanding, without attempting to legitimize it as original and recovered from somewhere in the past. This realization of the temporal character of our understanding should not be judged as negative — as misunderstanding — but as positive and productive understanding. If megaliths speak to us as living and associative reality then this situational understanding principally has, as Gadamer (1975) would have said, the quality of 'truth experience' (*Wahrheitsgeschehen*).

Does this leave us in a position where we have to accept any version of the past as 'true' or just another story about it? In other words, does the new epistemology of reading as suggested by Barthes impose an extreme relativism on archaeological interpretation? Obviously the answer will be 'yes' among those who cling to a position in which truth is a single and united thing which can be measured and revealed according to universal standards, and to whom 'relativism' denotes any position which goes beyond this objectivism. Unfortunately these two related terms of objectivism and relativism have been monopolized as complementary and exclusive in much of the western philosophical debate, making the epistemology of truth into a crude semiology of 'yes' or 'no'.

However, leaving this position aside we still have to consider what we will do to readings of the past we do not like (positivist, functionalist, rightist). Can the pluralism suggested by Barthes be used to legitimize readings which we find devastating, reactionary or racist? I do not think so if by this we mean our ability or 'legitimacy' to openly argue against such readings. If we consider a text such as the present one, it is obvious that I cannot control the readings of it. You who read it might read into it meanings far beyond my intention. Still, the sudden 'death of the author' does not deny me the right to argue against interpretations of this text that I do not like. Surely, what it denies me is the right to argue for any privileged interpretation based on authorial authority, but not my right as *another reader* to defend or reject certain readings of the text. Therefore, there is nothing in Barthes's project which denies us the right to argue for or against certain archaeologies or readings of the past. What it rejects is that such arguments can be legitimized by the existence of any external position of certainty, any universal understanding which is beyond society and history, or by reference to the authority of any preconceived centre or origin existing before and outside the text.

When I argue for a certain reading of the past I have to realize my own position as historically and culturally situated, i.e. that my struggle for an alternative view of the past is related to political and social values in a present academic sphere of western capitalist society, and has no automatic relevance outside it. What I consider as progressive and relevant attitudes to the past might not be considered to be such by an Australian Aborigine.

This leads on to another, more serious, problem, namely: who has the right to speak of the past? The present struggle for power among archaeologists and their archaeologies might blur the fact that the most important conflict of power today appears not within the discipline, but between the discipline and those outside it; between those who have the right to speak of the past (i.e. by publishing books such as this), and those who, for various historical, social and epistemic reasons, have been denied this right. The pluralism suggested by Barthes might lead to a rethinking of our own critical strategies and might deny us some of the weapons formerly used. However, for those 'outside the true' this pluralism can hardly be regarded as anything but a liberation since it rejects any authoritative and singular version of the past.

Writing archaeology is a way of turning the 'writerly' into the 'readerly'. The works of Roland Barthes have made us aware of our innocence regarding language, writing and representation; that writing constitutes a practice, and does not merely support one; that archaeological and fictional writing participate in the same structure and thus cannot be regarded as strictly opposed terms. His whole corpus of writing calls the mimetic notion of representation into question. However, an acknowledgement of the plurality of history and material culture is probably the greatest lesson to be learnt from the writings of Roland Barthes. Our task – as he declared was the task of the literary critic (*CE*: 260) – is not to recover a lost origin, but to create intelligibility for our own time.

ACKNOWLEDGEMENT

I am grateful to Chris Tilley for detailed comments and criticism of an earlier draft of this paper.

BIBLIOGRAPHY

This bibliography contains only publications actually referred to in the text. For a more complete bibliography of Barthes and works on Barthes see Lavers (1982) and Champagne (1984).

1 Books by Barthes

Abbreviations used are given after the titles. Original date of publication in the French is given in square brackets.

Writing Degree Zero (WDZ) [1953] (1967) Jonathan Cape, London. Trans. A. Lavers and C. Smith.

Michelet par lui-même (MPL) [1954] Seuil, Paris (not translated into English).

Mythologies (M) [1957] (1972) Jonathan Cape, London. Trans. A. Lavers. Republished in 1973 (and later editions) by Paladin Books, London.

On Racine (OR) [1963] (1964) Hill & Wang, New York. Trans. R. Howard.

Critical Essays (CE) [1964] (1972) Northwestern University Press, Evanston. Trans. R. Howard.

Elements of Semiology (EOS) [1964] (1967) Jonathan Cape, London. Trans. A. Lavers and C. Smith.

Critique et vérité (CV) [1966] Seuil, Paris (not translated into English).

The Fashion System (FS) [1967] (1985) Jonathan Cape, London. Trans. M. Ward and R. Howard.

Empire of Signs (ES) [1970] (1982) Hill & Wang, New York. Trans. R. Howard.

S/Z (SZ) [1970] (1975) Jonathan Cape, London; Hill & Wang, New York. Trans. R. Miller.

Sade/Fourier/Loyola (SFL) [1971] (1967) Hill & Wang, New York (1977 Jonathan Cape, London). Trans. R. Miller.

The Pleasure of the Text (PT) [1973] (1975) Hill & Wang, New York (1976 Jonathan Cape, London). Trans. R. Miller.

Roland Barthes by Roland Barthes (RB) [1975] (1977) Hill & Wang, New York; Macmillan, London. Trans. R. Howard.

Inaugural Lecture (Leçon) [1977] English trans. published in *A Barthes Reader* (see section 2). Trans. R. Howard.

A Lover's Discourse (LD) [1977] (1978) Hill & Wang, New York (1979 Jonathan Cape, London). Trans. R. Howard.

Camera Lucida: Reflections on Photography (CL) [1980] (1981) Hill & Wang, New York (1982 Jonathan Cape, London). Trans. R. Howard.

2 Collections of writings and lectures

Image – Music – Text (IMT) (1977) Fontana, London; Hill & Wang, New York. Essays selected and trans. S. Heath.

A Barthes Reader (BR) (1982) Jonathan Cape, London; Hill & Wang, New York. Ed. S. Sontag.
The Rustle of Language (ROL) (1986) Basil Blackwell, Oxford, Ed. F. Wahl; trans. R. Howard.

3 Articles by Barthes and interviews not in the above collections

'La théorie', *VH 101*, no. 2 (Summer 1970).
'Responses', *Tel Quel*, 47 (Autumn 1971).

4 Works on or discussing Barthes

Champagne, R. (1984) *Literary History in the Wake of Roland Barthes: Re-Defining the Myths of Reading*, Summa Publications, Birmingham, Ala.

Coward, R. and Ellis, J. (1977) *Language and Materialism: Developments in Semiology and the Theory of the Subject*, Routledge & Kegan Paul, London.

Culler, J. (1983) *Barthes*, Fontana (Modern Masters), London.

Egebak, N. (1972) *Fra tegnfunktion til tekstfunktion: Introduktion til semiologi*, Berlingske Leksikon Bibliotek, Copenhagen.

Johnson, B. (1980) 'The critical difference: BarthesS/BalZac' in B. Johnson (ed.) *The Critical Difference: Essays in Contemporary Rhetoric of Meaning*, Johns Hopkins University Press, Baltimore.

Lavers, A. (1982) *Roland Barthes: Structuralism and After*, Methuen, London.

Sontag, S. (1982) 'Introduction' in S. Sontag (ed.) *A Barthes Reader*, Jonathan Cape, London; Hill & Wang, New York.

Sturrock, J. (1974) 'Roland Barthes', *New Review* I, 2 (May 1974).

Sturrock, J. (1979) 'Roland Barthes' in J. Sturrock (ed.) *Structuralism and Since: From Lévi-Strauss to Derrida*, Oxford University Press, Oxford.

Sumner, C. (1979) *Reading Ideologies: An Investigation into the Marxist Theory of Ideologies and Law*, Academic Press, New York.

5 Other works referred to in the text

Braudel, F. (1980) *On History*, Weidenfield & Nicholson, London. Trans. S. Matthews.

Clark, S. (1985) 'The Annales historians' in Q. Skinner (ed.) *The Return of Grand Theory in the Human Sciences*, Cambridge University Press, Cambridge.

Clifford, J. and Marcus, G. E. (eds) (1986) *Writing Culture: The Poetics* and Politics of Ethnography, University of California Press, Berkeley.

Collingwood, R. G. (1939) *An Autobiography*, Oxford University Press, Oxford.

Collingwood, R. G. (1946) *The Idea of History*, Oxford University Press, Oxford.

Derrida, J. (1978) *Positions*, University of Chicago Press, Chicago.

Drummond, L. (1983) 'Jonestown: a study in ethnographic discourse' *Semiotica*, 46: 167–209.

Flannery, K. (1982) 'The Golden Marshalltown: a parable for the archaeology of the 1980s', *American Anthropologist*, 84: 265–78.

Gadamer, H. G. (1975) *Truth and Method*, Sheed & Ward, London.

Hodder, I. (1982) 'Theoretical archaeology: a reactionary view' in I. Hodder (ed.) *Symbolic and Structural Archaeology*, Cambridge University Press, Cambridge.

Hodder, I. (1986) *Reading the Past: Current Approaches to Interpretation in Archaeology*, Cambridge University Press, Cambridge.

Kristeva, J. (1975) 'The subject in signifying practices', *Semiotext (e)*, 1, 3.

Kristeva, J. (1986) *The Kristeva Reader*, ed. T. Moi, Basil Blackwell, Oxford.

Lentricchia, F. (1980) *After the New Criticism*, University of Chicago Press, Chicago.

Lévi-Strauss, C. (1966) *The Savage Mind*, London.

Norris, C. (1982) *The Deconstructive Turn: Essays in the Rhetoric of Philosophy*, Methuen, London.

Patrik, L. E. (1985) 'Is there an archaeological record?' in M. B. Schiffer (ed.) *Advances in Archaeological Method and Theory*, vol. 8, Academic Press, New York.

Ricoeur, P. (1981a) *Hermeneutics and the Human Sciences*, ed. J. P. Thompson, Cambridge University Press, Cambridge.

Ricoeur, P. (1981b) 'Narrative time' in W. J. T. Mitchell (ed.) *On Narrative*, University of Chicago Press, Chicago.

White, H. (1981) 'The value of narrativity in the representation of reality' in W. J. T. Mitchell (ed.) *On Narrative*, University of Chicago Press.

White, H. (1984) 'The question of narrative in contemporary historical theory', *History and Theory*, 23: 1–33.

5

Jacques Derrida: 'There is nothing outside of the text'

Timothy Yates

However the topic is considered, the *problem of language* has never been simply one problem amongst others. But never as much as at present has it invaded, *as such*, the global horizon of the most diverse researches and the most heterogeneous discourses, diverse and heterogeneous in their intention, method and ideology... It indicates, as if in spite of itself, that an historical–metaphysical epoch must finally determine as language the totality of its problematic horizon. It must do so not only because all that desire had wished to wrest from the play of language finds itself recaptured within that play, but also because, for the same reason, language is menaced in its very life, adrift in the threat of limitlessness, brought back to its own finitude at the very moment when its limits seemed to disappear, when it ceases to be self-assured, contained and guaranteed by the infinite signified which seemed to exceed it. (*OG*: 6)

The name of Jacques Derrida, perhaps more than that of any of the other critics featured in this book, is associated with the shift to a *post*-structuralism. It would be of little value to produce a list of post-structuralist 'concepts', but many of those we might wish to include stem from Derrida's work. And yet, despite his undoubted impact on other disciplines, Derrida remains (to an archaeological audience) the most enigmatic of the post-structuralists, and deconstruction the least understood of its critical 'motifs' and 'movements' (why these terms are inappropriate, and thus suspended in quotation marks, will become clearer below). This text could appear, therefore, to be called for, or even demanded, at a time when structuralist archaeology, having broken the hold of positivism, begins to perceive that its own project is crumbling away beneath its feet.

Yet despite the promise made under the title with which I have begun to write and you will have begun to read, this text will never have achieved the status of a commentary. Perhaps it sets itself this task, but Derrida's work is too enormous, too complex, as it intersects with different traditions and disciplines, and an empirical survey is more than adequately provided elsewhere (cf. Culler 1983; Leitch 1983; Norris 1983; and, more critically, Dews 1987). The question of a commentary is, anyway, too trivial. I make no claims to have understood Derrida. I don't even know who he is. Or rather, I know that he lives, teaches in the Ecole Normale Supérieur in Paris, that he is a philosopher whose work could never be reduced to a mere 'philosophy', that he has written on subjects as diverse as philosophy, psychoanalysis, literature, poetry, art history, contemporary politics and educational reforms, that his influence has been wide, but most marked in literary criticism where a (heterogeneous) 'school' of deconstruction is now well established... All this I know 'about' Jacques Derrida. But from the outset, his work has passed beyond the copyright, and it is this dissemination that I wish here to extend to a new framework, to read archaeology through my reading of Derrida. For us, therefore, the name 'Derrida' will name only a problem and a body of texts to which I will return (I will quote him often, reinscribing his statements) in order to describe this problem, a problem that must come to face archaeology however much it is resisted. To write 'on' or 'about' Derrida is to write around this problem and, by quotation and connection, to bring these texts into play. As soon as I write, therefore, I am assured that Derrida himself will not appear.

That we should have come to this point, a confrontation with the Derridean question, is by no means guaranteed or inevitable, but it is certainly becoming more irresistible. Structuralism, though young in archaeology, has already started to break down, as the holes, inconsistencies and contradictions in its logic have become exposed. In Britain, post-processual archaeology has emerged out of a desire to engage in the political implications of archaeological production, which are 'originary' and irreducible. A rigid or formal structuralism has both led the way to a break with orthodox archaeology, and, at the same time, held it back in reserve. Post-structuralism reopens the question, and working this through should begin with Derrida.

The Derridean 'problem' does not only operate within the structuralist tradition, however. Were this the case, its influence and significance would indeed be limited, and difficult to carry to the real, sedimented aspects of archaeological practice. Rather, it extends to invade all aspects of the archaeological project, with the laws and rules of which it must lead us to demand a radical break. It is not structurally limited because the problem lies at the heart of the structure of western thought, which Derrida describes under the blanket term 'metaphysics', a tradition based upon 'logocentrism' —

the privileging of presence — and its species 'phonocentrism', the privileging of speech (presence over absence, speech over writing). What is involved requires some explication; Derrida defines metaphysics in the following way:

> 1.   The hierarchical axiology, the ethical–ontological distinctions which do not merely set up value oppositions clustered around an ideal and unfindable limit, but moreover *subordinate* these values to each other (normal/abnormal, standard/parasite, fulfilled/void, serious/non-serious, literal/non-literal, briefly: positive/negative and ideal/non-ideal) . . .
> 2.   The enterprise of returning 'strategically', ideally, to an origin or to a 'priority' held to be simple, intact, normal, pure, standard, self-identical, in order *then* to think in terms of derivation, complication, deterioration, accident, etc. All metaphysicians, from Plato to Rousseau, Descartes to Husserl, have proceeded in this way, conceiving good to be before evil, the positive before the negative, the pure before the impure, the simple before the complex, the essential before the accidental, the imitated before the imitation. And this is not just *one* metaphysical gesture among others, it is *the* metaphysical exigency, that which has been the most constant, most profound and most potent. (LI: 236)

Metaphysics, then, conceives of the world on the basis of polarities, one side of which is valued over the other, the opposite side thus becoming secondary, distorting, unnecessary and even, as a result, contaminating and dangerous. Conceptual oppositions are arranged hierarchically, all determinations hinging on the desire to make one side present and pure while excluding the other.

What Derrida does is to locate the lacunae and blind-spots within this system, and to attempt to use their unforeseen and unperceived problems and contradictions to invert the terms, overturn the hierarchy and work differently within the field they demarcate. It is this reading that will be the concern of this chapter, and this reading that must commit us to an attempt to think an archaeology in terms other than those of archaeology, what we could call an archaeology 'after' archaeology (though only with enormous risk — the risk of irony, the risk of jumping too quickly to a poorly perceived 'outside' of the conventional arena, and the risk of complicity with the system we are seeking to transform).

Readings

Beyond Saussurian Difference

At that time, structuralism was dominant. 'Deconstruction' seemed to be going in the same direction since the word signified a certain attention to structures (which themselves were neither simply ideas, nor forms, nor syntheses, nor systems). To deconstruct was also a structuralist gesture or in any case one that assured a certain need for the structuralist problematic. But it was also an anti-structuralist gesture, and its fortune rests in part on this ambiguity. Structures were to be undone, decomposed, desedimented. (LJF: 2)

In the context of post-structuralism, it is appropriate to open with Derrida's critique of Saussurian structuralism and the concept of the sign. Saussure had begun to rethink linguistics at a time when it had, during the course of the nineteenth century, placed more emphasis upon the historical study of language than on 'philosophical' questions, accepting *a priori* the existence of elements in language in order to study their evolution over time.

The word ceased to be examined in terms of sign or representation, and attention was focused upon treating it as a form to be compared with other forms (cf. Culler 1976: 57ff.). Saussure argued against this general trend that linguistics could only be put upon a scientific footing if it adopted as its model for research a synchronic approach, one that treats language as a network of structural relations existing at any one moment in time, rather than the more orthodox diachronic approaches which abstracted elements from their systemic context in order to trace their development.

A synchronic approach was preferred over a diachronic in order to examine the relations of difference which articulate the signs of language. Saussure took over from nineteenth-century linguistics the concept of the sign, but only to break it up. He divided it into two parts, the signifier (acoustic element) and the signified (meaning content) as the sensible and the intelligible. The basis for research would be the relations of difference which articulate the signifiers of the system. For Saussure, the signifier is arbitrary, and only defined as an entity on the basis of its difference from the other signifiers of the system. Thus there is nothing necessary within the object world ('the referent') that requires an animal of a given type (set of attributes, etc.) to be called 'dog'; the signifier exists only because it is different from the other signifiers of the language system, and this difference is the only condition that any signifier must fulfil. Therefore, in signification, Saussure wrote, there are only differences *without positive terms*.

This emerges more clearly when one considers writing – the value of the letters is purely negative and differential. Thus individuals may write letters in radically different ways; all that is important is that the letter *d*, for example, should be distinct from the letter *l*, the letter *b* and so on. The elements of this differential system Saussure conceived as founded upon *langue*, a system of rules which underlie language, which condition the range of permissible and intelligible alternatives for combination made in any individual speech act (*parole*). These rules appear only as instantiated in language use, but are the means by which it is possible.

In an interview with Julia Kristeva, Derrida summarized his relationship with the thought of Saussure. On the one hand, the division of the sign into the signifier and the signified played 'an absolutely decisive critical role' (*P*: 18). It broke up the homogeneity of the orthodox concept, and, by emphasizing that the signifier and the signified exist as a 'two-sided unity', showed 'against the tradition, that the signified is inseparable from the signifier, that the signified and the signifier are two sides of one and the same production' (*P*: 18). Thus, through stressing the differential (sensible) and the formal (intelligible) characteristics of signification, Saussure began to turn back upon metaphysics the very concept he had borrowed from it. For if the signifier is differential, it is 'impossible for sound, the material element, itself to belong to language' (*P*: 18). This reconceptualization offered the potential to challenge notions of a fixed element of consciousness which is concomitant with a meaning anterior and external to the production of meaning through language, notions, no less than any other, of the Cartesian *cogito*.

On the other hand, however, Derrida stresses that this potential remains unrealized in Saussure's work, and he remains bound within the sign concept he seemed to have questioned, the concept which 'by its root and its implications is in all its aspects metaphysical . . . [and] in systematic solidarity with stoic and medieval theology' (*P*: 17). Thus, while Saussure maintains the distinction between the signifier and the signified, and thus moves towards the break-up of the self-sameness of the metaphysical concept of the word, he continues to retain that very concept within his theories, using the word 'sign' because he could not think of any alternative.

> No more than any other, this concept cannot be employed in both an absolutely novel and an absolutely conventional way. One necessarily assumes, in a non-critical way, at least some of its implications inscribed in its system. There is at least one moment at which Saussure must renounce drawing all the conclusions from the critical work he has undertaken, and that is the not fortuitous moment when he resigns himself to using the word 'sign', lacking anything better. (*P*: 19)

The retention may seem trivial, but then language is neither innocent or neutral, it is the language of the metaphysics Saussure was attempting to transform. By retaining the single concept of the sign, and with it the notion of the 'neutral' unity of the word, rather than finding another means to express its two-sided unity, Saussure left open 'the possibility of thinking a *concept signified in and of itself*, a concept simply present to thought, independent of a relationship to language, that is of a relationship to a system of signifiers' (*P*: 19). The term 'sign' leaves open recourse to what Derrida calls the 'transcendental signified', an origin before the sign, a sign that is itself not a part of the continuous productivity of signification that would be the implication of the signifier – signified relation. Such a transcendental signified would exist without any necessary connection to anything else, without mediation, beyond question – God, for example to a medieval theologian, or science and objectivity to a processualist drunk with reading Hempel.

This concession to metaphysics is underlined elsewhere in Saussure's lectures where he privileges the relationship of speech to meaning over that of writing, 'everything that links the sign to phonè [speech]' (*P*: 21). Derrida attempts to show how this position ends up contradicting Saussure's most basic conceptions and most important critical insights. 'The theme of the arbitrary, thus, is turned away from its most fruitful paths (formulations) towards a hierarchising theology' (*P*: 21). For by emphasizing in speech the unity of the signifier and the signified, and thus of speech and thought, Saussure collapses voice into consciousness. Signifier and signified become the sign – absolute identity and irreducibility around the same space. It is a notion of meaning most basic to the metaphysical tradition from Plato onwards. By privileging speech, not only do the signifier and the signified seem to become a single entity, a unity of two sides, but the signifier seems to disappear as speech becomes inseparable from consciousness. 'In this confusion the signifier seems to erase itself or to become transparent, in order to allow the concept to present itself as what it is, referring to nothing other than its presence. *The exteriority of the signifier seems reduced*' (*P*: 22, emphasis added). This reduction of the exteriority of the signifier contradicts Saussure's statement that the signifier, of itself, cannot belong to language, that it must be external to the intelligible, constituted only on the basis of difference, arbitrary in relation to the signified.

The privileging of speech as the model for linguistic analysis and the reduction of writing to a secondary and derivative space define the general movement by which the signifier as material exteriority is denied and the metaphysical sign as presence is reconstituted. Writing would be an impoverished model for language. If in speech the signifier and the signified seem to converge and conflate, in writing this opposition is maintained and underlined. Writing, in the absence of the author, can only re-present speech and consciousness: it is a technical device which, because of its distorting effects, is always 'evil'. Thus Plato, in his *Phaedrus*, condemns writing as a bastardized form of communication which, unlike speech, gives rise to failures of meaning, to misinterpretation and to misunderstanding. Philosophy must use writing, but its ideal form would be speech, with its irreducible connection to presence, and thus it has always aimed at putting an end to writing, an end to the signifier and residence in meaning only through the 'interiority' of the signified/sign.

Derrida turns this edifice upon its head, and rather than repeating the hierarchization of speech over writing, works from writing to speech. In interfering with the privilege of speech (phonocentrism), he not only threatens conceptions of communication on the basis of the sign, but also questions epistemology and ontology. He threatens all that unites these various motifs, the conception of meaning and existence on the basis of presence. What is writing? From Saussure, we know that it is constructed of signifiers in a differential relationship with each other. Derrida explores the question by following this most radical of Saussure's insights.

The debasement of writing and the elevation of speech has, Derrida writes, always been determined on the basis of presence. Speech would be privileged because it is closer to the presence of meaning as event, which is ultimately the immediate presence of meaning to the subject of an utterance. Thus the appeal made by Descartes to the 'I' that escapes radical self-doubt must rely upon the presence of the subject to itself (see p. 223). It is another form of the fetishism of presence which inculcates and underlines even the most basic comments and assumptions in language. The notions of 'making clear', 'showing what is the case', 'explaining', 'demonstrating' — all such notions, regularly used in everyday discourse — are based upon these very same assumptions, and demonstrate that ordinary language as much as the specialized forms of academic discourse are phenomena of a general metaphysical 'ideology', instances of this logocentrism. Presence, when clouded by a misunderstanding or an ambiguity, may immediately be approached, through interrogation, by a different route, a different set of signifiers. Such a capacity for immediate and spontaneous self-reflection is not a capacity found in writing. Loss of presence (the meaning in the author's mind) is not recoverable from the text in the same terms, and thus the text contains within it, through the non-presence of the author at its distribution and dissemination, the slide of the presence of the signified content of the text. Writing *re*-presents speech, the moment of conception or intention, but cannot do so directly, clearly or unambiguously. Writing is debased because 'of a speech dreaming of its own plenitude and self-presence' (*OG*: 110).

But if writing is no more than difference, then the logocentric connection between speech and writing can be inverted in its hierarchy. Speech is found to be already constructed through a system of signifiers articulated differentially, signifiers as arbitrary as those of writing. The phoneme is constituted in the same way as the grapheme, and the privilege of speech can no longer be sustained for that which it excludes (writing) is already within speech before these secondary distinctions. The problem has been to define writing only as linear and phonetic notation. The 'phonetic' sign is not privileged or primordial, but itself an identification made possible by and predicated upon differences amongst signifiers which are external to the signified, as *material* as the grapheme. Therefore it is writing, rather than speech, as Saussure thought, that should be the basis for research, since writing as difference is the structure that returns to underlie all the possibilities of signification, of signs written or spoken.

The Nambikwara studied by Lévi-Strauss as a 'pre-literate society' (see chapter 1 of this volume), who misunderstand the purpose and the meaning of the scribbles in his notebooks, are therefore found to possess an already-constructed writing system, in so far as signifiers are used through difference. Thus the very possibility of naming things and, significantly, people, shows that this society possesses already all the characteristics of writing, since these namings and this nomenclature are dependent upon '*arche*-writing' or 'writing-in-general', 'the violence of difference, of classification, and the system of appellations' (*OG*: 110). Out of the weighted opposition of speech and writing, Derrida extracts a new 'conceptual' framework which underlies both but which has itself no identity outside their operation (that is, outside the operation of the signifier). The possibility of writing is no longer dependent upon speech, is no longer an inhabitant of the structure of speech which it serves only to represent, but a possibility the origin of which lies outside voice and phonè, and comes from a space anterior to them. The possibility of writing, but also of speech, comes from an already-constituted writing, such that 'no reality or concept would therefore correspond to a "society without writing"' (*OG*: 109). 'If writing is to be related to violence [the fall from presence], writing appears well before writing in the narrow sense; already in the difference or the *arche*-writing that opens speech itself' (*OG*: 128).

But if writing is a structure upon which speech is also dependent, then the undoing of the opposition has serious implications for a philosophy and a language conceived on the basis of presence. The 'violence' of writing extends into the very heartland of metaphysics, of presence, that is speech itself. If in language there is nothing but a system of differences, we encounter unsettling effects upon the anchor of presence:

> The play of differences supposes, in effect, syntheses and referrals which forbid, at any moment, or in any sense, that a single element be *present* in and of itself, referring only to itself. Whether in the order of spoken or written discourse, no element can function as a sign without referring to another element which is itself not simply present. This interweaving results in each 'element' – phoneme or grapheme – being constituted on the basis of the trace within it of the other elements of the chain or system . . . Nothing, neither among the elements nor within the system, is anywhere ever simply present or absent. There are only, everywhere, differences of differences and traces of traces. (*P*: 26)

To be different the sign is founded not only upon its presence 'as such', but also upon the absence of that which it is not – it cannot simply be present because it is always referring constitutively outside 'itself' to an Other which is not present, but which functions as the source of the difference. This Other would also itself be differential, however, and not a 'present' Other, thus looking beyond itself for the source of its identity. This movement would go on indefinitely – there could be no natural or necessary end to the referral of the sign for the source of its difference. The name Derrida gives to this production – *différance* – is a neologism designed to express these effects. The substitution of the *a* for the second *e* in the French captures the verbs of to differ and to defer, both passive and *active*. It is a movement at once synchronic (dispersal through illimitable chains of signifiers) and diachronic (deferral, since the ends of these chains cannot be reached). Any boundary we might wish to set up to delimit this networking cannot itself escape these effects – it would be only a new mark and therefore a new signifier, presupposing the movement of a signifying chain in which it belongs as difference.

This movement causes enormous problems for structuralism. It has always, Derrida contends, reduced the potential of its own discoveries and propositions:

> Up to the event which I wish to mark out and define, structure – or rather the structurality of structure – although it has always been at work, has always been neutralised or reduced, and this by a process of giving it a centre or referring it to a point of presence, to a fixed origin. The function of this centre was not only to orient, balance and organise the structure – one cannot in fact conceive of an unorganised structure – but above all to make sure that the organising principle of the structure would limit what

we might call the *play* of the structure. By orientating and organising the coherence of the system, the centre of the structure permits the play of its elements inside the total form. (*WD*: 278–9)

The notion of structure is a totalizing device, within which the play of differences is controlled. But such organization does not only permit the play, it also functions to limit and reduce *différance*. The centre of the structure is the only point or mark within the structure that cannot come within the play of *différance*. At the centre, 'the substitution of contents, elements or terms is no longer possible . . . the permutation or the transformation of elements . . . is forbidden. At least this permutation has always remained *interdicted* (*WD*: 279). The centre, therefore, governs structure from the outside, escaping its effect, an element of play (structurality) which is at the same time beyond its reach and its law. '[T]hus it has always been thought', Derrida writes,

> that the centre, which is by definition unique, constituted that very thing within a structure which, while governing the structure, escapes structurality . . . The centre is, paradoxically, *within* the structure and *outside* it. The centre is at the centre of the totality, and yet, since the centre does not belong to the totality (is not part of the totality), the totality *has its centre elsewhere*. The centre is not the centre. (*WD*: 279)

The centre of the structure would appear to be both produced by the play of the structure and at the same time to lie outside that play, produced from some other, forgotten, space. By escaping structurality, the centre has been conceived as presence, 'on the basis of a fundamental immobility and a reassuring certitude' (*WD*: 279). Structuralism, therefore, removes from structures the very points which make them possible, the points around which they become structures.

Within the rediscovery of *différance*, however, the centre cannot escape play. It is no more than a new mark within a chain, referring necessarily to the marks from which it is different. Structure, which cannot come about without a centre, is overrun from the inside of the text it functioned to contain, in so far as it no longer escapes its effects and governs from the outside. 'There are only, everywhere, differences of differences and traces of traces' (*P*: 26).

Supplementarity and the Undecidable in the Language of Philosophy

it happens that this graphic difference (the *a* instead of the *e*), this marked difference between two apparently vocalic notations, between vowels, remains purely graphic: it is written or read, but it is not heard. It cannot be heard, and we shall see in what respects it is also beyond the order of understanding. (*SP*: 132)

Différance makes no pretensions to satisfy the desire for a pure and transcendental concept. It is unknowable in the terms of presence upon which metaphysics places the emphasis for knowledge. This neologism, through the silent *a*, binds differences that cannot be heard and can thus only appear in writing (undoing in the very concept the privilege of speech), divides itself, never effecting the join of the sense – it can only be known through its effects, but is always irreducible to any instantiation of these effects. 'No ontology can think its operation' (*OG*: 314). And yet, *différance* remains only a name, 'a metaphysical name; and all the names that it receives from our language are still, in so far as they are names, metaphysical' (*SP*: 158). *Différance* 'itself' is to be conceived as prior to the separation of sense introduced in the ambivalence or double sense of this term, for what this captures as movement (differing/deferral) is already an effect of what it purports to name.

Derrida's texts rehearse the operation of this field, displacing differences through a series of alternative names, drawn from the texts that are being read, that demonstrate the manner in which concepts escape the rules they had been set up to govern, the way in which they transgress the logical axioms of thought in which they seem to be inscribed, by what they are unable to describe within themselves and their own operation. Two of the most well-known examples of this conceptual displacement are to be found in Derrida's readings of Plato and Mallarmé in *D*.

Plato's *Phaedrus* has always had a prominent position in metaphysics, by virtue of the privilege he assigns to speech. In the text, Socrates condemns writing as a secondary form of communication, giving rise to failures of meaning, etc. In his dialogue with Phaedrus, Socrates is therefore led to proclaim speech (and the phonetic sign) as the proper vehicle for the discussion and formalization of truth.

Derrida, however, takes the *Phaedrus* and reveals how certain elements work against the argument Socrates seemed to be developing. Everything turns upon Plato's use of a single word to describe writing, *pharmakon*. In Greek, *pharmakon* has a double and contradictory meaning, signifying both 'poison' and 'remedy'. It is impossible, at any point, to isolate which of the two senses should be understood as that which would be intended. It is the translators of the *Phaedrus* that have imposed a single meaning on the word. The point, however, is not simply that of translating between languages:

it is a difficulty inherent in its very principle, situated less in the passage from one language to another than already . . . in the tradition between Greek and Greek; a violent difficulty in the transference of a non-philosopheme into a philosopheme. With the problem of translation we will thus be dealing with nothing less than the problem of the very passage into philosophy. (*D*: 72)

The two senses of *pharmakon* cannot be split, the meaning cannot be presenced as a distinction between the two senses. *Pharmakon* would be untranslatable into the terms of a metaphysics of presence. 'The "essence" of the *pharmakon* lies in the way in which, having no stable essence, no 'proper' characteristics, it is not, in any sense . . . of the word, a *substance*. The *pharmakon* has no ideal identity' (*D*: 125–6). But this property would, at the same time, *not* be that of a plurality of senses or essences; it is not an empirical composite of several meanings. It is the 'prior medium' through which differentiations of this sort are produced. 'The *pharmakon* is the movement, the locus and the play: (the production of) difference. It is the difference of the difference' (*D*: 127). It is the point at which dialectics emerges as both the birth and the death of philosophical concepts, those claiming to rule through some essence or identity which is pure and abstract but omnipotent. 'We will watch it infinitely promise itself and endlessly vanish through concealed doorways that shine like mirrors and open onto the labyrinth' (*D*: 128). The *pharmakon* cannot 'be', if by that we would imply an object or a sign homogeneous and complete. It 'is' a concept only in so far as it produces conceptual effects – effects of the trace of the opposites that cannot be reduced to simple points of translation. 'If the *pharmakon* is 'ambivalent', it is because it constitutes the medium in which opposites are opposed, the movement and the play that links them among themselves, reverses them or makes one side cross over to the other (soul/body, good/evil, inside/outside, memory/ forgetfulness, speech/writing, etc.)' (*D*: 127).

Pharmakon, in spite of the readings and translations proffered for the *Phaedrus*, is the closest 'concept' we can imagine that would approximate to a non-concept, by which would be meant a non-metaphysical concept, a concept no longer reducible to the conditions of presence. It is untranslatable into these terms at every point of its trajectory, transcending the polarities it seemed to describe. It both cures and reinfects. Its double sense would mean that the expulsion of writing which Socrates (seems to have) proposed in order to reconstitute speech as pure can only be made if writing is already within speech. The structure of *pharmakon* both produces the possibility of the boundary (speech as inside, writing as outside) but also causes both to be repossessed in the same space through the explosion of the boundary. The sense of the word cannot be split, cannot be decidable. Similarly, *pharmakos* (scapegoat), to which it is related, can be cast out of the city in order to cleanse its inside only if it is already on the inside, the opposition of out and in being created for the cathartic effect.

A similar point emerges from Derrida's discussion of the *hymen*, which is found in the works on mimesis by Mallarmé. *Hymen* in French has two meanings, signifying at the same time both the vaginal membrane and marriage — simultaneously, therefore, both virginity and consummation, both purity and impurity, inside and outside, self and other. *Hymen* both joins opposites and keeps them apart: 'it is an operation that *both* sows confusion *between* opposites *and* stands *between* the opposites "at once". What counts here is the *between*, the in-between-ness of the hymen. The hymen "takes place" in the "inter-", in the spacing between desire and fulfilment, between penetration and its recollection' (*D*: 212). Truths are located in the text by their names, points of dependency or 'centres', but they are discovered to be unable to govern and determine the whole so clearly, discovered to be 'undecidable', names that are only names for the movement named as *différance*.

The undecidable, if it is a concept, is a concept that can never function in accordance with orthodox conceptions about language and the grounds of presence. They are not 'added' by Derrida, but are produced from the inside of the text that is being read, from within its very resources. Another such undecidable is the *supplement*. In French, *supplement* has two meanings. It is both 'addition' and 'substitute', both 'to complete' and 'to substitute' and replace. 'Supply' in English might perform the same semantic ambiguity and self-contradiction (Leavey 1980: 20). By virtue of the workings of *différance*, therefore, not only is the meaning of the supplement impossible to formalize, but logically 'it produces that to which it is said to be added on' (*SP*: 89). The effects of the supplement upon philosophical and conceptual grounds can be illustrated by examining Derrida's reading of Rousseau's *Confessions*, from which it emeges as a 'concept' within deconstruction.

Rousseau discusses writing and masturbation, and their relationship to pure and natural intercourse (speech and copulation) is considered to be of a supplementary character. Thus writing is the representation of speech, a loss of the immediacy and presence of meaning that would characterize convesation, the direct expression of the self. Despite this philosophical presupposition, Rousseau confesses that he finds it easier to express what he means through writing rather than speech; in person, he admits to 'showing myself not only at a disadvantage, but as completely different from what I am', saying things on the spur of the moment that he does not mean or meaning things that he cannot speak (quoted in *OG*: 142). Rousseau thus explicitly, in personal reflection, finds himself unable to practise what he preaches, and contradicts the observation on the nature of language that he has already made, questioning its substance: 'Straining towards the reconstruction of presence, [Rousseau] valorizes and disqualifies writing at the same time . . . Rousseau condemns writing as destruction of presence and disease of speech. He rehabilitates it to the extent that it promises the reappropriation of that which speech allowed itself to be disposed. But by what, if not a writing older than speech and already installed in that place' (*OG*: 141–2).

Speech is characterized, ultimately, by precisely those qualities identified in writing and for which it has been condemned. Writing turns out to describe the qualities of speech as well. The presence of meaning which Rousseau claims for speech cannot be supported, and indeed it is not supported by his own experience, his own confessions. Writing as the loss of presence occupies the whole scene of language. Speech cannot be differentiated from writing on the basis of presence, for it is already writing before anyone speaks.

Where writing appeared, therefore, to supplement speech (as an addition to its communicative arsenal) it now functions to displace speech, to substitute for it and be able to replace that to which it becomes attached. The logic of Rousseau's supplement is reversible, the priority and value of the hierarchy undone.

Precisely the same movement is shown by Derrida to underlie Rousseau's distinction between masturbation and copulation. Both are characterized by desire for a real 'object' ('a real person'), but only in intercourse is the object of desire present to desire, Rousseau would maintain. Masturbation is a supplementary form of sexual activity, taking place in the absence of the object on which it nevertheless remains focused – an addition to normal sexual activity.

But both intercourse and masturbation share the desire for an object, and by virtue of the fact both possess only the impossibility of ever fulfilling that desire and possessing the object. Desire is caught in the irresolvable space between the desirer and the desired, pursuing an object that cannot be obtained but only presented back to the subject as an object. Desire is the structure of distancing and objectification. If masturbation is founded upon this difference, then so too is the 'union' of intercourse – neither can fulfil desire and capture the presence of the object. The hymen, even as it is broken, underlies the separation that divides desire. 'Both writing and auto-eroticism are necessary to recapture a presence whose lack has not been preceded by any fullness

— yet these compensatory activities are themselves condemned as unnecessary, even dangerous, supplements' (Johnson 1981: xii). If writing can come to replace speech, then it must share some of the fundamental qualities that permit the substitution. If masturbation replaces copulation, then it must be structured like intercourse. The structure and working of the supplement is everywhere reversible — addition/substitution. Both writing and masturbation can function as supplementary activities since their qualities — distance as the loss of presence — belong to their Other, the separation of which can never be final or absolute.

Rousseau's distinction is founded upon a difference between the meanings of *supplement* that he thinks he can control, but the rhetoric is nowhere compatible or in accordance with its explicit or logical meaning. Language *exceeds* the distinction he tries to make between addition and substitution. Unable to split the two senses, to drive a border between the two sides of the concept, *supplement* becomes a function of the movement of *différance*, leading to the most radical formulation:

> *There is nothing outside of the text.* And that is neither because Jean-Jacques' life, or the existence of mama or Thérèse *themselves* is not of prime interest to us, nor because we have access to their so-called 'real' existence only in this text and we have neither any means of altering this nor any right to neglect this limitation . . . What we have tried to show following the guiding line of this 'dangerous supplement' is that in what one calls the real life of these existences 'of flesh and bone', beyond and behind what one believes can be circumscribed as Rousseau's text, there has never been anything but writing; there have never been anything but supplements, substitutive significations which could only have come forth in a chain of differential references, the 'real; supervening, and being added only while taking on meaning from a trace and from an invocation of the supplement, etc. And thus to infinity, for we have read, *in the text*, that the absolute present, Nature, that which words like 'real mother' name, have always already escaped, have never existed; that which opens meaning and language is writing as the disappearance of natural presence. (*OG*, 158–9)

The Frivolity of Context: Writing as Parergon

The *supplement* intervenes in all conceptual grounds, all differentiations, to recapture through the Other that has been repressed the significance of the differentiation as a multiple tracing, in which the origin (speech, copulation) becomes the non-origin, disappearing at its root. 'There is nothing outside of the text' — no ground that escapes difference, that is not a mark within a signifying chain. No point escapes this system that will not be recaptured through its movement. All signifieds rejoin their signifying traces as marks in a chain in motion. We arrive at the shocking conclusion of deconstruction, the one that writes the 'post' into post-structuralism: 'One cannot determine the centre and exhaust totalisation because the sign which replaces the centre, which supplements it, taking the centre's place in its absence – this sign is added, occurs as a surplus, as a *supplement*. The movement of signification adds something, which results in the fact that there is always more' (*WD*: 289). 'An apocalyptic superimprinting of texts: there is no paradigmatic text. Only relationships of cryptic haunting from mark to mark. No palimpsest (definitive unfinishedness). No piece, no metonymy, no integral corpus' (LO: 136–7).

It might be objected here that the context of a signification (utterance, event, etc.) is the governing force of a structure. Context would position proper borders to the signifying chains, delimit their deferral and referral, control *différance* and play. According to this notion, utterances can have their meaning altered by their contextual associations. This would seem to externalize something from the signifying system – some element of the determination of meaning would escape that system, since the *same* utterance would produce different meanings. This involved Derrida in a debate with speech-act theory, the way in which we account for the meanings of statements (or, as J. L. Austin put it, their 'illocutionary force'). These theories would hold that in order to account for the different meanings a single utterance can produce, we must look towards the system and the context in which they are found.

Austin argues that it is not what the subject has in mind that determines meaning, but conventions and rules that surround and define the context in which the utterance is made. Austin draws a distinction between statements (*constative utterances*) which describe situations, facts, etc., and are either true or false, and *performatives*, statements which are not true or false but which perform the action they describe, such as the promise (Culler 1983: 112). Performatives can only take place if their failure is a part of the potential result of the act: 'If something cannot be used to tell a lie, conversely it cannot be used to tell the truth' (Umberto Eco, quoted in Culler 1983: 114). Promising relies entirely on the possibility that it may be broken, be insincere or fail. This force does not originate in the speaker's own mind, but in the discursive conventions in which the performative takes place. Context would thus compel certain obligations of the speaker, such that a marriage ceremony is meaningful but also binding if it takes place within certain conventional surroundings – a church or register office in Britain. Outside these locations, it would not have the same meanings. The promise is effective and binding, it *performs* what it says, only within prescribed circumstances which are a part of the discursive or speech-act formation.

Austin therefore tries to avoid both reducing the effectivity of speech to individual intention, and excluding failures from the analyst's attention. However, at one point he reintroduces precisely these categories, by requiring that the utterance be spoken (intended) 'seriously', if it is to conform to the conventions located in the context. He would thus have to exclude of necessity non-serious utterances since, although they may be uttered within contexts such as a church, they would themselves escape the determinations of that context. What implication, for instance, would a dramatization of a wedding scene from a novel have upon these ideas?

Searle, in his reply to Derrida's assult upon Austin's theories, tries to defend the (provisional) casting out of court of such exceptions, in order to preserve the methods and basic ideas that Austin had proposed – the functioning of context in determining meaning. But, Derrida writes, 'What is at stake is above all the structural impossibility and illegitimacy of such an "idealisation", even one which is methodological and provisional' (LI: 206). 'Are the prerequisites of context ever absolutely determinable?' he asks, 'Is there a rigorous and scientific concept of context?'

What is the context of a written text? There can, of course, be no question of the author, who is absent from the reading. The written text exists totally independently of the writer, and *must* do so in order to be understood. It must be iterable, repeatable, without the presence of the author or addressee: 'A writing that was not structurally legible – iterable – beyond the death of the addressee would not be writing' (M: 315). The death of the author/addressee is not a side-effect of writing, a secondary effect or property, but is inscribed within its very structure, absolutely necessary for its very existence. Thus 'a written sign carries with it a force of breaking with context, that is, the set of presences which organise the moment of its inscription. This force of breaking is not an accidental predicate, but the very structure of the written . . . no context can enclose it' (M: 317). The written sign, characterized by spacing through difference, cannot function otherwise. Thus writing cannot carry with it the determined meaning, cannot exist within a given context of situational determinants. It can constantly be inscribed within chains of signifiers, grafted on to new contexts and different situations, without the function of the grapheme, which is answerable only to difference and not to a signified, being distorted. If it were not capable of breaking with the present moment and the present space, if it could not be reproduced and reinscribed infinitely in this way, then writing would be impossible, since the sign would be constantly grasping for a relationship it can never have. Unable itself to anticipate all the contexts in which it can be read, the text is unable to signify unless it is repeatable regardless of context.

The same arguments would apply to speech. 'Across empirical variations of tone, of voice, etc., eventually of a certain accent, for example, one must be able to recognise the identity, shall we say, of a signifying form'. This identity is founded only upon difference and the possibility of iteration which rupture the sign's relationship with presence (space/time). It is independent of any context, and the identity is found solely upon repetition.

> The structural possibility of being severed from its referent or signified (and therefore of communication and its context) seems to make every mark, even if oral, a grapheme in general, that is, as we have seen, the non-present *remaining* of a differential remark cut from its alleged 'production' or origin. And I will extend this law even to all 'experience' in general, if it be granted that there is no experience of *pure* presence, but only chains of differential remarks. (*M*: 318)

Derrida concludes his reading of Austin with a reproduction of his own signature, what he calls 'the most improbable signature'. Alongside it is printed a teasing commentary:

> (Remark: the – written – text of this – oral – communication should have been sent to the Association des Societés de Philosophie de Langue Français before the meeting. That dispatch should thus have been signed. Which I do, and counterfeit, here – Where? There – J. D.). (*M*: 330)

Is the signature successful, viable, legitimate, even when the signatory denies that it is genuine? Is it legitimate when printed, in the total absence of the hand of the author? Is it possible to forge one's own signature? A signature is supposed to carry with it the conscious intention of the subject. It is supposed to be the *very* mark, unique and valuable, of the individual. But it must be both unique (an event of some importance, as when I sign a cheque and promise therefore to supply payment) and non-unique – repeatable, capable of being detached both from the moment of its inscription and from the body or presence of the signatory. What the signature assures us is, in fact, that the signatory will be absent, is absent, and that it is only from this very absence that the signature can have any power as a meaningful and legitimate device.

So the author's signature, as intentionality, origin, invoking the who and what and where of the desire to presence meaning, would be problematic in relation to these functions, undecidable. Thus the poet Francis Ponge, whose proper name precedes and invades his texts, finds himself dispersed rather than found. Ponge, the name, becomes 'sPonge', the sponge, a transformation which is among the most frivolous (non-serious) of Derrida's textual gestures. The sponge 'overflows' the limits of determination — able to 'hold gases or liquid alternatively' (S: 70), 'it takes in water everywhere' (S: 72). The sponge, the proper name becoming the common name, absorbs, takes over, is added to, it gives, loses, supplies, opens and is squeezed: 'it is sufficiently equivocal to hold the dirty *as well as* the clean, the non-proper as well as the proper' (S: 64, 72). The signature, the proper name, cannot control or frame a text, not only because the text becomes separate from the self, but because that self will already have been a text. 'Hence the signature has to remain and disappear at the same time, remain in order to disappear, or disappear in order to remain. *It has to do so, it is lacking*, this is what matters; (S: 56). To sign is to enter a text, not to frame it from an outside, where entry is possible only because already on the inside of this illimitable textuality. It is to lose the title of ownership over the text (and, as we shall see below, over one's own consciousness too).

The structure of signing is that of difference and iteration, not presence or intention which Austin/Searle expel only to reintroduce. The same is true of all utterances, including speech ('oral signatures'), for the moment of utterance by a speaker is always already spaced, distanced and removed from the site of its utterance. Intention is not removed from the scene,

> it will have its place, but from this place it will no longer be able to govern the entire scene and the entire system of utterances . . . given this structure of iteration, the intention which animates utterance will never be completely present in itself and its content . . . One will no longer be able to exclude, as Austin wishes, the 'non-serious', the *oratio obliqua*, from 'ordinary' language. (M: 326–7)

Our attention is therefore to be constantly displaced. Every boundary to context, like that of structure and its centre, is no more than a mark within a chain of signifiers in which there are no *a priori* fixed points, places of certainty or security. Each context is inscribed and carried off within the chains which break out of the inside in which their containment had been supposed.

What becomes of concern in context, therefore, is the status of the borders, all that would frame the interior in order to bring it about. Thus, where Kant would reduce the *parerga* (the drapery on a statue, the ornamental frame on a picture, the columns of a building) to secondary status with respect to the essence and ideality of the aesthetic, the *parergon* is shown to be absolutely indispensable within/ to this *ergon*, which cannot be thought without it. They are necessary to mark the difference between the outside and the inside, and yet the *parerga* ('*hors d'oeuvre*', 'accessory', '*supplement*') is indispensable for this marking, and therefore must be an addition that is at the very heart of what is primary, exceeding it. It is the structure of excess, displacing the centre and inverting its priority with respect to the border:

> No 'theory', no 'practice', no 'theoretical practice' can intervene effectively within this field if it does not weigh up and bear upon the frame, which is the decisive structure of what is at stake, at the invisible limit to (between) the interiority of meaning (put under shelter by the whole hermeneuticist, semioticist, phenomenologicalist and formalist tradition) and (to) all the empiricisms of the extrinsic which, incapable of either seeing or reading, miss the question completely. (*TP*: 61)

The *parergon* raises the question of the boundary, the context, which provides the possibility of the centre while at the same time displacing it, denying the possibility of a discourse on the context that did not exceed its object, 'the always open context which always promises it more meaning' (*MPM*: 116). Meta-commentary leads on to meta-commentary, for 'parerga have a thickness, a surface which separates them not only . . . from the integral inside, from the body proper of the *ergon*, but also from the outside, from the wall on which the painting is hung . . . from the whole field of historical, economic, political inscription' (*TP*: 60–1). To rethink the theory of context is to force the margins, by displacement of the structure, to signify and to reveal their role in the 'provisionality' of discourse, on the construction of essences and priorities from points located elsewhere, drawn from the *différance* of inside/outside, text/context, *ergon/parergon*, primary/ secondary, intrinsic/extrinsic. 'This is my starting point: no meaning can be determined outside of context, but no context permits saturation. What I am referring to here is not richness of substance, semantic fertility, but rather structure, the structure of the remnant and of iteration' (LO: 81).

Situating Subjectivity: The Self as Text

I refer to myself, this writing, I am writing, this is writing — which excludes *nothing* since, when the placement in abyss succeeds, and is thereby decomposed and produces an event, it is the other, the thing as other, that signs. (*S*: 54)

There is no point that can be said to lie outside *différance*. The most basic point raised by Saussure was that signification is not a function of the speaking subject, but that the subject is a function of language, an effect made possible by signification (cf. *SP*: 145; *M*: 15). Derrida underlines Saussure's situating or positioning of the subject in relation to meaning. 'Subjectivity – like objectivity – is an effect of *différance*, an effect inscribed in a system of *différance* . . . It confirms that the subject, and first of all the conscious and speaking subject, depends upon the system of presence, that the subject is not present, nor above all present to itself before *différance*, that the subject is constituted only in being divided from itself, in becoming space, in temporising, in deferral' (*P*: 28–9). There is no greater confirmation of this than the 'violence' of naming already referred to above, for personal or individual names themselves depend upon a general classificatory system, a system opened always by difference, a system already written. The proper name of the individual, which would appear to be the greatest sign of its identity, is in fact the obliteration of that identity in the very act of naming, of the individual disappearing in the face of the nomenclature even as it seemed to emerge, through being classified according to a general structure that extends before and beyond and engulfs it. 'Because the proper names are already no longer proper names, because their production is their obliteration . . . because the proper name was never possible except through its functioning within a classification and therefore within a system of differences' (*OG*: 109). Notions of intentionality, of consciousness and of the meaning and meaningful self are affiliated 'to the essence of logocentrism and metaphysics' (ODD: 89). They call out for decon- struction. And yet these conceptions remain pervasive, at the very root of the system Derrida is attacking. 'Speech and consciousness of speech – that is to say, simply consciousness as self-presence – are the phenomena of an auto-affection experienced as the suppression of *différance*. This *phenomenon*, this presumed suppression of *différance*, this lived reduction of the opacity of the signifier, are the origin of what we call presence' (*OG*: 166).

It is important to note here Derrida's encounters with phenomenol- ogy which, though less familiar, are as crucial as his critique of structuralism. Phenomenology, put very simply, set itself against metaphysics in order to rediscover the original aims of the metaphysi- cal project – the immediate juxtaposition of consciousness and its intended objects. Thus Edmund Husserl, whose theory of signs elaborated in his *Investigations* and *Cartesian Meditations*, is the subject of *SP*, founds his research on 'the living present', 'the self-presence of transcendental life' (*SP*: 6). For Derrida, this factor of presence is fundamental, and a factor of continuity that binds phenomenology to the metaphysics it was attempting to supersede; it can be taken apart on this basis.

As a result of the emphasis upon the indivisible present moment, Husserl comes to centre upon self-consciousness, which alone can keep and repeat this pure presence. Thus a distinction is immediately made between two senses of the word 'sign', between 'expression' and 'indication'. While both may be present in the same statment (phenomenon), a distinction is nevertheless necessary at the essence of being; the discursive sign, involved in communication, is always part of a system of indication, which must be set aside as an extrinsic and empirical phenomenon falling outside the content of absolutely ideal objectivity, outside the originality of expression as meaning and as relation to an ideal object. The indicative sign, we are told, is that which expresses nothing that could be called sense – it is *bedeutungslos*, *sinnlos*, meaningless and senseless. Only expression can participate in the absolute ideality of *bedeuten* – *bedeuten* intends an outside which is that of an ideal object. This outside is expressed and goes into another outside, which is always in consciousness, 'solitary mental life', for expression has no need of being uttered in a world of communication between subjects. The relation to objectivity thus denotes a pre-expressive intentionality aiming at a sense to be transformed into meaning and expression, an intention outside speech/indication but upon which they are dependent. Expression is directly associated with the will, whereas indication is separate and includes all that introduces spacing between *bedeuten* and intention (pre-expression). Indicative signs 'mean', but not in the same and specialized way that expressive signs mean; what separates indication from expression is precisely its non-self-presence in the living present, its delay and temporizing, which can be avoided only within the expressive consciousness where both speaker and interpreter are present in the same moment, without difference or distance.

Indication is therefore necessary wherever necessary wherever there is something to be communicated outside the self. It requires intentionality, and therefore expression, but this then becomes mediated by indicative signs as the content of intentionality is *indicated* elsewhere. Indication is the structure of representation, a representing of the thoughts of the solitary mind. Thus, Husserl maintains in the fifth of his *Cartesian Meditations*, as soon as the other appears, whose 'ownness' is closed to me, indicative language can no longer be effaced.

To remove indication, 'the relation with the other must perforce be suspended' (*SP*: 40). *Bedeuten* is thus reduced to expression as interior monologue, where the physical event of language appears to be absent, there being no delay in the identity and sameness of the manifesting and the cognition of it (*kundgabe/kundnahme*). In solitary mental life, we no longer use real words, but only imagined words – lived experience does not have to be indicated because it is immediately present to itself and certain.

The problem of this Cartesian elaboration is the problem of presence, the ideality of the present moment in (to) consciousness. 'Is this to say that in speaking to myself I communicate nothing to myself? Is not presence reduced and, with it, indication, the analogical detour, etc.? Do I not then modify myself? Do I learn nothing about myself?' (*SP*: 41). The structure of the difference between expression and indication is the structure of presentation (essence) and representation (derivative), the structure by which the sign comes to have an original point where it is unnecessary. Indication is absent at the origin, because there is no need for it – there is no need for communication, for 'I' am already present to 'myself'.

The temporizing of *différance* as the double meaning of both 'to differ' and 'to defer' undoes these priorities. 'We quickly see that the root of these expressions is to be found in the zero-point of the subjective origin, the I, the *here* and *now*.' (*SP*: 94). What ruptures this structure is the structuring of the sign which, as we have seen, cannot exist in a purely isolated present moment, but must rather be iterable, repeatable, the structural necessity of the breaking of any homogenized point. The sign depends upon repetition for its force. As soon as this is admitted, as soon as the consequence of Saussurian differance is drawn to the extent that the sign is relational rather than identical, then indication can no longer be extracted from expression, and no line can be drawn between them. Self-dialogue, the Cartesian formulation, cannot take place without already having invoked an Other without giving to the subject a representation of itself, without noting that within Descartes's formula there is the subject–object division. In order to verify its own existence, the subject must refer outside itself, use the resources of what does not originate on the 'inside', and thus obliterate itself even as it seems to have found it. It must enter into a structure of signs where no point exists without referring constitutively to other points. Already within expression, therefore, the difference between presence and repetition, self and other, as the *différance* of the subject, has begun to gyrate. Expression is already an indication. 'When in fact I effectively use words, and whether or not I do it for communicative ends . . . I must from the outset operate (within) a structure of repetition whose basic element can only be representative' (*SP*: 50). Self-consciousness, the present moment of solitary mental life, the moment that enables expression by removing delay and difference, is narcissistic, a misrecognition of unity for difference and difference for unity.

The intentionality manifested in expression cannot, therefore, be made present to itself – iterability, which makes it possible, introduces into the heart of self-presence a constitutive doubling that renders purity impossible. In soliloquy, I speak to myself, I divide myself. So I am not one, but two. Therefore I am not. When Husserl's phenomenology 'confirms the underlying limitation of language to a secondary stratum, confirms the traditional phonologism of metaphysics' (*SP*: 80–1), Derrida turns this upon its head. Rather than immediately focusing upon an abstract logic behind language and excluding the 'generalities', the ground of consciousness has first to be thought from language, within the indicative sign, for there is nowhere else. Silent self-knowledge is already a signifying trace of difference. Unable to approach primordial presence through anything other than the language it supposedly escaped, Husserl's expression collapses back into indication, and consciousness is dethroned, an effect only of a signifying chain. Thus the individual or proper name is no longer unique, it is iterable, general, differential.

The effect of *différance*, therefore, is to assult the whole metaphysical/phenomenological and onto-judicial concept of 'being', the true and present core of essence. Deconstruction, 'in examining the state just before all determinations of being, destroying the securities of onto-theology . . . constitutes, quite as much as the most contemporary linguistics, to the dislocation of the sense of being, that is, in the last instance, "the unity of the word"' (*OG*: 22). As soon as we ask the question 'What is the sign?', being in its philosophical, ontological and political role begins to regain its stature. It is the unity of the word – the formal essence of the sign conceived as the absolute identity and immediacy of the signifier to the signified, such that the signifier absents itself or at least appears to become transparent, and the signified reduced to something present only to itself. Essence, foundation, core, identity – the question demands these predicates, and the phenomenological and metaphysical question of being requires just such a question and just such a ground. The assumptions upon which it is based are hardly unproblematic within language.

Derrida returns the following formulation of what is at stake. 'The sign is that ill-named thing, the only one, that escapes the instituting question of philosophy, "What is . . . ?"' (*OG*: 19). The question in itself would reinstate metaphysics by virtue of the simple assumptions

about language that would posit an object as that which is represented. Derrida would ask the question only with the force of marked
reservations and precautions. In this instance he takes over from
Martin Heidegger the strategic practice of putting word-concepts 'sous
rature', 'under erasure' — writing the word, using language (we can do
no other) only if it is also crossed out, marked in order to emphasize
the differentiation by which it has been produced as sign, the system
of differences in which it is articulated and outside which it cannot
pass. Being (*Sein*), the ground of all grounds, the principle of all
principles, the name of absolute and irreducible presence, is erased by
Heidegger in order to mark the dependency of the conceptualization
upon a language that is impenetrable, that cannot be escaped, that
cannot have an outside that is anterior to the inside into which the
concept might disappear.

But where for Heidegger 'being' remains a master word, the name
of that which is existent but which cannot be approached, that which
remains reserved as a possibility indefinitely obscured, Derrida has
only the trace, the non-concept and the non-master word. For
Heidegger, the question of being sought to undermine and unground
all notions of meaning anterior to discourse. But he slips back into the
position of (negative) ontology by retaining the notion of being
however unapproachable. The transcendental ground is therefore still
present as a nostalgia within Heidegger's negative ontology (being as
absence). For Derrida, on the other hand, 'being' is no more than a
sign, has no independent ideality, and is no more valuable than any
other word for this function. All signs would be erased, no one more or
less than any other. And this would include his own concepts
particularly and primarily, the trace, *différance*: '*Différance* by itself
would be more 'originary', but one would no longer be able to call it
'origin' or 'ground', these notions belonging essentially to the history
of onto-theology, to the system functioning as the effacing of
difference' (*OG*: 23). We remain locked within that system, which we
cannot escape, but can only work to refuse its implications by playing
the system to its very limits. The desire to name and the requirement
of a naming are countered — the neologism of *différance* resists the force
of onto-theology by combining two senses within a single word, such
that if they cannot be split, neither can they be joined. *Différance*
cannot be formalized.

Deconstruction undermines and problematizes the ontological
grounds of metaphysics and phenomenology, but does not end up, as
did Heidegger, in confirming their propositions by producing a new
ontological ground. Language, inculcated with metaphysical presuppositions, is set to work against itself — *différance* is neither nameable

nor unknowable. Heidegger's 'being' would represent to deconstruction the last gestures of metaphysics and phenomenology and the first
writings of an 'epoch' that has refused its motifs. Refusing to concede
to the demands of metaphysics, deconstruction promises for the
structure in place what can only appear, as Derrida puts it, 'a
monstrous future', 'the play of *différance*, which prevents any word,
any concept, any major enunciation from coming to summarise and to
govern from the theological presence of a centre the movement and the
textual spacing of differences' (*P*: 14). The subject – and along with it
consciousness, subjectivity, objectivity, intentionality, etc. – is therefore caught up in a chain of signifiers which is constantly shifting and
moving. None should be privileged with respect to this *différance*,
which none can escape. Such points are to be erased. But this raises the
question, what articulates these chains of signifiers if not a connection
to a signified, a relationship somewhere to a fixed point (sign) around
which all these chains can pivot?

Jacques Lacan's re-reading of Freud in terms of Saussure seeks to
provide many of the answers. Lacan's notion of language is very similar
to that of Derrida, and indeed, Lacan has claimed to have been
working in advance of Derrida (MacCannell (1986: 20). Lacan draws a
dividing-line between the signifier and the signified, expressing it in
the algorithm

$$\frac{S}{s}$$

such that the signifier is 'over' the signifed, "over" corresponding to
the bar separating the two stages' (Lacan 1977: 149). This split, the
bar resisting signification, allows Lacan to focus attention on the
signifier, which can be said to 'float' or 'slide', engaging in multiple
relations with signifieds. Thus, the manifestation of the unconscious
in dream language is distorted (Freud's 'psychic distortion') as a
primary process of meaning, as metonymy, a relation in meaning that
exists only in 'the *word-to-word* connection' (Lacan 1977: 156), that is,
between signifiers, without introducing signifieds as a necessary
component at the root of the unconscious. To describe this, Lacan
(1977: 164) produces one of his characteristic formulas:

$$f(S \ldots S') S \cong S (-) s$$

Metonymy functions (f) by the displacement from one signifier to
another ($S \ldots S'$), where the first signifier, S, is equivalent ($\sim$) to the
second signifier, S', such that no signified (s) can appear except after

the barrier (−) which dislocates the unity of the sign opening the signified only through the system of signifiers (cf. Leitch 1983: 13). The unconscious is therefore always in process, movement, and cannot be made present as totalization in the reconstrcution through analysis.

It is through this system that the subject is constituted, for its identity is not essential (in the Cartesian.metaphysical/ phenomenological sense) but rather is *produced* by its insertion into something that lies outside its 'self'. subjectivity comes to the subject when it subjects its 'self' to the signifiers of the linguistic–symbolic system ('Language' and 'the Symbolic' are terms Lacan uses to describe the whole circuit of culture). Prior to this moment, the 'subject' (for it is not yet recognizable as such) experiences its 'self' as an unmediated totality – it has no sense of itself as the determinate element within the symbolic system (Frosh 1988: 132).

Subjectivity is established through two major shifts of identification that come to fill (incompletely) and to focus this lack. the first, 'the mirror phase' (Lacan 1977: 1–7) makes this identification of the !I' possible by beginning a process by which it is perceived to be separate. Gazing into the mirror at its own reflection, the child receives an image of itself as a unity, as complete, but this ego is 'imaginary', in the sense that the child is identifying itself with an image that comes from elsewhere. the 'Ideal-I' is possible only by entering into a relationship with 'the Other' (the external) through the mediation of which alone does the ego become possible, and will form the basis for all later identifications. the child identifies and focuses its 'desires' on the mother, who performs the role of this Other. As in Freud's account of the fort/da game, the comings and goings of the mother introduce the child into the alternatives of presence and absence, satisfaction and non-satisfaction, the structure of language, around which its whole life will be organized.

Yet the differences (between self and Other) remain to be completed – the signifiers into which the child has now entered must come to have a referent (Coward and Ellis 1977: 112). the mirror phase constitutes the subject by producing for itself a signifier – the mother – in the place of the Other, upon which its own identity relies and around which its desires will become centred, the child receiving back from the mother perceived as separate the verification of its own identity and separateness. Into this dialectic of introjection and projection, third term – the Other – breaks. The castration or Oedipal phase functions to relate the Ideal-I of the mirror phase to a series of categorical subject identities, specifically in the Oedipal myth, sexual difference and the structure of taboo placing a prohibition on the identification with the mother as focus of desire. The signifiers of the symbolic order are instituted at this stage, pivoting around a single point, the Name of the Father, the mythical father as the figure of the law, signified by the phallus which acts to determine the signifying chains. Identity shifts into the symbolic order as the presence or absence of the phallus becomes the feature that determines differences (male as presence, female as absence).

The central reality of subjectivity is therefore a construct coming to the subject from its outside. This identification is produced at the cost of producing an unconscious. The 'I' that I use to denote myself is given to me, and a split therefore exists between the 'I' that is represented in discourse by accepting the norms of its representation, and the 'I' that is not represented there, but is repressed as a part of all that precedes entry into the symbolic. Thus Lacan can write of the unconscious as structured 'like a language', since it comes into being as a result of the structurings that transform the 'subject' as it enters the symbolic and subjects itself to its codes.

Derrida's critique focuses upon the status of the phallus as signifier. Despite all Lacan's work on the differential structuring of meaning, this shifting is still resolved around the phallus as presence, a transcendental signifier (rather than a transcendental signified, since Lacan emphasizes that the phallus is not an organ, not the penis). Derrida is therefore attacking those moves in Lacan that allow the phallus to come to serve the role of the master word (Culler 1983: 271; Ryan 1976: 39) Thus Lacan's conception of language shifts back from its leanings towards Derrida's *différance* to what he calls a 'phallo-centrism' or 'phallogocentrism', for the phallus is no longer a signifier amongst other signifiers, but a signifier present to itself such that it can determine all the other differences of the signifying chain. In *PC*, Derrida focuses upon Lacan's reading of Edgar Allen Poe's short story 'The Purloined Letter' (Lacan 1988: 191–205), which is taken as a parable for the constitution of the unconscious and the psychoanalytic process. It hinges on an ambiguity of 'the letter', which can mean both an epistle or missive and a graphic, topographical letter. Put as baldly as possible, the story concerns the movements of a letter addressed to a high-ranking person, probably the queen, from an unknown person, concerning things that are never disclosed to us during the course of the tale. All that we know is that the content of the letter, should it be revealed, would be highly injurious to the royals and the established order. It is concealed by the queen from the king by being left in an obvious place on the table; only the minister perceives her strategy, and substitutes a letter of his own for that addressed to the queen who, because she cannot acknowledge the presence of the letter, cannot object. The police are engaged to recover it, but again because it is displayed in an obvious place – in a card-rack above the fireplace – they do not see it. Only Dupin, a detective engaged to recover the letter after the police have failed, sees through the deception, recovers the letter, and substitutes for it one of his own condemning the minister for his actions.

For Lacan the journey of the letter becomes a metaphor for the unconscious. The meaning of the letter/unconscious cannot be revealed or consciously acknowledged, for neither the queen nor the minister can reveal its contents because of the threat it represents to the (symbolic) order. It remains a singular unity, as the letter (signifier) is indivisible: like the phallus, it operates always to disrupt the duality (mother–child, king–queen, minister–queen) and to return to its proper place and reassure the triangularity of these structures, the Oedipal triangle. The displacement of the letter/signifier (the phallic signifier) determines the subjects in their acts, but remains intact through the course of itinerary, with its integrity (individuality) preserved, and always to be returned to its 'proper place'. The symbolic order remains unshaken. 'At every moment each of them, even their sexual attitude, is defined by the fact that a letter always arrives at its destination' (Lacan 1988: 205).

'Lacan leads us back to the truth, to a truth which itself cannot be lost. He brings back the letter, shows that the letter brings itself back towards its *proper* place via a *proper* itinerary . . . destiny as destination. The signifier has its place in the letter, and the letter refinds its proper meaning in its proper place' (*PC*: 436). Like the phallus, the letter is 'only', a signifier, but around it all the signifying chains (of the story) are aligned and follow the rules of the journey. The letter finds its proper meaning in the phallic law, represented by the king and guarded by the queen, the law which she should therefore share with the king but which (through the possession of the letter) she threatens to betray. From then on, Derrida writes, the letter will always have the same meaning as the symbol of the pact. The proper place is the place of castration – 'woman as the unveiled site of the lack of a penis, as the truth of the phallus, that is of castration' (*PC*: 439).

But where Lacan emphasizes the singularity and indivisibility of the letter, thus elevating the letter to a transcendental status, guaranteeing the closure of the Oedipal triangle (the return of what was purloined), Derrida emphasizes the workings of a fourth side, 'the *squaring* of a scene of writing played out in it' (*P*: 112). The letter cannot guarantee the law of the phallus: 'because it is written, at the very least, implies a self-diverting fourth agency, which at the same time diverts the letter of the text from whoever deciphers it, from the *facteur* of truth who puts the letter back into the circle of its own, proper itinerary' (*PC*: 443). The determination of truth, Derrida maintains, governs the entire Lacanian project, of which the seminar would be symptomatic, for within it metaphors of the identification of truth as the unveiling of presence are mobilized, such that 'the ultimate signified of this speech or *logos* is posed as a *lack* (nonbeing, absent, etc.) in no way changes this continuum, and moreover remains strictly Heideggerean' (*P*: 111). Thus, where Lacan ends his seminar by asserting that the letter always arrives at its destination, Derrida's response is that it always might not:

> Its 'materiality' and 'topology' are due to its divisibility, its always possible partition. It can always be fragmented without return, and the system of the symbol, of castration, of the signifier, of the truth, of the contract, etc., always attempt to protect the letter from this fragmentation . . . Not that the letter never arrives at its destination, but it belongs to the structure of the letter to be capable, always, of not arriving . . . Here dissemination threatens the law of the signifier and of castration on the contract of truth. It broaches, breaches the unity of the signifier, that is, of the phallus. (*PC*: 444)

The phallus, as the 'signifier of signifiers', cannot perform the role that Lacan attaches to it. It can only become a part of the movement of the shifting signifier. Thus, where the truth of the letter is found 'between the jambs of the fireplace' where the minister had 'concealed' it, as 'between the legs of a woman' (*PC*: 440, 444) where phallic law finds its realization as absence, Derrida finds the rules of the hymen rather than the phallus, the folds of undecidability and the division of presence or absence, 'the delicate levers that pass between the legs of a word, between a word and itself' (*PC*: 78). Lacan's focus on presence, on arrival, on the disclosure of truth, is dissipated by Derrida in his term 'dissemination'. If the phallus guarantees, then dissemination is the structure of arriving/detour, the divisible/indivisible. The letter (epistle/topographical character) is written, begins its journey, 'But the pen, when you have followed it to the end, will have turned into a knife' (*D*: 302). Semantics and semen are linked etymologically by Derrida, whose version of textuality invokes a sowing that does not fertilize, a semination without insemination, seed spilled in vain, 'an emission that cannot return to the origin in the father' (Spivak 1976: lvx). Where the phallus in Lacan seems to centre subjectivity on the male, defining female only as absence, for Derrida the effect is to install man within woman, woman within man, such that an original bisexuality constitutes both genders as 'variants of archi-woman' (Culler 1983; 171). Thus dissemination, which ungrounds the assurance of the phallus/letter, is feminine in French. 'If account be taken of what chides it, cuts its up, and folds it back in its very triggering, then the present is no longer simply the present' (*D*: 304). The rule of the hymen takes over from the functions of the phallus, complicates them by becoming that into which semen is spilt, and which can advance 'only in the plural' (*D*: 304).

Dissemination therefore breaks into the closed and assured triangularity of the Oedipal or symbolic, by 'castrating the castration', moving the death of the author/inseminator on the fourth side from which it moves but to which it will not return. Lacan's emphasis on the phallus amounts to nothing less than 'as reinstallation of the "signifier", and psychoanalysis in general, in a new metaphysics' (*P*: 109). To question the signifier in this function is to raise a whole problematic concerned with the boundary between consciousness and the unconscious, a question of heterogeneity, a question 'of knowing how, and up to what point, to administer the scene and the chain of consequences' (*P*: 112).

'The irreducibility of "effect of deferral" — such, no doubt, is Freud's discovery' (*WD*: 203). The reading of Freud conducted by Derrida exceeds the space available here for a review (cf. Culler 1983: 159ff.). The subject as origin, as homogeneous *cogito*/ego, is to be decentred into a chain of signifiers which constitute its identity by relating its signifier — the proper name — to other signifiers, for the proper name ('the sPonge') must always be attached, deferred, etc., while at the same time this subject is split into a conscious and an unconscious, neither of which appears anywhere as presence, or disappears anywhere as absence. Lacan's 'lack' runs the risk of shifting back into Heidegger's being, unapproachable but nevertheless ultimately of the species of being-present. Derrida, in the paper that announced *différance*, reads 'a certain alterity' in the place that Freud gave 'a metaphysical name':

> the unconscious is not, as we know, a hidden, virtual or potential self-presence. It is differed — which no doubt means that it is woven out of differences, but also that it sends out, that it delegates, representatives or proxies; but there is no chance that the mandating subject 'exists' somewhere, that it is present or is 'itself', and still less chance that it will become conscious . . . the unconscious can no more be classed as a 'thing' than anything else; it is no more a thing than an implicit or masked consciousness. This radical alterity, removed from every possible mode of presence, is characterised by irreducible after effects . . . With the alterity of the 'unconscious', we have to deal not with the horizons of modified presents — past or future — but with a 'past' that has never been nor will ever be present, whose 'future' will never be produced or reproduced in the form of presence. (*SP*: 152)

The subject and the unconscious are to be read in terms of *différance*. Against Cartesianism and humanism, the subject is nowhere present, has no essence 'as such'; against Lacan, the unconscious is never a form of presence, delayed or deferred, but rather the structure of the conscious/unconscious shifts and rebinds. 'What a mistake to have ever said *the* id' (Deleuze and Guattari 1983: 1). The subject is movement, is in process. It is decentred because it is now to be removed from its position at/as the centre and be situated elsewhere, to find its place within a signifying chain but (like the letter) it will never have arrived completely within the symbolic. The symbolic constitutes the solidity of the order; but dissemination will never allow the symbolic to contain the subject, its consciousness or unconsciousness, in 'its padded interior; (P: 86).

Strategies

Since language, which Saussure says is a classification, has not fallen from the sky, its differences have been produced are produced, effects, but they are effects which do not find their cause in a subject or a substance, in a thing in general, a being that is somewhere present, thereby eluding the play of *différance*. (*SP*: 141; *M*: 11)

It is precisely the production of meaning, its origin and *telos*, stability and identity, that deconstruction questions. Sign, text, context, subject, being – all concepts such as these attempt to account for the totality of meaning, and are imperial motifs in every sense of the word, in complete complicity with a system that is 'logocentric.' There is always more, deconstruction claims – this is the implication of the '*toujours déjà*', the always already, that all grounds and so-called essences are already constructs within a system that creates them, a system which may try to hide itself, but will always reappear through the tensions of *différance*, the lines of weakness which cannot be stabilized or obliterated, only repressed. Deconstruction heralds 'a sort of overrun', that spoils all the boundaries of conventional practice, wiping away the reference-points which had always, by curtailing the signifying chains, protected the system in place. 'Thus the text overruns all the limits assigned to it so far . . . all the limits, everything that was to be set in opposition to writing (speech, life, the world, the real, history, and what not, every field of reference – to body or mind, conscious or unconscious, politics, economics and so forth), (LO: 83–4). The most intimate places by which authority and its reproduction are assured are laid bare through the very resources of their possibility.

The Politics of Style

> The reproductive force of authority can get along more comfortably with declarations or theses whose content presents itself as revolutionary, provided that they respect the rites of legitimation, the rhetoric and the institutional symbolism which defuses and neutralises whatever comes from outside the system. What is unacceptable is what, underlying positions or theses, upsets this deeply entrenched contract, the order of these norms, and which does so in the very *form* of works, of teaching or of writing. (TT: 44)

'The scandal of deconstruction', Christopher Norris writes, 'is its habit of uncovering a disjunct relationship between logic and language, between the order of concepts and the order of signification' (1983: 7). Derrida's texts, certainly, mark the disturbance performed by rhetoric when it is refused to a philosophy that writes but has always, as far as possible, avoided its implications. Like the *pharmakon*, however, instances of the language of metaphysics can be identified that fall outside its rigid formalism and undermine the system they purport to promote. The translation of rhetoric into logic, of a 'non-philosopheme' into a 'philosopheme', is always and necessarily problematic. 'Is philosophical discourse governed . . . by the constraints of language?' (M: 177), Derrida asks, and affirms Nietzsche's observation that language contains an 'illogical element', metaphor − illogical because it operates at the heart of logic to establish relations between (to identify) the non-identical. And when, Derrida asks in 'The White Mythology' (M), is language other than metaphor? Is it not, as Nietszche argued, that metaphor is the very structure of language, of all concepts as their possibility? What the formalization of an appropriate philosophical language excludes (writing in Plato, frivolity in Condillac, the non-serious in Austin and Searle, the *parerga* in Kant) is always at a certain and constitutive point to return, precisely because the formulation and formalization depend upon it. Interiority/exteriority remain undecidable.

It is therefore impossible to split form from content, style from statement, rhetoric from logic. Derrida's own writing attempts to live this difference as a part of his challenge to metaphysics. '*To write otherwise*. To delimit the space of a closure no longer analogous to what philosophy can represent for itself under this name, according to a straight or circular line enclosing an homogeneous space' (M: xxiv; emphasis added). He mobilizes an often dizzying array of stylistic devices and textual strategies that exploit the disjuncture that deconstruction works. He writes double texts, juxtaposing two columns on the same page (G), one on Hegel and the other on Genet, or uses footnotes as a continuous commentary on (what is no longer) the main text, separate from it but intervening and commenting upon it (LO). The double text cannot be formalized; it forbids access within the terms of a reading founded upon presence, problematizing the concepts of origin, authorship, text and identity. This strategy, borrowed from a certain convention in translation, takes up this motif in order to emphasize not just the translation between languages but the translation within language, between language and philosophy and language and itself. 'We are all mediators, translators' (ID: 71). The double text denies simple authority, the authority of presence, the authority of philosophy to denounce writing and exclude its own rhetoric. 'If I write two texts at once, you will not be able to castrate me' (G: 65) Derrida taunts. How can a philosophical tradition seeking to ground itself on metaphysical presuppositions recapture this ground of debate? It can do so only by conceding what is in question.

Having written this, I anticipate a certain response from an archaeology accepting without question the notion of a transparent and representative language. We have already heard within archaeology a denunciation of Derrida's style as obscurantist, and the call for a more passionate and approachable discourse. It has been called pretentious, an argument that will always be both (il)logical and perverse. The fetish of an ordinary language does not escape this criticism. 'Now "everyday language" is not innocent or neutral. It is the language of Western metaphysics, and it carries with it not only a considerable number of presuppositions of all types, but also presuppositions inseparable from metaphysics, which, although little attended to, are knotted into a system' (P: 19). As soon as we ask for the logic to be simply and clearly put, we carry out a classical metaphysical strategy, reducing rhetoric and the rhetorical *parergon* to transparency and irrelevance. For what is at stake here is precisely this *pretence*, this presentation as an act of pretending or deception, which extends even to include this ordinary language, seeking always to present itself as essential, and therefore as other than it is. 'The appeal to the criteria of clarity and obscurity would suffice to confirm what we stated above: this entire philosophical delimitation of metaphor already lends itself to being constructed and worked by "metaphors". How could a piece of knowledge or a language be properly clear or obscure?' (M: 252) The structure of metaphor, which would consist in giving something a name that belongs to something else, can be infinitely multiplied, for the points of condensation that enter the relation are necessarily metaphors already in metaphorical relations.

Any form of language, all forms of discourse, are involved in power. This is emphasized in Derrida's reading of Warburton's essay on hieroglyphs. Warburton attempted to argue for a dislocation between writing as the servant of truth and knowledge, and writing as the 'crypt', as a means of power, obscurity and deception. And yet, when he takes the history of writing back to its root, he discovers that the difference between hieroglyphs as a tool for knowledge and hieroglyphs as a tool for power is nowhere essential, and they are in the hands of the priests and the state from the start. As soon as there is writing there is power. Attempting to describe why what should not have happened (according to his logic) did happen from the beginning, Warburton becomes involved in a distinction between types of hieroglyph, the 'tropical hieroglyph', designed to divulge, and the 'tropical symbol', designed to conceal and protect. But as these separate, they are rejoined, because the crypt effect is present from the beginning and is thus inscribed as an originary presence. There is no first text, Derrida writes, no virgin or originary surface on to which the hieroglyphs as the absence of power could be inscribed. 'Writing does not come to power. It is there beforehand, it partakes and is made from it. Starting from which, in order to seize it . . . struggles and contending forces permeate writings and counter-writings' (SWP: 117). As soon as there is writing, there is a battle over the forms and norms of meaning, over the representation of truth and therefore over what is the truth to be represented. 'And however far one goes back towards the limit of the first need, there is always a writing, a religion, already' (SWP: 146).

Writing text comes to problematize the whole notion of text, binding style and content, rhetoric and logic, and demonstrating their limits and divisions. Derrida's texts challenge authority, precisely because he refuses to accept that the ground or scene of politics is simply that of logic or the signified. The threat to metaphysics is to be offered in the *very form* of writings. If the double text works at the very heart of this philosophy to divide its legitimacy, that is because the body of all texts is not as it seems, is already doubled and redoubled:

Two texts, two hands, two voices, two ways of listening. Together simultaneously and separately. The relationship between the two texts, between presence in general . . . and that which exceeds it . . . Such a relationship can never offer itself to be read in the form of presence, supposing that anything can ever offer itself to be *read* in such a form. (M: 65)

In each text there is more than one voice, more than one statement. There can be no comprehensive reading that does not reduce other significations to silence in the process of highlighting the particular.

We need not assume, however, that this process is not structured, that there is not a system here, nor that what is most important is that which is noticed. A text is heterogeneous; so too is a reading.

The style is certainly difficult, loaded with puns, metaphors and allusions, challenges to conventions and to syntax, fortuitous word-plays, that resist simple consumption and disturb the vertical passage in a reading between the signifier and the signified. Pretentious, certainly, in the sense that language is being stretched to its very limits, limits which have always been menacing precisely because they lie at the heart of conventional values. The first criterion of science is that it should be serious – that it should, as a response to this demand, elaborate a language that excludes the frivolous. This is why Condillac could advance a new metaphysics as 'second first' (phenomena and relations, which metaphysics had placed second, would now come before essences and causes, which had been primary), a metaphysics of *phenomena* requiring a language founded upon the exclusion of the frivolous. Why? Becuase it is frivolity that unsettles the clarity and precision of philosophical statements. 'If philosophical writing is frivolous, that is because the philosopher cannot fulfil his statements' (*AF*: 125). For Derrida, in reading Condillac, all writing is frivolous, by virtue of this delay that enters into philosophy, and will always prevent it from putting an end to writing. Frivolity *is* writing, a part of its structure.

It is for the same reasons that Austin and Searle following him will come to exclude, however provisionally, the non-serious statement, the frivolous that would unsettle the structural formality and law of context because its intentionality is *illegal*. Searle's reply to Derrida's critique of Austin is submitted to the most detailed examination (LI). He is renamed 'SARL', the new spelling meant to indicate the 'Société à responsabilité limitée' or the 'Limited Inc.' of the paper's title, in order to problematize the idea that texts can be controlled by and belong to their authors. Thus Searle's text is reproduced in its entirety in different parts of Derrida's reply, playing upon the significance of copyright for the question of meaning and origin (always the institu-tionalized, legalized, judicial origin). Is it serious? This is precisely the point. Where, for the speech-act theorists, philosophy must operate first on the serious alone, casting out of court the non-serious, Derrida's text teems with an intermingling of indulgent plays and logical argument. Frivolity returns to writing because *différance* 'will have named *at once* the root of sensibility and instance of the frivolous' (*AF*: 128).

'Why is it that we seem to ask the philosopher to be "easy" and not other such scholars who are even more inaccessible to the same reader?

. . . I think that it is always the "writer" that one accuses of being unreadable . . . someone who is engaged in explaining things with language, i.e., with the economy of language, with the codes and channels of what is itself the very medium of understanding' (ID: 72). Derrida mixes genres, and blurs the territories of conventional territories. He reads philosophy as though it were literature, as though it were impossible to distinguish between the two. In *D*, Derrida explores some of the implications that arise when one treats philosophy as writing, and what conventions govern the accepted norms. It opens with a reflection on the notion of the preface, a preface on prefacing, writing around the function of this device in the construction of a text as philosophy. The preface would operate to create the figure of the book as one open to reading as, on and by presence. It states what the book will say before it is said, presencing the argument, its significance, essence or notable points; gives the text identifiable borders, points at which meaning begins and ends. It would stand in an ambiguous position, at one and the same moment inside and outside the text, promoting and transgressing the chains it seemed to establish and delimit. In the teleological scheme of the book, the preface stands before the text to which it cannot properly belong. But in anticipating what the text will say, it has already formed the book for us, introduced its themes, constructed as a present object the text it precedes, positioned the reader.

The preface, prescribed as an empty form, a convention, signifies. It is a totalizing device, one invested with the authority to introduce, form and pre-face a text, unifying its disparate elements, generalizing about its history, treating the text as transparent. And yet, for all this, we know that its position must assure us that all texts are already prefaced, already parts of systems. The preface is itself a part of metaphysics, implicated in its ideology and the reproduction of its conceptual framework. In Derrida's hands, the structure of the preface-text is exploded. 'The text has no stable identity, no stable origin, no stable end. Each act of reading the "text" is a preface to the next' (Spivak 1976: xii). The preface has no authority over the text, which is heterogeneous; reading is opened up as production and not merely consumption.

Style, then, is not to be cut out of the politics of the text. Rhetoric is 'illogical', it creates, sanctions and reproduces meanings. There can be no political practice that does not extend its challenge to elaborating a new language to undermine that which it opposes. Habermas's 'ideal speech community' cannot exist, as he admits, without repression to establish the norms and conventions of the debate. No ideal speech can be elaborated, because style is a material factor in meaning, because language is ideology and not simply its carrier (Ryan 1982: 113). The subject is located in language, situated in chains of signifiers which constitute its consciousness and its central reality. No purely ideal speech, operating only at the level of the signified, can transform the subject no longer conceived along Cartesian lines. 'Walter Benjamin said fairly much the same thing: the responsibility of the writer is not primarily to propose revolutionary theses. The latter are defused as soon as they are presented within the language and according to the norms of the existing cultural apparatus. And it is the latter that must *also* be transformed' (ID: 77). Appeals to Cartesianism as the destination of radical and challenging theories will always shoot wide of the mark, because the materialism of language will have been written out of consciousness. '[W]hat we need, perhaps, as Nietzsche said, is a change of style' (*M*: 135), a change of the norms of discourse that will break out of the enclosure of presence, consciousness and so on. The poet, s/he who invokes only language and affirms the play of metaphors to establish connections, may be more radical than the politician (cf. Kristeva 1984), and it is only a structure at work already, a structure of the exclusivity of genres as a protection of the system, that makes us think that style is empty, that this poetics will not be effective and not understood.

Paris and Yale: A Tale of Two Signifiers

[T]here is no sense in speaking of *a* deconstruction, or *simply* deconstruction as if it were only one, as if the word had a (single) meaning outside of the sentences which inscribe it and carry it within themselves. (*MPM*: 17)

What Derrida does not found through his encounters with various forms of philosophy is a philosophy 'of *différance*. The concept cannot come to replace all other ontological references, cannot be formalized, cannot be named as such without compromising its significance. The allusions which the silent *a* creates cannot be compacted into a name which can be imported into every kind of critical situation. But to be unnameable is not to deny its force – it is unnameable only in the sense of all that metaphysics would wish to invest in a name. 'This unnameable is not an ineffable Being which no name could approach: God, for example. This unnameable is the play which makes possible nominal effects, the relatively unitary and atomic structures that are called names, the chains of substitutions of names in which, for example, the nominal effect *différance* is itself *enmeshed*, carried off, reinscribed, just as a false entry or a false exit is still a part of the game, a function of the system' (*M*: 26–7). He is emphatic. Deconstruction is not a method, not even an activity. *Différance* is not a name, nor a concept (*P*: 39), it is a function of texts, an operation situated in their construction, their possibility. 'There is a crack there. Construction and deconstruction are breached/broached there. The line of disintegration, which is not straight or continuous or regular . . . On this condition alone, at once internal and external, is deconstruction *possible*' (*AF*: 132). It is not a hermeneutic technique, focused on revealing obscure truths in a text (Ormeston 1988: 43). 'It is not an analysis in particular, because the dismantling of a structure is not a regression towards a *simple element*, towards an *indissoluble origin*. These values, like that of analysis, are themselves philosophemes subject to deconstruction' (LJF: 3). It takes place, but it does not belong to a method, subject, era or genre. It deconstructs, and this would include deconstructing itself (LJF: 4). Everything is in/through deconstruction.

Thus deconstruction produces no convenient index or list of concepts. There is no dictionary and can be no dictionary in which we could look up *différance* and be provided with a convenient definition that would exhaust its potential. In the 'economy' through which deconstruction works, producing 'undecidables', 'the list has no taxonomical closure . . . because these are not *atoms*, but rather focal points of economic condensation' (*P*: 40). There is no question here of a new epistemology, a new ground for knowledge. Deconstruction yields only the activation of a certain spacing as the unravelling of existing conceptual (and non-conceptual) grounds. *Play* – 'the absence of the transcendental signified . . . that is to say as the destruction of onto-theology and the metaphysics of presence' (*OG*: 50). In a letter to Jean-Louis Houdebine, Derrida asks himself the rhetorical question, 'why deconstruct?' If there is no objective truth, no ontology, no solid corpus of critical ideas, why bother? 'Nothing here,' he responds, 'without a "show of force" somewhere. Deconstruction, I have insisted, is not *neutral*, it *intervenes*' (*P*: 93).

Yet despite these statements of prupose, in its success deconstruction has accumulated around *différance* as a new motif of interpretative authority. The American deconstructors, centred at Yale in New Haven, have vigorously pursued the ideas of 'free play' in signification, to the extent that the text has been wiped of any form of textual determination and left open entirely to the notion of a free reading. They have championed the idea of *aporia*, the *mise en abyme*, the abyss of meaning through which the reader traces a 'lateral dance' along the chains of signifiers in the text, 'and no one of these chains has archaeological or interpretative authority over the others' (Miller 1975: 58).

The theme of these formulations of deconstruction is that *différance* has the authority to deny all authorities, to supplant all forms of ontological agency, and that *différance* is sufficient in itself to supplant these structures and grounds. Discourse which would be unbounded in the Derridean sense, causing it to turn in once again, becomes unbounded in some absolute sense. All historically locatable forces are 'torn apart', in de Man's words; the past disappears, the slate is wiped clean. *Mise en abyme* – the end of the old system and the beginning of the new.

But, as Lentricchia has shown, this group has fulfilled Derrida's prophecy about such an easy victory, and left everything as it is. 'Such freedom is the corner-stone principle of formalist, idealist and aestheticist positions after Kant . . . [it] represents a new formalism . . . in the sense that it is the older formalism with its ontological freight thrown away' (Lentricchia 1983: 180). It is Miller who, of the Yale school, comes closest to formulating a powerful theory of history, based upon the heterogeneity of epochs, but fails to realize the potential, 'probably because the so-called non-principle of the *mise en abyme* functions in deconstructionist commentary as a universal shield which protects texts from difference rather than opening them up to it' (Lentricchia 1983: 184).

Thus, when de Man attempts a deconstructive reading of Derrida's *OG*, he can elevate the 'free play' of *différance* in the literary text to the extent that 'there is no need to deconstruct Rousseau', for he (Rousseau) has already done so. The text is privileged for its capacity to deconstruct itself, the literary text becoming the grandest form of this phenomenon, the opaqueness of the old interpretative systems and of language itself suddenly vanishing as the text becomes transparent, endlessly 'anticipating' all that can be said of it. Thus Miller, inspired by de Man, ends up prioritizing the object 'text' over the activity of reading/producing readings of it. The texts are 'ahead' of the critic, 'they have anticipated any deconstruction the critic can achieve' (Miller 1975: 31). The author is restored to place and literature is staged as a superior form of expression, criticism condemned to secondary status. It is the practice of structurally limiting deconstruction to the very concepts and identities it should have been challenging. Where Derrida emphasizes the general text, of which the literary would be one instance as it arises from *écriture*, the American disciples have restricted themselves to the literary, to high culture. the political implications of deconstruction are stripped away to leave only a new contender in the same old formal power strategies over the literary text in the institution. All deconstruction does in these hands is provide a vigorous philosophical justification for a pre-existent system of interpretation — the valorization of history and ideology in the face of a literary text endlessly multiplying readings of itself.

Derrida himself is surprisingly coy about these appropriations of his work. Speaking after Paul de Man's death in 1984, he seems conscious that in America deconstruction has been inserted into existing traditions — political, ethical, religious and academic — that have blunted its edge, but declines to speculate further on this because this would be to totalize a diverse movement, to objectify it. He does note, in relation to de Man's comments, that if Rousseau anticipates the deconstruction, this is because deconstruction as a concept must be erased 'since it only designates the explication of a relation of the work to *itself*' (*MPM*: 124). But there is also here the necessity for a reading to *produce* this deconstruction. If the word only names what will 'happen' to texts, what is a possibility, it remains that this possibility is historically constituted and does not therefore necessarily become realized. If the text 'deconstructs itself' in this sense, it does not follow that the critic is superfluous, that the text will reveal itself. Deconstruction is necessary as an action, as an intervention. Derrida's original expression of the relationship of the text 'to itself' is quite clear:

> It is certainly a production, because I do not simply duplicate what Rousseau thought of this relationship. The concept of the supplement is a sort of blind-spot in Rousseau's text, the not-seen that opens and limits visibility. But the production, if it attempts to make the not-seen accessible to sight, does not leave the text . . . It is contained in the transformation of the language it designates . . . We know that these exchanges can only take place by way of the language and the text, in the infrastructural sense that we now give to that word. And what we call production is necessarily a text, the system of writing and reading which we know is ordered around its own blind-spot. We know this a priori, but only now and with a knowledge that it is not knowledge at all. (*OG*: 163–4)

The text which has no outside is not the literary text, whose borders can thus be re-established. On the contrary, Derrida's working through *différance* is supposed to extend the question of the conventional text into realms which were hitherto not regarded as 'textual'. At the same time, however, the resources for this transformation are take from the 'inside' of the text. The *supplement* comes to overturn Rousseau's polarities, but by being neither addition nor subtraction, outside nor inside, accident nor essence, presence nor absence, it never becomes a third term, a new concept, coming to the text from the outside. If the *supplement* comes to govern Rousseau's oppositions, then it begins this process from the inside of the text it will transform.

The notions of the abyss and the authority of *différance* rest, as Marion Hobson (1987) has argued, on an inadequate and inaccurate reading of the original Derridean texts. Play (*jeu*) occupies a role in Derrida's work up to *OG*, but not the *free* play of meaning that these varieties of deconstruction have propounded. Bringing with it associations of freedom and equality amongst interpretations, 'free play' is highly inappropriate within deconstruction and rests upon a mistranslation of Derrida's seminal paper in the United States. The political ineptitude of American deconstruction can be traced to this root, the mistranslation of *jeu*. Play in Derrida's work belongs to a notion of *tension*, a force within structuring against which a structure emerges, and which it always retains within itself. Derrida does not offer the free play of the signifier or its associates, but the means of locating the supports of a system, and therefore its weak points and blind-spots in the chains that hold it in place.

Thus, in the same text in which he is supposed to have introduced and sanctioned 'free play', Derrida writes:

> There are thus two interpretations of interpretation, of structure, of sign, of play. The one seeks to decipher, dreams of deciphering a truth or an origin which escapes play and the order of the sign, and which lives the necessity of interpretation as an exile. The other, which is no longer turned towards an origin, affirms play and tries to pass beyond man and humanism, the name of man being the name of that being who, throughout the history of metaphysics or of onto-theology — in other words, throughout his entire history — has dreamed of full presence, the reassuring foundation, the origin and the end of play. (*WD*: 292).

The choice here, the apparent choice, would be that between Rousseau and Descartes on the one hand, with their dreams of full presence, and Nietzschean affirmation on the other, 'the affirmation of a world of signs without fault, without truth and without origin' (*WD*: 292). The choice would thus be offered between metaphysics and its 'after' or 'outside'. But although the question of the difference is important, these are not on offer as alternatives, and Derrida emphasizes that the question of choice is itself a trivial point, for the break or rupture that is announced by deconstruction with its transatlantic tongue is not the point of this passage. We cannot simply slip from one side to the other, wiping away structures as if (because we now have *différance*) they were no longer there. 'We must first try to conceive of the common ground and the *différance* of this irreducible difference' (*WD*: 293).

There is no choice, there is no escape. We cannot simply pronounce the end of the old system; we are bound within it. The structure may not simply be destroyed by constructing another position governing from the outside, such as the abyss; this only continues to reproduce the structure in question by playing its rules. The system can only be shaken from within, pushed irrevocably towards and through its points of tension, points located marginally, points condemned to a secondary function in a hierarchy. Deconstruction works from the inside of texts 'to avoid both simply *neutralising* the binary oppositions of metaphysics and simply *residing* within the closed field of these oppositions, thereby confirming it' (*P*: 41). How, and how successfully, this can be done within deconstruction will be the concern below.

After the Abyss: Deconstruction and History

Deconstruction is not, therefore, about releasing the reader from the formal restrictions through which s/he works, allowing her or him to produce something approximating to de Man's 'more interesting' or 'productive' literary texts. *Différance* performs a role, but it does not occupy the totality of the activity. There is no question of the abyss. 'I didn't say that there was no centre, that we could get along without the centre. I believe that the centre is a function, not a being – a reality, but a function. And this function is absolutely indispensable . . . It is a question of knowing where it comes from and how it functions' (*SC*: 271). Thus, Derrida asks of the critic, 'Where are the borders of a text? How do they come about?' (LO: 85). The question is wholly unlike that of the abyss, and we may take it as paradigmatic (I should eschew such a word, or at least erase it. 'Paradigm' carries with it associations of instances – practices perhaps – of a theoretical essence or core, a unifying point to which the instance is referent. Since deconstruction works within its object text, it is inappropriate to imply a division between theory and practice, as between instances and totality.) Exploring the questions so raised means exploding the categories and identities that structure orthodox work – situating all practices, all texts, beyond their borders in the other from which they are differentiated, in order to discover them as constructs within a system, and write into these texts the marks that surround the scene. There is nowhere an 'innocent' meaning, one which we can take for granted; all significations and productions are 'suspect', in so far as they are products and therefore implicated within a system that has produced them. In place of the text that anticipates all that may be said of it, a notion which seems to make a nonsense of ideology and transform the hedonistic into the reactionary, there is the space in which the air of freedom is breathed with that of guilt. Ideology is no longer masking or opaque, but opened up in its closure through the tension of the structure upon which it is constructed. Lentricchia puts the case succinctly: 'Derrida's point is that once we have turned away from various ontological centrings of writing, we do not turn to free play in the blue, as the Yale formalists have done. Rather, it would appear that our historical labours have just begun' (Lentricchia 1983: 173). This point, however, requires further elaboration. If deconstruction leads, against the excesses of the Yale school, to some kind of historical labour, then what form will this activity take? In Lentricchia's account, the question seems suspended within Derrida's work as the narrative moves quickly into the work of Michel Foucault. Whilst this is by no means prohibited, and is indeed demanded in approximating Derrida and Foucault, the former's *écriture* and the latter's *discours*, the question remains unaddressed, as do the differences between the concepts.

Some kind of historical labour is certainly what Derrida does call for – he uses the term often, though usually in inverted commas or with some other means of marking his reservations and precautions. In the essay 'Différance', he writes, 'If the word history did not in and of itself convey the motif of the final repression of difference, one could say that only differences can be "historical" from the outset and in each of their aspects' (*M*: 11; *SP*: 141). Obviously, the neologism *différance* attempts to convey as movement both spatialization and temporalization, 'the becoming-space of time and the becoming-time of space' (*SP*: 136), 'the gap of the present's relation to itself and still the present's self-relation in iterability' (*AF*: 128). *Différance* comes, therefore, to designate the movement through which language and all significations are 'constituted "historically" as a weave of differences' (*M*: 12), but only with the proviso that these concepts are shown to be in complicity with that which is questioned by *différance*.

The most useful debate around this point is to be found in Derrida's critique of Foucault's *Madness and Civilization*, in which the concept of history within deconstruction becomes more explicit. Foucault attempts to show how the relationship between madness and reason changed between the medieval and classical periods. From the beginning of the age of reason, what had previously been a vocal madness, a discourse in exchange with reason, was suppressed and silenced. The two examples Foucault uses to support his thesis are the Cartesian *cogito* and the use of leper houses to hold and contain the insane. Reason and the voice of reason come to dominate all discourse. What Foucault attempts to do is to write the history of the silence of madness, the 'outside' or the other side of reason, discovering it in its silence and letting it speak. He thus wants to step outside of reason and the boundary set up by reason, to let it speak for itself. He wants to write the history of madness *itself*.

In his reading, Derrida is concerned with the three pages in Foucault's text that deal with the passage taken from the first of Descartes's *Meditations*, which Foucault suggests demonstrates that madness is dismissed and excluded from philosophical attention, because the *cogito* could not possibly be mad, it must be rational through and through. First, is Foucault's interpretation of this passage correct? This is not an empirical question. Rather, it is asking whether it is possible for the historical project Foucault is writing of at the end of the eighteenth century to be totalized and thus whether it is possible to be so unequivocal about the significance of Descartes's statement. Does it have the historical meaning assigned to it by Foucault? 'That is, again, two questions in one: does it have *the* historical meaning assigned to it? Does it have *this* meaning, a *given* meaning Foucault assigns to it? Is the meaning exhausted by its historicity? In other words, is it fully, in each and every one of its aspects, historical, in the classical sense of the word?' (*WD*: 33). Second, he is concerned with the 'philosophical and methodological presuppositions' that underlie Foucault's project on the history of madness; that is, the dependency of madness on that '"other form of madness" that allows men "not to be mad"' (*WD*: 33), reason.

Derrida takes issue with Foucault's project of writing the history of madness. 'Of madness itself. That is, by letting madness speak for itself. Foucault wanted to be the subject of this book in every sense of the word . . . madness speaking about itself . . . and not a history of madness described from within the language of reason' (*WD*: 34–5). These are two points here. Foucault's attempt to make silence speak for itself can only be made from within the language of reason, and the attempt to found and make use of a language not so based and implicated is inherently problematic. 'We have a right to ask what, in the last resort, supports this language without recourse or support . . .? Who wrote and who is to understand, in what language and from what historical situation of the logos . . . this history of madness?' (*WD*: 38). Foucault's history can only be written in the language of reason, borrowing all the signs and the means of expression from precisely that which has walled up madness as the forbidden outside. '*Nothing* within this language, and *no-one* among those who speak it, can escape the historical guilt . . . which Foucault wishes to put on trial' (*WD*: 35). The very articulation and language, and therefore the trial itself, will simply reiterate and underline the verdict established in advance. Foucault's history of madness will repeat and reinforce the sentence.

Furthermore, is not history itself, as the concept guiding this writing, itself defined through and on the basis of rationality? So how can it be possible to write the *history* of madness *itself*, since these two terms are not independent. This history can only be written from the point of view of reason, and will therefore be a history that continues to impose a sentence on madness. The escape that Foucault wants and requires for his project cannot be imagined within these terms: 'The revolution against reason can be made only from within it . . . A history, that is an archaeology against reason doubtless cannot be written, for, despite all appearances to the contrary, the concept of history has always been a rational one' (*WD*: 36). By attempting to befriend madness, to convey its silence and write its history independently of reason, one must have already assumed the position of the jailer.

Within this 'historical' framework, what significance is to be attributed to Descartes's *Meditations*? Foucault places the emphasis upon the *cogito* as the philosophical underpinning of madness's exclusion from life, i.e. madness is to be excluded not only practically but philosophically. In the first *Meditation*, Descartes notes that sensory information can deceive and that we ought to mistrust that which is capable of deception. But also these sensory responses remain important – how, Descartes asks, could I deny that these hands and this body are mine? Such an argument would follow precisely the delusion that leads madmen to believe, for instance, that they are kings when they are only paupers. The result would then be to argue that such senses deceive only in relation to things that are hardly perceptible, or very far away. Sensory delusion finds its extreme form in dreams, which take place as experiences without the outside world. Yet the dream would itself be surmountable by truth, since its basis is real. So artists may imagine anything and everything, but truth remains within their fantasies as that which cannot be falsified – colour, for example. Thus everything that was previously admissible as madness has, according to Foucault, been separated from it. What was hitherto sanctioned within insanity is admissible in dreams, and insanity itself prohibited (i.e. the kernel of truth through sensory perception in madness is now to be included in dreams; madness is stripped of its dialogue, condemned to be absolute unreason).

Derrida contradicts Foucault's interpretation of Descartes. Descartes is not privileging madness for treatment, but, on the contrary, he is denouncing the sensory foundation of knowledge and asserting the 'intellectual' foundation of certainty. He notes the senses can deceive; he anticipates the response that he would thus have to end up denying the existence or testimony of his hands and body. So he uses an example which shows the poverty of the senses, dreams. It is sleep, not madness, that is at stake here in undermining the notion of a sensory origin for ideas. Madness is only one cause of sensory error. 'What must be grasped here is that *from this point of view* the sleeper, or the dreamer, is madder than the madman. Or, at least, the dreamer, in so far as concerns the problem of knowledge which interests Descartes here, is further from true perception than the madman' (*WD*: 51). Descartes does not exclude madness. Indeed, his formulation of consciousness and self-consciousness is specifically designed such that it works even in the case of madness. 'Whether I am mad or not, *cogito*, *sum*' (*WD*: 56).

The project of Foucault's work, which rests on the notion of the *Decision*, is therefore only one reading of Descartes. Where, for Foucault, the *Meditations* would be a sign of the historical structure he identifies, for Derrida the sign would itself be indeterminable as such – it does not simply represent developments taking place elsewhere; it signifies many things at the same time. 'The attempt to write the history of the decision, division, difference runs the risk of continuing this division as an event or a structure subsequent to the unity of an original presence, thereby confirming metaphysics in its fundamental operation' (*WD*: 38). Derrida therefore proceeds to take apart Foucault's whole conception of a radical epistemological break, for the division of reason from madness must be older than the medieval period. Foucault's 'Decision' is actually a 'dissension', a self-dividing action, 'interior to the logos in general' (*WD*: 38). Where Foucault defines the Greek *logos* as having no contrary, as pure presence, Derrida writes that for there to be a concept of reason, there must be a concept of unreason, its other, madness, which would of necessity be expelled in order for reason and rationality to establish and protect their foundations. Thus the decision must be older, and the free dialogue that Foucault identifies in the medieval period must be secondary in relation to this division: 'it must be assumed in general that reason can have a contrary, that there can be an other of reason' (*WD*: 41). *General* because it cannot be understood as an historical event, a *decision*, because the necessary exclusion of madness must be present *from the start* to enable this history to take place. Madness must thus become negative, the 'absence of the work' as Foucault puts it, necessarily divided from reason for the speaker to 'keep his distance, the distance indispensable for continuing to speak and live' (*WD*: 54). It is from this point, this realization, that historical analysis must proceed: 'It is therefore a question of drawing back toward a point at which all determined contradictions, in the form of given, factual historical structures, can appear and appear as relative to this zero-point at which determined meaning and non-meaning come together in their common origin' (*WD*: 56). It is necessary, therefore, to return *at first* to that point from which madness and its history emerge, for it is only relative to this that its development can be understood.

This account has been lengthy, but it is important because it shows precisely how a deconstructive reading can begin to examine historical structures. It opens by examining the conceptual frame in which history takes place. This means rejecting the notions of linearity or totality which govern historical writing. Thus Derrida, in situating the *Meditations* 'historically', questions the notion of Foucault's that this 'event' is a sign of a present feature, the emergence of a concrete genre inaugurated by 'the Decision', the classical period. '[W]hether it is a fundamental symptom or cause . . . whatever the place reserved for philosophy in this total structure may be, why the sole choice of the Cartesian example? What is the exemplarity of Descartes, while so many philosophers of the same era were interested or – no less significantly – not interested in madness in various ways?' (*WD*: 43–4). The text as sign is enmeshed in many chains of signifying traces, from which emerges the whole notion of genre, period, development, event. Derrida, therefore, uses the term 'history' 'in order to reinscribe its force and to produce another concept or conceptual chain of "history": in effect a "monumental, stratified, contradictory" history [Sollers]; a history that also implies a new logic of *repetition* and the *trace*, for it is difficult to see how there could be a history without it' (*P*: 57). The identity of the event must be iterable – repeatable outside itself, the present, the present moment – for it to signify. Thus Derrida subscribes, to a certain extent, to Althusser's criticisms of history, and his argument that there are histories of different type and rhythm (*P*: 58). The thing differs from itself, so history becomes possible as *time* only because the present cannot exist except by differing from itself. Thus, as Michael Ryan has written (1982: 24–5): first, the historical event is produced by chains that remove its homogeneity and determine it as multifaceted and heterogeneous, a fertile source of significations that cannot be exhausted; and second, if the event is determined, if difference is closed down, that determination is not natural, not a truth of the event discovered as essence and merely repeated or (re)discovered by the analysis, 'but instead an institution'.

Thus historical writing *adds*, it supplements and produces a new meta-level of determinations that are an addition that demands explanation. The concept of the period or genre therefore becomes problematic. The commentary on periods, 'whether it is a question of an individual work or of Western metaphysics, always has the value of a fiction or story we tell ourselves in order to dramatise, historically or teleologically, a non-historical argument' (*MPM*: 121). In the act of writing time itself must be stopped and presences produced, but this is something added to the historical context that escaped what is being explained. Thus if a text produces or participates in a genre/historical period, it can itself belong to no genre, because the frame that marks its belonging does not itself belong. Whatever contextualizes a text cannot itself simply belong to that context – so the frame of meaning becomes *parergon*, supplementary. 'The paradox of parergonality is that a framing device which asserts or manifests class membership is not itself a member of that class' (Culler 1983: 196).

The law of genre, then, like that of context/*parergon*, 'is a principle of contamination' (*WLO*: 206). What marks the belonging to a period divides itself from that period, because the supplementary trait does not properly belong to any genre or class. 'It gathers together the corpus and, at the same time . . . keeps it from closing, from identifying itself with itself' (*LO*: 212). Writing produces an endless play of meta-commentaries which define and exceed the event, period or genre in question. 'We cannot determine the centre and exhaust totalisation because the sign which replaces the centre, which supplements it, taking the centre's place in its absence – this sign is added, occurs as a surplus, as a *supplement*' (*WD*: 289). Historical writing exceeds itself, context is exploded, the object of history is displaced between past and present. The historical object has significance which exceeds its context by virtue of its writing, that overflows all borders and erases the 'ontology' of the event. It is no longer sufficient to show how an event is infused by multiple determining traces in its context, for the context of the event would itself be caught up in these traces, drawing the historian endlessly out of the comfortable security provided by the delimitation of a period. If history would be about what happened, then history is about what is still happening, 'A history of the possibility of history which would no longer be an archaeology, a philosophy of history or a history of philosophy' (*OG*: 28). The history of meaning and the meaning of history are bound up together.

Derrida's historical writing is, put glibly, located 'in' *différance* – between past and present, determination and under-determination, in the space traced out and traversed by the supplement as excess, therefore between binary poles or on the 'fourth side' of the triangle, Oedipal or more generally metaphysical. *Différance* as history has the effect, in fact, of reopening the present to the past, situating each in the terms of the other. Structuralism, therefore, is historically situated, emerging at/in a particular time and place, but it should be read at the same time in terms of history, because to write is to supply a context with all that is necessary for its operation as well as all that is necessary for its erasure, the reopening of context that would close down the question of the relation even as it works it, and protect the present from the past. How, for instance, could a history of structuralism be written, except in these terms?

> If it recedes one day, leaving behind its works and signs on the shores of our civilisation, the structuralist invasion might become a question for the historian of ideas, or perhaps even an object. But the historian would be deceived if he came to this pass: by the very act of considering the structuralist invasion as an object he would forget its meaning and would forget that what is at stake, first of all, is an adventure of vision, a conversion of the way of putting questions to any object posed before us, to historical objects – his own – in particular. (WD: 3)

An Incomplete Project?

> [T]he necessity of a deconstruction. Following the consistency of its logic, it attacks not only the internal edifice, both semantic and formal, of philosophemes, but also what would be wrong to assign as its external housing, its extrinsic conditions of practice: the historical forms of its pedagogy, the social, economic or political structures of this pedagogical institution. It is because deconstruction interferes with solid structures, 'material' institutions, and not only with discourses or with significant representations, that it is always distinct from an analysis or 'critique'. (TP: 19)

Since the late 1970s, Derrida's texts have been scattered with increasingly emphatic and explicit statements of the political implications of deconstruction, its potential for working not only within the 'academic' text but within a general textuality, within 'the world as text'. It is towards this constituting and constitutive exterior of intellectual culture that meanings are to be disseminated, the borders that guard the interior to be exploded and overrun. There has, however, been some doubt as to how this is to be realized; until very recently, Derrida has been content to confine his attention to the apparently 'philosophical' significance of logocentrism, and his principal involvement with the social has been his participation in the Group de recherches sur l'enseignement philosophique, an organization devoted to protecting the teaching of philosophy in French schools and involved in a critique of philosophy's role, institutionally, in forces regarded as marginal to its reflective content and significance (Culler 1983: 157–8). As Terry Eagleton has observed, it is Foucault rather than Derrida who has engaged in a dissemination of meanings into the institutional and social scene (Eagleton 1986: 79).

Certainly, it would be rash here to conclude without making some important reservations about deconstruction and Derrida's articulation of it. We should note, for instance, that the claims made for an 'immanent' critique (one that uses the resources of that which is being interpreted) rest upon a formalism that is basic to deconstruction and its procedures of analysis. Deconstruction, we are told constantly, is not a method or a means of analysis, because no critical system (no mere '-ism') can master or control *différance*, without itself being caught up and subjected to the same movements and shifts. *Différance* is less a critical motif than a force which operates within critical motifs, between the conceptual and the non-conceptual, etc. And yet this cannot remove the necessity of these frameworks if intervention is to take place – deconstruction will always be demanded, such that it will never end.

It would be as impossible, in fact, to operate without method or without a centre as it would be to work entirely within *différance*. Indeed, these notions remain indispensable. As many critics have pointed out, deconstruction must begin with a formalization of its object – it must presuppose a metaphysics, a text, operative and functional boundaries. Thus, while he bombards Foucault's *Madness and Civilization* with objections to its methods and explorations into its complicities with what it is attempting to escape, Derrida's own reading of Descartes's *Meditations* still rests on conventional assumptions about Descartes, his text, his period. As de Man points out, in order to open a text to deconstruction, that text has to have been/ become determined (de Man 1971). In order for a discursive formation or text to be deconstructed it has to have already been constructed, been determined and identified. For structures to be desedimented there must first be structures, and as Derrida himself admits, deconstruction must presuppose a structuralism in order 'to understand how an "ensemble" was constituted and to reconstruct it to this end' (LJF: 3).

This would not be too problematic were it not for the way in which structures have been received, for the ways in which texts are taken as objects for deconstruction. There has to be a determined, sanctioned metaphysics in order for there to be *différance*, and this might seem to render *différance* dependent upon presence (Wood 1988: 63). *Différance*, which 'alone exceeds dialectics' (*WD*: 256) and 'holds us in a relation with what exceeds . . . the alternative of presence or absence' (*SP*: 151), disrupts metaphysics while at the same time never being able to separate and only capable of inversion. For we know that there can be no possibility of overcoming metaphysics, of destroying it and beginning afresh – the notion of revolution is pre-eminently metaphysical. 'There is no sense in doing without the concepts of metaphysics in order to shake metaphysics. We have no language – no syntax and no lexicon – which is foreign to this history' (*WD*: 280). Hence *différance* remains a metaphysical name, and the sign, which must be taken apart, remains indispensable. But why the necessity of defining the system in which texts are to be located and through which they are to be opened up to deconstruction in terms of a grand, trans-historical structure of presence? This argument would reduce all historical development to sameness, and render Foucault's charge against deconstruction as a 'pedagogy which teaches the pupil that there is nothing outside of the text' (Foucault 1979: 27) worthy of further consideration.

And yet it is not, as was argued above, a question of historical investigation becoming prohibited with respect to logocentrism – on the contrary, it is an absolute necessity. 'It was never our wish . . . to transform the world into a library by doing away with all boundaries, all framework, all sharp edges . . . but that we ought rather to work on the theoretical and practical system of these margins, these borders, once more, from the ground up' (LO: 84). 'Does one have the right to speak of a – of *the* – Western metaphysics, of its language, of a single destining or "sending forth of being", etc.? Consequently everything remains open, still to be thought' (ID: 81). These statements should be taken as signs of where deconstruction leads. Not to the *mise en abyme* of the Yale interpretation of deconstruction, which sets *différance* to work in order to contain 'the full thrust of the Derridean question' (Riddel 1975: 62). Deconstruction should not lead to the erasure of all borders as a definitive act, which overturns the world in order to return it to a new ontology of textual work in the abyss, but to a discourse on the margins, on the hidden *parerga* of idealities and essences. To disrupt the identity of the sign and to set the signifier free from its connection to a natural and naturalized signified, to allow it to work through the full implications of Saussurian difference, to suggest that the sign would be arbitrary and that the play of structures would be infinite – all this, as the placement of the conditional tense causes us to turn in again from the abyss, which we cannot escape, and to focus upon that which, in constituting forms of presence, attaching a signifier to a signified, seeks to delay their transformation. 'For us, the rupture of that "natural attachment" puts in question the idea of naturalness rather than that of attachment' (*OG*: 46).

Thus the strategic role of *différance* is to open texts to readings that expose the functions of meanings and language as those of closure, convention, tradition and ideology. There are, however, problems in this transition that remain to be answered. As Dews has noted, Derrida is not concerned with challenging or transforming the relationship between subjectivity, truth, institutions, etc., and the presence that underlies them all so much as with laying bare their structure. To move towards a position that seeks to overturn the present, Derrida would have to depart from the immanent critique that allows him to work within established, given conventions and account for a position outside these traditions (Dews 1987: 37ff.) Thus when the question of determining the deconstructive reading is raised (of rendering it effective against the structure it inhabits), the response is through 'the double session' — both overturning the traditional conceptual hierarchy (speech before/over writing, and so on) and at the same time marking the interval, taking care, 'by virtue of the overturning and by the simple fact of conceptualisation, that the interval is not reappropriated' (*P*: 59). Thus *supplement*, which remains a metaphysical name, nevertheless cannot work Rousseau's text in quite the same manner as before. But the double session, as for deconstruction generally in Derrida's hands, takes us so far, only to unceremoniously dump us in a position where, although we cannot operate in quite the same terms, it is impossible to know how to act differently. We do not know where *then* to turn, as it offers us an alternative that cannot be thought and can offer no break, and therefore offers us, ultimately, no alternative whatsoever. If metaphysics cannot be superseded, then we need a means of distinguishing between different forms, manifestations and systems of presence.

Perhaps this is unfair. As Ryan has written, Derrida's vision of society is one that is constantly changing, reforming, displacing itself, a social formation that embraces rather than resists change, one whose closest political model might be that of the Paris Commune (1982: 7). Nevertheless, there remains, between the promise and the realization of the political implications of deconstruction, a lack, an incompleteness. How, for instance, is a logical contradiction to be converted into a social contradiction, a transformation crucial to our historical work, 'given that institutions are traversed by relations of force, it is difficult to see how deconstruction could be applied to them' (Dews 1987: 35). Political contradictions cannot so easily be reduced to the incompleteness and inconsistencies of a logic founded upon presence. Derrida, in fact, does not produce a theory of ideology, and as a consequence remains unable to explain *how meanings actually take place* — closures are closed, presences maintained against difference, how meanings come to be conventional and habituated, cemented into the cultural unconscious. We are offered an opening, a point of incision, but we need to know more about the particular form of logocentrism — capitalism, state communism or whatever — before we can proceed. And this may well, as Dews maintains, mean that deconstruction must return to those modes of discourse and analysis – dialectical, hermeneutic, Heideggerian – from which it had seemed to depart.

Derrida describes his project by stating that *différance* 'seemed to me to be strategically the theme most proper to think out, if not to master ... in what is characteristic of our "epoch". I start off, then, strategically, from the place and time in which "we" are, even though my opening is not justifiable in the final account, and though it is always on the basis of *différance* and its "history" that we can claim to know who and where "we" are and what the limits of an "epoch" can be' (*SP*: 135–6). If he has provided an account of how to open texts up, he is of little help in showing us how to conceptualize the conditions of systems of presence – of ideologies – or of establishing the limits of 'our' current epoch, however that is to be conceived.

It is precisely this lack that Ryan (1982) has identified and attempted to write through in his appropriation of deconstruction for Marxism. He notes – correctly – that deconstruction will be unable to disseminate meanings into their social and political contexts until it has developed a social theory that will allow us to convert a metaphysics of presence into a theory of ideology and social reproduction. This social text must be theorized if we are to know towards what we are working to relate structurally confined cultural practices.

There is no space here to evaluate Ryan's articulation in detail, but we should note that it is indeed appropriate. The opening of texts to their heterogeneity and the discourse on borders/margins offers a means of reading in terms of the social text. Deconstruction is well attuned to the exposure of hidden contradictions within ideology, 'a revelation of its hidden aporias' (Butler 1984: 114). Self-contradiction becomes ideology, and we can search for the 'not said' of the work, that about which it is silent, a silence that is necessary and integral to the production. Thus, for instance, it would be possible to forge a link with the work of Marxists such as Pierre Macherey (1977), concerned to develop notions of ideology as constitutive of subjects, while at the same time receptive to incisions and openings from within through which it can be exposed, allowing us access and transforming, to use Barthes's terms, the 'readerly' into the 'writerly'. We do not seek to show the unity and coherence of the work, even as a work of ideology, but its disunity and heterogeneity (Butler 1984: 117; Belsey 1980: 109). Marxism *supplements* deconstruction, and I would wish here, at the end of this account, to countenance Ryan's appropriation of Derrida, 'appropriate' being a deliberately chosen word since, in expressing the incompleteness of Derrida's own vision, it emphasizes that everything depends upon how deconstruction is set to work.

This is not, however, to end on a negative note, or to undo the importance of deconstruction. It is a question (and I am not trying to be ironic) of situating deconstruction within traditions concerned not only to expose (a metaphysical term) but to transform. Without this kind of external perspective, it becomes difficult, for instance, to defend the potential of deconstruction from what has been done under its name in the United States. Links with Marxism and indeed with psychoanalysis must form the way forward, the beginning of our 'historical labours', in Lentricchia's words. Lacan, in particular, needs to be reconstituted and reworked, for, when the 'logocentric' and 'phallocentric' (indeed, sexist) implications of his work and vocabulary are modified, the notion of the symbolic may provide the means with which to develop our point of entry into the social/general text. Deconstruction cannot be written in isolation. Coward and Ellis (1977) are right to place the emphasis upon the production of subjects which, as Ryan notes, takes away from us not only the possibility of Habermas's 'ideal speech community' but also the more orthodox Marxist notion of a pre-determined revolution. It requires that we explore ways, not of appealing to the subject, but of subverting it and the means by which subjects are produced. The institution of the Oedipal triangle – which has many names – cannot be closed. The fourth surface that is missing is death: the death of the author who is already dead as s/he lives and writes, the death that is dissemination, the semen that is not life-producing but is merely diffused, that may not return to the father because fertility exceeds the structure of return. Everything is conditional because nothing is any longer guaranteed. All the conventional anchors of truth, discourse, power, politics and so on are overrun, and we are offered points of incision, intervention, subversion, through the necessity of rethinking everything that is at stake:

> If you truly wish to investigate it from this particular point of view, dissemination would be not only the possibility for a mark to 'disembed' itself . . . not only the force – the force of repetition . . . which permits it to break with what fastens it to the unity of a signified that would not be without it, not only the possibility of bursting from this *clasp*, and of undoing the eider quilt of the symbolic . . . It is also the possibility of deconstructing . . . the symbolic order in its general structure *and* in its modifications, in the general *and* determined forms of sociality, the 'family' or culture. (*P*: 85)

Conclusion

~~Archaeology:~~ *Writing Difference*

[Archaeology. The name has signified. It has signified always and only within a metaphysical tradition conceived on the basis of presence. It is this presence that has always named the place of an archaeology, and this presence that it will always have been the task of an archaeology to name. At its root, in its history, historiography and practice, name and its etymology, it is wholly metaphysical. 'Archaeology' – 'the study of the past', from the Greek *archaios* (ancient), *arche* (origin and beginning), *logos* (discourse and truth). Each is the emblem of absolute presence, the name being the name of that which is dreamed and that which is pursued. To what else does the word 'reconstruction' refer other than to an original presence, an evidence sufficient to signify that presence, and an adequate science to study that evidence. These emblems are at work at every point of orthodox arachaeological practice, whenever we speak of 'material culture', of 'the neolithic', of burial, settlement and so on. The notion that we have, in fact, changed the structure of archaeological practice in the last twenty years is in many respects illusory. Has it been the role of these movements, these processualisms and post-processualisms, to extend the borders of the practice and push forward to new grounds, or have they functioned to renew the contract, police the territory and watch over the realm of presence, leaving the citadels untouched?

It would be possible, for instance, to describe the space of archaeology in terms of its accredited concepts. These concepts have always been metaphysical – of the structure (exclusion, opposition, prioritization, hierarchization) of metaphysical presuppositions, as dualities (past/present, material/written, object/subject, system/history, etc.) The primacy of the first oppositional term always delimits the space (epistemological, institutional) of archaeology. Moving through structuralism, whose potential has always been held back because it has, first and foremost, been archaeology, it is time to reopen the question, to release the past from the archaeology that contains it and *prevents it from signifying to us in the present.*]

From the Science of the Negative to the Margins of Identity

> this is why, as we will verify, there is no *space* of the work, if by space we mean *presence* or *synopsis*. (*WD*: 14)

It is generally accepted that, while it is not possible to study the past directly, archaeologists do none the less study the signs of the past – material culture. This name has two connotations, often emerging when, in the institutional structure of the university, archaeology attempts to differentiate itself from history. First, this material is the direct product of human activities, not detoured through the subjec-

262   Timothy Yates

tivity of an individual point of view or a lapse of time between the
event and its encoding. It is affected by various post-depositional
'distortions', but it is spatially and temporally closely related to the
point of origin. Second, material culture is raw, hard, physical,
tangible. Where ambiguity is the stuff of the written record, material
culture forms an indelible record. It is neither of the same order as
language nor subject to the same effects. Thus, for Binford, 'We do
not have to study mental phenomena. In fact we study material
phenomena. We study material things, matter in various forms and
arrangements' (1982: 162). The important thing about material
culture is its materiality, its non-ideal qualities which have the values
of solidity and durability. Even for Ian Hodder, whose brand of
structuralism has led to a shift from conceptualizations based on record
to those of text, 'The abtract analysis of signs and meanings is
particularly a problem in archaeology, which is primarily concerned
with material culture' (1986: 47). Artifacts and buildings play a role
in controlling ambiguity ('meaning variation'), by virtue of the fact
that they are 'durable' and 'concrete', 'restricting variability' (1986:
151, 123). Material culture performs the role of a framing device
within wider systems of meaning, a vital role in reproduction because
of its resilience. 'The material world therefore acts as a complex series
of *locales* within which meaningful and authoritative forms of discourse
can be sustained' (Barrett 1987: 8). As physical *presence* material
culture forms a distinctive meaningful scene within society, and thus
for processualist as for post-processualist alike, 'archaeology is
archaeology is archaeology' (Clarke 1968: 13; Hodder 1986: 1, 174).

All these points of view seek to find for archaeological data a
significant role in social reproduction. Although there would be
differences at other levels which I would not wish to conflate, around
this point all concur – on the specific nature of the phenomenon, its
material quality, juxtaposed in various ways to a language conceived as
idealistic, communicative and transparent.

And yet these statements, purporting to be logical statements
equivalent to some 'truth' or 'ontology' of material culture, are
undermined by the medium in which they are expressed. The
uniqueness of material culture, which allows it to enclose and perform
a role in determining non-material meanings, is based upon an
empiricism which conceives of the linguistic sign as wholly communicative and mimetic, as the formal unity of the signifier and the
signified, of the sensible and the intelligible. Rhetoric is completely
neglected. At what point, we must ask, has it ever been possible for
material culture to escape the (dis)order of language? The archaeological bandwagon, gathering within itself the motifs of a disciplinary

identity, never quite arrives at its destination, the outside of the language, the material privileged over the ideal. The linguistic sign is to be returned at that very moment when we seemed to have exorcised it from the start. So we have the right to ask what difference it makes to an archaeology if its rhetoric and its logic are found to be incompatible.

It is interesting to go back to a point before these developments emerged, before either a processualism or a post-processualism was identifiable, a point at which there was, strictly speaking, only one archaeology. As a nominal point, let us take the year 1962, which was in other respects momentous:

> We have used the word 'material' advisedly, and we must be clear at the outset of our discussions what we mean. The material which the prehistorian uses — which he interprets — is by definition and by fact unwritten. In the unwritten remains of the early past of man, the mute, silent witnesses of the origins and early development of prehistory — tools, weapons, houses, temples, farms, fields, forts, watermills — in a word it was all archaeological material. (Daniel 1962: 4–5)

Why this necessity to be clear at the outset? Of what are we so afraid that it is necessary to be sure before we start our discussions what it is that we will mean and what we will all of us be talking about? Because we know that in order to begin (to have begun) it is necessary to accept *a priori* the notion of material culture, to propose and to answer in the same moment what it is, how it operates or functions, where it comes from and where it is going. This *a priori* is advised because it is sanctioned in the legality of archaeology, because it is necessary at the outset to reduce the opacity of the sign in order to have immediately transcended it and to have begun to write the past.

And yet the very fact that we must begin with this statement emphasizes that in order to be clear there must be an act of clearance, with the result that what is *de facto* is not without already being *de jure* (the *arche* is also to be linked to authority). It assures us that in order to begin we must have already begun, that the foundation is itself produced, resting upon what it seems now to govern from the outside. If there is the necessity to be clear then there is the necessity of action, of a wiping away of the circumstantial, the obscure, the frivolous, the unnecessary, the contingent, the non-essential . . . all that will henceforth have become secondary to the essential core around which everything will turn. Thus the logical statement starts immediately by denying itself, its own figural form, the language in which it is announced.

In order to mark some points of incision into this conceptualization (which, in spite of everything, appears to be pervasive), it is necessary to read over it again, and to write around the concept and its expression. This performance could be sounded as follows:

(1) In the rhetoric of the expression, it becomes important from the outset, as material culture is announced, to define this identity in opposition to writing. The consequence of this is that archaeology, which takes its identity from writing about that which other disciplines ignore, will always find its material *in the negative of writing*, as that which is not written and that which writing is not. This, however, has other consequences; for, at the very moment at which we wish to cut off the relationship to writing from the outset, to make it prohibited and subject to censorship, to found material culture as exclusive and definitive, we can proceed only by marking its re-entry, by reintroducing that relationship to writing as a fundamental and indispensable foundation. Material culture is henceforth to be defined as the unwritten, in a direct but negative relationship to writing. The logical force of this assertion, which would have us concede the point and pass quickly on, should not allow us to forget that everything with which this archaeology proceeds emanates and radiates from a point of *absence* – the absence of writing – which will always therefore be the negative of an origin located elsewhere.

As such, and in order to trace the silent journey of this logic (its prehistory remains to be written), we do not – cannot – express this abstracted ideal *as it is*, though this has always been the assumption. We can only approach it, beat a logical path towards it, by starting from and presupposing as reference that which ought properly to have been excluded at the outset, and returning to this always at the end of our journey. It is therefore, within writing that archaeology, as the science of the negative, finds accumulated the prerogative of its research. Writing can be cast out, material culture can become the unwritten, only by speaking already and thus always from within writing. The structure of reference always remains in order to both permit and prohibit the difference. As material culture separates, it finds that its identity is already deferred in a structure of return that, from the first step of this logic, will always have established *already* a connection with what it is not, a connection it must follow in order once again to have found itself.

(2) Is not this attribution to material culture a strange historical argument, in so far as it entertains no relationship to history or, if it does have a place there, it is only to overturn our accepted teleologies

('prehistory' and others)? The definition as unwritten operates, in fact, to uproot all the anchor-chains of historical reference, by binding us to a space that is neither before nor after the inscription of writing, but somewhere in-between.

The logic of the unwritten is problematic historically. If material culture is to have an identity forged on the absence of writing, then it becomes necessary to divide history from logic in order for this identity to stand up. If material culture is always to be the absence of the written (and this is Daniel's first move), then this can only be taken to mean that the writing to which we refer (in the negative) must *precede* the appearance, distribution and development of empirical writing. For if we are to restrict the reference of the sign 'writing' to linear and phonetic notation (and this is clearly the model, however unacknowledged) then this can have only one of two consequences. Either material culture did not exist before this development (in Greece, China, Egypt, or wherever) *or* this appearance was itself only ever secondary. We know when we read this logical groundwork that without presupposing a writing already installed in place before these developments, and therefore an *arche*-writing within the archae-ology, without invoking a non-specific genus of the species writing, the statement that 'the material which the prehistorian uses . . . is by definition and by fact *unwritten*' (my emphasis) has no logical validity. It would be stripped of its force precisely because it requires that preliterate societies, in order to possess and use material culture, must anticipate that which is yet to come, that which has not yet appeared, that about which they would know nothing and of which they could have no conception, knowledge or understanding, since it assures us that in order to know material culture they must already know writing. This archaeology, we are reminded, can only 'come about' with(in) a concept of writing.

On what possible basis, therefore, can this anticipation take place other than upon a 'writing' already at work before writing, preceding its appearance, upon which material culture would depend in order to have become everything that we would mean by 'material culture.' The project of an archaeology as a prehistory is therefore upset because it can only take place within a writing *contemporary* with material culture, a writing about which we would know nothing.

(3) This unwritten resource of 'material culture' would, we are required to believe, escape the order of the sign, which must always be tied to language and writing, the concepts to which, before all else, material culture is to be opposed. The material artifact is *unwritten*, therefore it is not a sign, therefore it cannot signify, therefore it must

be mute and silent, the very expressions of the negative of the ideal. It is a witness of the event, but one that refuses to speak its testimony, which is the testimony on (at) the origin (*arche*). It is related to action, not reflection – 'a record of artefacts, of things made and fashioned by man' (Daniel 1962: 5). Outside of the sign, material culture would have no use for the sign, precisely because in the moment of function it has no need for mediacy, but is rather immediate, undivided, present. It is without utterance, without voice, silent; its testimony, therefore, will always be a silent soliloquy, which is to say that it is heard but it does not sound.

And yet this science of silence, this study in and of the negative of writing, can only ever write. 'In the unwritten remains of the early past of man the mute silent witnesses of the origins and early development of prehistory – tools, weapons, houses, temples, farms, fields, forts, watermills – in a word it is all archaeological material.' We note that when it becomes necessary to ascribe something positive to material culture, we will already have transgressed and effaced the laws of silence, and with them the conditions of identity that frame the unwritten. All these designations, promising to belong to material culture, make sense, sound, become possible, only within writing. Tools, weapons, houses, temples, farms ... the sign is put in place of the thing 'itself', in order to permit it to speak and to be heard.

The condition for an archaeology is therefore a structure of metaphor, which would consist of giving to a thing a name that belongs to something else. And the structure of metaphor will always be absolutely irreducible – it is present as soon as we find material culture ('in a word'), in the ascription of a realm of the unwritten. What this metaphorical structuring implies, however, is an absolute prohibition on this notion of representation, of a sign coming to material culture from its outside and functioning by mimesis. Material culture becomes conceivable only by approach through its Other, so its identity is constantly mediated by its non-identity, by the Other from which it is differentiated. The metaphor therefore does not come at a later stage – the practice of this science, for example – but is there at the beginning. Therefore, while we have been taught to say that the sign in writing the past comes to take the place of material culture, replacing it as a faithful representation, and therefore being only ever secondary and derivative, we know that before this can take place there is already a metaphor, that material culture is already metaphorical, already caught up in a play of differences that ruptures the binary codes of these systems, taking us back to and beyond the written/ unwritten. It can no longer make sense to think in terms of mimesis, since these identities are already carried off from themselves, already lying elsewhere.

(4) Let me reiterate. What disturbs the science of material culture is the irreducibility of the metaphor through which it is founded. For it is not simply, as part of the 'provisionality' of the reconstruction, to convert *a* into *b*, where both are prior to and independent of this relationship, which is entertained only in order for this science to write. But rather the fact that before either *a* or *b* can exist as alternatives, there is the metaphor as *différance* of *ab*. Before we arrive at tools, weapons, houses, temples – at material culture the categories of which are given names metaphorically – there will always already have been writing as *différance*. Metaphor is predicated upon an originary metaphor which overflows identities at their origin. It is the impossibility of ever reducing this writing to a material culture conceived as an *a priori*, as present, self-identical, independent, transcendent. Material culture is already metaphorical, already split from itself. We can only ever approach this identity sideways, through a detour into language as *différance*, which requires us to follow an indefinite tangent. 'Material culture' attracts and repels. The soliloquy of silence takes place only by a process of internal differentiation, division and delay.

This internal *dissension* and *disseverence* has the effect of splitting material culture as a sign from itself, drawing a line between the signifier and the signified as a bar to signification, as deferral of the present – the signified – along chains of signifiers. In the excess, the overflow, the sign is carried off, and with it all the signs of the past, all the signs and non-signs that anchor the past in place. Dispersed along chains of signifiers ('tools, weapons, houses . . .') these will never be absolutely determinable, because at no point will identity have come full circuit and met itself coming back, and so at no point in this dissemination will it have consummated its relationship to the past.

This is assured from the moment that Daniel, searching for a metaphor to describe this identity, strayed so far as law and writes of 'a mute, silent witness'. In the courts, the witness provides a testimony. It invokes a primary relation to the event, and a complete relation to the event. It is required to promise that it will tell the truth. And yet both of these are, in terms of a *de facto* relationship, already prohibited. The witness saw what happened, s/he/it furnishes *evidence* (Lat. *videre*, to see), introducing temporal and spatial delay into the heart of the testimony. It is at the origin, but it is already spaced from the origin, after the origin. The witness is a witness only of that which has taken place elsewhere. And this witness refuses to give evidence (it is (a) *mute*). Its testimony will always be incomplete, not simply because there are many other witnesses to be heard, but because the testimony will always itself have to be completed, because the silence will always already have been incomplete, demanding voice to complete its journey. Because out of the chaos that would have to characterize the *ergon* of material culture, someone will have to decide whether this is the truth that is spoken, someone will have to supply the testimony with a *parergon*, to frame it, complete it, add to it, and at the same time change it, replace it, overflow it, supersede it, carry it off. Something will have to produce the truth of the testimony, and this will never have been the witness, nor the essence of either event or account, but rather what, in a fortuitous moment, Daniel invokes as the legality of the metaphor establishing past and present.

It is this primordial division and delay which cracks presence, preventing it from ever presenting itself, and which opens material culture on to time. Metaphor leads on to metaphor, *a* to *b*, to *c* to *d*, revealing only a galaxy of signifiers that would exhaust the dictionary and still promise no return. Material culture, tools, weapons, houses, temples, farms, subjects, objects, institutions, eras, genres, proper and common names . . . on this condition alone, the condition of presence as its self-effacement, has archaeology ever been possible. There is no space of the archaeological record, and neither does it have any time. Ever eluding reduction, this difference plays a constant and illimitable chain of successive significations through the space and time of an archaeology — 'the operation of differing which at one and the same time both fissures and retards presence, submitting it simultaneously to primordial division and delay' (*SP*: 88).

All this is not to say that material culture does not exist, that it is not meaningful, social, historical. It is to say that it is all of these things, that it is structured like a language and it has only been the ahistoricism of this archaeology that has obscured this fact. Writing and material culture are to be seen as derivative effects of an underlying movement which is manifested only through them, Derrida's *arche*-writing. This ground would be that of the signifier as the 'material' element which, while not separable from the intelligible, nevertheless is not reducible to it. Material culture has its identity, it is real and active, but this identity must be thought outside the terms of an ontology. The difference operative at the root of identity, dividing it from itself, constituting it not as atom or axis but as *spacing*, as movement, as differing, deferring, delaying, dividing.

What is being proposed here is a practice that begins to reconceptualize archaeology as a textual practice. Partly this means beginning to read archaeological texts as texts, to assert the materiality of their writing, rather than conceiving of language as transparent and derivative in a structure of mimesis or representation from an original point considered present, pure, self-evident, stable. Lewis Binford, for instance, has gained much academic capital from the denunciation of structuralism as idealist, and therefore as inappropriate within a science founded upon 'material culture'. This supposition has been the foundation of a whole system. And yet, if we were to read his texts more closely, what we would discover is a materialism that, for all it supports and all that is claimed in its name, is more profoundly idealist than anything legitimated by the structuralist canon, although this profundity is tempered by a certain blindness after the fact.

'I know of no nomothetic science attempting to understand the archaeological record . . . the basic phenomena with which we work are (a) static, (b) material, (c) untranslated into symbols or clues to human thoughts' (Binford 1981: 23) All else, the structural projection of 'symbolism', is a hopeless idealism that is dangerous because it is 'remedial' (1982: 162). This is the very rhetoric of authority. And yet Ian Hodder, who is the object of these statements, accepts that there is, at the root of the sign, a division between the signifier and the signified, the signifier articulated as difference and therefore no longer within meaning but anterior and external to it. It is necessary to emphasize that at a certain level, which is by no means accidental (it is knotted into a system), Binford is *more of* an idealist than Hodder or any other post-positivist archaeologist; more so, because in the guise of disclaiming the idealism represented by the sign, and in order to excuse the absence from his work of any theory of the sign, he can only confirm it in place at the heart of his work, restore its original, metaphysical identity, and repeat the oldest idealist move of privileging the signified over the signifier.

It is only by confirming and reinforcing the priority established by idealism that the signs in material culture, of which it is composed, can appear to absent themselves and leave an archaeology founded on 'material phenomena', on system, function, behaviour, as unmediated expression. 'We do not find "fossilised" ideas, we find the arrangements of material which derive from the operation of a system of adaptation culturally integrated at some level' (Binford 1982: 162). Such an assertion is founded upon an idealism – the formal unity of the signifier and the signified – so essential and so indispensable that it no longer appears to be present or operative at all. And yet 'behaviour' still signifies, it is still within the order of the sign. The only function that allows it to appear otherwise is an idealism so profound that it seems to have elevated itself to such a lofty status that it can dispense with the concept altogether. Contrary to his claims, it is the *materialism* of structuralism that he will never be able to understand, and this materialism is set to unsettle the structure of archaeology, turning his comfortable little world upside down.

The effects of this materialism – the *différance* of the signifier – have been adequately detailed above, but it is important to note that as a result of releasing structuralism from the archaeology that contained it, we can no longer be satisfied with the notion of an archaeological record, *or that of the text which has come to replace it*. Both would invest within this space a presence that does not have a place within a system of difference, a signifier without any necessary connection to any other signifier. This signifier would be the very name of this record or text, and the name of the archaeological text in general, externalized from the significations they enclose. 'Text', if it is an advance, forecloses the question of structure even as it is opened by conceding to the system in place the notion of the sign as presence, a text containing meanings within a border which is itself not signifiable. Contrary to the claims made by Patrick (1985) the notion of the text as it has appeared in post-processual archaeology colludes with those premises it seemed to threaten, preserving the integrity of their space by the continued reduction of the exteriority of the signifier. If Patrick shows that to speak of an archaeological record is to carry with it certain metaphysical implications, as Barrett (1987: 6) has claimed, then these implications are reassured and reproduced rather than threatened by the mere action of renaming this analytical space 'text'. This action has the danger of leading us to think that, by virtue of the change in nomenclature, the problem has been solved.

Solved it has not been, however. The archaeological text is, according to Hodder, a structure of similarities and differences which are built up in order to form a network of meaningful associations. 'Abstractions are . . . made from contexts and associations and differences in order to arrive at meaning in terms of function and content' (Hodder 1986: 125). Conceptually, context operates to close these chains of signifiers, allowing us to conceive of a totality which refers each signifier in a differential network to another. Context thus becomes 'The totality of the relevant environment, where "relevant" refers to any significant relationship to the object – that is, a relationship necessary for discerning the object's meaning . . . the boundaries of the context only occur where a lack of significant similarities and differences occurs' (Hodder 1986: 139). Context, therefore, 'can be taken to mean "with text" . . . the context here is the structure of meaning into which the objects have to be placed in order to be interpreted. The argument is that objects are only mute when they are out of their texts' (Hodder 1987: 2).

This point is stated elsewhere. 'An object out of context is not readable' (Hodder 1986: 141). But what possible dimension could correspond to an object 'out of context'? To be identifiable, Hodder has conceded, is to be contextualized, so there can be no identification 'on the outside'. What is actually at stake here is the question of the *proper* context in which archaeological data should be interpreted. What we want to know is what sanctions, controls and permits these borders to operate. But Hodder has already defined these borders as 'lack', as where there are *no* significant similarities and differences, and therefore condemned these borders to insignificance and non-meaning.

Context would function as the centre of the structure, a centre that governs from the outside and prevents the structure from collapsing in upon itself. Context functions as a determining force within a system of meaning defined by contextual–structural archaeology as that of difference. And yet the question must constantly be asked of this conceptualization, by what means is context itself positioned in relation to the inside which it delimits, directs and determines? Is not the name of context – context itself – only a mark within a system of differences, referring to an inside but also therefore to an outside as its Other? How, then, does it become elevated above this system, the movement expressed by the silent *a* of *différance*? Context would alone be that which would be outside context, and therefore, by definition, unreadable. Context *only appears* to govern from the outside when it must in fact be a production of the very meaning it sought to contain.

The notion of context as determination rests upon a reduction of the exteriority of the signifier, for context is not, *at any point*, more than a new inscription within a system of differences. It is a totalizing motif, one which, more than anything else, is the emblem of stability and necessity. We cannot, as Hodder attempts, define context non-contextually. We retain the concept, but only to problematize both its ontology and its stability, those wider questions of borders and boundaries which are precisely those raised by deconstruction.

For the notion of context holds within itself, by virtue of its claims to totality and determination, the potential to concede all the ground that it had challenged to the structure in place. Thus Ian Hodder formulates two components of the analytical space, 'the past context in which meanings have a particular historical content' and 'the context of the archaeologist' (1987: 2). By splitting context into two parts, the way is left open for thinking of the relationship in terms of identity rather than difference. Despite all the best indications that context will have transcended the old polarities, the familiar binary of primary and secondary evidence is reintroduced at a crucial stage, repeating precisely that structure that should have been refused, allowing recourse to metaphysical division and prioritization.

This is precisely what has happened with the movement that has emerged in recent years in Britain and the United States, which styles itself the 'critical archaeology' (Leone et al. 1987). Through a very ambiguous relationship to the Frankfurt school, this movement has set itself the task of recovering the original project of positivist archaeology – objective, value-free knowledge of the past – adding to the New Archaeology of the 1960s consideration of the contemporary political context and producing 'more reliable knowledge of the past by exploring the social and political contexts of its production' (Leone et al. 285). Politics is no more than a distorting effect which can be filtered out, allowing us to recover the past as a pure origin, using, according to Alison Wylie, a 'methodological directive' based upon 'rational, empirical evaluation' (Wylie 1985: 142).

Context, which sought to presence in some way the ontology of the past and to preserve it from the play of differences, has functioned to restore to primary evidence both its identity and its priority by providing the conditions under which the signifier is internalized and merged with the signified. This is not an accidental occurrence, but the logical result of a theory of context which, however important, refuses to shift attention to the point which no longer signifies, to the *parergon* operating under the shadow of the *ergon* to which it is our task to return. A primary source is to be preferred because it is primary – with respect to what? Because it is closer to – what? Because it is more originary than – what? (Cousins 1987: 131). Because it is the integrity of the centre which, before all else, must be preserved, for to release context from this structure is to threaten to overturn the established priorities and hierarchies that determine its institutional identity. (Here, of course, in the institutional structure of appointments and commissions, s/he that would dissent runs enormous risk.) The primary source is to be preferred because it must be theoretically (pragmatically) closer to that which is closest to the event of the past, to that which is most distant from us, the here and now, the least threatening, at one and the same time the least present and the most present. It is this simultaneous reduction (reconstruction) and reproduction (archaeology) of distance, space and difference that context functions to reassure and that mandates the critical archaeologists to conceive of a past that is present but deferred, where what defers can be removed by appropriate techniques to leave the core intact and pure.

And yet the exteriority of the marginal, of the *parerga*, has already been returned. The movement of the trace of difference is absolutely irreducible, and the deferral and referral of meaning beyond the 'proper' context cannot be ended. However many traces of the present we remove there will always be more, not simply through the fertility of the trace that surrounds the origin, but because that origin – the past – has never existed except by virtue of the trace. If all meaning is structured according to difference, we can no longer conceive of a simple origin located in the past and present – ultimately – to analysis. The slide of the signifier, the instability and tension arising from the play of differences, pulls the carpet from underneath the feet of this archaeological ontology: 'The trace is not only the disappearance of the origin . . . it means that the origin did not even disappear, that it was never constituted except reciprocally by a non-origin, the trace, which thus becomes the origin of the origin' (*OG*: 61).

~~Archaeology~~: Writing the Difference of the Past

Material culture cannot be formalized. It cannot be reduced. It cannot be totalized, it cannot be exhausted. No writing – no science, no system, no middle-range observation, text or context – can contain it. The thing itself always escapes. 'The structure of an interlacing, a weaving or a web, which would allow the different threads and different lines of sense or force to separate again, as well as being ready to bind others together' (*SP*: 132). There is no proper scene, space or place in which this archaeology can take place. The past is a receptacle for significations which, while filling the vessel, overflow it and carry it off. Archaeology writes in the *différance* of identity, the *non-identity of identity*.

It has been possible to identify two dominant responses to the problem of the sign, language, etc. The one, which is called processualism, dreams of effacing the sign altogether, dreams of escaping its mediation, which has only been possible by uniting the signifier and the signified to the extent that it has been possible to make the former appear to disappear and cease to be a relevant problem. The other, which is called post-processualism, affirms rather than denies the mediacy of the sign, the irreducibility of its operation, and attempts to work within the Saussurian 'two-sided unity'. But at the same time it has remained faithful to the dream of an archaeology conceived on the basis of the materiality of material culture as the presence of the Binfordian 'already-ideal', and thus turned structuralism away from its most productive implications. We have thus, behind these differences, detected a certain rule, called 'archaeology', which has not been affected by the changes since 1962.

We should reformulate the scene. All the binary structures of containment (past/present, material/written, objective/subjective, science/society, etc.) cannot be transcended, but neither can they any longer function in the same way. The point is to work within them differently. Let us start with a rhetorical signification, which would nevertheless be important:

~~Archaeology~~: the study of the ~~past~~

Effacement because archaeology will never end – will never have put an end to – writing, so it will never become archaeology, will never have been archaeology. There can never be an end, so too there will never have been a beginning, for no *arche* can operate without anticipating some *telos* in which it will have found itself.

Putting the discipline and its interstices under erasure is not an empty gesture. It marks in a text the movement by which a signification is constantly supplemented by its other, that which a metaphysics has always sought to exclude in order to identify and protect that which sanctions its activity. Archaeology is no longer 'the study of the past', but must consider within itself the other which it is not but which remains, however obscurely, and continues to signify. It is a practice of writing located in the spacing between past and present. Through this space we trace a line of signifiers which mark out the terrain in which it takes place: subjects, politics, values, interests, institutions, societies, dogmas, histories. Within deconstruction, the pure object of study – the past as presence or the ontological origin – is dissipated and dispersed along chains of signifiers in which it is always implicated. The origin is always discursively produced, and it is impossible to locate either an *arche* where all can be said to begin and a *telos* where all can be said to end. The possibility of an archaeology is deferred *ad infinitum* within a chain that has neither beginning nor end, because the origin, if it were found, would always differ from itself. As spacing – the *différance* of identity – there is no question of defining a proper scene, a structure of belonging here and not there, a proper place for the past or a proper past. The one place where the past has never been is in itself. A megalith, a hill-fort, a piece of rock art or a medieval castle – all are receptacles for significations that could never be reduced to the identities and pure idealities of these names. The past is plural, multiple, contradictory, a line of force through the present. To write is to complete but also to add, to supplement, to replace and to connect. Archaeology is to write through the *parergon*.

And yet, if the text is plural, we do not seek to write plural texts, interpretations open to multiple readings in the self-conscious liberalism of recent suggestions. If the past is indeterminable in a metaphysical sense then this does not mean that it is not determining and determinative. The idea that we should present different pasts from which the reader may choose neutralizes the past in the present, and emanates from a naive conception of test and subject and the meaning systems in which they are located. It is a question of how the structure is set to work, for what end and for what objectives, what kind of knowledge to produce. There is no truth of the past, if by truth we would mean an ontology of the origin; the only truth of archaeology lies in the way it is set to work the scene between past and present.

'This constitutes', Wylie writes, 'the standard dilemma that once a radical critique of objectivism is accepted, it leaves us no ground for preferring one interpretation to its alternatives' (1985) 140). But on what standards is this to become a dilemma? There is more than a little residual nostalgia for a lost ontology here. Does it not upset this perspective and all the claims of liberal science to discover that this is how it has been all along, and so is a problem to be located already within liberalism, if it could but see it. We do not, in fact, lead to the spectre of an 'anything goes' – the scandal of Feyerabend (1982) is less in what he proposes in a free society than in the charge against liberalism, showing it what it would have to be in order to live up to its claims. What is at stake here is objective evaluation, not evaluation *per se*.

Deconstruction does not deny truth or claim that there is no truth. It is the link between truth and presence/ontology that is disputed. 'A possible plurality of truth descriptions does not imply a liberal pluralist vision of the equal validity of all positions' (Ryan 1982: 38). Truth is to be situated such that an absolute ground is indeterminable, and the question thus becomes, if no recourse to the transcendental is possible, what promotes, sanctions and supports all appeals to truths? Truth, Derrida would maintain, exists, it is real and 'material', but it is institutional and social, historical rather than ontological or transcendental. It is a construct, a function of a system, a projection outside of what lies within. We cannot appeal, as Wylie does, to the pragmatism of liberalism without contaminating the truth we are seeking to purify and preserve.

To strike against ontology and epistemology, against presence in general, is not to end up in a position of incommensurability. This is a liberal ideology, founded to obscure the fact that what is promised has never been delivered. It is true that some critics have argued themselves into something like this position, where all readings would be equally valid as misreadings, or where the only way forward is to prefer those readings which are 'strong' rather than 'weak', the most 'productive' or 'interesting'. At one level, deconstruction seeks to foreclose the problem by working from the inside of texts, undermining their logic from the inside by turning against them their own resources. And yet, as was argued above, this operation cannot ever be complete, for in order to function, deconstruction must possess theories of its own about what a text 'is', how it functions, how and where it is produced and reproduced and to what ends. For Derrida, this has been the operation of a metaphysics of presence or logocentrism, but in order to force the incision shown as the opening into all systems of presence, we need some theory more closely concerned with what historical irregularities as well as regularities articulate 'texts'. It is at this point that *écriture* should merge with Marx, with Foucault's *discours* or Lacan's 'symbolic'. Deconstruction opens text to new readings, situated in new areas of signification, examining meaning in terms of that which systems have obscured under writs of prohibition, precisely because they depend upon them.

The pattern for a deconstructive practice – what I have designated ~~archaeology~~ in order to emphasize the difference – is the practice of excavating a signifying chain, locating the tensions of the structure and pursuing them to rupture. The spacing of the archaeological work is that of the signifying spaces which connect past to present in an irreducible bind (the bind or weaving of an irreducible trace – difference, the supplement, and so on), a space in which there is no longer an *arche* as there is no longer a *logos*, if by these we would invoke something present to itself and without reference to an other. '[O]nly a genuine philosophy of history', Frederic Jameson writes, 'is capable of respecting the specificity and radical difference of the social and cultural past while disclosing the solidarity of its polemics and passions, its forms, structures, experiences and struggles, with those of the present day' (1983: 18). Deconstruction offers us the potential for just such a history. Where Jameson charges us to consider the claims distant monuments have on our own times, without naively imagining that we can split past from present, without continuing to dream of forcing the past to presence in an archaeological *parousia* that is assuredly theological, deconstruction offers us the means to read texts – material culture – for this difference. Why not call this reading an archaeology of metaphor, archaeology as metaphor? Metaphor, allegory, the unconscious – all these names attempt to describe that movement which threatens identity by no longer being content to respect its conditions, which forces us to consider that the text is other than it is, other than it claims, that it signifies differently and heterogeneously. Metaphor conjoins identities while retaining the distance, the difference of identity, as Derrida would put it, the *différance* of the difference. Metaphor names that writing which constitutes the neolithic period, the Iron Age, the Middle Ages as different/distant from us, while at the same time tearing down the boundary of the centuries and inserting it amongst us, establishing connections with the present. They can be closed, identified and written only by being reopened. To link this writing to notions of allegory and the unconscious is to open the past to the present and the present to the past. Deconstruction performs this transformation, opens us on to new texts to be written, raises new questions, new connections. Our historical labour as archaeologists is about to begin afresh, with new vigour and new objectives, for the problem raised by deconstruction, which I have attempted to describe at length in the preceding pages, is the *displacement* of a question: 'In some way yet to be determined, a genuine historicity is possible only on condition this illusion of an absolute present can be done away with, and the present opened up again to the drift from the other ends of time' (Jameson 1972: 187).

ACKNOWLEDGEMENTS

The writing of this chapter took place over a period of eighteen months. Throughout, I have had the benefit of discussions with many individuals, to whom I would like to extend my thanks, particularly Fred Baker, Ian Bapty, J. D. Hill, Willy Maley, Mike Shanks, Jane Wilson and especially Grant Chambers, Ian Hodder and Chris Tilley. Equally important has been the support of my parents and of Debbie Thorne: in their case, nothing written here, 'in parenthesis', would be sufficient, because no acknowledgement could ever say enough.

BIBLIOGRAPHY

1 Books by Derrida

Abbreviations used are given after the titles. Original date of publication in the French is given in square brackets.
Of Grammatology (*OG*) [1967] (1977) Johns Hopkins University Press, Baltimore. Trans. G. C. Spivak.
Speech and Phenomena, and Other Essays on Husserl's Theory of Signs (*SP*) [1967] (1973) Northwestern University Press, Evanston. Trans. D. B. Allison.

Writing and Difference (WD) [1967] (1978) Routledge & Kegan Paul, London. Trans. A. Bass.

Dissemination (D) [1972] (1981) Athlone, London. Trans. B. Johnson.

Margins of Philosophy (M) [1972] (1983) Harvester Press, London. Trans. A. Bass.

Positions (P) [1972] (1981) Athlone, London. Trans. A. Bass.

The Archaeology of the Frivolous: Reading Condillac (AF) [1973] (1987) University of Nebraska Press, Lincoln and London. Trans J. P. Leavey.

Glas (G) [1974] (1986) University of Nebraska Press, Lincoln and London. Trans. J. P. Leavey and R. Rand.

Signesponge (S) [1976] (1984) Columbia University Press, New York. Trans. R. Rand.

The Truth in Painting (TP) [1978] (1988) University of Chicago Press, Chicago. Trans. G. Bennington and I. McLeod.

The Post Card (PC) [1980] (1988) University of Chicago Press, Chicago. Trans. A. Bass.

Mémoires for Paul de Man (MPM) (1986) Columbia University Press, New York. Trans. C. Lindsay, J. Culler and E. Cadava.

2 Articles by Derrida

'Structure, sign and play in the discourse of the human sciences' *(SC)* (1972) in D. Macksey and E. Donato (eds) *The Structuralist Controversy*, Johns Hopkins University Press.

'Limited Inc. abc' (LI) (1977) *Glyph*, 2: 162–254.

'Living On: Border Lines' (LO) (1979) in H. Bloom et al. (eds) *Deconstruction and Criticism*, Seabury, New York.

'Scribble (Writing/Power)' (SWP) (1979) *Yale French Studies*, 58: 116–47. Trans. C. Plotkin.

'The Time of a Thesis: Punctuations' (TT) (1983) in A. Montefiore (ed.) *Philosophy in France Today*, Cambridge University Press, Cambridge.

'An Interview with Derrida' (ID) (1988) in D. Wood and R. Bernasconi (eds) *Derrida and Différance*, Northwestern University Press, Evanston.

'Letter to a Japanese Friend' (LFJ) (1988) in D. Wood and R. Bernasconi (eds) *Derrida and Différance*, Northwestern Univesity Press, Evanston.

'The Original Discussion of Différance' (ODD) (1988) in D. Wood and R. Bernasconi (eds) *Derrida and Différance*, Northwestern University Press, Evanston.

3 *Other works referred to in the text*

Barrett, J. (1987) 'Fields of discourse: reconstituting a social archaeology', *Critique of Anthropology*, 7: 5–16.

Belsey, C. (1980) *Critical Practice*, Methuen, London.

Binford, L. (1981) *Bones: Ancient Men and Modern Myths*, Academic Press, New York.

Binford, L. (1982) 'Meaning, inference and the archaeological record' in C. Renfrew and S. Shennan (eds) *Ranking, Resource and Exchange*, Cambridge University Press, Cambridge.

Butler, C. (1984) *Interpretation, Deconstruction and Ideology*, Oxford University Press, Oxford.

Clarke, D. (1968) *Analytical Archaeology*, Methuen, London.

Cousins, M. (1987) 'The practice of historical investigation' in D. Atridge, G. Bennington and R. Young (eds) *Post-Structuralism and the Question of History*, Cambridge University Press, Cambridge.

Coward, R. and Ellis, J. (1977) *Language and Materialism*, Routledge & Kegan Paul, London.

Culler, J. (1976) *Ferdinand de Saussure*, Fontana, London.

Culler, J. (1983) *On Deconstruction*, Routledge & Kegan Paul, London.

Daniel, G. (1962) *The Idea of Prehistory*, Watts, London.

Deleuze, G. and Guattari, F. (1983) *Anti-Oedipus: Capitalism and Schizophrenia*, Athlone, London.

Dews, P. (1987) *Logics of Disintegration*, Verso, London.

Eagleton, T. (1986) *Against the Grain*, Verso, London.

Feyerabend, P. (1982) *Science in a Free Society*, Verso, London.

Foucault, M. (1979) 'My body, this paper, this fire', *Oxford Literary Review*, 4: 1.

Frosh, S. (1988) *The Politics of Psychoanalysis*, Macmillan, London.

Hobson, M. (1987) 'History traces' in D. Atridge, G. Bennington and R. Young (eds) *Post-Structuralism and the Question of History*, Cambridge University Press, Cambridge.

Hodder, I. (1986) *Reading the Past*, Cambridge University Press, Cambridge.

Hodder, I. (1987) 'Introduction' in I. Hodder (ed.) *The Archaeology of Contextual Meanings*, Cambridge University Press, Cambridge.

Jameson, F. (1972) *The Prison House of Language*, Princeton University Press, Princeton.

Jameson, F. (1983) *The Political Unconscious: Narrative as a Socially Symbolic Act*, Methuen, London.

Johnson, B. (1981) 'Introduction' in J. Derrida, *Dissemination*, ed. B. Johnson, Athlone, London.

Kristeva, J. (1984) *Revolution in Poetic Language*, Columbia University Press, New York.

Lacan, J. (1977) *Ecrits*, Tavistock, London. Trans. A. Sheridan.

Lacan, J. (1988) *The Seminar of Jacques Lacan*, Book II: *The Ego in Freud's Theory and the Technique of Psychoanalysis*, Cambridge University Press, Cambridge. Trans. S. Tomaselli.

Leavey, J. P. (1980) 'The fractured frame, the seduction of fiction' 'Introduction' in J. Derrida, *The Archaeology of the Frivolous: Reading Condillac*, trans. J. P. Leavey, University of Nebraska Press, Lincoln and London.

Leitch, V. B. (1983) *Deconstructive Criticism: An Advanced Introduction*, Hutchinson, London.

Lentricchia, F. (1983) *After the New Criticism*, Methuen, London.

Leone, M. et al. (1987) 'Toward a critical archaeology', *Current Anthropology*, 28: 283–302.

MacCannell, J. F. (1986) *Figuring Lacan: Criticism and the Cultural Unconscious*, Croom Helm, London.

Macherey, P. (1977) *A Theory of Literary Production*, Routledge & Kegan Paul, London.

Man, P. de (1971) *Blindness and Insight: Essays in the Rhetoric of Contemporary Criticism*, Oxford University Press, Oxford.

Miller, J. H. (1975) 'Deconstructing the deconstructors', *Diacritics*, 5: 24–31.

Norris, C. (1982) *Deconstruction: Theory and Practice*, Methuen, London.

Norris, C. (1983) *The Deconstructive Turn: Essays in the Rhetoric of Philosophy*, Methuen, London.

Ormeston, G. (1988) 'The economy of duplicity' in D. Wood and R. Bernasconi (eds) *Derrida and Différance*, Northwestern University Press, Evanston.

Patrick, L. (1985) 'Is there an archaeological record?' *Advances in Archaeological Method and Theory*, 8: 27–62.

Riddel, J. (1975) 'A Miller's Tale', *Diacritics*, 5: 56–65.

Ryan, M. (1976) 'Self-deconstruction', *Diacritics*, 6: 34–41.

Ryan, M. (1982) *Marxism and Deconstruction: A Critical Articulation*, Macmillan, London.

Spivak, G. C. (1976) 'Introduction' in J. Derrida, *Of Grammatology*, Johns Hopkins University Press, Baltimore.

Wood, D. (1988) 'Différance and the problem of strategy' in D. Wood and R. Bernasconi (eds) *Derrida and Différance*, Northwestern University Press, Evanston.

Wylie, A. (1985) 'Putting Shakertown back together: critical theory in archaeology', *Journal of Anthropological Archaeology*, 4: 133–47.

6

Michel Foucault: Towards an Archaeology of Archaeology

Christopher Tilley

In this chapter an attempt will be made to discuss Foucault in a manner which I believe he would prefer; not as an author, a producer of a singular genre, a unified centre of consciousness inscribed into texts, but as a set of problems and problematizations of major areas within history, philosophy and social and political theory. Foucault, then, is the proper name we ascribe to a series of texts, problems and ways of thinking about these problems, and connecting them with past and present.

Foucault's work is both so extraordinarily wide-ranging and written in such a manner as systematically to defy any attempt to provide meaningful compression. He has written histories of madness, medicine, the human sciences, incarceration and sexuality, to provide a minimal description of his work. But he is not a historian, at least in the conventional sense. He has investigated areas such as discourse, power, truth, subjectivity, ethics and rationality. His work has sparked off debate and work within the spheres of literary criticism, art history, linguistics, philosophy, history, social and political theory, geography, anthropology and archaeology. His texts have been extolled as 'the most fully developed version of a new political "theory" and "practice" that is just beginning to emerge from the discrediting of Marxism and reformism' (Sheridan 1980: 221–2) and he has been criticized as 'a central figure in a disgraceful metamorphosis of continental philosophy [involving] the "subversive cynicism" of preaching irrationalism' (Merquior 1985: 159–60). Foucault himself has noted that:

> I think I have in fact been situated in most of the squares on the political checkerboard, one after another and sometimes simultaneously: as anarchist, leftist, ostentatious or disguised Marxist, nihilist, explicit or secret

anti-Marxist, technocrat in the service of Gaullism, new liberal etc. An American professor complained that a crypto-Marxist like me was invited to the U.S.A., and I was denounced by the press in Eastern European countries for being an accomplice of the dissidents. (*FR*: 383–4).

What follows is a discussion of a number of central themes in Foucault's texts: the manner in which we should write the past and the nature of discourse, power, history, space and time, subjectivity and politics. Foucault does not provide any overarching systematization with regard to either these themes or other areas; his work is fundamentally opposed to any attempt to provide a single all-embracing theoretical system for the study of society, history or whatever. There can, then, be no question of simply following Foucault or becoming a Foucauldian as one may become, or attempt to become, a Marxist or a rationalist. Foucault's abiding importance is to show us new ways to conceptualize and study the past and the present. Rather than attempting to follow exactly in his tracks into the thicket of the social constitution of reality the important thing is to use him to both construct and deconstruct our own conceptual clearings and insert different footprints within them. In the conclusions a few potential guidelines for using Foucault in relation to reading and writing material culture, or the archaeological study of past and present, are outlined: directions towards an archaeology (in Foucault's sense of the term) of and for archaeology.

The Past and its Writing

Consider the representation in figure 6.1. In *TP* Foucault amusingly uses Magritte's painting of a pipe, with its appended message 'Ceci n'est pas une pipe', to demonstrate the fundamental gap between

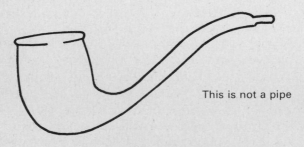

This is not a pipe

Figure 6.1

language and the world, between signifiers (e.g. words) and things. What is the relationship between the image and the words above it? Foucault identifies at least four possibilities:

1 This is not a pipe but a drawing of a pipe.
2 This is not a pipe but a sentence saying that this is not a pipe.
3 The sentence 'This is not a pipe' is not a pipe.
4 In the sentence 'This is not a pipe', *this* is not a pipe: the painting, written sentence, drawing of a pipe – all this is not a pipe.

The negations multiply, at no point can the image connect with the words. In *OT* Foucault remarks: 'it is not that the words are imperfect, or that, when confronted by the visible, they prove insuperably inadequate. Neither can be reduced to the other's terms: it is in vain that what we say we see; what we see never resides in what we say' (*OT*: 9). Stated in this way, all this appears strikingly obvious, but it is an obviousness we tend to forget when writing the past, that the meaning comes from syntax and not through a transparent relationship of language to the world. We need to understand that we *are* writing and the manner in which we write conveys as many messages in itself as the discursive objects discussed, illustrated and fitted together. In describing material culture we are producing discursive objects on which subsequent discourse may then set to work. At no point are we transparently dealing with the 'real'.

With the exception of *AK* all of Foucault's major works begin with vivid descriptions of points of historical detail encapsulating certain features of the subsequent arguments. *MC* begins with the closing of the great European leper houses and an account of the ship of fools conveying a cargo of 'madmen' set to drift in the liminal space of the sea; *BC* a contrast between the clinical practice of Pomme and Bayle; *OT* a description of the painting *Las Meninas* by Velasquez; *DP* details of the execution of Damiens the regicide set against a timetable for the correction of inmates at the House of Young Prisoners, Paris; *HS* a discussion of the anonymous Victorian memoir, *My Secret Life*, detailing various sexual activities; *UP* a kaleidoscope of various discursive images of gonorrhoea, principles of the devout life based on analogies with the sexual life of elephants, homosexuality, and the virtues of abstinence. On one level these obviously serve the rhetorical purpose of interesting the reader, but their meaning goes further. They point to two things, first, the importance of empirical detail ('data') which is subsequently integrated into the wider discursive arena of the texts. This detail provides clarification for the arguments rather than a weight of evidence to back them up or test them.

Furthermore, this detail is considered in all its specificity: it is not reduced to tables of statistical inference. Second, an integration of theory, data and practice.

Apart from *AK* Foucault has never written a book of theory and *AK* is more an attempt at systematization of the background informing the earlier studies *MC*, *BC* and *OT* than a book which stands on its own. For Foucault theory *is* practice, data *is* theory or theoretical. There can be no meaningful separation between these terms or areas. The texts systematically avoid a discursive strategy so common in the social sciences in general and archaeology in particular: the presentation of a theoretical structure followed by its 'application' to supposedly explain or test against a data set. Such scientism systematically precludes any success in understanding. At the outset theory and practice are divorced from data. Consequently their relationship can only remain arbitrary and contingent.

Foucault productively transgresses the theory – data divide as usually posited. For example, *HS* and *DP* are fundamentally to do with power, knowledge and agency. Foucault does not begin these books with a formal set of theses concerned with power which are then applied to discourses on incarceration or sexuality. His theoretical position is inseparable from and emerges in his discussions of history. We can, of course, extract and create a theory of power, the subject and discourse from the texts but what we are left with is often not all that satisfactory on a formal level and definitely has much more to do with the person carrying out this process of textual dissection than it may do with Foucault. Simply because of the way Foucault's theory, practice and historical discussions adhere to each other it is extraordinarily difficult to summarize what is stated. Any discussion of Foucault is necessarily a dim shadow of the texts themselves. This is precisely their strength. Foucault shows us through example, a new way to write the past involving neither an account of 'how the past really was' nor a reduction of its difference to being merely a pale reflection of the present.

Foucault is very conscious of the fact that he is not simply doing research concerned with the past. He is writing that past and the way in which he writes is of vital significance. Censoriously described as a 'prose-poet' (Rousseau 1972: 238), his writing style is far removed from the normal measured tones of academic analytical blandness, as the quotations throughout this paper illustrate. He plays on words and syntax to create meaning and turns language use into a productive space which is not conceived as a value-neutral representative system. Words may obscure as much as illuminate that which they are meant to signify. The relation of words to things or the signifier to the signified is problematic. Discourses do not simply consist of groups of signs. They are rather 'practices that systematically form the objects of which they speak. Of course, discourses are composed of signs; but what they do is more than use these signs to designate things. It is this *more* that renders them irreducible to the language (*langue*) and to speech' (*AK*: 49).

For Foucault positivist science is a myth and a dangerous one at that. He analyses its discourse to reveal its mythic status, its failed attempts at representation, and replaces it with a linguistic poetics in which signifiers become released. He refuses to inhabit the dank, drab and deadening discursive dungeon characteristic of all empiricist discourse. Discourse is a violence done to things linking desire and power. That which is important is to determine the nature of these powers and desires and their social effects.

Power

Foucault's conception of power can be summarized by the following points:

1 Power is not simply repressive. It is also productive and positive. No power means no social relations. Social relations are dependent on power. It works through them, in them and on them.
2 Power creates subjects of a certain kind in relation to historical and social circumstances.
3 Power is integrally linked to knowledge. Knowledge and power are dependent, they build on each other so we can speak of power–knowledge strategies. This does not mean that power collapses into knowledge or vice versa (S: 207). What is important is the intimate relationship between the two terms and their linkage, in turn, to truth and rationality.
4 Power relations are multiple. They do not simply flow from the top to the bottom of the social order.
5 The modalities power takes, and the way it operates, are historically specific.
6 Power is a networking of relations and practices throughout the social. It is found in e.g. institutions, forms of administration and family relations but is not exactly located in them. In other words power does not radiate out from specific points or nodes. It is more like a series of interlinked threads in the social which, when they cross, become more dense. Power is everywhere because it comes from everywhere. This means we must abandon any notion of

power arising in the economic or being 'held' and 'wielded' by individuals. A king may be a point of the *exercise* of power but he does not *hold* this power in his hands like a crystal ball. A definition: 'it is the name that one attributes to a complex strategical situation in a particular society' (*HS*: 93).

7   Power comes from below so that relations of domination on a societal or global scale are effects of and sustained by power in families, local groups, offices, etc.

8   Power is not a property. It is a strategy which is 'both intentional and nonsubjective' (*HS*: 94). Power is exercised with aims and objectives but these cannot be simply reduced to a framework of intentional agency in relation to either individuals or social classes.

9   The rationality of power is characterized by its tactics: 'the logic is perfectly clear, the aims decipherable, and yet it is often the case that no one is there to have invented them' (*HS*: 95).

10   Where there is power there is always resistance. These resistances are inscribed into power as its irreducible opposite. Like power resistances are dispersed and heterogeneous.

11   The principal modalities of the operation of power in the modern state are disciplinary procedures coupled with a bio-power managing populations.

We can now consider some of these themes further. It is apparent from the argument in *DP* and elsewhere that for Foucault the supposed humanitarianism of the Enlightenment merely results in a fresh system of domination linked to new modes of surveillance technology. Truth, reason and science are simply slogans of a new, more systematic and totalizing technology of power and Marxism is itself embroiled in such a conception. Foucault radically decentres power from any sort of specifiable context or location such as residing in individuals, institutions, classes, the economy, the state or whatever. His work marks a radical break with previous Weberian individualizing theories of power, locating power in a determinate set of relationships between power-holders in positions of authority and power-subjects over whom power is wielded, and structuralist accounts locating power as a structural feature of the social order. He reverses such a thesis, maintaining that such contexts can only be understood in relation to the kind of power that inhabits them.

Power, Truth, Ideology

The linkage of power to knowledge and so to discourse means that such knowledge and discourse can never be regarded as dispassionate or disinterested. Knowledge is always useful, a *will* to truth, a will to social domination. Power is linked to truth: it creates truths which cannot be detached or liberated from power. Truth therefore cannot be a condition for, nor a means of, liberation. Neither can any appeal be made to rationality or processes of rational argument. Here again we have to ask what power–knowledge–truth strategies do an appeal to rationality in any argument make. That these strategies run through rather than omit from agents, i.e. they are intentional strategies without the need for the postulation of a human subject(s), is entirely consistent with Foucault's dissolution of the subject into history. If modalities of the networking of power in the social field result in social domination this is because of their capacity to create empirical truths and not through ideological mystification. Rather than oppose truth to falsity the emphasis of such a perspective shifts over to the historical investigation of why some truths are accepted in society rather than others. The concomitant is that there can be no Marcusian deep-seated human nature to liberate and set free from the chains of capitalist repression. Furthermore any notion of ideology becomes difficult to make use of as Foucault regards any talk of ideology as being necessarily founded on some deep-grounded distinction between falsity and truth (*PK*: 118). Power cannot simply be repression because:

> In defining the effects of power as repression, one adopts a purely juridical conception of such power, one identifies power with a law which says no, power is taken above all as carrying the force of prohibition . . . If power were never anything but repressive, if it never did anything but to say no, do you really think one would be brought to obey it? (*PK*: 119)

Avoiding Essentialism

Foucault's emphasis on the positive aspects of power in society act as a useful counterweight to the melancholy of Critical Theory. Both domination and resistance are expressions of power. Foucault's position leads us to a concept of power which can perhaps be most broadly understood as referring to a capacity in social life to bring about outcomes and effects in the world. Such an understanding of the concept underlines the fact that power has a plethora of meanings as an integral feature of social life. This avoids essentialism: power is not to be automatically linked solely to systems of social oppression or conceived as simply an effect of economic processes. Power has two sides or faces. It may be regarded as a facet of all social encounters, a positive production of social effects. So without power the social world would not and could not exist. The negative side of power cannot be unequivocally linked with discipline and social control since these may be necessary for the positive outcomes of social action. Although power is neither directly positive or negative the picture Foucault leaves us with is that it generally results in new forms of domination.

Foucault's decentring of power from agency, class or institutions or the state means that what we are left with is power strategies without there being any necessary purpose to them. Where these power strategies operate there is always resistance to them because strategies are not necessarily coherent but operate within a contradictory and conflictual field of social articulation.

Power and Resistance

Many commentators have regarded both Foucault's conception of power and his portrayal of contemporary society as incredibly nihilistic. The workings of power are everywhere. No one escapes. The disciplinary apparatuses seem to be so profound and all-embracing that to hope for any other political future seems merely an exercise in self-deception. Struggles against power–knowledge–truth strategies seem only to reinforce them. A critique, for example, may merely reinforce the status, influence and power effects of that criticized. Poulantzas has argued that for Foucault the power relation never has any basis but itself and the question 'what power and power to do what?' becomes a mere obstacle. Poulantzas goes on to argue:

> his famous resistances, which are a necessary element of every power situation, remain a purely gratuitous assertion in the sense they are given no foundation: *they are a pure affirmation of a principle* . . . if power is always already there . . . if every power situation is immanent in itself, *why should there ever be resistance? From where* would resistance come, and *how would it be even possible?* (Poulantzas 1980: 149)

This charge that Foucault extends the concept of power so far that it becomes a virtual metaphysical principle is a common one. Poulantzas sees power and resistance to it as operating in terms of class struggle and division involving exploitation, the location of classes in terms of power apparatuses and in state mechanisms. In other words power and resistance are located in the social relations of production. Resistance to the exploitative effects of power take the form of class struggle. Foucault's position fails from such a perspective because he develops an over-radicalization of the concepts of power and resistance coupled with a total decentring of these concepts from the economy, classes or the state and this is why he has so little to say about resistance apart from noting its presence. Foucault comments: 'What I find striking in the majority — if not of Marx's texts then those of the Marxists . . . is the way they pass over in silence what is understood by *struggle* when one talks of class struggle' (*PK*: 208).

Governmentality and the State

For Foucault what is needed is not so much an analysis of classes or the state in relation to power in modern society but one concerned with what he terms 'governmentality' (G; OS; SP). The tactics of government make possible a continual series of definitions and redefinitions of what the state can do, how it may intervene, how it may decide between, for example, public and private issues. Governmentality allows the state to survive: it is more fundamental. By this term Foucault means very broadly a complex linkage of institutions, procedures, analyses and reflections targeting power on entire populations and linking it with knowledge of those populations (G: 20). Although historically power relations have become increasingly linked to state control they cannot be reduced to state apparatuses. This is because such an analysis would evade consideration of the manner in which the political structures of the state relate to the construction of definite forms of individualization. Foucault's specific contention is that the governmentality which secures the conditions of existence for the modern state has its roots in a Christian ethic of pastoral power. Pastorship is a form of power involving an aim of individual salvation; it is a power which does not simply command subjects, it is also sacrificial; it is a type of power looking after not just the whole community but each individual in that community during their lifetime; it is a kind of power dependent on knowing people's minds, exploring their souls (SP: 214). This pastoral power has, according to Foucault, ramified and spread into the secular form of the modern state. The effects are individualization and totalization (OS: 254). In the state such pastoral power operates to ensure the health, well-being and security of the population: worldly, secular aims. In order to do this the officials of this pastoral power increase in the form of public institutions, such as the police (Foucault points out that in the eighteenth century the police force appears as an administration heading the state together with the judiciary, army and exchequer yet its tasks, as outlined in documents, include virtually everything which will create a live, active and productive population (OS: 248). Prior to the modern state pastoral and political power, the power of the sovereign, were to a large extent separated. In the modern era pastoral power invades the entire social body, becoming linked to political power. The result: 'there was an individualizing "tactic" which characterized a series of powers: those of the family, medicine, psychiatry, education and employers' (SP: 215). According to Foucault the problem is not to try and liberate the individual from the power of the state and its institutions — power is not *located* there — but to liberate the individual both from the state and its manner of individualizing, the way in which subjects of a certain sort are created so as to be compatible with its ends and strategies. The totalizing power of the state, its totalitarianism, cannot be separated from its powers of individualization.

Foucault's analytics of power can only be adequately understood in relation to those of discourse, history and subjectivity considered below.

Discourse

This single term 'discourse' may be held both to provide one succinct description of Foucault's entire work and its subject matter. But what does this term mean and, in the light of the statement made above, is it impossibly broad? Foucault's most explicit formulations occur in three texts: *OT*, *AK* and *OD*, and these will be considered in turn.

The Notion of an Episteme

In *OT* an analysis is made of the changing historical discourses of the human sciences, those concerned with what we would call today biology, linguistics and economics. The aim is to show that diverse sets of discursive practices are ordered according to underlying codes and rules which change radically through time, govern what may be thought or said at any one time, and are culturally specific (Foucault's is an analysis of Western culture). *OT* sets out to show how cultural order is created and sustained through discursive practices. Consider the following passage:

> Towards the middle of the eighteenth century, Pomme treated and cured a hysteric by making her take 'baths, ten or twelve hours a day, for ten whole months'. At the end of this treatment for the desiccation of the nervous system and the heat that sustained it, Pomme saw 'membranous tissues like pieces of damp parchment . . . peel away with some slight discomfort, and these were passed daily with the urine; the right ureter also peeled away and came out whole in the same way'. The same thing

occurred with the intestines, which at another stage, 'peeled off their internal tunics, which we saw emerge from the rectum. The oesophagus, the arterial trachea, and the tongue also peeled in due course; and the patient had rejected different pieces either by vomiting or by expectoration'. (*BC*: ix)

What do we make of this account? Written by a doctor it was intended as a serious description of a pathological condition and its treatment. In such a piece of writing what is to count as an observation? And how do we distinguish a true from a false statement? How can *we* be sure that Pomme did not observe what he reports? Foucault uses such accounts not as evidence of later scientific advance towards the truth, a happy condition existing for us today, but to problematize any claims to truth or progress. In taking Pomme's description seriously and bracketing off the question of meaning content, he aims to demonstrate that such accounts are not at all fantastic or wild but obey a discursive lógic which is at the same time internally consistent and utterly different from our own. Such statements represent an ordering of reality which was once accepted and taken seriously. The implication is, of course, that our own thought will, no doubt fairly soon, be regarded in a similar manner as we are inclined to think about that of Pomme.

In *OT* four periods of discursive coherence are distinguished, from the sixteenth century to the present day (Renaissance, Classical, Modern and Post-Modern). These are termed 'epistemes': total sets of relations uniting the discursive practices giving rise to various epistemologies, sciences and formalized systems. An episteme is a historical and a social *a priori*. It is impossible to think, write, learn or discover beyond an epistemic framework. An episteme constitutes the very grounds on which to distinguish between true or false statements. Between each of the epistemes is a gulf so deep as to be beyond meaningful discussion. Epistemes are totally incommensurable, historically they arise from ruptures in the ordering of experience. Why such ruptures take place is of no interest to Foucault. He analyses these epistemes vertically rather than horizontally, to uncover the rules underlying the discourses produced. Epistemes are like islands separated by an unbridgeable gulf of water going down to uncharted depths. *OT* alights on each of these islands and digs down to uncover their discursive strata, strata that permit them to take the form of an island. It is this process of digging down to reveal that which underlies discursive practices that Foucault terms 'archaeology'.

The book has no historical 'plot' (of, say, development). It is like a play with four separate acts totally disconnected rather than building on each other. The fundamental concern is with the relationship between an order of things (discursive objects) and an order of language that deals with these objects. A new episteme 'crystallizes' alongside an already established one, filling up and compiling a fresh discursive space. Not only do the representations of the 'real' change, but so do the definitions of the real — what actually is supposed to count as a discursive object. Discourses are examined as sets of self-sufficient representations, i.e. they are not simply effects of underlying social or economic processes. *OT* resolutely refuses such a reductionism. If anything, epistemes explain the social and the political rather than the other way round. Here Foucault has a very real problem. He has no reason to criticize an episteme, to think one is any better than another, yet it is quite clear that the episteme he does detest is that of modern science subsuming forms of social oppression under claims to true knowledge. An analysis situating discourse in relation to power only begins to emerge in *OD*.

In each of the four epistemes an analysis is made of connections between the representation of language, wealth or economic exchange, and living organisms. Each episteme orders the relationships differently. The last is only beginning to emerge with the structuralism of Saussure and the psychology of Freud. A new episteme 'forgets' a previous one working on a new set of discursive objects in a new way. For the Post-Modern episteme Foucault is not just describing a set of discursive practices, he is in a sense predicting and promoting their full realization: the dissolution of humanity into the word (see p. 313). In *OT* we have a picture of discourses as ways in which reality is historically ordered and accepted. Discourse is the combination of a theory (or meta-theory) which is historically specific. The notion of the episteme is continued and amplified in *AK*.

The Inadequacy of a History of Ideas

In *AK* a dominant intellectual tradition in both the social sciences and philosophy provides a foil for Foucault's own conception, as it did in *MC, BC and OT*, but for the first time he explicitly sets out to attack it in detail. This tradition he broadly refers to as 'the history of ideas', a particular way of writing intellectual history or the manner in which conceptual structures are developed, become accepted and/or subsequently rejected. It should be immediately noted that the kind of framework Foucault is criticizing has totally dominated all work in archaeology which has dealt with the history of the discipline. If we reject such a framework and take Foucault's criticisms seriously the implications are quite profound: we will have to rewrite archaeology's history.

The history of ideas is dependent on a number of related notions: genesis, continuity, totality and authorship/consciousness. An emphasis on genesis assumes that knowledges have specific points of origin either in terms of individuals or the collective consciousness of an age. These knowledges develop through time as definite traditions of thought (continuity). We can trace the development of these ideas to the present day. Ultimately it will all add up to a single story of progressive intellectual development of knowledges (totalization) which is to be related back to (ideally) named individuals and the writings or ideas they produce. Ideas constitute a series of representations of the world, developing through time and providing a coherent object of study for the intellectual historian or for those interested in writing the history of specific disciplines such as archaeology. Such a perspective has the following results:

1 It reduces knowledges to being either an expression of or representation of other social relations.
2 It relates knowledge to the consciousness of imaginative individuals.
3 This means that the history of ways of thinking about the world is to be derived from the manner in which theories and ideas are passed down (modified, extended or replaced) from one generation, or one individual, or one tradition of thinking, to the next.
4 All this implies a separation between an abstract non-material realm of ideas and a non-discursive realm of real material objects and relations which lies beyond it.

Foucault is rejecting a perspective in which knowledge is conceived solely in terms of sets of ideas developed by individuals and given a 'lifespan' by being subsumed into a wider notion of tradition linking together a number of individuals and texts and also sometimes being related to 'the spirit of an age'. Not only does he suspend the categories of ideas, thought traditions, periodizations of ideas, but also those of the discipline, the author, the book and the *oeuvre*. Knowledges are not simply produced differentially in discrete disciplines by 'authors'; they are not located in books; nor is there any necessary unity in the texts an individual named author produces (an *oeuvre*). Here what is being challenged is any supposition that the discipline, book, author or *oeuvre* may be held to be self-sufficient categories closed in on themselves.

Our notions of the academic discipline or types of discourse, e.g. economics, politics, literature, are of very recent date. We can only rather dubiously and retrospectively define and designate a discourse as 'economic' or 'archaeological' two hundred years ago on the basis of making a series of anachronistic assumptions which assume what we think of as economics or archaeology has always existed in a more or less stable form. Furthermore our disciplines are entirely artificial creations whose boundaries are far from clear although enthusiastic attempts are always being made to maintain them (e.g. archaeology proper is the study of the distant past and not the present). Foucault points out that academic disciplines are themselves products of a particular type of discourse and need to be analysed as such.

Books do not form any simple or unitary category. There is little in common between a collection of poems, a history book, a work of philosophy or between Balzac's novel-cycle and the stories of Stephen King. Furthermore, each text forms a vast web of references and interrelations with other texts – nodes within a wider network – and have different forms in the cases of mathematical treatises or literary commentaries. Authors who put texts together are the medium through which webs of references and relations run rather than a distinctive point of origin. There is no necessary unity to an author's *oeuvre* – what he or she produces under a proper name. Does the name of an author designate in the same way a text that he has published under his or her name, a text under a pseudonym, an unfinished draft, a collection of jottings, a notebook, texts intended for publication and not completed, first drafts, crossings-out, sketches, letters, notes, reported conversation, ultimately shopping-lists? What is the essential and the inessential, who is to decide, and why, if there is any connection at all between any of these?

Discursive Formations and Statements

AK attempts to introduce a radically new set of concepts from those utilized in the history of ideas approach and we will now examine what these are, their implications and their adequacy. Foucault wants to clear away all the conceptual baggage referred to above to open up an entirely new field for the analysis of discourse. This means that before we approach what happens in archaeological discourse, a book of an individual archaeologist or any statements ('archaeological' or otherwise, written or spoken), the material we are dealing with is 'a population of events in the space of discourse in general'. This leads to a project which attempts to describe these discursive events in order to search for internal unities which will not be those of the book, author, discipline, tradition, etc., but may in themselves lead to a different conceptualization and form of understanding of these displaced categories (*AK*: 27).

Knowledges are to be located in 'discursive formations'. These discursive formations consist of a body of related statements. A statement is neither a sentence nor a proposition (although in certain circumstances it may be) so, for example, if we were to say: 'Lewis Binford is an archaeologist who thinks it is important to study bones' we would not necessarily be making a statement in Foucault's sense of the term. Consequently a discursive formation does not simply consist of a set of related sentences or propositions of this kind. A discourse does not reside in a set of statements conceived as related but nevertheless fundamentally discrete entities; it is a group of thoroughly mediated statements existing within the specificity of a discursive formation. In other words discursive formations and statements dialectically provide conditions for each other's existence. As a statement cannot be conceived according to linguistic or logical categories it has no unitary essence. It is not a thing or unit but an 'enunciative function'. What this means is that the statement is a function relating to signs. Statements have *effects* on both what is said and written and how this is realized.

Analogies, graphs, maps, experiments, qualitative or quantitative descriptions, biographical accounts, deductions, statistical calculations, may all be statements (*AK*: 50). Statements relate to linguistic or, equally, non-linguistic signs, marks or traces. They are not simply reducible to language. According to *AK* to describe a statement means 'defining the conditions in which the function that gave a series of signs . . . a specific existence can operate . . . [in] relation to a domain of objects' (AK: 108). Elsewhere it is stated:

> In examining the statement what we have discovered is a function that has a bearing on a group of signs, which is identified neither with grammatical 'acceptability' nor with logical correctness, and which requires if it is to operate: a referential (which is not exactly a fact, a state of things, or even an object, but a principle of differentiation); a subject (not the speaking consciousness, not the author of the formulation, but a position that may be filled in various conditions by various individuals); an associated field (which is not the real context of the formulation, the situation in which it was articulated, but a domain of coexistence for other statements); a materiality (which is not only the substance or support of the articulation, but a status, rules of transcription, possibilities of use and re-use). (*AK*: 115)

What all this appears to mean is that statements are functions with effects taking place in relation to linguistic or non-linguistic sign systems. The statements have existence only within the space of particular discursive formations and their material effects may emerge in particular representations (e.g. graphs) and the use of particular signifiers in particular sentences or propositions rather than others. Statements when considered together become sets of functions that may articulate to form rules and rule-governed systems underlying particular discourses and knowledges. Together, statements form conditions of existence for propositions and sentences. However, they have no necessary unitary essence. They are fundamentally oscillating in form, always shifting and changing according to both context and circumstances. They are never available to the consciousness of the social actor. Such statements are usually never 'stated' or 'known', but nevertheless they may be acted upon in a fairly routine way. In order to operate statements require sets of referentials differentiating between objects and elements of social reality, subjects (agents) through which they pass, finally, a field of operation and articulation provided by the discursive formation.

An analysis of statements leads one to investigate why particular discourses are produced at particular times and places rather than others and according to what rules discourses are produced. It is not to search for deeper meaning in the manner of hermeneutics. Rather than 'depth interpretation' it is 'surface description' that refuses to treat discourses as a mere gloss on deeper meaning residing in them, a sign of something else, such as the workings of capitalism. Discourses to Foucault are not *documents* to be interpreted which will finally reveal their inner meaning, but *monuments* to be described (see the discussion on history).

In the passage cited from *AK* on p. 295 two terms: 'the referential' and 'materiality' require further consideration. Dreyfus and Rabinow (1982: 48–9) argue that Foucault's use of the term 'statement' is more or less equivalent to what they refer to as 'serious speech acts' and this is a most helpful insight. Foucault is exclusively concerned in his early works up to *AK* with the discourses of those individuals we might term professionals: doctors, psychiatrists, economists, linguists, natural scientists. It is their statements derived from written documents that he analyses. He is not at all interested in analysing in detail the discourses of those subjected to the practices of these professionals (e.g. patients, madmen — with the exception of *IPR*). In other words he is not interested in everyday speech or discourse but that produced by professionals or specialists.

If an archaeologist were to say 'This find of obsidian on Melos is evidence of the operation of a prehistoric exchange system' this would count as a serious speech act, whereas if Andris Michalaros, a local farmer, were to make the same proposition this would count as an everyday speech act, not automatically to be taken seriously. Why?

Any speech act can be serious providing that validation procedures are set up involving, for example, a community of experts of which the archaeologist rather than the farmer is a member, and institutional sites which legitimize speaking and writing as serious claims to knowledge and meaning.

The materiality of the statement does not simply refer to the fact that it has real material effects in the form of 'concrete' utterances or graphic marks on a page. It also means that statements as valued or serious speech acts tend to be copied, repeated, disseminated and commented upon. Stressing the materiality of the statement is also part of a refusal to draw any clear dividing-line between what may be taken to be discursive and another realm, that of the non-discursive.

We will now examine the relation of statements to the discursive formation. A discursive formation is a historically specific and socially contingent ordering of discourse. Initially Foucault proposes that a discursive formation may perhaps be identified if the statements refer to one and the same object; their is a repeated style or series of regularities underlying statements; the same or similar concepts are employed in making statements and if these statements relate to a common expositional theme. He rejects all these possibilities on the basis of his own previous investigations in *MC*, *BC* and *OT*. For example, in the discourse of psychiatry, there is no common object — madness — to refer to. The meaning of madness is historically variable as is the style in which it is written about, the concepts employed and the themes invoked. Consequently the relation of statements to each other in a discursive formation cannot be one of identity in relation to objects, concepts, etc., it is rather one of a regular and non-random *dispersion*. So a discursive formation is a system determining the manner in which statements are dispersed in relation to each other. It is not a neat, logical dove-tailing and may, therefore, embrace non-correspondences and contradictions (*AK*: 155). Discursive formations are irregular rather than regular, differentiated rather than undifferentiated, multiple rather than singular, a set of oppositions rather than a series of unifications. And if all this sounds difficult to visualize it is only because Foucault bravely attempts to bring out real complexities and real differences rather than subsume these features into a simplistic and reductionist model.

The dispersion of statements within a discursive formation is governed by what Foucault terms 'rules of formation' relating to the formation of the objects of a discourse, the types of statement that are made in relation to these objects (enunciative modalities), the manner in which concepts are formed and certain discursive strategies are actualized. We will briefly consider each of these in turn.

Discursive objects   Objects of discourse are by no means natural or pre-ordained but created in particular historical and social circumstances. At any particular time or place 'surfaces of emergence' may occur from which fresh discursive objects take on a recognizable shape and particular form. Foucault gives a particular example of this from an earlier study (*MC*). At the beginning of the nineteenth century the confinement of those individuals socially designated as mad in special psychiatric hospitals created madness as a fresh object of study and investigation bearing little real relationship to a previous discursive object going under the same name 'madness'. In archaeology the creation of a typology of objects based on certain properties – stone, bronze and iron – created a new discursive object which through time became increasingly differentiated from other objects, e.g. fossils and stuffed animals previously collected together in the same curio cases. Processual and post-processual archaeologies have created their own discursive objects, artifacts as, respectively, adaptive objects and part of a significative system. Different discourses are not simply to be differentiated between on the basis of the objects they deal with. They actively *produce* the objects of which they speak, internally limit their own domains, define that which they are purporting to talk about and make these objects manifest and subject to further descrip-tion.

    Foucault proposes to differentiate between two sets of practices that operate to bring about the surfaces of emergence of discursive objects, the realms of non-discursive and discursive practices. The former include relations between institutions, economic and social processes, norms and value systems. These relations do not define what the objects of discourse are but enable them to appear in the first place, to be subjected to analysis. Discursive practices 'determine the group of relations that discourse must establish in order to speak of this or that object . . . These relations characterize not the language (*langue*) used by discourse, nor the circumstances which it is deployed but discourse itself as a practice' (*AK*: 46). What Foucault is proposing is that non-discursive and discursive practices are autonomous and that the latter govern the manner in which the former actually arise. Rather than making a radical separation of the discursive from the non-discursive as Foucault wishes to do in order to 'save' the autonomy of the former as a 'pure form', it would seem to be better to argue that both reside in a relation of mutual mediation, mutual determination, from which definite objects of discourse arise and emerge.

Discursive statements   The statements arising in discourse – what are referred to as 'enunciative modalities' in *AK* – set to work on discursive objects. Discourse becomes instated not as a description of these objects but as a practice working in relation to them. Here the basic questions to be asked of a discourse are: Who is speaking? What is their institutional site? What position is occupied by the subject who does speak or write in relation to discursive objects? These questions all arise from and are related to Foucault's consideration of statements as involving the production of serious speech acts (see p. 297). If we analyse those who are accorded the *right* to speak on any particular occasion this involves criteria of competence and knowledge in relation to institutions, pedagogic norms and legal systems. These allow particular subjects to practise and extend their knowledge claims. In other words archaeological statements cannot come from anyone. Their value, effectivity and influence are to be related to an institutional and educational system, qualifications and legal rights: only the trained archaeologist may be permitted to excavate and decide that which is worth excavating and that which is not. Institutional sites (the academic department, the seminar-room, the finds-processing laboratory, the museum and the library) all provide supports for the making of serious speech acts and differentiate hierarchically betwen those who may and may not make them (the professor, the lecturer, curator, the student and the man or woman in the street). These all act so as to create definite positions that subjects may occupy *vis à vis* the past and its objects, its re-telling.

Concept formation   Consideration of modes of discursive object formation and the manner in which statements are and can be made immediately suggests that discourses are not merely sets of concepts. What we must investigate according to *AK* is how concepts arise at a particular time and place and precisely which concepts may be placed alongside each other and those which are incompatible. What kinds of conceptual statements are permitted and which are not? Here *AK* argues that historical shifts in conceptual structures are not to be automatically regarded as being the result of progress, truer or better ideas replacing those which are false. Such a position bears a strong relationship to Kuhn's work on conceptual revolutions where one paradigm replaces another because of shifts of interest within the academic community. However Foucault goes further than this, wishing to search for rules *internal to discourse* that may be held to account for changes in conceptual structures: 'the rules of formation operate not only in the mind or consciousness of individuals, but in discourse itself; they operate therefore, according to a uniform anonymity, on all individuals who undertake to speak in this discursive field' (*AK*: 63).

Discursive strategies Within any particular discursive formation there is space for change in what is said, how it is said, which concepts are employed, objects created and the kinds of statements that occur. Analysis involves a search for regularities both within and between traditionally defined disciplines. *AK* argues that in the human sciences sets of rules underlie particular discourses at particular times, determining the kinds of discursive strategies (ways of speaking, writing, investigating, performing analyses, etc.) which can be undertaken and/or accepted. These rules will account for the fact that some modes of investigation etc., are carried on and others ignored. These rules result in discontinuities relating to real historical differences in discourse rather than continuities and gradual development towards a fuller and truer picture.

Bracketing the Self

Although Foucault is exclusively concerned with what may be taken to be seriously intended discursive formations and the serious statements residing within them he does not take the question of meaning seriously nor the question of truth. The first thing he does when confronted with a text is to laugh at it — at least metaphorically, sometimes literally (*OT*: xv). He has, of course, a serious purpose and precisely for this reason he considers all discourses in the same way. Discursive formations do not replace each other in a successive advance towards the truth, they just change. Discursive formations create truths according to time and place and if we are to study them we must, according to *AK*, bracket off both ourselves and any claims to real meaning made in a discourse. This is why *AK* refers to the project of a pure description of discourses (see p. 296).

Consideration of truth or meaning would only contaminate or actually prevent such description taking place. Discursive formations are merely the space in which statements become linked together in various ways. They have a history — they emerge and fall away — but Foucault is not interested in providing any reasons for why one type of discourse replaces another. Such an interest, with its search for underlying meanings, would again block possibilities for pure description. Discursive formations are simply anonymous rule-governed historical systems. Agency (people using discourse) is quite irrelevant to their understanding and moreover, as we have already seen, discourses are autonomous from non-discursive practices.

The Discursive and the Non-discursive

Discourses are, of course, meaningful to those who participate in them, but *AK* refuses to seek for any underlying meaning residing in the relations between discourse and that outside, the realm of the non-discursive. From a structuralist position we might regard discourses as being structured in the same manner as non-discursive practices according to an underlying relational logic. Discourse would in no sense be a privileged manifestation of this logic. On the other hand, from a hermeneutic perspective, discourses would be regarded as determined by non-discursive factors. Only particular discursive practices at any given time or place are possible given the presumed existence of a horizon of intelligibility beyond which agents cannot speak, think or act. From a structural–Marxist perspective discourses would form part of the ideological instance, operating so as to legitimate the social order, interpellating agents, and being derived in the last instance from the economic. *AK* does not relate discourses to the economic nor to wider questions of the distribution of power within the social order. It attempts to avoid reducing discourses to a particular manifestation of a structural logic underlying all social practices or an outcome of the contextualized matrices of social life underlying all social being and forms of consciousness.

AK's insistence that we should study discourse as an autonomous pure form creates major problems. First, discourse becomes discon-nected from power yet discourses are not merely documents to be interpreted or monuments to be described but have definite power effects on the way the social world is organized. Such a conception is present in *AK* but remains largely latent. Second, if *AK* stands outside any horizon of intelligibility merely cataloguing differences it remains problematic (i) how the book could be written in the first place; (ii) whether *AK* itself is supposed to have any meaning or make any difference to the way discourses are produced. If we totally bracket ourselves off from a discourse and discourses as meaningful, how can we be expected to identify statements?

Discourse and Power

In *OD* Foucault begins to make a much clearer linkage, subsequently amplified in *DP* and *HS*, between the discursive and the non-discursive, discourse and the operation of power and social domina-tion. Discourse is not just connected to power, as in *AK*, it is a form of power. In the history of Western thought it is argued, there has been a persistent tendency to invalidate ordinary speech acts and convert more and more statements into serious speech acts produced by specialists within institutional settings. This is a manifestation of a 'will to truth' constantly growing stronger and deeper (*OD*: 56).

Discourse is to be linked with individual desire on the one hand, wanting discourse to be open and unrestricted and institutional constraint on the other, dividing off what may be said and what must be left unsaid and insisting on the restraint, control and formalization of discourse. It is only through this restraint that discourse may possess power, be taken as being expressions of serious meaning.

Foucault identifies controls acting so as to constrain discourse. These may be external to the discourse, internal to it, or both inside and outside it. The extra-discursive controls he identifies are prohibitions, divisions and oppositions. Prohibitions prevent statements being made according to the context of the discourse, what it is supposed to be about and what the subject speaking has a legitimate right to say. These are all familiar. In the archaeology seminar-room only those individuals who have a legitimate claim to being archaeologists or having an interest in the past may be permitted to speak, and they must speak seriously about some aspect of archaeological interest concerning archaeological discursive objects according to dominant definitions of what these interests and objects are supposed to be. Anyone writing an archaeological text must similarly constrain him- or herself or discourse would threaten to fragment and shatter. For example, any text will inevitably be judged archaeological to the extent that it deals with the distant past. Deviations such as modern material-culture studies will always be judged warily. Discourses become divided into a hierarchy of importance serving to distinguish between those which are accepted and sanctioned and those to be banished from serious consideration. Of oppositions structuring discourse by far the most prominent is a division between truth and falsity. An archaeological will to truth involves filtering out those statements designated to be true from those considered false. Foucault notes that '"true" discourse, freed from desire and power by the necessity of its form, cannot recognise the will to truth which prevades it' (*OD*: 56). A true discourse, for the very reason that it is supposed to be true, is supposedly not linked with the exercise of power. Yet it is this very (social and historical) ascription of truth that gives a discourse power and social effects. Any power a 'scientific' archaeology might have is based on its claims to be 'in the true' as opposed to other archaeologies out of it. A vision of apolitical truth supports particular discursive forms such as 'cultural resource management' in which archaeologists establish a legitimate right to a hegemonic control over, and ordering of, the distant past. Prohibitions and divisions of discourse cannot operate without the possibility of violence and coercion. These two external controls are historically being integrated into the opposition between truth and falsity: denials of the right to speak require 'scientific' justification.

Internal constraints on discourse involve various types of 'rarefaction' resulting in a scarcity rather than a plenitude of meaning. Here *OD* points to principles of the commentary, the author and the discipline. Commentaries are dependent on a gradation of discourses into everyday speech acts, and those speech acts giving rise to new ones, taking up, transforming, interpreting and translating from the original. The latter allow the endless production of new texts and paradoxically demand that one must 'say for the first time what had, nonetheless, already been said, and must tirelessly repeat what had, however, never been said' (*OD*: 58). It should be immediately remarked that this piece of writing does exactly this. Right now (11.30 p.m. 18 December 1987, Lund, Sweden) I would like to say so much, to deviate entirely from this present task of exegesis, and produce something different. I would like to consign Foucault to my bookshelves, to resurrect him in certain texts in ways he probably would not like. Should I go on? Aware that I am infringing permitted boundaries . . . *OD*'s remarks about the author concern the manner in which consciousness of being an author, working out a 'genre' limit what is and can be stated (see pp. 321–2).

Possibly the most important internal control on discourse is that of the discipline. Disciplines are supposedly defined by specific domains of objects (for archaeology artifacts and their associations), methods and corpuses of propositions considered true and proper, rules and definitions for producing truths and technical aids and instruments constituting an anonymous system at the disposal of anyone who wants or is able to use it. For archaeology to exist as a discipline there must be the endless possibility of producing new archaeological statements. However, such statements can only be accepted if they address whatever are defined as proper or true archaeological objects or the manner in which archaeological statements are supposed to be represented in archaeological texts. Disciplines police themselves, preventing the production of inappropriate or non-disciplinary statements. If you transgress these rules you are no longer an anthropologist, archaeologist, sociologist, etc., and can no longer expect anyone to either read what you write or take you seriously at all. And all this is productive of knowledge?

OD concludes the discussion of constraints on discourse with this cogent remark: 'What, after all, is an education system, other than a ritualisation of speech, a qualification and a fixing of the roles for speaking subjects, the constitution of a doctrinal group . . . a distribution and an appropriation of discourse with its powers and knowledges?' (*OD*: 64). This would appear to be an appropriate note on which to end this section.

History

Foucault tells us in the preface to *OT* that the 'fundamental codes of a culture — those governing its language, schemes of perception, its exchanges, its techniques, its values, the hierarchy of its practices — establish for every man, from the very first, the empirical orders with which he will be dealing and within which he will be at home' (*OT*: xx). At a distance from these cultural codes are forms of reflection, scientific theories or philosophical interpretations, which attempt to explain why this order exists. Situated in-between the 'encoded' eye and reflexive knowledge are discourses which are more obscure, providing general theories as to the ordering of things and the interpretation such an ordering involves. These are the discourses which directly confront and transform the world of appearances, and it is primarily these in which *OT* is interested.

Difference

Whatever we may think of the term 'episteme' (Foucault himself abandons it after *AK*), what *OT* manages to do most brilliantly is to show us how to think historical and cultural specificity. Orthodox history may sometimes attempt to show us the different social and cultural objects that have been perceived by different encoded eyes. What Foucault does is actually to present us with those encoded eyes and enable us to see just how obvious an utterly alien world can be through them. The immense descriptive richness of *OT* (a richness which could only be dissipated by an attempt to summarize 400 pages in this small space) stands as a monument to how an alternative archaeology and an alternative history could be written, one emphasizing specificity, particularity and difference, what Foucault terms the historical *a priori*. There is a double refusal here: to write history using present-day terms or to write history by attempting to show that present-day conceptions operated in the past but were perhaps more blurred and/or went under different names: 'the men of the seventeenth and eighteenth century do not think of wealth, nature, or languages in terms that had been bequeathed to them by preceding ages or in forms that presaged what was soon to be discovered' (*OT*: 208). Foucault's is a production of a history which takes history seriously. By contrast a cross-cultural atemporal and aspatial generalizing perspective promoted so much in recent archaeology does not take history seriously; it does not recognize real and irreducible historical differences. History becomes the endless repetition of the same.

Precisely because Foucault takes history seriously he defamiliarizes it. He does not write of conceptions in the seventeenth century by translating them into modernist terminology. Rather than domesticating the past by using the terms of the present he reactivates it as utterly strange, an alien world. *OT* begins by citing a passage from Borges in which a 'certain Chinese encyclopaedia' classifies animals in a variety of bizarre ways, e.g. belonging to the emperor; embalmed; sucking pigs; that from a long way off look like flies, drawn with a fine camelhair brush; included in the present classification... Such a classification is clearly impossible for us to think, utterly incomprehensible; but the Renaissance naturalist Aldrovandi's *Treatise on Serpents and Dragons* is not all that different. Snakes are considered alongside dragons and other mythological beasts. A chapter discussing 'On the serpent in general' includes information on anatomy, nature and habitats, coitus, sympathy, monsters, gods to which it is dedicated, proverbs, coinage, riddles, historical facts, statues, use in human diet and much more (*OT*: 39). *OT* describes the Renaissance episteme as being based on a vast series of resemblances, an attempt to link everything together by recovering the same in the different. This search for resemblances included not only relations between things but between these things and the words signifying them. Aldrovandi's work is entirely comprehensible within such a framework in which nature was from top to bottom written: 'when one is faced with the task of writing an animal's history, it is useless and impossible to choose between the profession of naturalist and that of compiler: one has to collect into one and the same form of knowledge all that has been *seen* and *heard*, all that has been *recounted*, either by nature or by men, by the language of the world, by tradition, or by poets' (*OT*: 40).

'Archaeology' and Genealogy

Foucault uses these two terms to describe his historical method. They imply two parallel rather than conflicting approaches, archaeology characterizing *MC, BC, OT* and *AK*, and genealogy *DP, HS* and *UP*. Foucault uses the word 'archaeology' as a metaphor for his early work, suggesting digging down, uncovering concealed layers, letting archival fragments stand for the whole, reconstructing that which has been forgotten As we have seen, this metaphorical use of the term accompanies its use to construct rules for specifying discursive objects and relations between these objects based on a principle of *rarity*: why is it that of all the things that could have been said just these things were said and not others? His use of the term 'archaeology' to describe his history is also tactical – to differentiate between his concerns and the traditional concerns of historiography. Rather than being simply a different history, Foucault's is an anti-history. He denies all the conventional types of explanation and approach – comparative method, the erection of typologies, cause-and-effect-type explanations and any appeals to the collective consciousness of an age. His emphasis on discursive formations as a dispersed relational order of statements remains utterly distinct from the normal unities proposed as binding ideas, such as traditions, books or authors.

Foucault's work is rightly anti-evolutionary, the emphasis on origins (what was the first civilization?), continuities (what links can be set up between various temporal segments in the archaeological record?) and notions of progress found in traditional history and archaeology are replaced with fundamental ruptures and discontinuities. He suspends any notion of a total history. By 'total history' is meant forms of explanation such as systems theory in contemporary archaeology in which it is proposed that there is one set of processes uniting all areas of human society from economy to religion. Instead of the coherences of processes, Foucault has the dispersions of events. An emphasis on total history also implies that ultimately history is, or should be, a single story the writing of which is divorced from the social and political concerns of the present. Total history is dependent on the unwarranted assumption that all pieces of 'evidence' can be slotted together into one unified picture of the past which ultimately leads up to the present. A total history tries to reconstruct the past as it really was. Instead of this Foucault interrogates the past, relating evidence to specific problems being investigated and this has, apart from the emphasis on problems, nothing to do with the hypothetico-deductive method. There can be no question of testing or independently verifying a theory or hypothesis. Instead, theory practice and evidence are thoroughly interwoven together. Archaeological evidence or historical documents do not simply 'stand for' the past to be interrogated or interpreted to free *the* meaning inhering in them. What this implies is that a potentially infinite number of events can be brought out from a series of potsherds, rock carvings or written sources. The criteria deciding their status as events has nothing whatsoever to do with the past. It has everything to do with the purposes and values of the analysis being undertaken in the present.

If we wish to search for a 'break' in Foucault's work it would be quite easy to locate this between *AK* and *DP*, in which the term 'archaeology' as a general description is displaced by 'genealogy'.

Foucault is now prepared to recognize longer-term continuities as well as transformations in Western culture. The abandonment of the concept of the 'episteme' no longer requires him to regard historical differences in various phases as so profound there is no point of contact. History becomes a more complex web of continuities and discontinuities. In constructing genealogies what Foucault is doing is seeking out the discontinuous in the continuous, what appears to be a directional 'flow' of meaning and social practice. Foucault's genealogical history can be regarded as supplementing or extending rather than contradicting his 'archaeologies'. An 'archaeological' study forms a necessary basis for carrying out a genealogical analysis. The major difference in Foucault's later work, compared with that carried out earlier, is that he is far more concerned than previously with the relationship between discursive and non-discursive practices. The lack of an adequate theorization of the latter created major problems which remained unresolved in *AK*. An emphasis on the supposed autonomy of discourse is abandoned by investigations which show how the discursive and the non-discursive mediate or serve to form each other. Discourse is linked with power and forms of social domination. We might state that while archaeology is a descriptive analysis concerned with what statements are actually made, genealogy is a critical analysis of the social conditions of existence of these statements, their relationship to power. In 'archaeology' statements in discursive formations have surfaces of emergence which are considered as being beyond further intelligibility, whereas in genealogy these statements emerge as the result of a linkage between the discursive and non-discursive in a longer-term historical field. Furthermore, as the statements and their related field of social practices are linked with power, they can no longer be regarded as meaningless permutations; they have profound consequences for those involved. Whereas Foucault the 'archaeologist' can bracket himself off (or attempt to do so) from questions of meaning and seriousness, as genealogist he can no longer do so. Genealogy does not revert to a search for deep meanings or an evolutionary trajectory in history. It rather questions the political status of meaning and discourse in relation to power.

On the Interpretation of the Past

Foucault persistently derides hermeneutic attempts at interpreting the past. This does not mean that Foucault does not interpret. His entire output is an active interpretative engagement. To describe is to interpret, to write is to interpret, to think is to interpret, to study objects whether discursive or non-discursive is to interpret. So

Foucault cannot deny the importance, indeed the necessity, of interpretation. His remarks about archaeology being a pure description of discursive events are essentially empty. A 'pure' description would be an impossible description. Choices, for example, are always involved in how to describe discourses. A further claim, which must be taken much more seriously, is his denial of the necessity for 'deep interpretation', which is what hermeneutics is all about, trying to recover hidden meanings and moreover to pin down these meanings in the form of statements such as 'The real meaning of this design is . . .'. Evaluation of such questions inevitably involves us in determining between various truth claims, whether meaning is restricted or infinite and at what level meaning itself can be located. For Foucault truth and meaning are both dispersed, and lie on the surface of things rather than being hidden in their interiority: 'If interpretation is a never-ending task, it is simply because there is nothing to interpret. There is nothing absolutely primary to interpret because, when all is said and done, underneath it all everything is already an interpretation' (AS: 189, cited in Dreyfus and Rabinow 1982: 107). Truths, not truth, meanings not meaning. Human existence *is* interpretation and any and all interpretations are equally imposed on the 'real'. Interpretations are contingent. The questions that arise are, as with the analysis of discourse: Why *these* interpretations? Why *these* ascribed meanings rather than others? A belief in deep, essential, coherent, and non-dispersed meaning might be described as merely a Western cultural malaise. What Foucault wants to show is that when looked at (interpreted) in the right way meaning is visible on the surface in small concrete details, shifts in the forms of practices, in paintings, in architecture, in and between the lines of texts rather than that beyond the lines. Fine. But we can ask why only the surface? Why not surfaces and depths? Part of the reason seems to be that as Foucault has chosen to totally oppose hermeneutics this means he must reject any 'depth' interpretation. If we agree with Foucault that meaning is irrevocably dispersed there appears to be no necessary corollary that this must be only a surface dispersion. This whole problem is, in any case, dependent on what we mean by 'surfaces' and 'depths', and this raises questions of agency, consciousness and social totalities, space and time.

Space and Time

Integrally bound up with Foucault's historical investigations are the uses of space and time in relation to social practices. Space and time are constructed in relation to these practices rather than acting as containers for them. Furthermore they act so as to construct themselves, the spatial is interwoven with the temporal, but we might say that this interweaving is not like that of the canes or straws in a basket, criss-crossing one another at regular intervals, but a much more irregular and dispersed set of linkages. For the sake of convenience I will unpack these notions of space and time, discussing them separately.

Space

Foucault suggests that a general distinction might be drawn between the Middle Ages constituting a 'space of emplacement' and modern uses of space embracing specific sites with differentiated oppositions and functions (OOS: 22–3). A space of emplacement is one made up of hierarchies; sacred spaces and profane spaces; protected places and open, exposed places; urban and rural spaces broadly corresponding to cosmological theory with its supercelestial, celestial and territorial places. In social practice the celestial provides a map for the worldly and vice versa. The map becomes a medium for inquiry into the form and nature of these spaces (PK: 74). Microcosm mirrors macrocosm within such thought, finding expression in the constructed space of the architectural form; structures such as churches have definite experience effects within such a context. Galileo opened up and dissolved such a place of emplacement and for it an infinitely open space became substituted, and in the modern era such an open space becomes increasingly localized in terms of sites with their relations of proximity, accessibility or inaccessibility. The problem becomes that of knowing what relations of propinquity, storage, circulation, marking and differentiation and classification of spaces should be developed for given ends. The division and utilization of space becomes a fundamental anxiety and it is largely desanctified. In the disciplinary society the control and distribution of people in space becomes of central concern. The map becomes a means of inquiry and examination and control: distribution maps of various elements, electoral maps, taxation maps, maps of ethnic groups, etc. Techniques of social control become increasingly invested in varied institutional architectural forms: hospitals, prisons, factories, schools, office buildings. In the context of the modern disciplinary society, Foucault comments, it is hardly surprising that prisons resemble hospitals which resemble schools which resemble prisons (DP: 228). The aim in all these institutions is to create a space for surveillance. Below we will consider the cases of the hospital and the prison.

In *BC* Foucault contrasts a 'medicine of species' with one of 'social spaces', the latter developing in France in the final years of the eighteenth century. The former was one based on a nosological classification of diseases, usually in the family and at home. Health is individualized and is simply considered as the converse of a morbid state. It inheres in the humours and sympathies of the body. By contrast, the new medical gaze constitutes bodies as objects for study and dissection and disease resides entirely in what is open to the gaze of the doctor. The medicine of social spaces is concerned with populations rather than individuals and more with the prevention of disease than its cure. The health of the individual becomes measured against that considered a norm. What is important to Foucault in this context is a fundamental change in medical practice involving a tripartite spatialization: (i) the spatialization of the medical gaze over the surfaces of the body: only that which was visible could now be studied; (ii) the location of this new medical gaze in specific institutions, its institutionalization; (iii) the concern with entire populations rather than individuals. A politics of health involves itself in housing regulations, drainage systems, the marketing and consumption of food – in short, with the administration, control and 'well-being' of the population. Society becomes medicalized and medical knowledge becomes a fresh means for surveillance and control. The architectural form of the hospital is both an effect of and a support for the new medical knowledge, involving a new set of problems in which bodies are simultaneously individualized and brought under a centralized system of observation. Such space must be divided up so as to permit both a global and an individualized surveillance (*PK*: 146). By contrast, in the old-style houses of the sick the purpose of the institution was to protect the healthy from the sick or the sick from the ignorant or to treat those in penury. The distribution of space within the hospital duplicated that of the family, the natural locus for disease producing a specific configuration of the world of pathologies: 'there beneath the eye of the hospital doctor, diseases would be grouped into orders, genera and species, in a rationalized domain that would restore the original distribution of essences' (*BC*: 42). In the instance of the birth of modern medicine a specific manner of spatialization can be linked to discourses and the observation of bodies, to specific architectural form, and to urban planning. Doctors were, along with the military, the first managers of collective space according to a principle of hygiene. Thus an administrative and political space became articulated upon a therapeutic space. Discipline creates a medically useful space which then sets to work on this space further in order to ensure the smooth functioning of bodies. A healthy population is a productive one.

Just as medical practices create and control and distribute subjects in space, so do prisons, and here the principle of surveillance is even more clearly manifested. Foucault uses Bentham's plans for a 'panopticon', although never actually built, as signifying the particular form of the redistribution of space required in the disciplinary society that both individuates and transforms subjects:

> at the periphery an annular building; at the centre, a tower; this tower is pierced with wide windows that open onto the inner side of the ring; the peripheric building is divided into cells, each of which extends the whole width of the building; they have two windows, one on the inside corresponding to the windows of the tower; the other, on the outside allows the light to cross the cell from one end to the other. All that is needed, then, is to place a supervisor in the central tower and to shut up in each cell a madman, a patient, a condemned man, a worker or a schoolboy. By the effect of backlighting, one can observe from the tower, standing out precisely against the light, the small captive shadows in the cells of the periphery. They are like so many cages, so many small theatres, in which each actor is alone, perfectly individualized and constantly visible. (*DP*: 200)

This sublime scheme permits the prisoners to be constantly observed with a minimum of effort in all their individuality. Surveillance is constant for the simple reason that they can never be sure when they are being watched. Contact between prisoners, perhaps resulting in resistance, is prevented: if they are criminals they cannot plot an escape, if children they cannot copy, if workers they cannot thieve or chat. The principle remains the same. It does not matter that the panopticon was designed as a prison since Foucault demonstrates similar uses of space in other institutions: 'power has its principle not so much in a person as in a certain concerted distribution of bodies, surfaces, lights, gazes; in an arrangement whose internal mechanisms produce the relation in which individuals are caught up' (*DP*: 202). Discipline can be effective only through the control and structuring of space — enclosure and measured subdivision or partitioning, fixed positions, paths for circulation — complex spaces at one and the same time architectural, hierarchical and functional. Such spatial divisions are not just restricted to institutions, they also determine the arrangement of private space. Gone are the large open rooms of the medieval house in almost any one of which guests could be received. Instead: 'the working class family is to be fixed; by assigning it a living space with a room that serves as a kitchen and dining-room, a room for the parents which is the place of procreation, and a room for the children' (*PK*: 149). A whole field of morality becomes spatially circumscribed.

Time

Conventional historians have been constantly exasperated with Foucault. He appears to have no concept of time and place, constantly mixing the two up together. His periodizations in *OT*, *MC* and *DP* go against the normal grain. He is supposedly careless about dates yet his books contain them and are packed with historical detail. Is he then incapable of a proper temporal systematization or does he take a cavalier attitude? Of course, Foucault does have a conception of time – his entire work depends on it – but it is not the temporality of a uniform, spatial, chronometric and calendrical time. Time instead is understood to refer to social processes and discourses. His work denies homogenous time, the time of evolutionary theory, which is the same anywhere and everywhere. Foucault understands time as a series of differences inextricably bound up with social practice, hence a simple reference to date cannot provide an organizing principle for analysis. Any periodization of history is contentious because if removed from social practice it remains an arbitrary slice. The way to carve up the past is not in terms of time-slices but in relation to events and connections between these events. Differing types of events each require their own periodizations, their own times. There can be no one periodization applying to all events and no one time corresponding to these events. So something that happens in France in 1839 may belong to the same time as another event occurring sixty years later. It is up to the historian or the archaeologist to organize his or her periodizations according to the specific temporalities of the events under investigation (*AK*: 187; *DP*: 160). This, again, clearly mitigates against the study of societies as coherent temporal wholes. Such a notion of wholeness is always imposed. It is not a reflection of reality.

In *UP* time is shown to be bound up with sexual activity and a moral problematization of pleasure among the ancient Greeks. Morality was an art of the 'right time' and this right time demanded consideration of age (body time), the time of the seasons, dietary regulations and the passage of day and night (*UP*: 57–9). An entirely different conception of time (our own) occurs in societies of the modern era and, as with space, it is linked to disciplinary practices. Activities become precisely controlled in terms of measured intervals in army drill, in factories, in schools and places of correction. Time is to be added up and capitalized. Disciplinary power is articulated on to a particular time corresponding to its usage of space.

The Subject and Subjectivity

Foucault has examined subjectivity throughout his work in relation to madness and rationality, in the formation of the historical and social sciences, in clinical and psychiatric practice, with regard to punishment, sexuality, notions of death, the soul, the physical body, crime — to compile a minimal list. He has gone so far as to describe his own work as being 'to create a history of the different modes by which, in our culture, human beings are made subjects' (SP: 208).

Forging a Materialist Conception

Foucault has provided a strident critique of humanist conceptions of the person, agent or subject and a reconsideration of the place of subjectivity in discursive and non-discursive social practices. It can be claimed that he goes further in this direction than Althusser, Barthes, Kristeva or Lacan, who have similarly 'de-centred' the subject. By de-centred subject is meant, in general terms, a notion of the subject as not the unified subject of consciousness, linking together a body and an ego, but the subject as a variable and dispersed entity, whose very identity, position and place is constituted in language and social practices.

Whereas Lacan, Barthes and Kristeva displace the subject into language and Althusser into ideological practices mediated through language, Foucault displaces the subject into history. In so doing he eliminates both subjectivity and consciousness (individual or collective) as having any prime explanatory significance in considerations of the social or historical change. Subjectivity and consciousness become instead problems for analysis and discussion. Rather than appealing to a realm of ideas which supposedly explain social action (often going hand in hand with the kind of idealism that postulates an immanent rationality or teleology in historical development), Foucault adopts a thoroughly materialist conception of the subject. The subject becomes something attached to the materialism of the physical human body and is historically constituted. Physical and biological bodies do not of course alter historically but the types of subjectivity engraved into them through discursive and non-discursive practices do. The subject is formed through a dialectic of power and knowledge. We will further examine Foucault's notion of the subject in four texts, OT, DP, HS and UP.

The Emergence of the Subject

OT, somewhat gleefully, charts the historical birth and predicted death of humanity. The notion of man/woman is merely a fairly transient mutation in Western culture not even 200 years old, a fold in knowledge which will disappear as this knowledge takes a new form. So humanity simply has not been there from the moment he or she can be identified in the palaeolithic until the present but is a very recent creation. An astonishing claim indeed! On what basis can it be established? In order to understand this proposition it is important to remember Foucault's materialist conception of subjectivity and the manner in which he links subjectivity to discourse. The main protagonist in *OT* is not humanity but language and its relationship to things or objects. The human body is one of these objects. In the Renaissance episteme this relation was one of resemblance. Attempts were made to establish resemblances between words and things (see p. 305). In the Classical episteme of the seventeenth and eighteenth centuries the relationship between words and things transmuted into one of representation, which at the same time and in the very act of representation simultaneously provided an analysis of their essences. Words were to represent things in a universal language of signs. These signs standing for things could be used to represent the order of the world by their tabular ordering, by establishing taxonomies of re-lations. To know was to tabulate and signification was both represen-tation and analysis. Things reside in their representation as discourse and not just in it. If a correct table could only be established this would permit the relationships established between the discourses on living beings, wealth and general grammar to be manipulated through and by further work on their sign systems. Humanity, while con-structing the vast tables of signs, never appears in them:

> In Classical thought, the personage for whom the representation exists . . .
> he who ties together all the interlacing threads of the 'representation in the
> form of a picture or table' — he is never to be found in that table
> himself . . . The Classical *episteme* is articulated along lines that do not
> isolate, in any way, a specific domain proper to man . . . Classical language
> as the *common discourse* of representation and things, as the place within
> which nature and human nature intersect, absolutely excludes anything
> that could be a 'science of man'. (*OT*: 308–11)

The Modern episteme issues in this science of humanity, so constitut-ing a fundamental break with the Classical episteme. Humanity emerges as we know this category today. Humanity is no longer an object amongst other objects but a subject among objects, a subject *in* discourse and *of* discourse. Humanity becomes not only a subject and object of knowledge but the organizer of the theatre into which he/she inserts him-/herself. Part of this theatre is an emphasis on history and more broadly the development of the human sciences, such as anthropology, sociology and psychology. The general grammar of the Classical episteme, searching for an originary language to slot into the great table of things, switches to the philologies of nineteenth-century linguistics. Analogy and succession become the primary principles at work (*OT*: 218). 'Man' becomes an 'empirico-transcendental doublet': a fact among other facts studied empirically and yet also attempting to provide a transcendental grounding for this knowledge; surrounded by mysteries which cannot be comprehended yet the source of all intelligibility; a product of history whose origins could not be traced but the source and foundation of this history. The root and branch of the problems created by all this and attempted philosophical solutions, such as existentialism or phenomenology, is that the Modern episteme is incapable of posing a satisfactory relationship between language and representation. This leads to the putative Post-Modern episteme in which humanity, in effect, threatens to collapse forward into subjectiveless objectivity. Intimations of this process are emerging in considerations of structure, language and the unconscious in which humanity becomes deconstructed as a unitary essence or subject of consciousness. Humanity vanishes as an effect of the linguistics of Saussure, the structuralism of Lévi-Strauss and Lacan's re-reading of Freud: 'The idea of a "psychoanalytic anthropology" and the idea of a "human nature" reconstituted by ethnology, are no more than pious wishes. Not only are they able to do without the concept of man, they are also able to pass through it, for they always address themselves to that which constitutes his outer limits . . . they dissolve man' (*OT*: 379).

Genealogies of Power and Subjectivity

Foucault also intends actively to aid and abet this dissolution of humanity but into historically mutable forms of subjectivity in the genealogies of incarceration and sexuality, *DP, HS* and *UP*.

DP traces the constitution of subjectivity in relation to a nexus of power–knowledge and truth. It contrasts forms of the operation of power in the absolutist and capitalist western state through a specific examination of penal history. In the absolutist state punishment, taking the form of torture, was an excessively violent and ritualized public spectacle operating directly and physically on the body with differing degrees of gradation of the torture according to the crime.

This public display of violence represented a display of the force of the sovereign and his ability to punish transgressions. The actual power of the monarch in the absolutist state over the daily lives of the subject population needs in some respects to be de-emphasized. In one respect, of course, it was total: power over life or death. On the other hand, its degree of effective penetration throughout the population remained relatively low. The kind of subjectivity produced by sovereign power was essentially one based on ritual, memory and commemoration of the type found in crests of arms, family trees, portraits, statues, noble tombs, etc. In such a manner the rich and the powerful were subjectified, the great mass of the population remaining anonymous unless transgressing the law. The greater the transgression the more they tended to be marked out, the ultimate being the act of regicide. The scaffold becomes a symbolic and commemorative theatre by an extension of the same logic that creates subjects, the purpose being to render theatrically the transgressor of the law powerless and thus reaffirm the position of the sovereign. The body of the condemned becomes a kind of text:

> torture . . . revealed truth and showed the operation of power. It assured the articulation of the written on the oral, the secret on the public . . . it made it possible to reproduce the crime on the visible body of the criminal; in the same horror, the crime had to be manifested and annulled. It also made the body of the condemned man the place where the vengeance of the sovereign was applied, the anchoring point for a manifestation of power. (*DP*: 55)

The problem was that the visible display of punitive violence to a 'textual' body on a theatrical stage could be read in different ways for its moral and theological significance. Were the death cries of the condemned perhaps anticipations of the punishments to be expected in hell? Or penitence to God? Signs of guilt? Or innocence? (*DP*: 46). This fundamental ambiguity and the reactions of the crowd made such ritualized public torture increasingly ineffective. The victim was sometimes likely to evoke the sympathy rather than the vilification of the crowd, which on occasion expressed resistance by revolt. By the eighteenth century the public spectacle of controlled torture began to have definite political risks. The subsequent reforms, often considered to be more humane, shifted discipline from the public application of force on the body to systems of incarceration and finely tuned observation which required the creation of the 'soul'.

The advent of incarceration as the principal means of punishment is associated with disciplinary procedures taking on a major role in structuring social life in the context of the development of industrial capitalism. The contrast Foucault wishes to draw is that between pre-modern and modern modalities of the exercise of power and social domination in the West and the manner in which they create subjects of a certain sort. In the emerging industrial societies of the capitalist West disciplinary procedures and surveillance of the population provide the primary modes of social subjection. The prison is merely the most visual and obvious manifestation of this new focus of power, a microcosm of all institutional forms. Discipline creates subjects of everyone. Power does not just operate on a few tortured bodies to serve as an example but radiates throughout the entire social fabric, creating subjects and simultaneously subjecting. As power spreads throughout the social field it simultaneously becomes more anonymous and less visible. Discipline is located and exercised in a wide variety of institutions: factories, schools, hospitals, university departments of archaeology, military organizations, to name but a few. This discipline creates subjects by providing procedures for the training or coercing of people through hierarchical observation, the normalizing judgement (of, for example, the teacher or the social worker), and the examination involving the compilation of documents and the constitution of case histories. Surveillance takes place in the workplace, increasingly separated from the home, and through the systematic collection and organization of information that can be stored and used to monitor populations. The factory-based labour process renders bodily behaviour routine, repetitive, subject to codifiable rules and accessible to surveillance and calculation. The factory's logic is thus political rather than purely economic. It is simply more efficient in terms of an economy of power, as is incarceration as opposed to the public spectacle of torture. In capitalism the body is

> directly involved in a political field; power relations have an immediate hold over it; they invest it, mark it, train it, torture it, force it to carry out tasks, to peform ceremonies, to emit signs. This political investment of the body is bound up . . . with its economic us; it is largely as a force of production that the body is invested with relations of power and domination; but, on the other hand, its constitution as labour power is possible only if it is caught up in a system of subjection (in which need is also a political instrument meticulously prepared, calculated and used); the body becomes a useful force only if it is a productive body and a subjected body. (DP: 25–6)

The point is that discipline does not just crush, negate and alienate people. It is a far more insidious process producing subjects who *will* work for the capitalist. Power can only subject if it first subjectivizes.

Power–knowledge creates appropriate subjects for its further operation, the means and political technologies fostering subjectification and sets of strategic objectives orientating these power relations. The way discipline creates subjects can be seen in perhaps its most manifest form in the figure of the soldier. In the seventeenth century the soldier bore natural signs marking him out as noble, such as bodily posture, strength and physical condition: 'a lively, alert manner, an erect head, a taut stomach . . . dry feet' (Montgommery in *DP*: 135). In the late eighteenth century the soldier is no longer discovered – he is made. This results in a 'general theory of *dressage*, at the centre of which reigns the notion of "docility"' (*DP*: 136). Docile bodies are more efficient, they may be used, transformed and improved, made to perform. So discipline creates a docile and useful body while controlling it, stripping it of its dangers. Dressage is merely a form of normalization found in the school examination and a multitude of other specific forms located at particular institutional sites: hospitals, factories, offices. The school examination permits subjects to be forced into conformity and simultaneously allows their individualization. Discipline thus permits the standardization of subjects (measurement against a norm) and allows a careful gradation of individual differences. The ideal is a constant surveillance – to observe and to detail in dossiers and to know. Modern society is a carcereal archipelago in which power–knowledge strategies individuate to subject.

Foucault conceives of two major axes of subjectification in the modern state. First, disciplinary technologies or power over forms of living optimize the capabilities of the body and ensure political docility. The second dimension does not so much concern individual bodies (persons) as entire populations, involving interventions in terms of reproduction, mortality and health. He considers this in relation to what he considers to be the central role of sexuality. It provides a 'pivot of the two axes along which developed the entire political technology of life. On the one hand it was tied to the disciplines of the body . . . On the other it was applied to the regulation of populations . . . Sex was a means of access both to the life of the body and the life of the species' (*HS*: 145–6). Foucault argues that sexuality emerges historically as a central element in the surveillance and control of populations. Sexuality, like madness, is a historical construct, during the nineteenth and twentieth century becoming a major object of investigation and adminstrative control with wide-ranging social consequences. The social and political ramifications of AIDS today underline the strength of such an argument. Sexuality and its control and development affects the entire population. Power and knowledge work through and on sexuality.

This is an important part of Foucault's contention that power is not just negative. Power–knowledge strategies create a discourse on sexuality, permitting an object to emerge which may then be utilized as an instrument of subjectification and domination. In *HS* the repressive hypothesis with regard to sexuality is impugned. According to this hypothesis from a time of shameless sexual liberty the pleasures of the body became suppressed during the Victorian era only to be partially released very recently. Reich, Marcuse and others associate this repression of sexuality with the development of capitalism. Sexual pleasures were incompatible with a work ethic. Sexual and political liberation go hand in hand. Here power, conceived as repressive, just says 'no' to sex. Instead, *HS* argues, power creates sexuality. The power relation has been productive of an ever-increasing discourse and knowledge of sexuality extending, intensifying and elaborating its forms and practices. Power produces domains for its exercise (in this case sexuality) and the very reality of the field in which it operates. In the nineteenth century sexuality became a 'police' matter: 'that is, not the rigor of a taboo, but the necessity of regulating sex through useful and public discourses' (*HS*: 25). These 'useful' discourses involved (and still involve) (i) statistical studies of the population: birth rates, marriage rates, frequency of sexual relations, legitimate and illegitimate births, impact of contraception, etc. and (ii) a proliferation of discourses concerned with the body and the mind through the agency of doctors, psychiatrists, sexologists. Here Foucault identifies four major themes: hysterization of women's bodies, a pedagogization of children's sex dealing principally with the problem of masturbation, a socialization of procreative behaviour within the family and a psychiatrization of perverse pleasures (*HS*: 104–5). These were not so much a repression of sexuality as its positive production, a production which may then be integrated today in fresh forms of power:

> What was the response on the side of power? An economic (and perhaps also ideological) exploitation of eroticism, from sun-tan products to pornographic films. Responding precisely to the revolt of the body, we find a new mode of investment which presents itself no longer in the form of control by repression but that of control by stimulation. 'Get undressed – but be slim, good-looking, tanned!' (*PK*: 57)

Sexuality being produced by power–knowledge strategies cannot be free of them. Its effects are to bolster up the effects and operations of bio-power working together with disciplinary technologies to both create the modern subject or person and the very conditions for his or her individualization and subjection, subjection to power. Both bio-power and disciplinary mechanisms are integrally bound up with the development of capitalism, involving the insertion of controlled bodies into the production process and the adjustment of populations into the economic process (*HS*: 141).

In *DP* and *HS* what is of almost exclusive concern is the analysis of sets of practices external to subjects that construct them in specific ways. *UP*, the second volume in *The History of Sexuality*, marks a change in the analysis in that here the concern of the analysis is the manner in which individuals turn themselves into subjects. In a sense this is the opposite side of the coin and complementary to those external practices analysed previously. However, the analysis is not of modernity but of fourth-century BC Greek texts. Foucault terms the process of self-imposed subjectification 'techniques of the self'. These are means by which agents affect their bodies, souls, thoughts and conduct hence transforming themselves. Foucault refers generally to 'prescriptive' texts, suggesting rules of conduct, but for the Greeks such rules took more the form of guidelines for the conduct of the self than sets of rigid prohibitions or taboos. Sexuality was problematized as a moral matter associated with a need for moderation and austere conduct, and sexuality was intimately linked with three main arts or techniques of living: dietetics (the subject's relation to his or her body involving diet, exercise and the risks and pleasures associated with sexual activity); economics (the conduct of the head of the household); and erotics (the relationship between men and boys). All these formed areas through which the conduct of the self could be conceptualized. For example, in the realm of dietetics, the food one ate depended on (i) the activities engaged in during the day and their serial arrangement, and (ii) the relation of the self to an external world over which one had no control: the climate, seasons, the hour of day, degree of humidity and dryness, heat and cold, directions of the winds, regional geography and the layout of a city (*UP*: 106). In winter conduct of the self should have a drying and warming effect, hence one should eat roasted rather than boiled meats, whole-wheat bread, dry vegetables accompanied by numerous vigorous exercises and more frequent sex. All these aspects of conduct of the self would have warming effects, whereas in the summer sex should be reduced to a minimum, diet consist of barley cakes and boiled or raw vegetables and exercise should be limited – all to produce cooling and moistening effects (*UP*: 110–14).

Foucault's aim in the *History of Sexuality* series, of which *UP* is only an instalment, is to determine how

> Western man had been brought to recognise himself as a subject of desire . . . Not a history that would be concerned with what might be true

in the fields of learning, but an analysis of the 'games of truth', the games of truth and error through which being is historically constituted as experience; that is, as something that can and must be thought . . . The object was to learn to what extent the effort to think one's own history can free thought from one it silently thinks, and so enable it to think differently . . . [The] goal is a history of truth. (*UP*: 6–11)

Foucault more than any other modern writer has been concerned to dissect this truth, to disperse it into history as truths to be situated in, of, for and by the subject.

The Role of the Author

Foucault's consideration of the subject extends to the role of the author (*LCMP*: 113–34). His position, quoting Beckett, is 'what matter who's speaking?' What he wants to do is to dispel any notion of the author as a natural fixed point by which we can ascribe meaning to a text or indeed material culture in general. The attribution of a text to an author only has a functional significance within our culture and is very much to be related to wider social features of discursive practice embodied in property relations, legal rights, and questions of accountability and, ultimately, censorship. The author-function serves as a means of classifying texts and grouping them together in what may be an entirely spurious way. The notion of authorship is not simple. First, we have a whole host of problems concerning what is to count as a text belonging to an author (see the discussion of the history of ideas, pp. 292–4). Second, what reason do we have to group texts under a single proper name rather than with different proper names when differences can be enormous within the 'works' of an author? The concept of an author results from a series of complex operations whose purpose is to construct and maintain a rational entity involving notions of creativity, intentionality, continuity, consistency, personal identity, maturation and development. These are all *projections* and are themselves dependent on the manner in which we deal with a series of texts. In academia, it might be noted, the concept of the author is ideally suited to uphold and foster a value-system wishing to maintain competition and which treats ideas like any other commodity.

Foucault subjects the author to exactly the same fragmentation as discourse. The author is, if anything, a discontinuous series rather than a unitary entity. The author is a function of discourse rather than discourse being a production of the author. The questions then become not Who is the real author? Have we proof or his or her authenticity and originality and creativity? What he or she revealed about his or her most profound self in the text? How can we fit such and such a text into this author's genre? but: What are the modes of existence of this discourse? Where does the discourse come from? How is the discourse circulated and who controls it? What placements are determined for possible subjects in the discourse and who can fulfil these diverse functions of the subject? (*LCMP*: 138).

Rather than grasping for the coherency and creativity of the author what is required is an analysis of the way the author-subject fits into discourse in general, i.e. what can be stated and how can it be stated. Traditional notions of authorship are mistaken because they are dependent on non-analytical psychological themes. Instead we must analyse how authors are themselves produced and constructed and inserted into discourse. The author may of course make certain decisions of what and how to write but these are nevertheless thoroughly determined.

Truth, Rationality and Political Critique

If Foucault questions truth, rationality, the author, the subject as a concrete discrete entity and centre of consciousness, a view of power as repressive and moreover disperses all these categories into history and discourse we are pehaps entitled to ask exactly which power–knowledge–truth strategies Foucault himself is embroiled in. In short, why is he writing and can he expect to change anything? This raises the question of the politics of Foucault's work and, somewhat inevitably, the relationship of Foucault to Marxism. Is Foucault a supplement to Marx, a fiancé, following on from the post-war exist-entialist, phenomenological, hermeneutic and structuralist brides? Or does he provide an alternative? It should be immediately noted that his work has been used both by those on the left and the right, to reinforce and to condemn socialist practices. Does the fact that Foucault's work can be open to such radically different sociopolitical interpretations in itself tell us anything about it? As a means of entry into these questions we can consider one of the texts in some more detail.

Science and Rationality

MC analyses changing conceptions of madness from the sixteenth to the twentieth century. It is not so much a history of insanity as a critique of this category and the development of psychiatric practices. *MC* investigates how an object of discourse came to be created and its social and political effects in turning people into objects of knowledge and subjects of discourse. Madness is considered not as a given and unchanging fact but a specific product of the 'civilization' of Enlightenment thought. Foucault problematizes the whole question of madness: Why was it created? What historically mutable forms does such a category take? What ends does such a category serve? Madness is a social achievement rather than a preordained and self-evident category. It is not a product of psychiatric science but something this science can set to work on once madness has been produced. Furthermore madness did not develop as the result of the operation of a historical unfolding of reason — rationality — it was rather a chance development, a product of a whole host of social, economic and political factors which could have been otherwise. MC thus challenges conventional histories of psychiatry which would regard madness as an unchanging fact released into a proper framework of understanding through the progress of medical reason. MC argues that in fact psychiatry only becomes possible when madness becomes defined, and negatively evaluated, as the converse of reason and when those designated as mad are isolated and confined as a special social category. Both these developments precede that of psychiatry. Its role was merely to strengthen a category which had already been created. It is thus a discipline with ignominious rather than noble origins. The history of madness in MC is a history in which a series of changing social conditions give rise to discourses which justify the confinement and special treatment of those individuals or groups who are deemed to threaten society at any particular time.

In the sixteenth century the mad did not constitute a homogeneous social category. Madness was not a mental pathology or sickness and indeed the fool could be a source of wisdom. The insane were in some sense a liminal category, between God and humanity: in the world and yet not of it. It was not the mad who were locked up on a consistent basis but lepers. At the end of the sixteenth century a profound shift occurred in conceptions of the mad. They now became a dangerous category and the emptying of the vast leper houses of medieval Europe was accompanied by the filling of this social space — a space of confinement and exclusion — with the mad, who effectively became objects rather than subjects. But the mad were confined not as an isolated class but with all those other social categories deemed dangerous: the poor, the sick, vagabonds and criminals. Madness was not designated a sickness but merely the converse of reason: unreason. It was alternatively conceptualized as a regression to a childlike state or as a form of bestiality. The mad were not properly human and thus could be treated as animals. Another shift in conception occurs at the end of the eighteenth century, represented by such reformers as Tuke and Pinel who released the mad from their chains. Insanity becomes regarded as an illness to be treated through medicine. The insane become segregated from other antisocial groups but Foucault argues that this was a product of political interventions rather than a result of an advancement in understanding the insane. The mad began to be isolated in a specific institutional site, the asylum, not as an effect of liberal concern for their plight but because other social groups were now treated differently. It was economically inefficient to confine the poor: large populations of workers were now required to fill the factories of the Industrial Revolution. The criminal class, now considered even more a menace to private property, should not be mixed with the insane for the hope of reforming them. The birth of the asylum for the sole treatment of the mad rather than being a liberation resulted in an even more profound confinement, and the development of a special class of practitioners to deal with the problems the mad posed – psychiatrists. An opposition between reason and madness became complete. Madness is no longer simply unreason but a pathology to be cured, and the psychiatrist working at his or her institutional site decides who is mad. Commital to an asylum defines someone as mad. Foucault comments:

> It is thought that Tuke and Pinel opened the asylum to medical knowledge. They did not introduce science, but a personality, whose powers borrowed from science only their disguise, or at most their justification. These powers, by their nature, were of a moral and social order; they took root in the madman's minority status, in the insanity of his person, not of his mind. If the medical personage could isolate madness, it was not because he knew it, but because he mastered it; and what for positivism would be an image of objectivity was only the other side of this domination. (MC: 271–2)

Stated in other terms, power–knowledge mechanisms create a discursive object, madness, which is then refined and extended as mental illness in modern psychiatric practice, becoming an instrument of subjectification and domination. Madness, rather than being an invariant objective truth, is socially constituted through the changing relationships between those falling on either side of the couplet sane/insane.

Knowledge, Truth and Rationality

The human sciences have their 'technical matrix in the petty, malicious minutiae of the disciplines and their investigations' (DP:

226). In other words, they are linked to the kind of disciplinary power Foucault takes as being characteristic of contemporary society. Each society has its own regime of truth and rationality. There is no absolute form of truth or rationality to evaluate statements against. Different social practices determine alternative forms of rationality and truth. Rationality is the historical production of rules and procedures for creating true discourses and legitimating these discourses by providing them with reasons and principles. In modern society the following statements can be made about truth: (i) it is taken to be embodied in science; (ii) there is a constant striving after this truth, a 'will to truth'; (iii) these true discourses are diffused widely; (iv) truth constitutes a battleground. Truth is 'this-worldly' so that which should concern us about truth is not an analysis of an ensemble of statements taken to be true but of the rules and codes whereby truth and falsity are separated and the former linked to power. Power does not stand opposed to truth, it rather invests truth to make it acceptable. To speak the truth is supposedly to be beyond power, i.e. beyond the interests power serves (of domination in a conventional conception), but for Foucault both power and truth invest each other. They are not external and opposed. It is only through the operation of power that truth claims can be made. In Foucault's analytics we must turn our attention to how statements come to be counted as true, and why. Truth is relative to the social practices producing it, inextricably linked with them. Convention guarantees truth rather than the usual philosophical candidates, correspondence with the world or the internal coherence of statements.

Politics and the Analysis of Discourse

In May 1968 Foucault's answer was published to the following question put to him by the editors of *Esprit*: 'Doesn't a thought which introduces discontinuity in the history of the mind remove all basis for a progressive political intervention. Does it not lead to the following dilemma: either the acceptance of the system, or the appeal to an uncontrolled event, to the irruption of exterior violence which alone is capable of upsetting the system?' (HDD: 224). Foucault's reply dealing with his earlier work up to and including *OT* is fascinating in that he attempts to produce, or bring out, a politics in his work. His thesis is that in presenting discourses as involving: (i) limited *practical* domains with boundaries, rules of formation and conditions of existence rather than a world of slumbering texts, history as a completely filled intellectual space without ruptures; (ii) roles and operations for discoursing subjects as opposed to the theme of subjects constituting meanings and transcribing them into discourse (originary founding subjects); and (iii) emphasizing historical difference in opposition to continuity and a search for origins and thought traditions, he is liberating the study of discourse from a nineteenth-century historical–transcendental structure, creating an intellectual space for a critique of the present. He cogently asks why a progressive politics should be linked to themes of meaning, origin and the constitutent subject:

> In short to all the themes which guarantee to history the inexhaustible presence of the Logos, the sovereignty of a pure subject and the profound teleology of an original destination . . . to all the dynamic, biological, evolutionary metaphors through which one masks the difficult problem of historical change . . . to the devaluation of discursive practices, so that a history of the mind, of conscience, of reason, of knowledge, of ideas or opinions might triumph in its çertain ideality?

Foucault wants to destroy all these idealist and ultimately conservative themes. To 'liberate discourse' is to take it seriously. That is to understand it as having real material effects, the kinds of effects described in *MC*. A progressive politics recognizes the historical specificity of particular practices rather than ideal necessities or the free play of individual initiatives; it defines possibilities for transformation rather than relying on uniform inbuilt abstractions such as evolutionary process; it does not make a conscience of humanity but defines the roles and places subjects can occupy; it recognizes the link between the discursive and the non-discursive, between the sociality of discourse and the sociality of oppression (HDD: 246).

Writing the History of the Present

Elsewhere (*DP*: 31) Foucault has proposed that he is a historian of the present. He is not writing about the past because it may be interesting to do so. There is no antiquarian desire to study the past for its own sake, therefore evading the issues of the present. Nor is he writing the past simply from the standpoint of the present. The results of such studies found in evolutionary studies or histories of various disciplines are familiar: How dreadful it was! How brutal the tortures! How confused and inadequate the knowledges! How far we have advanced towards truth and enlightenment and consideration for human freedoms and justice! Foucault more or less reverses such platitudes. By emphasizing the difference of the past and its own internal coherency he systematically undercuts the legitimacy of the present and its portrayal as either necessarily embodying rationality or truth. The rejection of any historical teleology throws into focus the contingency and arbitrary nature of the present, that the present could be otherwise, and the future will be different. What Foucault cannot and does not do is engage in utopian speculations as to the form of the good society, and neither did Marx. The difference is that while for Marx the overthrow of the capitalist present would necessarily open up a road to genuine human fulfilment, non-ideological truth and justice, Foucault is much more sceptical, and this term would seem to be more appropriate than the one with which he is usually branded: 'nihilist'.

For Foucault 'the history which bears and determines us has the form of a war rather than that of a language: relations of power, not relations of meaning' (*PK*: 114). It is through the understanding of these relations of power that a radical critique of the present may be maintained through a study of the past. It is to show that knowledges are not disinterested and neither are truths. They are historically constituted in relation to struggles. So Foucault suspends any notion of ahistorical and natural categories. There is no such thing as madness, criminality or sexuality with a dangerous internal essence to be dissected or analysed. There are rather changing discursive objects formed through power–knowledge strategies. Foucault does not write a history of sexuality, he rather writes a history of how sexuality ever came to be invented in the first place as an object in and of discourse.

The Politics of Totality

Foucault has never attempted to provide a self-sufficient theoretical system for the study of discourse or social totalities, or indeed of individual concepts such as power or subjectivity. His emphasis on dispersion – of statements in discourse, of power in terms of strategies, of subjectivity in history – and his discussion of power–knowledge directly mitigate against any such attempt. If anything he tends towards the disunification of theory rather than its systematization: '"The whole of society" is precisely that which should not be considered except as something to be destroyed' (*LCMP*: 233). Any totalizing theory, a theory that attempts to take account of everything, is not only impossible, it is socially and politically suspect, a manifestation of domination and the 'will to truth' Foucault is so concerned to attack. Perhaps the worst of all is evolutionary theory, postulating a longitudinal as well as a latitudinal totality. Foucault's own emphasis on the episteme in *OT*, it should be noted, was only a unity of statements in dispersion. There was no postulation of a necessary coherency that is found, for example, in functionalist theories or certain dialectical models.

The Universal and the Specific Intellectual

If Foucault abandons the attempt to create a totalizing theory then it is entirely consistent that he should abandon any notion of the universal intellectual, found in Marxist theory, whose job is to provide a blanket political critique of modern society and so raise the social consciousness of the masses. He sees the role of the intellectual as a specific and localized intervention operating at specific institutional sites and in relation to specific knowledges (*PK*: 126–30; *LCMP*: 205–17). The Renaissance scholar who could attempt to master and incorporate all or most aspects of knowledge within a single framework is clearly a thing of the past. Foucault is simply proposing that as knowledges and social practices in general have become more differentiated and specific then so should their analysis and critique; this certainly does not mean that such critiques should necessarily be restricted within current disciplinary boundaries or within specific institutions or technologies for the operation of power – at least if we are to attempt to follow the example of Foucault's own discourses.

It should, however, be noted that although Foucault has spoken of the active political role of the specific intellectual in relation to the 'micro-powers' that inhabit society he has never self-reflexively described himself as one or addressed the question 'What should be done?'. All we find, for example in *HS*, in opposition to the fresh form of domination he argues is issued in by the repression hypothesis, is talk of a return to 'bodies and pleasures' which does not appear to be all that helpful. We look to Foucault in vain for recommendations of how to act, how to change the present. After Foucault we are always left with the question as to whether any proposed reforms may merely be a fresh act of domination. If Foucault can, as he wishes, leave us with a feeling that we simply do not know what to do (*QM*: 12) (will the new museum exhibition be even worse than the last?) perhaps he has achieved what he can only hope to do: to make us think harder, more critically, more intensely, more self-reflexively.

Marxism

A supplement to Marx? Foucault, at one point, suggests that he is: 'one might even wonder what difference there could ultimately be between being a historian and a Marxist' (*PK*: 53). However, he has also stated in interviews that he has never been a Marxist (*S*: 198) and whether he is or is not labelled a Marxist does not appear to be a matter for great concern anyway. Foucault's great strength is his attention to detail and historical specificity, and tracing through the social and political outcomes of various discourses and social practices. He provides no alternative to Marxism and has never set out to do so. If his work has been linked by some (certainly not by himself) to the concerns of the new right (the 'Nouvelle Philosophie'), this is only in a naive and superficial manner. In relation to Marxism, Foucault's work can be regarded as both a serious critique and an extension which, of course, leads to a need for reformalization and revitalization.

First the critique: for some, such as Althusser, it is absolutely essential to determine the scientific credentials of Marxism as opposed to other forms of knowledge. Marxism can be effective only if it is grounded in the truth as opposed to the ideologies of non-Marxist discourse. For Foucault this is both the wrong direction and the wrong battle to fight (*PK*: 84–5). To claim that Marxism is a science is, of course, to grant it definite power effects within the framework of an Enlightenment discourse bound up with wider themes of modernity and rationality. It is this very notion of scientificity that Foucault wishes to dispel, for it merely inserts Marxism within a form of discourse which it *ought to be challenging*. By contrast Foucault claims that his genealogies attempt to emancipate historical knowleges from this subjection, 'to render them, that is, capable of opposition and of struggle against the coercion of a theoretical, unitary, formal and scientific discourse' (*PK*: 85). By basing itself on an ultimately mystical notion of scientific truth and rationality, Marxism in a sense only serves to neutralize itself or at the very least cut away the grounding for a more radical critique. It might be added that such a position does not convince or persuade anyone outside the ranks of the Marxists although it may have the effect of promoting internal solidarity within them.

Much Marxist theory, whether operating in terms of the very broad and very ambiguous foundations laid down by Marx or in subsequent structuralist ramifications, has been consistently prone to economism, the total or partial reduction of social practices and forms of consciousness as an effect of the working through of the internal logic of the economy. To use traditional Marxist terminology all of Foucault's work is concerned with the superstructure. However, what his work clearly shows is that any neat division between economic base and ideological superstructure is misplaced; both form part of each other. Foucalt's 'discursive formations' are not simply an ideological icing on the basic processes of economic determinancy in a social formation. They actively 'select for', i.e. help to create, bring into existence, certain forms of social and economic organization rather than others. This does not mean we simply replace a materialist Marxism with a Hegelian idealist Marxism. It rather extends the notion of materialism to include discourses which can be argued to have effects in and on the world in a similar manner to more obviously economic processes. Foucault's conception of modern societies as disciplinary is a powerful one. Indeed having read *DP* it seems almost impossible to regard them in any other way (his discourse *has* power). This concept of discipline cannot be reduced either to the realm of ideology or to economics: it unites them. Discipline operates materially on the body in the production process and simultaneously acts so as to maintain hegemony, producing forms of political subjugation. If we take Foucault seriously rather than automatically denouncing him for challenging certain of the commandments of Marx, it is obvious that what is required is a rethinking rather than a complete abandonment of classical Marxist concepts such as alienation, ideology, class exploitation and notions of power, domination and resistance. His particular scattered critical remarks on concepts such as ideology are hardly decisive but what they do point to is a need for greater debate and theorization.

Second, the extension: if for the Frankfurt school writing and research is intended as an active means of social intervention, with the aim of social emancipation, then for Foucault it is a more muted matter of a social analytics, which takes the form of a discourse on discourses in which the intention is not to try to establish a general theory of power but only to reflect on certain aspects, such as the relation of power to knowledge to rationality to subjectivity. However, it can be argued that precisely the advantage of Critical Theory is that there is a systematic refusal to abandon the whole problem of repression, ideology and social domination as Foucault might appear to do with his emphasis on the positive effects of power. He does not take sides with resistance against social domination but rather wants to establish 'a topological and geological survey of the battlefield. But as for saying, "Here is what you must do!", certainly not' (*PK*: 62). This appears to lead inevitably to a theme of increasing personalized resistance, found, for example, in his discussion of the specific intellectual. We might ask if this is itself a manifestation of the greater entrenchment of power and domination today and political despair in the face of it?

Nevertheless, Foucault's work can be regarded as providing a form of social and political critique in a similar manner to the Frankfurt school of Critical Theory. Radically different premises result in different forms of critique. It is the notion of, and importance assigned to, intellectual labour as an act of cultural and political critique that links

Foucault with Adorno or Habermas, and perhaps it is this similarity that should be stressed rather than the differences. His argument that 'there is no power relation without the correlative constitution of a field of knowledge, nor any knowledge that does not presuppose and constitute at the same time power relations' (*PK*: 109) does not leave any possibility whatsoever that work can, is, or should be, value-free. All writing, all speaking, all knowledge has power effects. The implication: be careful (self-reflexive) as to what you do or do not say and how you say it. Nor does such a statement allow us to cling to notions of primary objectivity to evaluate various discourses or statements. The objects we deal with are always *discursive objects*. All discourses deal in truths, discursive rather than absolute truths. The point of critique is to detach the *power of truth* from present-day forms of hegemony and social oppression. That is, it is to analyse how certain truths come to be accepted or formulated rather than others and the social and political ends these truths serve: 'liberation can only come from attacking . . . political rationality's very roots' (OS: 254). The fundamental area Foucault directs our attention towards is the politics of truth. The kinds of truth claims Foucault is particularly concerned to demolish are precisely those that have been of concern to critical theory: those involved in the positivist social sciences, which simultaneously turn people into objects and subjects of a certain sort, thus all the better for surveillance, control and manipulation.

Conclusion: Some Directions for Use

> I often quote concepts, texts and phrases from Marx, but without feeling obliged to add the authenticating label of a footnote with a laudatory phrase to accompany the quotation . . . For myself, I prefer to utilise the writers I like. The only valid tribute to thought such as Nietzsche's is precisely to use it, to deform it, to make it groan and protest. And if commentators then say that I am being faithful or unfaithful to Nietzsche, that is of absolutely no interest. (*PK*: 52–4)

There are a large number of possible areas or topics around which this conclusion could be structured, but I wish to tackle two broad areas of fundamental concern, each of which embrace's a number of key points: reading and writing material culture in discourse, and in history.

Discourse, Material Culture

Foucault's work on discourse opens up a vast field for archaeology and material-culture studies more generally. Here I will initially separate out three areas: (i) the question of how the past and material culture should be written; (ii) the manner in which archaeology's history could be produced; (iii) the means in which the production of archaeological knowledge can be understood as a discursive practice.

Writing the past   The inscription of artifacts, their attributes, context and associations into a textual medium is something that needs to be problematized. Any writing of material culture is transformative. It is not and cannot be a transparent medium for expression and analysis. The associations made between artifacts and their context occur as much in the linguistic medium of the text as they do in that which the text may attempt to describe or discuss. Here it is important to deny a nihilistic assertion of incommensurability in which we would assert that the text is a free-floating medium, an endless play of meaning which can only refer back to itself. This would, if followed through to its logical conclusion, only result in a self-denying ordinance that any meaningful study of material culture is impossible. By meaningless-ness is meant, in this context, an assertion that writing material culture is an entirely fictional enterprise. It is not, of course. Studying material culture means transcribing artifacts. The end product is both something more and something less than the raw materials worked upon. The text *mediates*: it is neither a direct expression of reality, nor is it totally divorced from it. So meaning in the text is dual. It is both to be found in the text's organization and syntax and in the relation of the text to the world. These two aspects of meaning creation cannot be separated out, they inhere in each other and help to form each other.

The artifact in the text is always a *discursive object*. This object is formed through language acting on the world. No description is pure nor can it be total. Listing the attributes of a pot does not allow one to arrive back at that pot. The textual embodiment of an artifact is always partial, less than that artifact. It is more than that artifact because it transports it into an entirely different medium, a medium which then sets to work on it. This means that we are never dealing with the artifact, or more generally the past or the present, in itself and for itself. Our knowledge and understanding comes through a linguistic, textual medium. The need to place artifacts into texts is simultaneously a violence done to those artifacts and a productive and creative exercise. Writing material culture is producing material culture.

Now, this linguistic production of material culture has to be taken very seriously indeed for the *meaning* of material culture is created in the text. It does not reside outside the text. From the beginning to the end meaning resides in what the text does to material culture.

Meaning is internal to the text and its language use. It does not reside externally except in so far as discourses have effects in the world. They help us to interpret and understand it. But it needs to be recognized that this exercise is always already an interpretation of an interpretation of an interpretation.

It is possible furthermore to regard discursive and non-discursive practices as equally material. The notion of materiality needs to be extended so as to properly include discourse. Both discursive and non-discursive practices have effects in the world. Second, they mediate each other. There can be no clear dividing-line. Material culture is non-discursive in the limited sense that it is a set of objects. However, these objects (e.g. pots) are multidimensional in that they act both physically in an instrumental sense and so as to frame and constitute significative systems of meaning. Meaning again has to be understood as a form of materiality, a production rather than an abstraction (something which just occurs within thought). Every material object is constituted as an object of discourse. What this means is that objects only become objects *in* discourse. Such a position does not deny that a pot or a rock carving exists outside thought but that a pot or a rock carving could constitute itself in a particular manner without discourse.

We must write material culture and we must write the past and the present. Part of the creation of an alternative past and an alternative understanding of material culture will of necessity be to write it in a different way. Foucault provides us with a whole series of examples of how this might be accomplished. First, and as implied by the discussion above, we need to abandon any longing for, or striving after, a basic originary and primary objectivity. Rather we have to understand that the subjective is the form of the objective. Objectivity and subjectivity do not stand opposed. They both form part of each other. Second, producing meaning is an expressive and formative exercise. Consequently the manner in which statements are made is an important as their propositional content. The creation of meaning is in part a literary exercise. This implies that we should perhaps write material culture in a manner that has more similarities to novels or poetry than to a treatise on constant acceleration equations. However, it is important to avoid any simplistic notion of returning to, or falling back on, 'common-sense' everyday discourse. The manner in which Foucault writes is dense, some would say 'difficult'. He does not write like Balzac, or like Oppenheimer. His writing is, in a sense, a mixture of technical discourse and literary creation. Both are articulated to create a space for meaning and neither aspect can be singled out. This is important because writing material culture is not like writing physics or biochemistry, nor is it simply writing a good, bad or indifferent story. In writing material culture we need to distance ourselves both from writing with a spurious scientism, which regards language merely as a technical medium to state things using an abstract terminological system, and from writing as a novelist, who may create anything and destroy anything at will.

Third, we need to pay much greater attention to detail, being empirical while avoiding empiricism. The artifact cannot be reduced to its visible surfaces. Meaning resides both in these surfaces directly open to observation and beyond them. By paying attention to detail and specificity we impugn any notion that material culture can be adequately understood by reducing it to tables of measurements and statistical correlations of various traits. These may obscure just as much as they may help us. Such types of analysis have a place but should be shorn of the rhetoric of objective neutrality which normally accompanies their use.

Fourth, data should be used as a means of clarification for an argument rather than as its sole basis. In other words, our texts should incorporate a genuine dialectic between theory, data and practice. Rather than regarding these three areas as separate they should be understood as mediating or helping to form each other. There can be no question of testing theories against data since they form part of each other. Nor can we simply apply a theory to data since by doing so we are making the unwarranted empiricist assertion that the two are essentially separate.

Fifth, texts should be produced that open out a field of meanings for material culture rather than attempting to pin it down as precisely as possible to one meaning: plurality rather than unidimensionality. One way of achieving this will be to create 'dense' texts: texts which the reader actively has to work at to understand. This is precisely what Foucault does. A reading of *AK* demands precise attention. This opens out an active rather than a passive role for the reader. Part of the creation of the meaning is undertaken by the reader. His or her role is not simply to absorb ideas or information. In a similar way, texts on material culture need to be written in such a manner as to actively involve the reader rather than to shut him or her out. The role of the reader should be not simply to absorb information or ideas but to engage in a productive critical dialogue within the spaces of the text. This also draws attention to the fact that an author has no necessary priority with regard to the meaning of a text. The meaning goes entirely beyond the writer.

Writing archaeology's history   Taking into account Foucault's cogent attack on the history of ideas, if we were going to write the history of archaeology or any other discipline or a set of disciplines we would *not*: (i) regard archaeology as a 'natural' and unproblematic field of inquiry; (ii) envisage any necessary continuity in thought from a supposed point of origin (e.g. the moment when archaeology can first be conceived as existing as a body of thought) to the present day; (iii) regard archaeology merely as a set of ideas about the past; (iv) locate archaeology as developing in tandem with other types of investigations into the past or present as merely being part of the way people thought at particular times and places; (v) attempt to trace the manner in which ideas such as the concept of culture are developed or rejected from one archaeologist to the next; (vi) conceive of knowledge of the past as simply residing in archaeology books, which through the progressive influence of one individual archaeologist on another, or one generation of archaeologists on another, provide closer and closer accommodations to the way the past really was; (vii) think there is any necessary unity between a series of books or articles because they have a single name (e.g. Childe; Clarke) stamped on them, or regard changing ideas about the past as the result of innovations in thought developed by those individuals who label themselves, or become labelled, as archaeologists.

If we suspend this entire edifice as inadequate or downright misleading we have seriously called into question the validity of all histories of archaeology written to date. We need to re-write archaeology's history. The manner in which this might be attempted must include consideration of archaeology as a set of discursive practices linked to power and the non-discursive, which will now be briefly examined.

Analysing archaeological discourse One aspect of contemporary archaeology that is quite shocking is its comparative lack of self-reflexivity or awareness of itself as a contemporary activity being forged by women and men today. Here we need to be constantly aware of two features: archaeology as a practice within contemporary capitalism and archaeology as an active production of statements about material culture, whether past or present. Part of the process of understanding material culture has to be about the form and nature of this practice as carried out today, an awareness that archaeology is not just about events or material culture but itself is an event and a material production. It is necessary to understand archaeology as a discourse, as a set of dispersed statements, codes and rules which actively form the objects of which it speaks. Archaeology needs to be examined in terms of power–knowledge–truth strategies for the creation of meaning. The only way to alter archaeology and our understanding of material culture is to attempt to analyse what is being done now, and what has been done in the past. Foucault's analyses of discourse provide us with some important directions with which to situate archaeological texts both in relation to each other and contemporary capitalism.

In analysing archaeological texts a necessary preliminary must be an attempt at creating a certain degree of personal distance. In other words, we should try to read a contemporary archaeological text as if it were written, say, in 1066. To put it another way, in order to take a text or a series of texts seriously we first need to treat them as a joke and laugh at their attempts to seriously represent material culture. In many cases, no doubt, this may be rather difficult but it is worth a try! The distance created by laughing at the claims to serious meaning produced in the text may have a productive cathartic effect. Next, we need to look at texts from the perspective of a principle of rarity. Why is it that, given there are an almost infinite number of aspects of material culture patterning to be discussed, only a limited number of statements tend to be made, disseminated in various ways, and repeated? We can begin to analyse various discursive formations within archaeology as sets of rule-governed statements in a relation of dispersion. We will be analysing the regularities governing this dispersion and their effects. Needless to say, we will not be concerned with the psychology of individual authors. We do not reduce texts to simply being the products of individual imaginative consciousnesses. Furthermore, we need to analyse the social and political implications of producing one version of material culture rather than another. In other words, what linkage is there between a text and its social context of production? We have to try to analyse the relationship between archaeological knowledges and power, both within the academic community and without. We have to understand the manner in which archaeology creates its own discursive objects — never the only possible ones — and the manner in which these are framed and worked upon in texts. The archaeological record is variously and continuously being constituted by all that has been said about it, the manner in which it is named, divided up into segments, the way in which these segments are correlated with each other, described, understood, explained, and judged. The archaeological record exists only within the space of the discourses that have purported to deal with it. Objects of archaeological discourse are actively created, they have no objectivity except through the medium of their subjective constitution. Furthermore, any notion of archaeological objects as objective categories on which mathematical or other operations may be performed only makes sense in terms of certain forms of discourse in the present. An assertion of objectivity has got nothing to do with the past; it has everything to do with the present. Archaeological discourse does not merely use a linguistic medium as a group of signs to represent the past. These signs create the past, its objects and its objectivity.

An important area to analyse will be the manner in which prohibitions are placed on what 'proper' archaeological discourse is supposed to be about, who has the right to speak about material culture, to engage in serious speech acts about it, and who does not. Some remarks about this have already been made in the section on Foucault's analysis of discourse and will not be repeated here. We also need to analyse discourses in terms of the micropolitics of power in the academy. One way to do this might be to study the networking of references in texts in terms of individual and institutional influence and power; various tropes of writing and critique also need to be examined. Studies need to be conducted of who obtains employment and how, and who does not, who gets grants and who does not, who gets published and who does not, who has praises heaped upon them and who does not, why some books are read and others are ignored, why some debates take place rather than others. All these and others are not secondary issues. They are of some considerable significance in understanding how archaeology polices and constrains itself.

Choices are always made as to what to study and why to study it. A positive outcome of analysing contemporary archaeological discourse will be to open out fresh choices, new discursive objects. Contemporary empiricist discourse puts the study of material culture into a brittle, crystalline discursive structure which it is vital to shatter in order to open up fresh meanings, new ways of seeing, fresh truths. A focus on material culture and its study today threatens to dissolve the normal discursive boundaries archaeology erects around itself and this is productive—productive of fresh discourses and fresh knowledges. In fact it would be just as well to abandon the disciplinary label 'archaeology' altogether. Instead a new set of discourses needs to be developed, one that focuses on material culture and its relation to social practice irrespective of whether this be in the past, in the present, in our own society or others. Contemporary material-culture studies need to be undertaken, for example, because they are important studies in their own right, not for the sole purpose of trying to understand the past more adequately. Such a focus would be truly interdisciplinary. The purpose of most so-called interdisciplinary studies in archaeology today is merely to reinforce the unreality of present-day disciplinary boundaries.

It is important to abandon simplistic notions of an opposition between truth and falsity in analysing texts and statements made in these texts. Rather we should ask why these statements rather than others are made and what ends they serve. Archaeology is not so much about reading the signs of the past but writing these signs into the present. Correct stories of the past are dependent on a politics of truth linked to the present because all interpretation is a contemporary act. This interpretation is active. There is no original meaning to be textually recreated in an analysis of a set of artifacts. Meanings are always to be linked to the practices producing them, whether of prehistoric artisan or contemporary archaeologist, and discourse is a willed act of struggle for and against the production of particular types of statements.

History, Material Culture

Archaeology—history is constituted by concrete social practices, practices which relate to the production of material culture and the discourses which construct it within the framework of particular significative systems. Foucault is concerned to demonstrate that these practices are always material. They go beyond being mere expressions of systems of ideas. They also have a context. The use, production and meaning of material culture is not a context-free event. Equally, material culture does not simply consist of a set of signs to be read in which inheres a teleology of intentional meaning. Consequently, to understand social practice and its link to material culture we cannot (i) reduce material culture to a set of ideas either on an individual or societal basis; (ii) regard it simply as having utilitarian or social functions; (iii) carry out context-free cross-cultural studies; or (iv) adopt an evolutionary frame of reference. Material culture instead exists in a space falling between rules and principles for action and actual social practices. The rules do not govern the practices in the manner of norms or laws because they are dispersed and multifarious but dialectically relate to them. By uncovering the dispersions of rules and principles we can begin to account for both the form and variability of social practices. These practices are to be linked with power—knowledge strategies both producing material culture and constraining the forms it may take according to context. So the use and form of material culture can be understood in relation to power and knowledge as can the social practices producing it. The production of material culture and its societal significance cannot be understood by attempting to reconstruct sets of goals or motives on the part of subjects. It goes entirely beyond them. Regularities (systems of dispersed rules) define the limits of both social practice and material culture: they make them intelligible but the intelligibility and the regularity involved here is not that of an overall structural logic with everything in its place in a system of pure difference. The regularities may embrace contradictions, conflicts, and may superficially appear incoherent.

Foucault's work points to the centrality of power and its various forms of linkage with knowledge and truth as a crucial area for understanding the relation of material culture to social practice. The emphasis on power as dispersed throughout the social field avoids the essentialism involved in locating power solely in the economy or other areas such as the state apparatus in contemporary societies. We can clearly link this conception of power–knowledge to an understanding of the social conditions of production of material culture and the manner in which it may act back so as to have definite effects within the social field. Foucault's discussion of architectural forms shows quite clearly how definite forms of social practice are articulated with and in part mediated through the built environment. Constructed space helps to produce certain forms of action and agency as opposed to others. Material culture is shown to be actively involved in processes of perception, surveillance and the manner in which forms of subjectivity, subjugation and domination are constituted.

Material culture, agency, society   In reaching an understanding of the relationships between material culture and social practices Foucault shows us that there is a need for recognition of the fact that we can achieve an adequate understanding of material culture *without* attempting to reconstruct the specific intentions of individual agents or the whole of society. Given the extreme difficulty of doing either in prehistory this can only be a relief! An understanding of material culture in relation to social practice is not dependent on giving priority to the individual or society. The production of material culture is always social and goes beyond the individual but there is no necessity to locate it within an all-embracing social totality. Rather than suggesting that all the way across whatever entity we might like to define as 'society' all social relations and material culture are linked in some continuous manner, we could suggest that social relations are *discontinuous*, lacking any overall processes of connection or forms of determination. Such a standpoint would seem to have particular relevance in forms of prehistoric social organization that lack any overall political or state apparatus to connect them together. So rather than linking in material culture with a notion of systems or other conceptions of social wholeness we would have to regard its connection with social practices as both more specific and more dispersed, i.e. less unified.

Taking the past seriously Foucault takes history – historical difference – seriously and so should we. There are two aspects to this. First, material culture can be understood only by locating it in a specific historical context: specificity and detail, not generalization. The latter only destroys what we should be trying to understand and makes it meaningless. Second, the very concepts we use in analysis need to be historically located. What this means is that any search for a general theory of material culture good for all times and places is futile. Understanding must be always relational, related to history. Similarly, attempting to define individual concepts such as power, ideology, agency, domination, class, forces of production, relations of production, space and time, etc., as precisely as possible only makes sense within a historical context. These concepts and others need to be defined and redefined continually according to the historical context under investigation. For example, in a study of the distant past we will be dealing with social practices operating in and through spaces and times radically different from our own, times which are not chronometric and spaces which are not Euclidean, and differing events may again have their own times within such times. In a similar fashion, subjects or agents in the neolithic cannot at all be thought to possess exactly the same sorts of attributes or capacities as agents in the modern Western state. This has nothing to do with either a positive or negative valorization *vis á vis* the present. What it does mean is that it is important to recognize that the subject and subjectivity have no enduring essence. There is no such thing (except ideologically) as human nature. The subject is thoroughly constructed and the only thing which we are likely to have in common with a palaeolithic social actor is the possession of a physical body of more or less the same kind. The men and women of the past did not just think or conceive the world differently from us, they *were* totally different and part of this difference will run through to the very conception of an agent (peculiarly modernist) as a discrete centre of emotion, awareness and consciousness.

History and critique The purpose of writing the past should not be simply to try to reconstruct an aspect of it for its own sake, thus attempting to escape from the contingencies of the present. such a purely antiquarian concern has little relevance today and furthermore is invariably associated with a conservative politics. The past is, in part, politically created and this needs to be recognized. Material-culture studies have to be undertaken both critically and as an exercise in social critique. Here we can try to understand the relationship of material culture to patterns of social domination and repression and also the way in which material culture positively contributes to the fostering of particular forms of social practice rather than others. Studying contemporary material culture, if done in the right way, may have a constructive contribution to make as a form of social and cultural criticism. It is admittedly less easy to immediately envisage how studies of prehistoric material culture can aid social construction in the present. Here two points may be very briefly made. Part of the conception of the present lies in the past, so writing that past critically and self-reflexively will have an impact. One possible means of approach will be to perform genealogical studies of the kind Foucault has undertaken, identifying an issue of strategic social and political significance today, such as gender representation, and undertaking highly specific studies that cross-cut standard archaeological conceptions and periodizations of materials. More generally, what is required is an emphasis on the difference of the past in the analyses being undertaken to make the present appear as strange and exotic as possible in order to undercut its legitimacy and seeming necessity. The past can be a very powerful tool in the defamiliarization of the present, as Foucault has shown us.

Dialogic understanding and evaluation   Mention has already been made of the need to rework and situate historically concepts used in analysis. This also applies to knowledge, truth and rationality, which have definitely been over-valorized in the recent history of Western thought. It might be argued that if we deny that criticism is fundamentally grounded in epistemology then we are simply condemned either to a self-defeating acknowledgement of the 'truth' of the position we criticize or we have to resort to an appeal to some kind of natural reality or perspective outside discourse. This is not the case at all. We can regard the trinity of knowledge, truth and rationality as having a dialogic and historical resolution that is not reducible to abstract epistemological and ontological arguments. Rationality can be regarded as an attribute which allows us to make problematic what once seemed self-evident, to examine statements critically, to think self-reflexively about thinking. Such a process is historically and culturally grounded and the same applies to truth and knowledge. We always operate in terms of knowledges and aim to write truths. The problem is (or rather is not) that these knowledges and truths are always changing and always linked to power. We can well do without the self-congratulatory stance that this is in a unilineal progressive direction. The truth is to be found in history, history is not to be found in the truth. The resolution of opposing critiques or differing explanations is structured through processes of persuasive argumentation within the perspective of the present. Foucault expresses this well:

> In the serious play of questions and answers, in the work of reciprocal elucidation, the rights of each person are in some sense immanent in the discussion. They depend only on the dialogue situation. The person asking the questions is merely exercising the right that has been given to him: to remain unconvinced, to perceive a contradiction, to require more information, to emphasize different postulates, to point out faulty reasoning etc. As for the person answering the questions, he too exercises a right that does not go beyond the discussion itself; by the logic of his own discourse he is tied to what he has said earlier, and by the acceptance of dialogue he is tied to the questioning of the other. (FR: 381)

Foucault is laughing at you reading this, he was laughing at me scripting it. If it is possible to laugh at failed representations and failed discourses, no doubt including this piece, perhaps there is hope for the future.

BIBLIOGRAPHY

This is a select bibliography. Comprehensive listings of Foucault's publications can be found in PK and Cousins and Hussain (1984). Since this chapter was completed the following book has appeared with a full bibliography of Foucault's work: J. Bernauer and D. Rasmussen (eds) (1988) *The Final Foucault*, MIT Press, Cambridge, Mass.

1 *Books by Foucault*

Abbreviations used are given after the titles. Original date of publication in the French is given in square brackets.
Madness and Civilization (MC) [1961] (1967) Tavistock, London, Trans. R. Howard.
The Birth of the Clinic (BC) [1963] (1973) Tavistock, London. Trans. A. Sheridan.
The Order of Things (OT) [1966] (1970) Tavistock, London. Trans. A. Sheridan.
The Archaeology of Knowledge (AK) [1969] (1972) Tavistock, London. Trans. A. Sheridan.
The Order of Discourse (OD) [1970] (1981) in R. Young (ed.) *Untying the*

* *Both only available to me after this chapter was completed.*

Text. Also in *Social Science Information* vol. 10, no. 2, and appears as an appendix to the US edition of *AK*.

I. *Pierre Riviére, having slaughtered my mother, my sister, and my brother . . . (IPR)* [1973] (1975) Random House, New York. Trans. F. Hellinek (a collaborative work with others).

This is not a Pipe (TP) [1973] (1983) University of California Press, Berkeley. Trans. and ed. J. Harkness.

Discipline and Punish (DP) [1975] (1977) Vintage, New York. Trans. A. Sheridan.

The History of Sexuality, Vol. 1: *An Introduction (HS)* [1976] (1981) Penguin, Harmondsworth. Trans. R. Hurley.

The Use of Pleasure (UP) [1984] (1986) Viking, London. Trans. R. Hurley (vol. 2 of *the History of Sexuality*).

The Care of the Self [1984] (1987) Viking, London. Trans. R. Hurley (vol. 3 of *The History of Sexuality*). ★

Death and the Labyrinth [1963] (1987) Athlone, London. Trans. C. Raus. ★

2 Collections of writings, lectures and interviews

Language, Counter-Memory, Practice (LCMP) (1977) Cornell University Press, Ithaca. Ed. D. Bouchard; trans. D. Bouchard and S. Simon.

Power, Truth, Strategy (PTS) (1979) Feral Publications, Sydney. Ed. M. Morris and P. Patton. (Contains also articles by Patton, Morris and Foss.)

Power/Knowledge (PK) (1980) Ed. C. Gordon; Trans. C. Gordon, L. Marshall, J. Mepham and K. Soper. Harvester Press, Hassocks, Sussex. (Contains also an afterword by Gordon.)

The Foucault Reader (FR) (1986) Penguin, Harmondsworth. Ed. P. Rabinow.

3 Articles by Foucault and interviews not in above collections in English

'On the archaeology of the sciences: questions to Michel Foucault' (AS) (1971) *Theoretical Practice*, 3–4: 108–127.

'History, discourse and discontinuity' (HDD) (1972) *Salmagundi*, 20: 225–48.

'The politics of crime' (1976) *Partisan Review*, 43: 453–9.

'The political function of the intellectual' (1977) *Radical Philosophy* 17: 12–14.

'Power and sex: an interview with Michel Foucault'(1977) *Telos*, 32: 152–61.

'Governmentality' (G) (1979) *Ideology and consciousness*, 6: 5–21.

'*My body, this paper, this fire*' (*1979*) *Oxford Literary Review*, IV. (1): 9–28.

'Georges Canguilhem: philosopher of error' (1980) *Ideology and Consciousness*, 7: 51–62.

'Questions of method: an interview with Michel Foucault' (QM) (1980) *Ideology and Consciousness*, 8: 3–14.

'War in the filigree of peace. Course summary' (1980) *Oxford Literary Review*, IV (2): 15–19.

'Omnes et singulatim: towards a criticism of "political reason". (OS) (1981) in S. McMurrin (ed.) *The Tanner Lectures on Human Values*, University of Utah Press, Salt Lake City.

'The Subject and power' (SP) (1982) 'Afterword' in H. Dreyfus and P. Rabinow (eds) *Michel Foucault: Beyond Structuralism and Hermeneutics*, Harvester Press, Hassocks, Sussex.

'Structuralism and post-structuralism: an interview with Michel Foucault' (S) (1983) *Telos*, 55: 195–211.

'Of other spaces' (OOS) (1986) *Diacritics*, 16: 22–7.

4 *Work on or discussing Foucault*

During the past six years there has occurred a veritable explosion of Foucault studies. What follows is an extended listing of secondary literature on Foucault published before September 1987 with brief comments.

Baudrillard, J. (1980) 'Forgetting Foucault', *Humanities in Society*, 3: 87–111. [A parody taking the form of a metaphorical critique.]

Carroll, D. (1978) 'The subject of archaeology or the sovereignty of the episteme', *Modern Language Notes*, 93: 695–722. [Discussion of *OT* and *AK*.]

Cousins, M. and Hussain, A. (1984) *Michel Foucault*, Macmillan, London. [Best introduction, concentrating on Foucault's specific studies. Complementary to Dreyfus and Rabinow.]

Dews, P. (1987) *Logics of Disintegration: Post-Structuralist Thought and the Claims of Critical Theory*, Verso, London. [Chapters 5, 6, 7. Very useful discussion of Lacan, Foucault, Derrida and Lyotard in relation to the Frankfurt school of Critical Theory. Comes down on the side of the latter.]

Dreyfus, H. and Rabinow, P. (1982) *Michel Foucault: Beyond Structuralism and Hermeneutics*, Harvester Press, Hassocks. [Best thematic introduction. Complementary to Cousins and Hussain.]

Fardon, R. (ed.) *Power and Knowledge*, Scottish Academic Press, Edinburgh. [Useful paper by Hirst on space and architecture.]

Gane, M. (ed.) *Towards a Critique of Foucualt*, Routledge & Kegan

Paul, London. [Collection of articles originally published in *Economy and Society*. Sympathetically critical. Discussions centre largely on discourse and power.]

Golstein, J. (1984) 'Foucault among the sociologists; the "disciplines" and the history of professions', *History and Theory*, 23: 170–92. [Draws out implications, especially from *DP*, for study and critique of professions, and discusses Parsons.]

Gordon, C. (1977) 'Birth of the subject', *Radical Philosophy*, 17: 15–25. [Useful and interesting discussion along with Gordon (1979) of Foucault's later work.]

Gordon, C. (1979) 'Other inquisitions', *Ideology and Consciousness*, 6: 23–47.

Harland, R. (1987) *Superstructuralism*, Methuen, London. [Chapter 9 discusses *OT* and chapter 12 *DP* and *HS*. Draws out spurious Hegelian analogies and rather glibly written.]

Hirst, P. and Woolley, P. (1982) *Social Relations and Human Attributes*, Tavistock, London. [Chapter 9 contains a good discussion of *MC*.]

Hoy, D. (1979) 'Taking history seriously: Foucault, Gadamer, Habermas', *Union Seminary Quarterly*, 34: 85–95. [Short discussion drawing out similarities in conceptions of history of these thinkers.]

Hoy, D. (ed.) (1986) *Foucault: A Critical Reader*, Basil Blackwell, Oxford. [A series of critical analyses. Those by Hacking and Taylor are particularly useful.]

Keat, R. (1986) 'The human body in social theory: Reich, Foucault and the repressive hypothesis', *Radical Philosophy*, 42: 24–32. [Discusses similarities between the two opposed theses of Reich and Foucault and makes interesting remarks about Foucault's conception of the body.]

LeCourt, D. (1975) *Marxism and Epistemology*, New Left Books, London. [P. 187ff. Tries to insert Foucault into Marxism and claims *AK* is primarily about ideology.]

Lemert, C. and Gillan, G. (1982) *Michel Foucault: Social Theory as Transgression*, Columbia University Press, New York. [Interesting attempt to introduce Foucault while writing like Foucault. Tends to gloss over differences in his work, and in order to understand the book you need to have read Foucault first.]

Lentricchia, F. (1982) 'Reading Foucault (punishment, labour, resistance)', *Raritan*, 1: 5–32 and 2: 41–70. [Excellent discussion of *DP*.]

MacDonell, D. J. (1986) *Theories of Discourse*, Basil Blackwell, Oxford. [Chapters 5 and 6. A brief introduction largely ignoring *AK*.]

Mcdonnell, D. (1977) 'On Foucault's philosophical method', *Canadian Journal of Philosophy*, 7: 537–53. [Discussion of *AK*.]

Megill, A. (1985) *Prophets of Extremity: Nietzche, Heidegger, Foucault, Derrida*, University of California Press, Berkeley. [Chapters 5 and 6. Practises on Foucault exactly the type of 'history of ideas' approach he detests.]

Merquior, J. (1985) *Foucault*, Fontana, London. [More a eulogy to the rationalism of Gellner than a serious discussion of Foucault.]

Miel, J. (1973) 'Ideas or epistemes: Hazard versus Foucault', *Yale French Studies*, 49: 231–45. [Compares the historian Hazard with Foucault's *OT*]

Minson, J. (1985) *Genealogies of Morals: Nietzsche, Foucault, Donzelot and the Eccentricity of Ethics*, Macmillan, London. [Stimulating discussion and extension of themes in Foucault's later work.]

Poster, M. (1984) *Foucault, Marxism and History*, Polity Press, Cambridge. [Discusses relation between Foucault, Sartre and Critical Theory. Usefully suggests that Foucault extends the latter and is especially relevant in the understanding of late capitalism.]

Poulantzas, N. (1980) *State, Power, Socialism*, Verso, London. [A revisionary Althusserian study attempting to incorporate and criticize some of Foucault's work on power.]

Racevskis, K. (1983) *Michel Foucault and the Subversion of Intellect*, Cornell University Press, London. [Useful general discussions of most of Foucault's work. Defends Foucault against Baudrillard.]

Rajchman, J. (1985) *Michel Foucault: The Freedom of Philosophy*, Columbia University Press, New York. [Suggests Foucault cannot be taken to be a nihilist and argues that he puts forward a fresh conception of freedom, history and ethics.]

Rose, G. (1984) *Dialectic of Nihilism: Post-Structuralism and Law*, Basil Blackwell, Oxford. [Chapter 9. Argues that Foucault is a pessimistic nihilist involved in a more general post-structuralist misappropriation of Heidegger in an extremely dense discussion.]

Roth, M. (1981) 'Foucault's "history of the present"', *History and Theory*, 20: 32–46. [Brings out aspects of the critical side of Foucault's studies.]

Rousseau, G. (1972) 'Whose enlightenment? Not man's: the case of Foucault', *Eighteenth Century Studies*, 6: 238–56. [A historian's denouncement of Foucault's earlier work.]

Said, E. (1978) *Beginnings. Intention and Method*, Johns Hopkins University Press, Baltimore. [Chapter 5. Discusses Foucault's work on discourse in relation to literary theory.]

Said, E. (1984) *The World, the Text and the Critic*, Faber & Faber, London. [Chapter 9. Makes a comparison between the work of Derrida and Foucault on discourse and thinks Foucault better.]

Sheridan, A. (1980) *Michel foucault: The Will to Truth*, Tavistock,

London. [First introduction to Foucault to appear in English by Foucault's main translator. Provides a good summary but is perhaps a little over-enthusiastic.]

Smart, B. (1983) *Foucault, Marxism and Critique*, Routledge & Kegan Paul, London. [Good general discussion of Foucault's later work in relation to Marxism and critical theory. Similar view to that of Poster.]

Smart, B. (1985) *Michel Foucault*, Tavistock, London. [A general introduction concentrating especially on Foucault's later work. Better for a beginner than Dreyfus and Rabinow or Cousins and Hussain.]

White, H. (1973) 'Foucault decoded: notes from the underground', *History and Theory*, 11: 23–54. [A good summary and sympathetic discussion of Foucault's earlier work, especially *OT*, by a philosopher-historian.]

White, H. (1979) 'Michel Foucault' in J. Sturrock (ed.) *Structuralism and Since*, Oxford University Press, Oxford. [Discussion of discourse and Foucault's style.]

Williams, K. (1974) 'Unproblematic archaeology', *Economy and Society*, 3: 41–68. [Strident structural-Marxist attack on *AK*.]

5 *Work in archaeology discussing and using Foucault*

Miller, D., Rowlands, M. and Tilley, C. (eds) (1989) *Domination and Resistance*, Allen & Unwin, London. [Introduction and chapter 2. General discussion of conceptions of dominance and resistance in Foucault and social theory. Discussion of *OD* in relation to Cambridge inaugural lectures in archaeology.]

Miller, D. and Tilley, C. (eds) (1984) *Ideology, Power and Prehistory*, Cambridge University Press, Cambridge. [Chapters 1, 3, 4 and 8. Discussion of Foucault's conception of power in relation to ideology and linked with studies of modern architecture, eighteenth-century gardens and prehistoric societies.]

Shanks, M. and Tilley, C. (1987a) *Re-Constructing Archaeology*, Cambridge University Press, Cambridge, [Chapter 8. Foucault's conception of discipline used in a study of contemporary beer-can design, social relations structuring drinking and attitudes towards alcohol consumption.]

Shanks, M. and Tilley, C. (1987b) *Social Theory and Archaeology*, Polity Press, Cambridge. [Chapters 3, 4 and 7 especially. contains discussions of Foucault's conception of the subject and subjectivity, power, totality, and nature of social and political critique.]

Index